THIRD EDITION

RESEARCH STORIES FOR INTRODUCTORY PSYCHOLOGY

JOSHUA DUNTLEY

The Richard Stockton College of New Jersey

LARY SHAFFER

State University of New York at Plattsburgh

MATTHEW R. MERRENS

Dartmouth Medical School
Dartmouth Psychiatric Research Center

PEARSON

Boston ∎ New York ∎ San Francisco
Mexico City ∎ Montreal ∎ Toronto ∎ London ∎ Madrid ∎ Munich ∎ Paris
Hong Kong ∎ Singapore ∎ Tokyo ∎ Cape Town ∎ Sydney

Series Editor: Stephen Frail
Marketing Manager: Karen Natale
Production Editor: Patty Bergin
Editorial Production Service: Progressive Publishing Alternatives
Composition Buyer: Linda Cox
Manufacturing Buyer: JoAnne Sweeney
Electronic Composition: Progressive Information Technologies
Cover Administrator: Elena Sidorova

For related titles and support materials, visit our online catalog at
www. ablongman. com.

Between the time website information is gathered and then published, it is not unusual
for some sites to have closed. Also, the transcription of URLs can result in typographical
errors. The publisher would appreciate notification where these errors occur so that they
may be corrected in subsequent editions.

Library of Congress Cataloging-in-Publication Data

Duntley, Joshua.
    Research stories for introductory psychology/Joshua Duntley, Lary Shaffer,
Matthew R. Merrens. –3rd ed.
        p.   cm.
    Includes index.
    ISBN-13: 978-0-205-52065-7
    ISBN-10: 0-205-52065-0
        1. Psychology—Research—Methodology.   2. Psychology.
    I. Shaffer, Lary.   II. Merrens, Matthew R. III. Title.
    BF76.5.S43   2008
    150.72—dc22

                                                              2007037214

Printed in the United States of America

10

For Alice, Anna, Benjamin, Grace, Helena, Olivia, Reese, Sam, and Zoë
To the faculty and students who use this book:

Pollis Non Docere Scientiam

CONTENTS

CHAPTER 4

Zipping Up the Genes   32

INCORPORATING THE RESEARCH OF BOUCHARD AND MCGUE, "GENETIC AND REARING ENVIRONMENTAL INFLUENCES ON ADULT PERSONALITY: AN ANALYSIS OF ADOPTED TWINS REARED APART"

CHAPTER 5

The Nose Knows   44

INCORPORATING THE RESEARCH OF THORNHILL AND GANGESTAD, "THE SCENT OF SYMMETRY: A HUMAN SEX PHEROMONE THAT SIGNALS FITNESS?"

PART III   Learning

CHAPTER 6

Being Sick of the Hospital   57

INCORPORATING THE RESEARCH OF BOVBJERG, REDD, MAIER, HOLLAND, LESKO, NIWDZWIECKI, RUBIN, AND HAKES, "ANTICIPATORY IMMUNE SUPPRESSION AND NAUSEA IN WOMEN RECEIVING CYCLIC CHEMOTHERAPY FOR OVARIAN CANCER"

CHAPTER 7

Yoking Smoking   69

INCORPORATING THE RESEARCH OF ROLL, HIGGINS, AND BADGER, "AN EXPERIMENTAL COMPARISON OF THREE DIFFERENT SCHEDULES OF REINFORCEMENT OF DRUG ABSTINENCE USING CIGARETTE SMOKING AS AN EXEMPLAR"

PART VIII   Stress and Health (Health Psychology)

CHAPTER 20

To Catch a Cold   212

INCORPORATING THE RESEARCH OF COHEN, TYRELL, AND SMITH, "NEGATIVE LIFE EVENTS, PERCEIVED STRESS, NEGATIVE AFFECT, AND SUSCEPTIBILITY TO THE COMMON COLD"

CHAPTER 21

Spaced Out   219

INCORPORATING THE RESEARCH OF BAUM AND DAVIS, "REDUCING THE STRESS OF HIGH-DENSITY LIVING: AN ARCHITECTURAL INTERVENTION"

CHAPTER 22

Weight Loss That Works   230

INCORPORATING THE RESEARCH OF SBROCCO, NEDERGAARD, STONE, AND LEWIS, "BEHAVIORAL CHOICE TREATMENT PROMOTES CONTINUING WEIGHT LOSS: PRELIMINARY RESULTS OF A COGNITIVE-BEHAVIORAL DECISION-BASED TREATMENT FOR OBESITY"

PART IX   Behavior Change

CHAPTER 23

I Think I Can, I Think I Can   242

INCORPORATING THE RESEARCH OF MARTOCCHIO, "EFFECTS OF CONCEPTIONS OF ABILITY ON ANXIETY, SELF-EFFICACY, AND LEARNING IN TRAINING"

CHAPTER 24

Betting on the Winners   252

INCORPORATING THE RESEARCH OF SYLVAIN, LADOUCEUR,
AND BOISVERT, "COGNITIVE AND BEHAVIORAL TREATMENT OF
PATHOLOGICAL GAMBLING: A CONTROLLED STUDY"

CHAPTER 25

Behavioral Treatment to Change Vocalization Patterns in
a Person with Schizophrenia   263

INCORPORATING THE RESEARCH OF WILDER, MASUDA,
O'CONNOR, AND BAHAM, "BRIEF FUNCTIONAL ANALYSIS AND
TREATMENT OF BIZARRE VOCALIZATIONS IN AN ADULT WITH
SCHIZOPHRENIA"

CHAPTER 26

Tokens Against Aggression   271

INCORPORATING THE RESEARCH OF LEPAGE, DELBEN, POLLARD,
MCGHEE, VANHORN, MURPHY, LEWIS, ABORAYA, AND MOGGE,
"REDUCING ASSAULTS ON AN ACUTE PSYCHIATRIC UNIT USING A
TOKEN ECONOMY: A 2-YEAR FOLLOW-UP"

PART X   Social

CHAPTER 27

I Confess   278

INCORPORATING THE RESEARCH OF KASSIN AND KIECHEL,
"THE SOCIAL PSYCHOLOGY OF FALSE CONFESSIONS:
COMPLIANCE, INTERNALIZATION, AND CONFABULATION"

CHAPTER 28

INCORPORATING THE RESEARCH OF FEIN AND SPENCER, "PREJUDICE AS SELF-IMAGE MAINTENANCE: AFFIRMING THE SELF THROUGH DEROGATING OTHERS"

CHAPTER 29

INCORPORATING THE RESEARCH OF STONE, ARONSON, CRAIN, WINSLOW, AND FRIED, "INDUCING HYPOCRISY AS A MEANS OF ENCOURAGING YOUNG ADULTS TO USE CONDOMS"

PART XI   Applied

CHAPTER 30

INCORPORATING THE RESEARCH OF LATOUR, SNIPES, AND BLISS, "DON'T BE AFRAID TO USE FEAR APPEALS: AN EXPERIMENTAL STUDY"

CHAPTER 31

INCOPORATING THE RESEARCH OF WOGALTER, ALLISON, AND MCKENNA, "EFFECTS OF COST AND SOCIAL INFLUENCE ON WARNING COMPLIANCE"

CHAPTER 32

INCORPORATING THE RESEARCH OF BUSHMAN, "EFFECTS OF TELEVISION VIOLENCE ON MEMORY FOR COMMERCIAL MESSAGES"

■ ■ ■ ■ ■

The goal of this book is to help you see psychological studies in a larger scientific context and to understand the reasoning that provides a foundation for empirical research. We do not believe that introductory students need to be protected from the research procedures of scientific psychology. The approach we use in this book is to explain research methods as part of the stories of contemporary research studies. In order to think critically, you need to know that the findings of psychology are tightly linked to the methods. It makes little sense to talk about one without the other. By reading about both scientific methodologies and the findings derived from them, you can come to appreciate what scientific psychology is really about. You will see that the results of studies discussed in this book may contradict the kinds of commonsense guesses about behavior that permeate the pop psychology of television, the Internet, magazines, and newspapers.

Although the research stories in this book have been retold, they have not been dumbed down. You will find appropriate levels of challenge as you master the material. Some details have been eliminated. Other detailed notions that are required for understanding by the beginning student have been introduced or expanded. Moreover, scientifically terse introductions and procedures have been more fully explained and discussions of statistical analyses have been reduced to understandable dimensions.

Sometime when you have a few minutes, you should go to the library and look at one or more of the original research articles that have been discussed in this book. The primary reference for each chapter is found in the footnote on the bottom of the chapter's first page. It might interest you to know how much editing and rewriting have been done in bringing this material to you.

While reading these chapters, you will see the gears and wheels of the process that generate knowledge about psychology. You must understand the methodological processes to be able to critically assess the validity of assertions about behavior. In a general sense, good methodology is more likely to produce valid research results. The kind of critical thinking you will develop with this book is a set of highly transferable skills. Critical thinking is essential for you in the job market, as a graduate school applicant, and as a critical consumer of the information you encounter in the world.

Psychology is unique among disciplines in the broad applicability of the skills you should learn. It is probably safe to say that all of you will be required to evaluate assertions about human cognition and behavior as part of your adult lives. Particularly in the age of the Internet, professional advancement will go to the person who can effectively evaluate the validity and value of information.

The Internet is packed with information about human behavior. That information is only as good as the research methods that produced it. A requisite professional skill for the new century is the ability to sort information along continuums of quality or accuracy.

At the very least, when you are finished with these readings, we hope that you will critically challenge assertions about behavior. Your first questions should be, "Who found that out and what methods did they use?" Once you have answers, you can use your knowledge of research methods to assess the validity of claims about human cognition and behavior. The toolkit of skills you will get from this book will be useful in other courses and, more importantly, out in the world. The studies in this book are examples of good, contemporary psychological science. Because these stories are real science, they have flaws, limitations, and shortcomings. No study is perfect. Any study can be criticized. One of our goals for an introductory course is to take you along with us while studies are critically examined for strong and weak points. Our experience suggests that this activity will leave you with a mature and practical grasp of psychology. We do not want you to accept study findings uncritically. Instead, we want you to understand that a well-designed study is a powerful tool for gathering knowledge, even if there are practical limitations within the methods. The "facts" in any science are certain to change over time, but the ability to evaluate these facts is of lasting value.

You should be aware that this book consistently offers a scientific viewpoint about psychology. We believe that science is the most powerful method yet developed for understanding cognition and behavior. We think a great disservice would be done to you if we were not steadfast in our commitment to science.

ACKNOWLEDGMENTS

This project would not have been possible without the tireless assistance of Ms. Mary Turner, Ms. Cheryl Lafountain, and Ms. Cynthia Pratt of the Feinberg Library at SUNY. They showed endless patience with requests for interlibrary loan and document copying. Bryan Kieser kindly helped us with Latin translation. Additionally, we gratefully acknowledge several of our undergraduate students for help with earlier versions of this material. Alan Morrison has been with us from the start of the project. We told him not to be shy about tearing chapters apart, and he took us at our word. He read the chapters multiple times and made insightful suggestions. Carrie Shapiro worked hard on the teaching materials that are used with the book. When Jen Edmonds laughed at our attempts to draw a few apparatus pictures, we challenged her to do better and she did. Introductory psychology students Lori Christopherson, Lachlan Chambliss, Surjit Chandhoke, Michael Harrington, and Sharon Clarke voluntarily made detailed corrections to each chapter while reading it as course material. Advanced undergraduate student Chelsie Connolly read several chapters and provided very helpful feedback. Psychology department secretary Judy Dashnaw also volunteered to read the chapters and has made numerous improvements. Special thanks go to Paula Duntley, who made insightful suggestions on all of the new chapters and revisions for the third edition, and created the new figures. The keen intelligence, detailed work, and generosity of these people have made this a better book.

Several of our colleagues have been willing to adopt this book and they have given us valuable feedback. Dr. Renee Bator, Dr. Katherine Dunham, Dr. J. Stephan Mansfield, and Ms. Cori Matthews at SUNY-Plattsburgh, as well as Dr. G. Terry Bergen, Dr. John Klein, and Ms. Julie Volkens at Castelton State College, Castleton, Vermont, have used it in duplicated draft from the beginning. We also wish to thank the Psych1 staff at the University of Vermont: Dr. Justin Joffee, Dr. James Rosen, Mr. Joshua Cooper, Ms. Julianne Krulewitz, and Mr. David S. Henehan. The experience and comments of these supportive and enthusiastic scholars have made this a better book, and we are very grateful to them. We are also grateful to Gordon D. Atlas, Alfred University; George T. Bergen, Castleton State College; Terry D. Blumenthal, Wake Forest University; Gary Greenburg, Wichita State University; Paul Greene, Iona College; R. Steven Schiavo, Wellesley College; Linda J. Skinner, Middle Tennessee State University; and Fred Whitford, Montana State University, who offered helpful suggestions and comments that have strengthened the book. Finally, we are grateful to our editors at Allyn & Bacon, who have stuck with us through three editions of the book.

ABOUT THE AUTHORS

Joshua Duntley (Ph.D., The University of Texas) is an assistant professor of social and behavioral sciences at The Richard Stockton College of New Jersey. He received his undergraduate degree in psychology at SUNY-Plattsburgh where he worked with Professors Shaffer and Merrens on earlier writing projects. He conducts research in the areas of evolutionary psychology, forensic psychology, and human mating. He has authored numerous chapters and papers and has co-edited a volume titled *Evolutionary Forensic Psychology*.

Lary Shaffer (D. Phil., Oxford University) was a State University of New York Distinguished Teaching Professor at SUNY-Plattsburgh before retirement. He has also coauthored a book of research stories for life span development. He now lives in coastal Maine and makes fine furniture and cabinetry.

Matthew R. Merrens (Ph.D., University of Montana) is a visiting Professor of Psychiatry at Dartmouth Medical School and the Dartmouth Psychiatric Research Center. He was Professor of Psychology at SUNY-Plattsburgh, where he served as chair of the psychology department. He received the SUNY Chancellor's Award for Excellence in Teaching. He has written and edited books in the areas of evidence-based mental health, personality, development, social, and introductory psychology.

CHAPTER 1

OH RATS!

If you ask most people, they will tell you that a psychology course is supposed to teach you to analyze people's minds. As a demonstration, we are going to try to analyze your mind. This reading describes an experiment about rats. Now, here is what is on your mind:

> "Rats! *Rats?* Let's see, (flip, flip, flip) how long *is* this chapter, anyway?"
> or
> "Rats! *Rats?* I wonder if the bookstore would still give me all my money back if I sold this stupid book and dropped this course. After all, the book has hardly been used."
> or
> "Rats! *Rats?* This is probably just some junk they put in the first chapter. The rest of the book must be about the unconscious and interesting stuff like that."
> or
> "Rats! *Rats?* Damn! I thought that this was going to be a cool course and now, one page into it, I am reading about **RATS**."

Did we read your mind? If we did, it was because we have common sense, rather than because we know about psychology. If we didn't, it shows that psychologists cannot read minds. Either way, there is no evidence here for mind reading. Hold that thought. You have only been reading this book for two minutes, and you already may have learned something: people who tell you that they can read your mind are not psychologists. Psychologists know better than to say things like that.

Psychologists study behavior. Sometimes a lot can be learned about behavior from the study of rats. This chapter is really about behavior, not rats. Okay, so we lied when we implied that this chapter was about rats. If you were inclined to believe everything found in textbooks, then you have learned something else:

Incorporating the research of C. Kim, L. Kalynchuk, T. Kornecook, D. Mumby, N. Dadgar, J. Pinel, and J. Weinberg, "Object-Recognition and Spatial Learning and Memory in Rats Prenatally Exposed to Ethanol," 1997, *Behavioral Neuroscience, 111,* pp. 985–995.

textbooks sometimes lie. We will not lie to you (again) on purpose, but we may well lie accidentally. Psychology is a vital discipline and, as such, is changing all the time. Although we intend to describe psychology as it is today, new research may alter current concepts, theories, and beliefs at any time.

STUDYING RATS

Because psychologists study cognition and behavior, rather than a particular organism, not all research in psychology involves the study of humans. Sometimes other animals are used because the researcher really wants to know about the behavior of that animal, often to answer questions about its evolution or ecology. In other cases, nonhuman animals are used as participants because they are more convenient. Many studies of learning have used rats because they are economical to maintain in large animal colonies that have rows and rows of drawerlike cages. The researcher who could use rats as participants had easy access to research participants from the animal colonies that used to be part of psychology departments in most universities. The behavior under investigation in basic studies of learning can sometimes be so similar from species to species that it does not matter what type of animal is studied. Nonhuman animals also have been the participants of choice when researchers believed that a study was too dangerous for human participants. In this case, the researchers may want to know about humans, but believe that other animals are sufficiently similar to permit their findings to be applied to humans. The experiment with rats to be discussed next was one of these important investigations in which humans could not be used as research participants.

AN EXPERIMENT

In this book, we will use the word *experiment* in a restricted and special sense. When most people speak of an experiment, they are talking about unsystematically trying something, as in: "I'm going to do an experiment to see if dogs like carrots." You toss the dog a piece of carrot. If he eats it, dogs are presumed to like carrots and if he spits it out, they dislike them. *One* dog in *one* state of hunger with *one* piece of carrot does not tell us much of anything about dogs and carrots. Alternatively, someone might say "I am going to do an experiment to see what will happen if I go to bed early tonight." Aside from all the problems of drawing conclusions based on one person doing something on one day, there is the additional problem that no particular outcome has been anticipated. In a real experiment, there is a clear statement about what is expected to occur as a result of the procedures. The experiment is a test of the correctness of this statement, called the *hypothesis*. In the example of going to bed early, there is no hypothesis. Nothing is being tested, so nothing important is likely to be learned. Going to bed early might be accompanied by a variety of outcomes, such as getting more sleep and feeling rested or waking up earlier and feeling tired the next day. In any event, there is little basis for the conclusion that going to bed early caused either of these—they might easily have occurred regardless of bedtime.

C. Kwon Kim and colleagues (Kim et al., 1997) did an experiment to demonstrate the effects of learning in rats that had been exposed to alcohol. We have chosen to discuss this particular study because of the importance of the question. In addition, it has the structural characteristics of a well-conducted experiment. First, we are going to do an overview of this experiment and then we will go back and highlight the features that permit this study to belong to the rarefied and elite class of research called the experiment. As with other studies discussed in this book, this one is important for its findings, but it is also important for its methods. For reasons that will become clear, not every scientific study can have all the procedural elements that are part of the experiment reported by Kim et al. (1997). Each of these elements is important to ensure that the conclusions drawn from the study are accurate.

THIS EXPERIMENT

Kim and coworkers obtained both female and male rats of a well-known genetic strain from a breeder. Because rats from the same strain are genetically quite similar, the differences found in the experiment were not likely to be the result of genetic differences among the sample of rats in the study. The rats were all maintained in cages in a room that had controlled temperature and lighting. Here, again, an effort was made to avoid differences that might affect the outcome of the study. The males and females were housed together until the females became pregnant. Pregnancy in rats is indicated by the loss of a mucous vaginal plug. When the females lost this plug, it was known that they were on Day 1 of their pregnancy, and they were moved to individual cages.

At this point, each female was randomly assigned to one of three groups. Group E was fed a totally liquid diet—a sort of liquid rat chow—which contained adequate food but derived 36 percent of the calories from ethanol. Ethanol is the same kind of alcohol that is in beer, wine, and other alcohol-containing drinks. There were 21 rats in Group E. A second group was called the *pair-fed*, or PF, group. This group was fed throughout pregnancy on a liquid diet that was the same as that of Group E, except that a sugarlike substance, maltose-dextrin, was substituted for the alcohol in their diets. This group was called pair-fed because each rat in this group was fed the same amount of liquid food (in grams per kilogram of body weight) as one of the Group E animals. Through its own consumption, each Group E animal determined how much a Group PF animal would be allowed to eat. In this way, these two groups were directly comparable except that one group had alcohol as part of every meal and one did not. A third group of 21 pregnant females, Group C, for *control*, was fed usual rat food and water. The special diets of Group E and Group PF were replaced with standard rat chow and water on Day 22 of gestation. The rat pups were born on about Day 23.

There were no differences among the three groups of rats in the number of live or stillborn offspring. On the day following birth, Group E and PF pups weighed less than Group C pups, but they caught up on subsequent days. By the time of birth, Group PF mothers weighed less than Group E or C mothers, but not alarmingly less. The weights of these mothers caught up, and they were not different by Day 15 after birth. The mothers raised all the pups until they were weaned at 22 days old. Then the pups were housed in groups by litter and sex until testing began. One male rat from each litter was randomly selected for testing. These rats were called the *participants*. When the participants were 16 months old, their learning was tested in a maze task.

The Test Situation

Two different tests were conducted on these rats. One of these involved a visual discrimination task that we will not discuss further because it showed no significant differences among any of the participants. The other was a maze learning task called the Morris water maze. The Morris water maze was a large (180-cm-diameter × 60-cm-high) tank that was filled to the 22-cm level with water made opaque with nontoxic white paint. This opaque water was a maze because somewhere in it, 3–4 cm below the surface, there was a 12-cm-diameter circular platform. From trial to trial, the platform remained in the same place within the maze. The other features of the research room also remained the same and could act as visual-orienting cues to help the rat find the invisible submerged platform on successive trials.

The rat was put in the maze and would swim around until it found the platform. Finding the platform was rewarding for the rats because they could stop swimming and climb up on it. The rat could not see the submerged platform; it had to find the platform in space. Once the rat had found it, learning was measured by putting the rat back in the water and timing how long it took to find the platform again. This measure is called *latency*. It is the amount of time it takes to perform a specific task. As learning progresses, we would expect the latency to get less and less as the rats learned the exact location of the platform and found it faster.

The researchers would place the rat in the maze and then retreat behind a screen so that the rat could no longer see them. While concealed behind the screen, the researchers watched the rats by means of a video monitor. The video monitor was connected to a video camera directly above the maze, permitting observations to be made without interfering with the swimming rat. Researchers watched the rat on the monitor and timed the latency for finding the platform. The experimenters who worked with the rats in the maze did not know which group the rats belonged to: Group E, PF, or C. Each trial in the maze began when a single rat was placed in one of four equally spaced positions around the rim of the pool. The start position was randomly selected from one of these four. Once started, the rat would swim until it found the platform. If it did not find the platform in 90 seconds, the trial was over and the rat was removed from the pool. Each rat was tested by giving it six trials a day on each of 10 days in a row. This kind of procedure is often called testing the animal in "blocks of six trials over 10 consecutive days."

The last two trials were different. On the 59th trial, the platform was raised up to the point where it was visible. The 59th trial was conducted to test whether some rats failed to find the platform in earlier trials because they were merely unable to respond to visual stimuli within the maze. The researchers believed that rats who had been exposed to prenatal alcohol had complex cognitive disabilities, not merely visual deficits. If they were correct, then all groups of rats would be expected to do well on Trial 59. On the 60th trial, the platform was removed, and the rat was allowed to search for it for one minute. On this trial, the data consisted of the number of times the rat swam directly over the area where the platform had been located. The researchers used a clever way to make a permanent record of the swimming path of the rat: they secured a piece of thin paper over the screen of the video monitor and traced the image of the moving rat with a marker as it swam about. The result was a tracing of the route taken by the swimming rat. The measure of success was called *annulus crossing*. An annulus is a ring. The rats were scored correct for each crossing of a ring drawn on the paper around the location where the platform used to be. The 60th trial was a test of the persistence of the rat in seeking the approximate location of the platform. *Persistence* was another behavioral outcome that might have been affected by prenatal exposure to alcohol, and Trial 60 was designed to investigate this possibility. The researchers did not expect to find differences among the rats in persistence at the task, but conducted Trial 60 to confirm this belief.

Results

Although all rats improved, the rats from the ethanol group had significantly longer latencies when the task was to find the hidden platform (see Figure 1.1, top).

As always when behavior is measured, there was some variability. Looking at the bottom graph in Figure 1.1, for example, you can see that on Day 4, the ethanol group had shorter latencies than the other groups. Statistical analyses can help to determine if this particular data point is sufficiently important to be considered more than chance variation. Something accounted for this difference, and it might be interesting to know what it was, but, in the absence of that information, the overall trend is clearly one of longer latencies for the ethanol group.

Figure 1.2 shows what happened on Trial 59, in which the platform was visible, and on Trial 60, in which the platform was missing and the rats were swimming across the area where it was previously found.

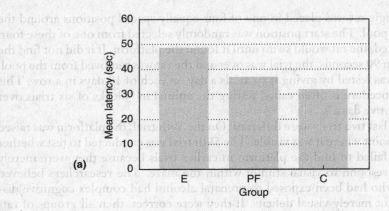

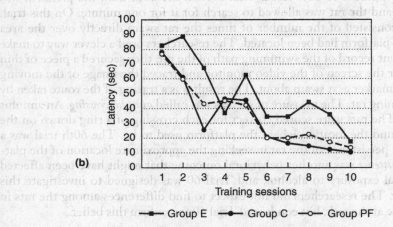

**FIGURE 1.1   (a) Mean Latency to Find the Platform by
Group (b) Latency to Find the Platform across Sessions**

Although there might appear to be differences in latency making the ethanol group appear to be slower, these differences were so small that they were not statistically significant. Likewise, the numbers of annulus crossings when the platform was missing were also determined statistically to be no different from random or chance fluctuations in behavior. When differences are very small, statistical tests can help determine if they are meaningful. In contrast, differences might merely be the result of small, ordinary, and unsystematic variations in behavior.

Discussion

Kim et al. (1997) concluded that prenatal exposure to alcohol could negatively influence the ability of rats to learn tasks involving the position of objects in space. Spatial learning may be different from some other kinds of learning that

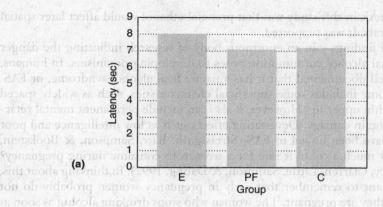

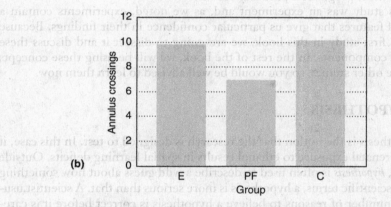

FIGURE 1.2 **(a) Latency to Find the Visible Platform (b) Annulus Crossings at Site of the Missing Platform.** (a) Latency (in seconds) to find the visible platform in Trial 59 and (b) annulus crossings in searching for the missing platform in Trial 60. None of the differences shown are statistically significant.

have been found to be less susceptible to the influence of prenatal alcohol exposure. This study supported the findings of a number of other studies of spatial learning and prenatal ethanol exposure. In contrast to the public perception, no one study "proves" anything for most scientists. Instead, it is recognized that all studies could have been more complete in some way. However, when a number of different studies by different researchers all point in the same direction, we may begin to have confidence in the overall findings. People who have training in science rarely talk about "proven" facts. That is the jargon used in advertisements and the news media. In contrast, when research outcomes are discussed, scientists acknowledge possible shortcomings by choosing words such as the findings *demonstrated* or *supported* the hypothesis that was being tested.

The hypothesis in this study was that prenatal ethanol would affect later spatial learning in rats. It was supported.

These findings join an enormous body of research indicating the danger that maternal alcohol consumption poses to developing organisms. In humans, this is so well documented that it has a name: fetal alcohol syndrome, or FAS. This syndrome includes some superficial characteristics, such as widely spaced eyes and a thin upper lip. However, it also can include permanent mental retardation and brain damage. Devastating effects such as low intelligence and poor judgment have been linked to FAS (Streissguth, Barr, Sampson, & Bookstein, 1994). How much alcohol is safe for a woman to consume during pregnancy? None (Astley, Clarren, Little, Sampson, & Daling, 1992). In thinking about this, it is important to remember that early in pregnancy women probably do not even know they are pregnant. The woman who stops drinking alcohol as soon as she knows she is pregnant is probably too late.

This study was an experiment and, as we noted, experiments contain a number of features that give us particular confidence in their findings. Because this is the first study in this book, we are going to dissect it and discuss these important components. In the rest of the book, we will be using these concepts to describe other studies, so you would be well advised to learn them now.

THE HYPOTHESIS

The hypothesis is the notion that the research is designed to test. In this case, it was that prenatal exposure to ethanol results in spatial learning deficits. Outside of science, *hypothesis* is often used to describe a wild guess about how something works. In scientific terms, a hypothesis is more serious than that. A scientist usually has a number of reasons to believe a hypothesis is correct before it is carefully tested. Past research or informal, less-structured observations may suggest correct hypotheses. Sometimes researchers will do pilot tests, which are incomplete versions of research that can be quickly done, to suggest the correctness of a hypothesis. Following pilot testing, a formal study may be undertaken. Usually scientists believe their hypotheses are correct, and they are trying to convince others by doing careful research to test their beliefs.

THE INDEPENDENT VARIABLE

The independent variable is the *difference* that is directly created or arranged by the experimenter. In this study, the independent variable was the difference in diet of the rat mothers: ethanol, maltose-dextrin, or rat chow. It is often said that the experimenter *manipulates* the independent variable. This literally means that the experimenters *handle* that part of the study. Conceptually, the researcher is trying to create one or a few differences to see what effects they will have on outcomes. In this study, researchers were as careful as possible to eliminate any differences other than the ones they wanted to study, the differences in diet. Perhaps a good way to think about a variable is to consider its opposite, a constant. In an experiment, most things are held constant, so that differences in outcomes can be seen to be the result of the independent variable.

THE DEPENDENT VARIABLE

The dependent variable is the important measured outcome of the study. It is the measure of the particular behavior that is being studied. This name is easy to remember because it *depends* on the independent variable. In this study, a dependent variable was the latency for finding the platform. Dependent variables are also sometimes called dependent *measures* or dependent *outcomes*. In some studies there may be several independent variables or several dependent variables. In this study, prenatal diet was the independent variable but there were several dependent variables. Latency to find the submerged platform was one. Latency to find the platform when it was raised was another dependent measure. Annulus crossing was a third dependent outcome.

Usually a two-sentence description of a study can be constructed if you identify the independent and dependent variable. Identification of the variables in a study is the first step to understanding it. For example, in research about the effects of loud music on studying, the loud music would be the independent variable and some measure of study effectiveness—maybe a nice little quiz—would be the dependent variable. Once you have found the variables, you can begin to ask if these particular variables constitute an adequate test of the hypothesis.

OPERATIONAL DEFINITION

An operational definition is the definition of some psychological characteristic in terms of the way it is measured. For example, an IQ test result might be the operational definition of intelligence. In the study discussed in this chapter, latency was an operational definition of learning, and the number of annulus crossings was the operational definition of persistence. One way to critically evaluate studies is to examine the operational definitions to see if they are adequate. For example, intelligence might be operationalized by asking people how smart they are. For most purposes, that operational definition would probably not be adequate.

RANDOM ASSIGNMENT

In this study, rat mothers were randomly assigned to Groups E, PF, and C. This means that any rat had an equal chance of ending up in any group. There was also another random process at work because among the litters of rat pups, one animal was randomly selected to be in the study. Any other method of assigning rats to groups might have resulted in some other characteristic of the rats playing a role in the dependent measure. The differences observed in the dependent variable were supposed to be the result of the independent variable the experimenter has manipulated. Random assignment to groups was the best way to ensure that the groups were not different before the independent variable was presented. For example, instead of random assignment, if the largest rat mothers were placed in Group C, the next largest in Group PF, and the smallest in Group E, there would be no way to be sure that latencies observed in their pups were a result of alcohol exposure. In this case, latencies might also have been the result of maternal size.

No researcher would purposely assign all the big rats to one group, unless size was going to be studied as a variable. Nevertheless, the researcher wants to eliminate all systematic differences among animals in the groups to ensure that the only systematic difference remaining is the independent variable. The best way to achieve this is through random assignment to groups. Unless assignment is random, it is easy for an investigator to unknowingly introduce some kind of systematic differences into groups of participants. In a study like this, imagine that the rat parents arrived from the breeder in five crates, stacked one on top of another. Further imagine that the experimenters removed rats from the top crate, assigning them to Group E until Group E was full, then to Group PF, and last to Group C. This might be fine, but it might not. These rats were born and grew up in a rat colony. These colonies are racks of cages, usually five or six cages high and six or eight cages wide. Viewed from the front, the rat colony has the appearance of a rat apartment house, with each rat, or rat family, in its own little space. We do not know how the breeder decided which rat to put in which crate. The breeder might have loaded the crates by emptying cages in the top row of the rat colony first. Rats who had grown up in bottom cages might be behaviorally different than rats who grew up in top cages. You think this is far fetched? Imagine growing up only being able to see people's knees. Unless this difference was to be the independent variable, a way to overcome it is to randomly assign rats to groups on arrival at the lab where the experiment is to be conducted. Even if researchers think that such early experiences would make no difference, every effort is made to see that the only systematic difference between groups is the one created by the researcher: the independent variable.

Random assignment is not always possible. Nevertheless, part of thinking critically about research is being able to ask the right questions. If you were to read a study in which participants were not randomly assigned to groups, you should immediately begin to ask yourself about factors other than the independent variable, accidentally introduced into groups, that might have effects on the dependent measures. Sometimes research articles do not say whether assignment to groups was random. When this happens, it is probably safest to conclude that they were not and to adjust your confidence in the findings accordingly.

Randomization may also appear in other aspects of a study. In this study, the swimming began at randomly assigned places in the pool. Something like a lottery was conducted ahead of time to determine where each rat would start. This was an additional attempt to remove bias. Imagine that two or three different experimenters are actually working with the rats in the pool. If one of them always starts the rats at the same location around the edge of the maze, this might influence the latency measure for these animals. If it also happened that this particular researcher started most of the rats from Group C, then the observed latencies might be merely a result of starting position, not the independent variable of alcohol exposure. This is another instance in which you can ask critical questions about studies. If some procedure was not randomized when you think it should have been, you might have less confidence in the findings.

"BLIND" STUDIES

Usually, if the participants in research do not know details, such as what group they are in or what the independent variable is, they are said to be *blind*. A study in which this is part of the procedure is sometimes called a *single-blind* study. If the participants are told what is going on in a study, there is an increased chance that their responses will be different. In this study, the rat pups were not aware that other groups had been prenatally exposed to different things, so we somewhat facetiously suggest that this study qualifies to be thought of as single blind.

The term *blind experimenters* is used to indicate that the experimenters who actually worked with the participants did not know the group assignment of any particular participant. It is usually desirable that both the participants and the researchers who work with them in the experiment be prevented from discovering the details of group assignment or the nature of the independent variable. In a famous study, Robert Rosenthal (1973) gave students the task of teaching a rat to run a maze. The rats were randomly selected from a large group and given to individual students. However, some students were told that they had a smart rat and some were told that their rat was not very smart. Although the rats were really randomly assigned to student experimenters, the students who believed that their rats were smart ended up with rats who did better in the maze-learning task. Further study indicated that these students, without being aware of it, treated their rats differently. For example, they handled the rats more often, and this was associated with better maze performance. If experimenters can transmit their expectations to rats, it is probably even easier to do so with humans. For this reason, whenever possible, neither participants nor researchers should have knowledge that would allow them to react differently to the independent variable. When this is done, a study is called *double blind*.

The American Psychological Association (APA) now discourages the use of the term *blind* because it considers this to be an insensitive label that is often easy to avoid. New studies in psychology are more likely to say that participants were *unaware* rather than *blind*. Nevertheless, the concepts of *single blind* and *double blind* are used in many other scientific fields and universally in older studies, so it is important that you understand what this means. There is a large section in the APA's *Publication Manual* that offers additional guidelines designed to help authors to reduce bias in the language of research reports (APA, 2001).

CONTROL GROUPS

You know by now that the independent variable is the difference that the experimenter handles, or manipulates. To see the effect of prenatal ethanol, it was essential to compare the behavior of some rats who were exposed to prenatal alcohol with some who were not exposed to it. The rats who were exposed to prenatal alcohol were called the experimental group, and any rats who were not exposed to prenatal alcohol were said to belong to *control groups*. Sometimes there are two or more control groups. In other research designs, participants can serve as their own control group by receiving one version of the independent variable at one time and another one later. In this study, both Group PF and Group C were control groups. The reason why there were two control groups may have been obvious to you as you read about the study. The experimental group had a liquid diet with alcohol as a component. If they had been compared only to Group C, the researchers would not know if the effects observed had been a result of alcohol compared to no alcohol, a solid diet compared to a liquid diet, or both. Group PF had a liquid diet but had no alcohol. The alcohol was replaced with a calorically equal substance in the diet of Group PF. To be sure that the quantity of liquid diet was the same in Group E and Group PF, each rat in Group PF was given the same amount of food as a rat chosen from Group E. This is called pair-feeding in this study, but a more general term for it is to say that the control group was *yoked* to the experimental group. A yoke is an old-fashioned wooden device that hitches two farm animals side by side so that they can pull a vehicle. The scientific use of this term means that the behavior of one participant determines what happens to another participant.

CAUSE AND EFFECT

The experiment is a powerful way of testing hypotheses. However, it is often not possible to do an experiment. Other scientific methods must be used. The advantage of a carefully conducted experiment is that it allows us to draw conclusions about cause and effect. One of the reasons why psychology exists is to find causes for behavior. The experiment is the only way to do this with any confidence. In our everyday lives, we do not generally require an experiment before we conclude that some event has caused a certain behavior. For example, if you are backing your car out of a parking space and hit a telephone pole, you may become angry. It is quite likely that the event of hitting the pole was the cause of your anger. We do not need to do an experiment in which a large group of randomly assigned people damages cars and another group does not in order to believe that accidents make us feel angry. This is not an important question. However, there are many important questions that psychology can address using the most powerful method yet developed for determining cause and effect: the experiment. Nonexperimental methods may tell us a great deal about behavior, but they should not be used to conclude that an independent variable is the cause of a dependent outcome or effect. As you will see, even true experiments are always limited in their scope, and we believe that conclusions about cause and effect from experiments should be made with appropriate caution.

There are many other scientific approaches discussed in this book, as well as a number of other experiments. As we will stress, these scientific methods are not perfect or flawless, but they are a great deal better than other approaches to knowledge such as hunches, guesses, intuitions, individual experiences, or the uncritical opinions of others.

RIGHTS OF RESEARCH PARTICIPANTS— THE ETHICAL ISSUE

There are committees in research institutions that examine each research proposal to ensure that the rights of the participants are considered. Even in research with rats, it is required that the research not be trivial and that the research design be sufficient to permit robust conclusions to be drawn. For humane reasons, researchers would have to describe what was going to happen to the rats at the conclusion of the research. The rights of research participants have been a major issue since the late 1960s, and, as a result, it is now fairly difficult to do psychological research on any organisms. When the participants are people, the ethics of deception is an issue: is it fair to allow humans to participate in an experiment when they are not fully aware of the hypothesis?

Informed consent is now required before people can be research participants. People must be given quite a bit of information about what will happen to them in the study before they finally decide to participate. In some cases, this may mean that it is not possible to conduct an experiment in which the participants are unaware, or blind, to the conditions. It must also be made clear to participants that they are free to leave, without penalty, at any time during the experiment.

REFERENCES

American Psychological Association (APA). (2001). *Publication manual of the American Psychological Association* (5th ed.). Washington, DC: Author.

Astley, S. J., Clarren, S. K., Little, R. E., Sampson, P. D., & Daling, J. R. (1992). Analysis of facial shape in children gestationally exposed to marijuana, alcohol, and/or cocaine. *Pediatrics, 89*, 67–77.

Kim, C., Kalynchuk, L., Kornecook, T., Mumby, D., Dadgar, N., Pinel, J., & Weinberg, J. (1997). Object-recognition and spatial learning and memory in rats prenatally exposed to ethanol. *Behavioral Neuroscience, 111*, 985–995.

Rosenthal, R. (1973, September). The Pygmalion effect lives. *Psychology Today, 1*, 56–63.

Streissguth, A. P., Barr, H. M., Sampson, P. D., & Bookstein, F. L. (1994). Prenatal alcohol and offspring development: The first fourteen years. *Drug & Alcohol Dependence, 36*, 89–99.

■ ■ ■ ■ ■

CHAPTER 2

PSYCHICS AND SCIENTISTS

Do you know what this chapter is about? Then you must be psychic! (Or maybe you read the title.) This illustrates the main point of the chapter: although many people believe in psychic phenomena, there are also perfectly normal explanations for these seemingly paranormal happenings. There is no need to resort to unknown powers of the mind.

Many of us have had the experience of thinking about someone when the phone rings, and the phone call turns out to be from the person about whom we were thinking. Is this really *precognition*, the ability to predict the future through psychic means? It is possible to collect a little data to study this question. Keep a piece of paper near the phone and, each time it rings, guess who it is and write the guess down before answering. Circle the guesses that turn out to be correct. If someone in particular usually calls you at about the same time every day, you are likely to be correct in guessing his or her name because you would recognize the time he or she usually calls. Time of day explains those cases, so set them aside. The real test of your precognitive ability is to be able to correctly identify the unexpected callers. You will be correct once in a while just by chance. These unusual occasions on which you are correct are likely to be remembered clearly. The thousands of times you are not correct are forgotten; they are too ordinary to be memorable. Keeping a record will illustrate this for you, if you need illustration. The failure to remember thousands of disconfirming instances while remembering a few successes probably explains psychic precognitive identification of phone callers. The correct guesses are examples of coincidences.

Coincidence is a technical term that means that two events have occurred together either by accident or by chance. When someone you have not heard from in years phones you while you happen to be thinking of him or her, it is probably a coincidence. To think clearly about these things, you need to know that in a large set of events, coincidences are highly probable. They are almost *certain* to happen. Imagine that you have five unbiased coins. If you toss all five at once, the probability

Incorporating the research of R. Wiseman, D. West, and R. Stemman, "An Experimental Test of Psychic Detection," 1996, *Journal of the Society for Psychical Research, 61*, pp. 34–45.

that they will all come up heads is 1 in 32, or about 3 percent. If you toss them 100 times, however, the probability of getting five heads at least once is 96 percent. It is almost certain to occur. Media reports often speak of "remarkable" coincidences as if they were unexpected. In a large series of events, coincidences are not unexpected or remarkable. If you receive about five phone calls a day you will have almost 10,000 calls in five years. With that many opportunities, it would not be at all surprising if you were to occasionally guess the correct identity of an unusual caller in advance.

Cable television and the Internet have many advertisements for psychics who claim to be able to use special powers to delve into your life and predict what will occur in the future. We believe that if they could really predict the future, they would be in Las Vegas predicting the future of roulette wheels and raking in the money. Of course, at the $4 a minute they charge for talking to people on the phone, they are making $240 an hour, so they are not doing too badly. One of the best-known psychics in recent times was the late Jeanne Dixon. Some people believe that in 1956 she predicted the assassination of President Kennedy seven years before it occured. What she actually predicted was that the person, unknown to her, who won the 1960 election would "be assassinated or die in office, but not necessarily in the first term." This vague statement was a reasonable surmise given that seven of the early twentieth-century presidents either died in office (McKinley, Harding, Roosevelt), were very seriously ill (Wilson and Eisenhower), or experienced assassination attempts (Truman). It is also noteworthy that Jeanne Dixon failed to predict her own death in 1997.

The words *psi* and *parapsychology* are used as blanket terms to refer to unusual human processes of information or energy transfer, such as sensing or moving things, that are currently unexplained in terms of known physical, biological, or psychological mechanisms. This includes a variety of supposed happenings such as:

Telepathy—knowing others' thoughts

Psychokinesis—moving and otherwise affecting objects in the physical world through thought processes

Clairvoyance—receiving information about remote events using pathways other than recognized sense organs

Some people who want to believe in psychic phenomena feel that the scientific community has somehow "ganged up" to suppress evidence of psi because it violates accepted theories or beliefs. This is not the case. There have been hundreds of research studies investigating paranormal phenomena, and nothing of substance has been found (Blackmore, 1996). Psi has not been rejected because it violates accepted scientific notions. It has been rejected as an explanation because there are plenty of ordinary rational explanations for the observed phenomena. The scientific arena is rigorous. Methods and procedures are scrutinized carefully before studies are accepted for publication. Yet, many initially unpopular ideas have passed the test of this scrutiny and have been accepted. Ideas such as continental drift and circulation of the blood received acceptance in science because the evidence for them was compelling. At this point, there is no convincing evidence for psi. Magician James Randi, who has been a crusader in exposing fake psychics, offered $10,000 to anyone who could demonstrate psi in properly controlled conditions (Randi, 1982). He made this public offer in 1968 and has not yet had to pay the reward money. In a typical case of an attempt to win the prize money, a psychic claimed that he could use psychokinesis to turn the pages of a phone book without touching them. Randi gave him the chance to do so, but being a magician himself, Randi knew that these tricks are usually accomplished with small streams of compressed air emanating from somewhere, such as the psychic's sleeve. In what was to be a television demonstration of psychic page turning, Randi instituted a simple but elegant control. He scattered Styrofoam beads around the phone book, which would move at the slightest puff of air. The psychic walked around the book for 10 minutes sweating and scowling before claiming that bright lights were inhibiting his psychic powers (Gardner, 1989).

Although it may be widely believed that police use psychics in finding solutions to crime, the data available present a different picture. Sweat and Durm (1993) conducted a survey of police departments in the 50 largest cities in the United States. Although 17 percent of the police departments that responded said that they handled information from psychics "differently" than information from the general public, *all* police respondents noted that psychic information was no more helpful than information from the general public.

Psychics have frequently claimed to be able to use their powers to assist law enforcement agencies in the solution of baffling crimes (Nickell, 1994). The difficulty is that the reports are anecdotal. When scientists speak of *anecdotes*, they are referring to stories that people tell of personal experiences or hearsay. The intention is to use the story as evidence for some assertion about behavior. In this case, someone might say, "I heard about a psychic who was able to solve a murder that stumped the police." If you are thinking critically about this assertion, you should begin to question the source and the quality of the information. Psychics may make several vague and sometimes conflicting predictions about a crime. Once the real story of the crime is known, the correct predictions are remembered and the incorrect ones are forgotten (Hoebens, 1985; Rowe, 1993). This situation is similar to the one we described concerning precognition and telephone calls. The rare instance that seems to confirm psi is remembered, and all the failures to confirm are forgotten.

An additional problem in evaluating the work of psychics in crime detection was identified by Lyons and Truzzi (1991). They pointed out that success in information about crimes should be measured against a baseline expectation. For example, a psychic may have told police that a person who suddenly disappeared is now dead, and this was later found to be accurate. To evaluate critically the extent of clairvoyant abilities, it would be necessary to know what percentage of people who suddenly disappear are later found to be dead. If this was a high-frequency outcome, then there may be nothing spectacular or important about the accuracy of the prediction. Anyone could have made it with no knowledge about the crime. If the psychic prediction referred to a highly unusual means of victim disposal, then it might have warranted more attention.

One of the earliest scientific investigations of psychic ability in crime detection involved four psychics who were shown photographs and objects that might have been related to crimes. Some of this material was evidence in criminal cases, and some had nothing to do with any crimes. The psychics were asked to describe the crimes that might have involved the pictures and objects. The final report of this demonstration concluded that nothing of interest to police was produced by the psychics (Brink, 1960). Martin Reiser of the Los Angeles police department and his colleagues carried out a similar study with 12 psychics (Reiser, Ludwig, Saxe, & Wagner, 1979). Each psychic was presented with physical evidence from real crimes. The procedure was double blind: neither the psychics nor the experimenters knew anything about the crimes in advance. Psychics made predictions that were sorted into categories such as type of crime, victim, and suspect. These descriptions were compared with actual information about the crimes. The performance of the psychics was poor. On one crime, police had established 21 real facts. The psychics averaged 4 correct. On another, 33 facts were known, and the psychics averaged 1.8 correct descriptions. Lyons and Truzzi (1991) have criticized this study and similar ones for methodological flaws. The data collected involved assessing a match or mismatch between each psychic statement and the key facts in the case. Other things that psychics said were simply discarded. For example, one crime involved the murder of a church historian. One of the psychics believed that the crime had something to do with a church, but there was no way in the data collection scheme to categorize this small, but accurate, assessment. Another methodological problem was that if psychics produced no information about a particular key fact, it was scored as a wrong response. This meant that, for example, not stating the sex of the victim was scored the same as saying the victim was male, when, in fact, she was female. These methodological issues might seem to put psychics at a disadvantage, thus lowering their scores and ignoring responses that did contain some correct information.

The research that is the focus of this chapter is from a study by Richard Wiseman, Donald West, and Roy Stemman (1996). They compared three self-proclaimed psychics against three college students in a test of psychic ability. One of their goals was to overcome shortcomings of earlier studies. The authors were contacted by a television production company that wanted to produce a program about psychic ability for a syndicated television series, *Arthur C. Clarke's Mysterious Universe*. The producers wanted to film a well-controlled test of psychic ability, and they were prepared to allow the psychologists to design the study and to specify the details of methodology to be followed.

PARTICIPANTS

Participants included three well-known psychics residing in Great Britain. One of these people had recently received considerable attention in the British news media because of claims that he had consistently and accurately predicted several crimes, terrorist attacks, and airplane disasters. He claimed that these predictions occurred in dreams. Although he had not been subjected to any formal assessment of accuracy, his local police department issued a statement saying he was "taken seriously" and that the information he provided was "acted upon immediately." The other two psychics in the study both worked as professional psychics. The participants in the other group for the study were three students recruited from the psychology department at the University of Hertfordshire. None of them claimed to have any psychic powers or any particular interest in solving crimes.

PROCEDURE

This study is an example of a research design called a quasi experiment. A difference between a quasi experiment and a true experiment is that the participants are not randomly assigned to groups. They cannot be, because they already belong to the groups to be compared before the research begins. In this case, they were either psychics or nonpsychics (students). Within psychology, opinions differ about whether this difference should be called an *independent variable*. There is no disagreement when this term is used to designate an experimental manipulation done to randomly assigned participants. Issues arise when the researcher does not create the input variable; rather, it is already a characteristic of the participants before the beginning of the study. In the strictest sense, being a psychic or being a student is not an independent variable because the experimenter has not created it. We will adopt this strict sense. We do this not to be pedantic or picky, but because occasionally precision of thought and of phrasing is warranted. Unless there is an experimenter-created independent variable, no evidence has been produced for cause and effect. Often the main interest in behavior is to attempt to uncover causal components, and we believe that the somewhat common broad use of *independent variable* only clouds critical analysis of results. The only reason we raise this issue is that published studies sometimes say that preexisting group characteristics, such as *gender* or *intelligence level*, are independent variables. Some statistical analyses also refer to preexisting group differences as independent variables. Although we allow that this is a judgment call, we are going to use the strict definition of an independent variable as something created by an experimenter. Instead, terms such as *predictors, antecedents, correlates,* or *participant variables* may be used to describe the relationship between group membership and outcomes measured in a quasi-experimental design.

The Essex Police Museum supplied three objects, each of which had been involved in a different actual crime. These objects were an old and rotting shoe belonging to a woman who had been murdered and buried, a deformed bullet recovered from the scene of a gunshot murder, and a red scarf that was used in a strangulation. Each of the crimes had been solved, and a great deal of detail was known about each one. Great care was taken to ensure that the people with whom the participants interacted in the lab had no knowledge of the crime. Sergeant Fred Feather, curator of the police museum, brought the objects to the lab, placed them on a table, and labeled them A, B, and C. He left the test area and waited in a distant part of the building while the tests were being conducted. The researcher who interacted with the participants during the tests knew nothing about the crimes or the objects. Participants were brought, one at a time, to the room where the objects were laying on a table. They were encouraged to handle the objects and to speak aloud any ideas, images, or thoughts that might be related to the crimes. They were told they could take as much time as they wanted and could say as little or as much as they liked. During the test, they were left alone in the room. With their full cooperation and knowledge, everything they said or did was filmed through a two-way mirror.

In advance, Sergeant Feather had supplied information for each crime. This information permitted one of the researchers to construct six statements that were true of that particular crime, but untrue of the other crimes. These statements referred to specific aspects of the particular crime that were not likely to be true of crimes in general. This was done to eliminate correct answers from educated guessing that had nothing to do with psychic powers. For example, one might guess that a stabbing crime in a home occurred in the kitchen because that is where most knives are kept. The three sets of 6 statements were combined and randomly ordered into a single list of 18 statements. Examples of these were:

An accomplice involved
Perpetrator aged in his twenties
A link with milk
Victim had only one son, aged four

After each participant was finished handling the objects and talking about them, one copy of the list of 18 crime descriptors was provided for each object. Participants were told that 6 of the statements were true for the crime associated with each object. Their task was to make check marks beside the 6 true statements for the particular crime connected with each object. They were allowed to take as much time as they wanted to complete this task. When they finished, they were ushered to a waiting area away from participants who had not yet been tested.

RESULTS

The number of correctly identified statements for each participant, out of six possible, is shown in Figure 2.1.

The data in Figure 2.1 are the average number correct for each participant averaged across all three objects. The mean correct for the psychics as a group was 2.09 and for the student group it was 2.33. None of the means, individual or group, were statistically significantly different from the rest. The psychics did not appear to be better or worse than the students in identifying correct statements about crime objects.

Wiseman et al. (1996) wanted to be sure that the ability of the psychics was not underestimated by the methodology of the study. Choosing statements from a list did not take into account correct statements that the psychics might have made in handling and talking about the objects. To assess this qualitative information, a rater who was not involved in the test transcribed and separated each comment made by any of the participants. A list was made of all comments each participant made relating to a single crime. On this list, the order of these statements about each crime was randomized. These lists were then presented to two additional people, who had read about the crimes, acting as judges. The judges were asked to rate each statement about the crimes on a scale from 1 (very inaccurate) to 7 (very accurate). The ratings of the two judges for each participant were averaged and are shown in Figure 2.2.

The psychics made a total of 39 statements, and the students made 20 statements. There was no significant difference between the mean accuracy of the psychics and of the students (psychic mean = 3.83, student mean = 5.63). The reason why the accuracy level of these statements was so high is that many

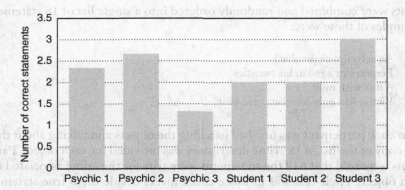

FIGURE 2.1 Participant's Identification of Statements. Average number of correct statements selected by each participant for all three objects combined. The statements about a crime were chosen from a list of 18 statements, 6 of which were correct. Total possible correct was 6.

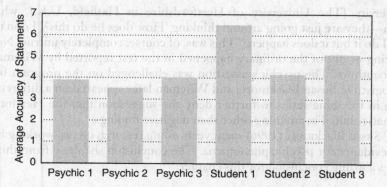

FIGURE 2.2   **Comments Judged To Be Accurate.** Average number of unrestricted comments and statements made about crimes that were judged as being correct. Total possible correct was seven.

of the comments were obvious from the nature of the object. For example, one of the objects was a scarf and most of the comments correctly predicted that it had been used in a strangulation murder. A deformed bullet elicited comments such as "loud bang heard," "involved a shooting," and "looks like a squashed bullet." These are accurate, but unsurprising. Wiseman and his colleagues noted that no participant produced even one piece of information that would have been helpful to police in the investigation of the crimes.

DISCUSSION

The results in this study showed that the psychics were as unsuccessful as students at choosing correct statements about crimes. Neither group performed above the chance level. In addition, a more qualitative analysis of free comments also showed that the psychics performed at the same level as the students. After the study, all the participants were told about the findings. When presented with their results, none of the students thought that they had performed very well. However, all three psychics thought they had been "very successful." Throughout the study, the psychics appeared eager and willing to participate under the test conditions. As the psychics happily talked about their performances, they began to rebuild the history of what happened. They emphasized small, vague, or somewhat correct statements and seemingly forgot they said things that had been contradictory or wrong.

Following the test, one of the psychics appeared on a nationally televised talk show and said: "I have proved it [my psychic ability] in laboratories. In fact, only three weeks ago I did a test at the Department of Psychology at Hatfield

University [The University of Hertfordshire in Hatfield, U.K.], which—I mean—they are just going around thinking 'How does he do this?' I don't know how I do it but it does happen." This was, of course, completely untrue. Nothing amazing or out of the ordinary happened in the test reported by Wiseman and his coauthors. The psychic's assertion was challenged on the program by psychologist Dr. Susan Blackmore, and Wiseman later appeared on a different program in the same series to further deny the suggestion that the Hertfordshire test had resulted in anything other than negative findings.

Susan Blackmore (1996) spent years doing research on psi, working hard to find evidence for psychic phenomena. The conclusion she drew from this work makes a fitting conclusion for this chapter:

> I now know that the very idea of psi has got me nowhere. Parapsychology is often held up as the science of the future, the science that will tackle all those questions about the nature of mind or the farther reaches of human experience, the science that will force a new paradigm to topple the old and serve as a route to spirituality. But it does not deliver.

REFERENCES

Blackmore, S. J. (1996). *In search of the light: Adventures of a parapsychologist*. Buffalo, NY: Prometheus Books.

Brink, F. (1960). Parapsychology and police investigations. *International Criminal Police Review*, *134*, 3–9.

Gardner, M. (1989). *How not to test a psychic: Ten years of remarkable experiments with Pavel Stepanek*. Buffalo, NY: Prometheus Books.

Hoebens, P. H. (1985). Reflections on psychic sleuths. In M. Truzzi and P. Kurtz (Eds.), *A skeptic's handbook of parapsychology*. Buffalo, NY: Prometheus Books, pp. 631–643.

Lyons, A., & Truzzi, M. (1991). *The blue sense*. New York: Warner Books.

Nickell, J. (1994). *Psychic sleuths: ESP and sensational cases*. Buffalo, NY: Prometheus Books.

Randi, J. (1982). *Flim flam: Psychics, ESP, unicorns and other delusions*. Buffalo, NY: Prometheus Books.

Reiser, M., Ludwig, L., Saxe, S., & Wagner, C. (1979). An evaluation of the use of psychics in the investigation of major crimes. *Journal of Police Science and Administration*, *7*, 18–25.

Rowe, W. F. (1993). Psychic detectives: A critical examination. *Skeptical Inquirer*, *17*, 159–165.

Sweat, J. A., & Durm, M. W. (1993). Psychics! Do police departments really use them? *Skeptical Inquirer*, *17*, 148–158.

Wiseman, R., West, D., & Stemman, R. (1996). An experimental test of psychic detection. *Journal of the Society for Psychical Research*, *61*, 34–45.

CHAPTER 3

YOU'RE DRIVING ME CRAZY

On February 20, 1994, drivers—Michael Blodgett, 42, and Donald Graham, 54—became entangled in a disagreement while in traffic. After several miles of driving, they pulled off the road and confronted each other. In the trunk of his car, Graham had a crossbow of the sort used for deer hunting. He retrieved it, pointed it at Blodgett, and killed him. It is not unknown for people to give reasons for murder on the highways such as "He couldn't care less about the rest of us—he just kept blocking traffic" or "He practically ran me off the road—what was I supposed to do?" (American Automobile Association [AAA], 1997).

These are examples, admittedly extreme, of the phenomenon that has come to be called "road rage." Reports of road rage have become commonplace in all the news media. The reports are so common that a controversy has sprung up concerning the real frequency of road rage events. One of the issues involves the operational definition of road rage. A review of news stories might suggest that any incident that takes place on or near a road is likely to be tagged with this label. If a car accidentally splashes mud on a pedestrian and the pedestrian responds by shouting and shaking a fist, is this road rage? Road rage is an attention-getting catchphrase and because the media are trying to get our attention, it is not surprising that road rage appears in so many news stories.

Ellison-Potter, Bell, and Deffenbacher (2001) presented an approach to the problem of a more precise definition of road rage. They made a distinction between aggressive driving and road rage based partly on legal terminology. Acts of aggressive driving include tailgating, horn honking, obscene gestures, and blocking the passing lane. Aggressive driving is a traffic offense. In contrast, road rage is a criminal offense. It includes such behaviors as assault with intent to cause bodily harm and, in the most extreme cases, attempted or actual homicide.

According to a 1997 report of the AAA, violent aggression has increased dramatically in recent years. For example, from 1990 to 1995 their data suggest a 51 percent increase in road violence. There were 10,037 incidents of road rage

Incorporating the research of J. L. Deffenbacher, R. S. Lynch, E. R. Oetting, and D. A. Yingling, "Driving Anger: Correlates and a Test of State-Trait Theory," 2001, *Personality and Individual Differences*, *31*, pp. 1321–1331.

during that time period (AAA, 1997). These data were questioned on the web-page of The Atlantic (www.theatlantic.com) by science writer Michael Fumento. Fumento contended that the data may overstate incidents of aggressive driving and road rage because there is no law specifically against some of the behaviors involved, and therefore, police tickets have to be interpreted, not merely counted. In addition, the AAA data may not have taken sufficient account of the increased numbers of drivers on the road and the miles driven by these drivers.

CORRELATIONAL RESEARCH

Chapters 1 and 2 exposed you to two different research designs, the experiment and the quasi-experiment. A third type of research method that is very common in the study of humans is the correlational study. The correlational approach to research looks at the relationship between variables under investigation. As you will see in reviewing the results of the research in this chapter, the findings are expressed in terms of a statistic called the correlation coefficient. The correlation coefficient is often symbolized by the lowercase letter r. A correlation coefficient gives two pieces of information about the relationship between variables: the strength of that relationship and its direction. The strength component of the correlation coefficient occurs on a scale ranging from -1.00 to $+1.00$. The closer the number is to 1.00 (+ or −), the stronger the magnitude of the relationship between variables. At maximum strength of $r = +1.00$ or $r = -1.00$, the relationship is perfect: if you know the magnitude of one variable, you can perfectly predict the magnitude of the other. For example, if there are 30 students enrolled in a kindergarten class, there will be a perfect correlation between the number absent on Monday and the number attending school on Monday. If you know how many are absent, you can make perfect predictions about how many are present. As correlation coefficients approach zero, it is likely that the variables studied have little relationship to one another and little predictive power. The relationship between hair length and IQ is probably near zero, as is the relationship between shoe size and family size.

The direction of the relationship is indicated by the sign (+ or −) of the correlation. Correlations that are negative reflect an inverse relationship between the two variables being measured. An inverse relationship means that as the measure of one variable increases, the measure of the other variable decreases (or vice versa). In contrast, a positive correlation means that both variables being assessed either increase together or decrease together. In other words, the sign (+ or −) tells you how the variables are related (directly or inversely). Table 3.1 provides an illustration of the range of correlation coefficients with qualitative descriptions of the strength of the correlations at various points, while Table 3.2 presents some examples of variables that are likely to be correlated positively, negatively, or near zero.

TABLE 3.1 Range of Correlation Coefficients

"APPROXIMATE" CORRELATION STRENGTH	CORRELATION COEFFICIENT
Very strong	-1.0 to $-.80$
Strong	$-.80$ to $-.60$
Moderate	$-.60$ to $-.30$
Weak	-30 to $-.10$
No correlation	$-.10$ to $+.10$
Weak	$+.10$ to $+.30$
Moderate	$+.30$ to $+.60$
Strong	$+.60$ to $+.80$
Very strong	$+.80$ to $+1.00$

TABLE 3.2 Examples of Positive, Negative, and No Correlation

STRONG POSITIVE CORRELATIONS
Study hours & grade point average
Calories consumed & body weight
Watching TV violence & engaging in aggressive behavior

STRONG NEGATIVE CORRELATIONS
Altitude & percentage of oxygen in air
Optimism & illness
Shyness & number of friendships

LITTLE OR NO CORRELATION
College ID number & grade point average
IQ in infancy & IQ in adulthood
Blood type & level of depression

As the absolute value of the number in the correlation coefficient increases, either toward -1.00 or $+1.00$, the strength of the relationship is greater. For example a correlation of $-.86$ is stronger than a correlation of $+.59$. After you have thought about this and looked at the examples in Table 3.2, test yourself by deciding whether the perfect correlation in the previous example of kindergarten class attendance and absences is positive or negative. Remember, the strength of the relationship is solely based on the number and not on the sign. Initially, many students make the mistake of assuming a correlation with a positive sign is stronger than a negative one; again, the sign tells you about the direction of the relationship, and the number tells you how powerful it is. This means that as the number increases toward 1.00, in either a positive or negative direction, the strength of the relationship, and therefore the predictive "power," is increased.

In real life, the predictive power of strong correlations can be important because if you know the value of one variable, you can make a fairly good prediction about the value of the other. If I were the admissions director of a college and knew there was a strong positive relationship between a college entrance exam and final college grade point average, entrance exams would be a powerful tool for making admissions selection decisions. If I, as the admissions director, wanted solely to consider accepting students who would have high grade point averages at graduation, such an examination would be an excellent selection tool because of its predictive power.

Be aware that even a strong relationship between the two variables in correlational research does not ensure that those two variables are linked in a causal relationship. If there is a strong correlation between two variables, one may cause the other, or there may be no causal relationship; even a strong correlation provides no evidence either way. Making causal assertions from correlational data is a common error in everyday life. Just because there is a relationship, that does not necessarily mean that one factor causes the other. For example, the number of churches in a city and amount of criminal activity are positively correlated. If we were to make the assumption that these two measures are causally related, then it would mean that churches are a breeding ground for crime or criminal activities leads to church construction. This example illustrates how a variable that is not being measured and is not under study can influence the two variables being studied. In this example, population is a likely "causal" factor that affects both the crime rate and the rate of church construction. Where the population is large, there are more churches and more crime. Other factors such as income and education levels may also contribute. Of course, it may be the case that two variables that are correlated do have a causal relationship, but a correlational approach alone does not provide evidence for a causal relationship. Strictly speaking, it takes an experimental design to explore causality; however, in some cases, experimental designs cannot be used to study behavior. For example, the presumed link between smoking and cancer in humans is correlational because we cannot randomly assign humans to smoke or not. If we employed human participants in such an experimental study, our dependent variable, the data we would be collecting, would be symptoms of a disease that we, as researchers, initiated by placing participants in various smoking groups. This is obviously unethical. In this case, correlational research is better than nothing. If studies are repeated to gain more confidence in the findings (a process called *replication*), the weight of evidence may begin to suggest casual links, even though they cannot be confirmed without an experiment. As a general rule, we think it is important to be cautious about drawing causal conclusions based solely on simple correlational research designs.

RESEARCH ON DRIVING ANGER

It will not surprise you to learn that much of the past research on all types of driving anger has been conducted using archival data, such as court records, or by using surveys. However, there have been a handful of attempts to investigate driving anger with field studies. In these field studies, researchers have typically set up a situation and then observed the behavior of drivers who encounter the setup. Diekmann, Jungbauer-Gans, Krassnig, and Lorenz (1996) created a situation in which German drivers were blocked by the researcher's car at a busy intersection. When the traffic light changed to green, the research car did not move, and the researchers recorded the reactions of the driver immediately behind them. One of the interesting findings from this study was that the drivers of more expensive cars reacted more quickly with responses such as horn honking or light flashing. McGarva and Steiner (2000) did a somewhat similar study in North Dakota, only their drivers were students who volunteered to be in a study about "driving behavior." The participants were unaware that they were driving into a setup where they would be blocked. Their behavior while experiencing a blocking vehicle was recorded by a researcher riding with them. In the high status condition, it was found that participant drivers accelerated more quickly following provocation.

These bold researchers probably went about as far as it is possible to go in the design of field studies of driving anger. Stronger manipulations invoking more anger could present participants or researchers with unacceptable levels of risk. Another approach to a field study was taken by Deffenbacher et al. (2001) in a correlational investigation of driving anger. Instead of directly observing the drivers, they asked drivers to observe themselves in naturally occurring situations that might invoke driving anger.

Participants

The participants were students from an upper-level psychology class. They volunteered to take part in the study and were rewarded with points amounting to a 1 percent increase in their final grade in the course. About 7 percent of the students in the class either chose not to participate or produced unusable data. In total, 61 men and 118 women participated. Ninety percent of them were white non-Hispanic.

Procedure

Four weeks into the semester, participants were given driving logs to complete on each of three days of the following week. These logs contained structured items that participants used to report on their own driving. They recorded factors such as the amount of driving they did on an observation day and situations they encountered that produced anger on that day. They rated the anger on an intensity scale from 0 (= no anger) to 100 (= the most anger they had ever experienced). They also indicated aggressive and risky behaviors they had performed by choosing them from a printed list. Aggressive behaviors were things such as angry gestures and swearing, and risky behaviors were things such as speeding or drinking and driving.

Also at four weeks, the participants were given the short form of a psychological test called the Driving Anger Scale or DAS (Deffenbacher, Oetting, & Lynch, 1994). As you will see in subsequent chapters, psychological tests are also sometimes called "scales," "instruments," or "measures." The version of the DAS used in this study had 14 items. Although the items asked about different aspects of driving anger, the scale was considered to measure overall driving anger, rather than the specifics detailed by any particular question. In taking the DAS, participants were asked to read short descriptions of driving events. They were supposed to imagine that these had happened to them, and then they were asked to rate the severity of the anger that the situation would produce in them. They rated this anger intensity on a 5-point scale where 1 indicated "not at all" angry, 2 indicated "a little," 3 indicated "some," 4 indicated "much," and 5 indicated "very much." Examples of the individual items were things such as "A slow vehicle on a mountain road will not pull over and let people by," "Someone speeds up when you try to pass them," and "Someone backs right out in front of you without looking" (Deffenbacher et al., 1994, p. 86).

Results

The data gathered from the three days of driving logs for each driver were averaged together. This helped overcome the effects of a single, unusually bad incident. Responses collected on the driving logs were correlated with each other and with the responses from the DAS. Correlations between the DAS and the driving log responses are shown in Table 3.3.

There was almost no relationship between DAS score and the miles driven or frequency of driving. Driving farther or more often did not predict aggressive

TABLE 3.3 Correlations between Driving Anger as Measured by the Driving Anger Scale and the Responses from Three Days of Driving Logs

DRIVING LOG MEASURE	CORRELATION (r) WITH DAS SCORE
Miles driven	−.03
Frequency of driving	+.04
Frequency of anger	+.31
Intensity of anger	+.40
Frequency of aggressive behavior	+.28
Frequency of risky behavior	+.23

driving. There were moderate correlations between the DAS score and frequency of anger, as well as intensity of anger. It was expected that these correlations would be at least moderate because the DAS is designed to measure driver anger. Correlations were weaker between DAS score and frequency of aggressive behavior as well as frequency of risky behavior.

Although not shown in Table 3.3, strong correlations were found between a few of the items on the driving log. Frequency of aggressive behavior and frequency of anger were correlated $r = +.69$. Frequency of aggressive behavior and intensity of anger were correlated $r = +.62$. This suggests that the angry driver is also the aggressive driver. Because this relationship is what might be expected, it suggests that the driving log is accurately quantifying these responses. The correlation between frequency of risky behavior and frequency of aggressive behavior was $r = +.43$. Although this was only moderate, it makes the interesting suggestion that many drivers who are likely to drive at excess speed, for example, are also more likely to be aggressive.

In research about human behavior, correlations are not usually strong. There can be many things that might influence the behavior that is being studied. When a researcher selects only one of these factors, it should not be surprising that resulting correlations are less than perfect. We selected these particular data for discussion because there were a number of moderate to strong correlations. If you examine published studies in the psychology journals and look at the magnitude of correlations that are reported, you sometimes will find that conclusions are based on rather weak relationships. It is important to become a skeptical consumer of information. In everyday conversation, people will say "there is a correlation between" one thing and another. That statement has little meaning until you know the magnitude and the sign of the correlation. Literally, the only information carried in that statement is that the relationship is not zero.

RELIABILITY AND VALIDITY

In the discussion of the data about driving anger, we noted that moderate to strong correlations were evidence that the measures were accurate. When there is evidence that measures are accurate, we say that they have a claim to validity. The term *validity* has a special technical meaning within psychology, and it refers to accuracy. A measure is valid if it is accurate. Sometimes an entire piece of research may be said to have validity. Validity is often divided into two categories, *internal* and *external*. A study has internal validity if it thoroughly and rigorously tests the correctness of its hypothesis. Appropriateness of control conditions, operational definitions, and sample representativeness are examples of factors to consider in judging internal validity. To some extent, validity is a matter of opinion; however, a validity judgment is not merely some wild and crazy guess. To evaluate the validity of a study, one must carefully consider all aspects of the methodology, using the kinds of critical thinking skills that are discussed in this book. It is probably never the case that a study is either valid or not. More often, strengths and weaknesses have to be considered, and a judgment is made that places the findings somewhere between absolute truth and complete lie.

The term *external validity* is used to indicate that the findings of a measure or an entire study can be generalized to the real world and do not merely apply to a contrived laboratory environment. The correlations between DAS outcomes and driving behavior in the real world are evidence for the external validity of the DAS.

There is a related concept called *reliability*. Reliability means repeatability. A measure would be considered reliable if it could be given twice and the outcome was the same. If a person took the DAS on Monday and again on Friday and the scores were the same or very similar, the DAS would be considered to be reliable. The same could be said for an entire study. If the replication of a study is conducted and the outcomes are the same, the study might be said to be reliable.

Although they are related concepts, it is important to understand that reliability and validity are not the same thing. If the fuel gauge on your car is stuck and always reads one-quarter of a tank, it is reliable, but not valid, except in the coincidental case where there really happens to be a quarter of a tank of fuel. This is an unusual example, but it illustrates the difference between reliability and validity. In psychology, reliability is often taken to be an indication of validity. Imagine that two observers are watching a behavior and collecting data about it. If their recordings are the same, or very similar, they are reliable, and this reliability may also be taken as an indication of validity. We phrase this cautiously because it is possible that the observations are not valid because both observers may be observing inaccurately in the same way, but this would not be a typical case.

Probably few students ever read the prefaces to textbooks. We did not read them when we were students. If you happened to read the preface to this book, you would have found out about our goals for your learning. In the simplest terms, we want you to appreciate the value of scientific evidence, but we also want you to be skeptical about claims that are made concerning behavior. For many of these assertions, there may be little or no evidence. Where evidence does exist, we want you to be able to take some introductory steps at evaluating it. Often, this will mean evaluating the methodology used to collect the data. There is enormous variability in the quality of the information about behavior available to you. How much of it are you going to believe? This vast quantity of information is almost valueless unless you can evaluate the methodology and make a decision about the validity of the studies that underpin the information. To be able to make these judgments based on an understanding of the research process is a precious skill that few people possess.

REFERENCES

American Automobile Association (AAA). (1997). *Aggressive driving, three studies.* Washington, DC: AAA Foundation for Traffic Safety.

Deffenbacher, J. L., Oetting, E. R., & Lynch, R. S., (1994). Development of a driving anger scale. *Psychological Reports, 74,* 83–91.

Deffenbacher, J. L., Lynch, R. S., Oetting, E. R., & Yingling, D. A. (2001). Driving anger: Correlates and a test of state-trait theory. *Personality and Individual Differences, 31,* 1321–1331.

Diekmann, A., Jungbauer-Gans, M., Krassnig, H., & Lorenz, S. (1996). Social status and agression: A field study analyzed by survival analysis. *Journal of Social Psychology, 136,* 761–768.

Ellison-Potter, P., Bell, P., & Deffenbacher, J. (2001). The effects of trait driving anger, anonymity and aggressive driving stimuli on aggressive driving behavior. *Journal of Applied Social Psychology, 31,* 431–443.

McGarva, A., & Steiner, M. (2000). Provoked driver aggression and status: a field study. *Transportation Research Part F, 3,* 167–179.

CHAPTER 4

ZIPPING UP THE GENES

When psychologists speak of personality, they are talking about the stable psychological traits people possess that lead them to respond in similar ways across different situations. The trait perspective in personality psychology argues that people possess many different personality traits that are stable from one situation to the next, just as physical characteristics such as eye color and height are stable across different situations. For example, people vary in how extroverted or introverted they are. A person who is very extroverted is likely to be this way across a variety of social situations. At the same time that an individual person is likely to behave similarly across situations, different people may respond differently to the same situation. When this happens, it is attributed to differences in their personalities. Some people are consistently the life of the party, while others are wallflowers.

Where does personality come from? As you will come to understand, there is no single source of personality; rather, it is part of a complex interaction among many factors. We wish it was possible to give you simple answers, but, for this question, simple answers are wrong answers. One of the differences between high school students and upper-level college students is that college students are better able to deal with multiple answers to a single question (Perry, 1981). High school seems to prepare students to seek THE answer, whereas college seems to help people to understand that this is often too simple. The style of thinking exhibited by high school students has been called *dichotomous thinking*. They are likely to see the world in terms of dichotomies; that is, they see the world as being one way or another. Often, this is expressed as seeing the world in black and white rather than appreciating the shades of gray. In dichotomous thinking, a national sports figure may be either a god or pond scum, not a realistic mix of various attributes. In the distant past, the field of psychology thought the same way as a high school kid. Mind *or* body and nature *or* nurture are examples of discarded dichotomies. Psychology now takes a multidetermined approach to areas where dichotomous thinking was once common. As an example of this, genes are now appreciated as an important influence on behavior that act in concert with many other influences.

Incorporating the research of Bouchard, T., & McGue, M. (1990). Genetic and Rearing Environmental Influences on Adult Personality: An Analysis of Adopted Twins Reared Apart. *Journal of Personality, 58*, 263–292.

THE MEASUREMENT OF VARIABILITY

In trying to find out where personality comes from, we are really asking why some people have different personalities than others: why there are so many differences in personality? Usually, the question is about a particular trait: why are some people so optimistic and some so pessimistic? Differences among people can be measured with a statistic called *variance*. Variance is a measure of the differences that can be found within a particular trait among members of some group. If you have taken statistics you may know how to calculate variance, but doing this calculation is not required to understand this chapter.

If you line up a group of 12-year-olds, you will be able to see considerable variation in the extent of their physical development. A statistical measure of that variability, such as the variance, would yield a high score for the physical development within that group. To take a behavioral example, the variance in juvenile delinquency would probably be quite high within most junior high schools. Some kids would commit many delinquent acts, some would commit none, and there would be a group in the middle. Because of the high degree of variability in delinquency, the value of the variance would be high.

Variance only can be measured within a specific group of individuals. It may be possible to imagine measuring the variance in juvenile delinquency for All-American kids in all junior high schools, but practically speaking, we could not. To do that would involve assessing the delinquency of each individual kid. Usually, if you are interested in the variance of some population (e.g., all kids in the United States), you will try to take a *representative* sample of the population and assume that the variance of that sample is similar to variance in the population. A truly representative sample captures the diversity, and therefore the variance, of the range of characteristics that exist in a population in the correct proportion.

If the sample is large, a random sample will probably be representative. Small samples are less likely to achieve representativeness, even if the samples are randomly selected. One reason is that small samples are more greatly affected by extreme values, which are also called outliers. Like the grades you receive in your classes, the numerical data that are collected from different research participants are averaged together. You can understand the problem of outliers in small samples by considering the grades you receive in your classes. Imagine a class in which your grade was based on four exams and your exam scores were 3 As and one F. Now imagine another class in which your course grade was based on 20 short quizzes and your scores were 19 As and one F. In both classes, we could argue that the grade of F was an outlier because it was extremely different than the other test scores in the class. However, the failing grade will have a much larger impact on your final grade in the first class than in the second class because the total number of scores in the first class is much smaller. The grade of F in the second class will not affect the overall course grade as much because there are such a large number of As to pull it up when you average the scores together.

Like the majority of research in psychology, research on personality is conducted on samples of people drawn from the overall population. We cannot know how much variability there is in optimism between all individuals who live in the United States, but we might be able to infer it with research samples that are representative of the people who live in the United States. These samples can be difficult to construct, but if they are large and carefully selected, they can yield good estimates of the variation within a large population.

SOURCES OF VARIABILITY

An important comparison can be made here between life sciences, including psychology, and some of the physical sciences. In physical sciences, variability is often largely the result of errors made in the scientific procedures. Imagine a simple demonstration of the physics of falling objects. If you want to know the speed at which objects fall, you might drop 10 bricks, one at a time, from a tall building and have a friend measure the falling time of each brick with a stopwatch. Variability might be introduced because you dropped some bricks end first and some side first. Additional variance might appear because bricks are not precision devices and some might have a bit more surface area than others, causing them to catch more air friction and fall more slowly. Perhaps some of the bricks hit window ledges on the way down. The person who is timing the fall of the bricks may also introduce some variability because he or she might not be paying full attention to the task after a number of bricks have fallen. This variability found in brick falling would be the result of errors and imprecision.

In psychology, variability may also be the result of error and imprecision but, much more important, the variability may reflect real differences among people. For example, the driving ability of elderly people has been shown to deteriorate as they get older, partially because of slowing of reaction time (Hakamies-Blomqvist, Johansson, & Lundberg, 1996). This variability is more than measurement error—some people are better drivers than others. In psychology, the variability is usually more than error—it can be the main focus of the study. Among people, the differences are usually more interesting than similarities. If we were to tell you that all kids in a particular classroom have IQs that are about average, you might think "So what?" In contrast, if we were to tell you that there was a classroom in which some kids had very low IQs and some kids had high IQs, then you would immediately have a question for psychological science: why are these kids different? This could also be phrased as "What accounts for the variance in IQ in this classroom?" Either way, it is the same question.

The answer to the question "Where does personality come from?" requires a clear understanding of the nature of variability within a group. Variance is one measure of this variability. We believe you can understand this, no matter how skilled or unskilled you are in statistics. Statistics are an important part of measurement in psychology, but at the introductory level it is probably more important to understand the concepts than it is to understand the math.

Once variability itself is grasped, the next step in finding out *where* individual differences in personality come from. We need to determine how much of the variability in a personality trait across members of a group is the result of the variability in any one specific factor. We might, for example, ask how much of the variance in a personality trait is accounted for by variability in genes, parenting, schooling, nutrition, or socioeconomic status. Note we are *not* asking how much of *personality* is accounted for by each factor. Rather, we are saying that we can measure personality, find a range of variation in a trait, and find out how much of *the variation* in the personality trait is the result of the variation in some other specific factor (see Figure 4.1). The research and statistical methods exist to enable us to answer this question.

You should be able to guess that variability in only a single factor, such as genes, parenting, or school, will never account for 100 percent of the individual differences in a psychological trait or a behavior. Nevertheless, some factors have been shown to account for rather large amounts of measured variation. It may come as a surprise to learn that for personality, painstaking research has indicated that a large amount of the variance is the result of variation in genetic factors. With proper research methods, it is possible to find out how much of the variation in certain characteristics is the result of individual, nongenetic components and how much is the result of genes. The amount of variance in a trait that is the result of genetic factors is called the *heritability* of that trait. The field of research that explores how much variance in a trait can be explained by differences in genes is called *behavior genetics*.

Heritability can be a difficult concept for people to grasp, so it is worth spending some additional time discussing it. Heritability refers to the amount of differences between individuals in a group that are due to differences in their genes. Differences in people's genes are not the only source of variability in the characteristics of individuals in a group. The other important source of differences between people is differences in their environments. People experience many aspects of their environments. Some of their experiences are the same, and others are different. As such, when people experience the same environments, it should lead them to be more similar to one another. When they experience different environments, it should lead them to be more different from one another.

If we agree that the two sources of differences between individuals in a group are differences in their genes and differences in their environments, we can conduct two quick thought experiments to demonstrate the logic of research on heritability. First, imagine a group of people who are exactly the same age and experience exactly the same environment in every possible way for their entire lives. If we observe differences between those people in how aggressive they are, for example, the differences must be the result of differences in their genes. Because their environments are and always have been identical, there is no other possible source of variance in aggression. In this case, the heritability of aggression would be 100%. One hundred percent of the variance in aggression between individuals in the group is due to differences in their genes.

Next, imagine a group of people who are exactly the same age and have exactly the same genes. If we observe differences between these people in how aggressive they are, the differences must be the result of differences in their

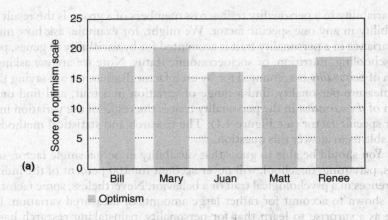

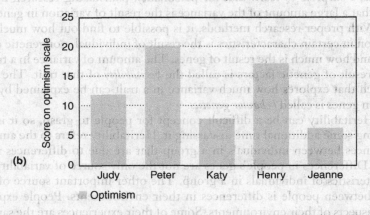

FIGURE 4.1   Illustration of Variance. (a) Optimism for Group A. (b) Optimism for Group B. Imagine that these are data on samples of students who have been selected from two classrooms, Group A from one class and Group B from another. Both have been given a pencil-and-paper optimism scale designed to measure their outlook about life. It is easy to see that there is more variation in Group B than in Group A. It would be interesting to do a larger study to find out why the members of Group A are so similar. The study we would do would ask why Group A has less variability than Group B. It would also ask what is the source of this variance. Perhaps, for example, the scores in Group B also have considerable variance, and the people who are not very optimistic, Judy, Katy, and Jeanne, are doing poorly in the class. As you can see, one way to approach this problem would be to calculate correlations between grades and optimism score. That might explain some of the variance. If Group A is a small class where students get a lot of individual attention and Group B is a large class, this might also explain some of the variance. You can, perhaps, think of other factors that might explain some of the variance.

environments. Since their genes are identical, there is no other possible source of variance in their aggression. In this case, the heritability of aggression would be zero. None of the variance in aggression between individuals in the group is due to differences in their genes.

TWINS

The usual way to approach the measurement of heritability in a human population is to measure the trait in question among individuals of known genetic related-ness—fathers and sons, siblings, half-siblings, cousins, or other relatives. A team of scientists at the University of Minnesota has been working on the heritability question for a number of years. Rather than relying on other family members who may share only small amounts of genetic material, this team has concentrated on twins. There are two kinds of twins: dizygotic and monozygotic. Dizygotic (DZ) twins are the result of two eggs being fertilized at the same time by two different sperm: *di* means two and a *zygote* is a fertilized egg. These individuals are no more closely related genetically than any other siblings. This means that they share, on average, half their genes. They just happen to have been conceived at the same time. Monozygotic (MZ) twins are the result of one fertilized egg splitting into two individuals: *mono* means one and a *zygote* is a fertilized egg. Because they came from one zygote, their genetic material is the same. These twins are sometimes called "identical twins." They are interesting as research participants because dif-ferences between them cannot be caused by genes—their genes are the same. The similarities between MZ twins certainly *may* have a genetic explanation, but these similarities also may have something to do with the shared experiences and envi-ronments that are usual for MZ twins. Again, *similarities* between MZ twins do *not* have to result only from their shared genes.

    The data in this study were collected as part of a large, longitudinal research project. Longitudinal research involves evaluating the same group of people over an extended period of time, usually a period of years. Longitudinal research is valuable in the field of psychology because researchers can directly observe how people change or stay the same as they age. Longitudinal research is expensive and difficult to do. Researches need to devote years of their lives to a longitudinal research project. They need to keep tabs on where research partici-pants live and stay in contact if the participants move. Researchers using a longi-tudinal design also need to keep participants interested in the research to try to prevent them from dropping out of the study.

Participants

To sort out the effects of genetic influences on personality, Thomas Bouchard and the research team from Minnesota located a group of twins, MZ and DZ, who had been separated early in life and raised apart in different environments.

These were called *MZA* and *DZA*, short for *MZ apart* and *DZ apart* (Tellegen, Lykken, Bouchard, Wilcox, Segal, & Rich, 1988).

If personality measures of monozygotic twins raised apart show strong correlations, we might be able to conclude that the similarities are the result of genetic influences. The dizygotic twins in this study form an important control group. The dizygotic twins share no more genes than ordinary brothers or sisters. On average, this is 50%. If the DZAs show about half as much similarity as the MZAs in personality, then we have some additional evidence for the role of genes in personality.

It might seem that it would be difficult to find many separated twins, and, once found, some of these twins might not want to be studied. The research team from Minnesota found that, indeed, separated twins are quite rare. However, with hard work, quite a number of pairs were located. Bouchard and his colleagues noted that the twins seemed to enjoy being studied. The Minnesota team worked hard to make the lab visits of all twins interesting and worthwhile so that they would remain in the study (Lykken, 1982).

Twins do not always know if they are MZ or DZ. In everyday life, this decision is usually made based on physical appearance: if the twins look quite similar, they are assumed to be MZ twins. Clearly, this is not good enough for genetic research because some DZ twins may appear to be quite similar, in the same way that nontwin siblings may sometimes look alike. Bouchard and McGue verified the MZ and DZ status of all twins in the study by testing blood samples to examine a variety of indicators of genetic relatedness. In addition, they examined fingerprints and other physical indices. Given these measures, the probability that a DZ pair would end up misclassified as an MZ pair in this research was less than 1 in 1,000.

Participants were 45 MZA pairs and 26 DZA pairs. In a study such as this, it is important to know how much contact the twins had with each other. In a perfect study, the twins would have been separated at birth and would not have been reunited until after personality had been assessed. However, real life does not produce this situation very often. Nevertheless, Bouchard and McGue were able to assure themselves that their twin pairs had been apart for a sufficiently long time so that shared environmental conditions were unlikely to account for personality similarities. Extensive interviews were conducted to collect information on the length of time that had passed before the twins were separated and on the amount of time they had spent together after they were reunited. The mean values for separation time are found in Table 4.1. This table also shows the range for each mean. The range is the lowest score in the group and the highest score in the group. It is a fairly crude measure of variability because if there is one individual with an extreme score, that person will distort one end of the range. If you look at the means and at the ranges together, you can get a better picture of the variability than you will get from looking at one or the other alone. For example, one MZA twin pair was together for 48.7 months before they were separated, but that could not be typical of many other MZA pairs or the mean for the whole group would be greater than 5.1 months.

Total contact months shown in Table 4.1 is the amount of time before separation combined with the amount of contact twins experienced after reunion.

TABLE 4.1   **Means and Ranges for Age and Contact in MZA and DZA Twins**

	AGE	% FEMALES	MONTHS PRIOR TO SEPARATION	YEARS PRIOR TO CONTACT REUNION	TOTAL CONTACT MONTHS
MZA (N = 45)					
Mean	41.0	65.2	5.1	30.0	26.5
Range	19–68		0–48.7	.5–64.7	.3–284.5
DZA* (N = 26)					
Mean	42.0	75.0	12.7	37.3	13.1
Range	25–61		.1–54.8	17–57.9	.2–54.2

*There were three opposite sex sets of twins in the DZA sample.

Procedure

When the twins were brought to the Minnesota lab, they engaged in about 50 hours of medical and psychological assessment. The researchers were interested in collecting as much information as possible on them because this may have been the last research of this kind to be done. Adoption agencies are now reluctant to separate twins. In contrast, this was commonly done when the people in this study were kids. Although we are primarily presenting information about personality, quite a bit of other information has been collected about twins by the Minnesota researchers (Lykken, Bouchard, McGue, & Tellegen, 1993).

The personality measure used by Bouchard and McGue was the California Psychological Inventory, or CPI. The CPI is a widely used personality test, probably selected because it has been shown to be a valid measure of personality. The form of the CPI that was used had 480 items designed to measure "aspects and attributes of interpersonal behavior that are to be found in all cultures and societies, and that possess a direct relationship to . . . social interactions." In addition, Bouchard and McGue asked the twins to assess their rearing environment using the Family Environment Scale, or FES. The FES is a self-report questionnaire made up of a wide range of statements about family environments. The twins' spouses were used as a comparison control group to ensure that the twins were not in some way different in personality simply because they were separated twins. The spouses were useful for this comparison because they were not twins and they had not been separated from siblings.

Results

The combined CPI scores of all MZA twins look about the same as the scores for all DZA twins combined. These combined scores for a few of the CPI scales are shown in Table 4.2.

These scores are not different than those found for typical adults, nor were they different from those found for the control group made up of the spouses of

TABLE 4.2 Examples of Mean CPI Scores for MZA-Combined and DZA-Combined Samples

SCALE ON CPI	MEAN MZA	MEAN DZA
Dominance	25.5	24.2
Sociability	22.5	19.5
Self-acceptance	19.4	18.3
Tolerance	20.7	20.0
Responsibility	26.9	26.2
Self-control	30.1	30.0
Flexibility	9.3	8.1

the twins. In terms of personality, as a group, the twins looked about like the rest of us. As a group, MZA and DZA twins were also similar in their responses to the FES measures. On FES family variables such as *cohesion, expressiveness, conflict, independence, achievement orientation, intellectual-cultural orientation, active-recreational orientation, moral/religious orientation, organization and control*, the two groups of twins were not different. Both MZA and DZA samples had similar FES scores to the group of nonadopted spouses, suggesting that any differences or similarities between twins were not merely the result of having been raised in adoptive homes.

The twins were separated early in life. When comparisons were made within a pair of twins, the data from the FES showed that there was no reason to think that their adoptive environments were particularly similar. Obviously, if both twins of a pair were placed in highly similar adoptive homes, similarity between twins in adulthood could be a result of home characteristics, shared genes, or both. Correlations were calculated for the FES ratings of each twin pair. High correlations would mean that the different adoptive homes were quite similar in family interaction style. Only a few of these correlations were significantly different from zero, suggesting that the adoptive homes were not very similar when one member of a twin pair was compared to the other twin in the pair.

In contrast, the members of a twin pair, particularly the MZA pairs, showed fairly strong correlations for personality when one twin was compared to the other. The MZA twins appeared to be more alike in personality than the DZA twins. Table 4.3 shows some examples of correlations for MZA pairs and DZA pairs. A third column shows the heritability for the listed factors. These heritabilities have been calculated from the twin data in this study and represent, as you will remember, the proportion of differences in personality that result from differences in genes. Heritability may range from zero—where there is no genetic influence, to a theoretical 1.00—where genes are the only cause of observed variation.

The difference between correlations for MZA twins and DZA twins is striking, and the heritabilities are all close to a value of 0.5, suggesting that about half of the variation observed in the personalities of these people was a result of genetic factors. A few personality traits not shown in Table 4.3 had lower heritability, such as *communality* (=.104) and *flexibility* (=.051), but these were rare.

TABLE 4.3   Examples of Correlations for MZA and DZA Twins and Heritabilities for California Psychological Inventory Scales

CPI SCALE	CORRELATION FOR MZA	CORRELATION FOR DZA	HERITABILITY*
Dominance	.53	.24	.541
Capacity for status	.60	.39	.652
Self-acceptance	.62	.11	.616
Well-being	.59	.17	.583
Responsibility	.48	.34	.626
Socialization	.53	.39	.577
Self-control	.68	−.28	.612
Tolerance	.55	.22	.602
Good impression	.53	−.19	.464
Achieve via conformance	.44	.02	.414
Achieve via independence	.62	.25	.665

Note: Be careful not to confuse heritability with the correlation coefficients. Although the arrangement of the digits is superficially similar, they are very different measures. Heritability is the proportion of variance for a particular trait that is the result of genetic factors.

DISCUSSION

This is not an isolated finding. Research using other personality assessments (Tellegen et al., 1988) and other groups in other countries (Rose, Koskenvuo, Kaprio, Langinvainio, & Sarna, 1988) have found substantially the same thing. Bouchard and McGue note that our intuitive estimates of the effects of environmental factors in personality are often inflated. Although we have not presented the data for MZ twins reared together, you may be quite surprised to learn that MZ twins show about the same levels of personality correlations when reared together as when reared apart. Summing up the literature, Bouchard and McGue say, "We are led to what must for some seem a rather remarkable conclusion: The degree of MZ twin resemblance on self-reported personality characteristics does not appear to depend upon whether the twins are reared together or apart, whether they are adolescent or adult, in what industrialized country they reside . . . degree of personality similarity between reared-apart and reared-together twins suggests that common familial environmental factors do not have a substantial influence upon adult personality."

If 50% of the variance in personality is accounted for by genes, what about the rest? As in the introductory example involving falling bricks, some of it will be a result of error in measurement and other unsystematic factors. One twin may have had more rest than the other on the day of testing. The personality test questions may mean slightly different things to the different members of the twin pairs.

Aside from heritability and error, Bouchard and McGue conclude that most of the rest of the variance is accounted for by idiosyncratic environmental factors.

Idiosyncratic factors are those that are different from one person to the next, even from one twin to the next. One way to understand these factors is to think about your own experience compared to that of other people raised in what may be naïvely called "the same environment." If you had siblings, you may be able to use them as examples; if not, think of a setting such as a school room. Homes and schools may seem like the *same* environment for the kids in them, but the current thinking in psychology suggests this is not the case. As Sandra Scarr (1992) pointed out, the actual experience of these contexts varies greatly from one individual to the next because, among other reasons, different people elicit or evoke different responses from the so-called *same* situations. Many of us may remember being hunted down and punished for specific behaviors while siblings and classmates seemed to get away with the same behavior. Perhaps when others told the teacher that the dog had eaten their homework, the teacher expressed concern for them. When you said the same thing, the teacher yelled at you and expressed concern for your dog. On the flip side, many of us will also remember having a special relationship with a teacher, very different from that person's relationships with our classmates. Parents may love all their kids, but the kids get treated differently from one another. These are the idiosyncratic factors that can make a superficially similar environment into a very different place for each individual.

Behavior genetic research involving twin studies has also demonstrated significant heritabilities for other personality traits and characteristics, including aggression (van Beijsterveldt, Bartels, Hudziak, & Boomsma, 2003), how people cope with stress (Kato & Pedersen, 2005), people's susceptibility to depression (McGue & Christensen, 2003), and perfectionism, which can be associated with the development of anxiety disorders, eating disorders, depression, and suicidal ideation (Tozzi et al., 2004). Psychologists who have reviewed the scientific literature on the role that genes play in the development of differences between individuals have come to some interesting conclusions. First, the majority of individual differences between people that have been studied to date, including height, weight, personality, vocational interests, and criminality are moderately heritable, ranging from values of 0.3 to 0.6. Second, evidence suggests that the heritability of characteristics increases as people age, a finding that is perhaps explained by the fact that, as people move from childhood to adulthood, parental influence decreases and people have more freedom to choose and shape their own environments (DeFries, McGuffin, McClearn, & Plomin, 2000; Rowe, 2005).

So, after all this, where does personality come from? You will now recognize that there is no easy answer to this question. Bouchard and McGue have demonstrated that genetics play a considerable role in personality differences among people. This is likely to be one reason why, as in other personality chapters in this book, personality seems to be quite consistent across situations and over parts of the life span. Does this mean that personality cannot change? No. At the same time that research on heritability demonstrates that genes are an important influence on variability in personality, it also demonstrates that the environment is an important influence. Researchers in the field of neuroscience have also documented that specific inputs from the environment can activate and deactivate certain genes (Jaenisch & Bird, 2003). We will have a more complete understanding of changes in personality when we know more about the idiosyncratic environmental factors that influence it. The first step in that understanding has been a big one. It has involved the acceptance of the idea that personality is not merely the result of learning *or* biology. Whatever the future holds for this line of research, it is already clear that there are important things going on down there in your genes.

REFERENCES

Bouchard, T., & McGue, M. (1990). Genetic and rearing environmental influences on adult personality: An analysis of adopted twins reared apart. *Journal of Personality, 58*, 263–292.

DeFries, J. C., McGuffin, P., McClearn, G. E., & Plomin, R. *Behavioral Genetics* (4th ed.). New York: Worth.

Goldsmith, H. H. (1991). A zygostiy questionnaire for young twins: A research note. *Behavior Genetics, 21*, 257–270.

Hakamies-Blomqvist, L., Johansson, K., & Lundberg, C. (1996). Medical screening of older drivers as a traffic safety measure—A comparative Finnish-Swedish evaluation study. *Journal of the American Geriatrics Society, 44*, 650–653.

Jaenisch, R., & Bird, A. (2003). Epigenetic regulation of gene expression: How the genome integrates intrinsic and environmental signals. *Nature Genetics, 33*, 245–254.

Kato, K., & Pedersen, N. L. (2005). Personality and coping: A study of twins reared apart and twins reared together. *Behavior Genetics, 35*, 147–158.

Lykken, D. (1982). Research with twins: The concept of emergenesis. *Psychophysiology, 19*, 361–373.

Lykken, D. T., Bouchard, T. J., McGue, M., & Tellegen, A. (1993). Heritability of interests: A twin study. *Journal of Applied Psychology, 78*, 649–661.

McGue, M., & Christensen, K. (2003). The heritability of depression symptoms in elderly Danish twins: Occasion-specific versus general effects. *Behavior Genetics, 33*, 83–93.

Perry, W. G. (1981). Cognitive and ethical growth. In A. Chickering (Ed.), *The Modern American College* (pp. 76–116). San Francisco: Jossey-Bass.

Rose, R. J., Koskenvuo, M., Kaprio, J., Langinvainio, H., & Sarna, S. (1988). Shared genes, shared experiences and similarity of personality: Data from 14,288 adult Finnish co-twins. *Journal of Personality and Social Psychology, 54*, 161–171.

Rowe, D. C. (2005). *The Limits of Family Influence* (2nd ed.). New York: Guilford Press.

Scarr, S. (1992). Developmental theories for the 1990s: Developmental and individual differences. *Child Development, 63*, 1–19.

Tellegen, A., Lykken, D. T., Bouchard, T. J., Jr., Wilcox, K. J., Segal, N. L., & Rich, S. (1988). Personality similarity in twins reared apart and together. *Journal of Personality and Social Psychology, 54*, 1031–1039.

Tozzi, F., Aggen, S. H., Neale, B. M., Anderson, C. B., Mazzeo, S. E., Neale, M. C., & Bulik, C. M. (2004). The structure of perfectionism: A twin study. *Behavior Genetics, 34*, 483–494.

van Beijsterveldt, C. E. M., Bartels, M., Hudziak, J. J., & Boomsma, D. I. (2003). Causes of stability of aggression from early childhood to adolescence: A longitudinal genetic analysis in Dutch twins. *Behavior Genetics, 33*, 591–605.

CHAPTER 5

THE NOSE KNOWS

Why do people have hearts? It is difficult to answer this question without explaining the specific function of the heart. One explanation is that people have hearts to pump blood throughout the body. Blood delivers nutrients and hormones to our cells and carries away metabolic waste. At this point, a lot of people might think that we have explained why people have hearts. However, we have only given part of an explanation. We have explained the *proximate* function of the heart. There is another question we need to answer: why do people have hearts in the first place?

For scientists, there is only one answer to this question. It is the same as the answer to a broader form of the same question: why do people possess complex, adaptive mechanisms? Complex, adaptive mechanisms are any traits or characteristics that are too complex and functional to have arisen by chance or accidentally. They function so well that they appear to have been specifically designed for the function that they carry out. So why do people possess these mechanisms? Why do people have hearts, eyes, lungs, and skin? The answer to these questions is that improbably useful functional characteristics were shaped by the process of evolution by natural selection (Darwin, 1859).

EVOLUTIONARY THEORY

The term *evolution* refers to change. The term *natural selection* refers to a process by which some characteristics are selected or favored by natural environments and other characteristics are not. The process of evolution by natural selection has occurred since the origin of life on the planet, and likely earlier. The process itself is simple, but its products can be incredibly elegant. For the process to work, it requires (1) individual variation in characteristics, (2) a mechanism of inheritance for those characteristics, and (3) a process of selection that favors some variants over others.

Incorporating the research of R. Thornhill and S. W. Gangestad, "The Scent of Symmetry: A Human Sex Pheromone That Signals Fitness?" 1999, *Evolution and Human Behavior, 20*, pp. 175–201.

VARIABILITY

We know that individuals vary in the functional characteristics that they possess. For example, some people have brown eyes; others blue eyes; and still others green eyes, grey eyes, or hazel eyes. We also know that some variation in characteristics, such as variability in eye color, is heritable.

INHERITANCE

The mechanism of inheritance at work in humans is genes. Genes code for the reliable development of the functional characteristics we possess, such as, hearts, eyes, lungs, and skin. Genes are passed on from parents to offspring through reproduction.

SELECTION

Some of the variability in characteristics may affect how successful individuals are at reproducing compared to others. Individual characteristics that make the individuals who possess them more successful at reproducing than others who possess different characteristics will be selected for. The genes that code for the development of the more successful characteristics will be passed on in greater numbers to future generations. If a particular variant is recurrently successful in contributing to better reproductive success compared to other variants across multiple generations, then it may eventually become a shared characteristic of all or most normally developing members of a species. When this occurs, the characteristic is classified as an *adaptation*. An adaptation is an evolved, functional characteristic that either *directly* contributes to successful reproduction (e.g., adaptations to prefer healthy mates) or *indirectly* contributes to successful reproduction by helping an organism survive long enough to reproduce (e.g., adaptations to circulate nutrients to all the cells in the body, such as the heart, arteries, veins, and capillaries).

LEVELS OF EXPLANATION

Why do people have hearts? There are at least two scientific explanations for this question. The first is a proximate level explanation: people have hearts to pump blood throughout their bodies.

The second is an *ultimate* level or evolutionary explanation: hearts are an adaptation, an evolved product of the process of selection. The hearts that humans possess were gradually shaped into their current form across millions of generations because of the beneficial effects each design feature of hearts (e.g., four chambers, valves governing blood flow direction) had on the survival, and indirectly, on the reproduction of our ancestors who possessed them. Individuals in the past with other design features in their hearts (e.g., three chambers, different valves) were less successful at surviving and reproducing. Our ancestors passed on the genes for the more beneficial heart characteristics in greater frequency than others who possessed genes for less beneficial heart characteristics.

The key to the process of evolution by natural selection is *differential reproductive success based on heritable variants*. Everyone has ancestors, but not everyone leaves descendants. In fact, more than 99.9 percent of individual organisms that were ever born in the history of life on Earth were not successful at reproducing for one reason or another. That makes all life on the planet, including you, an incredibly improbable success story. Every single one of your ancestors since the beginning of life managed to survive and reproduce. They were able to do this because they possessed characteristics that, on average, were better adapted; that is, they provided better solutions to the problems of survival and reproduction that they faced than others in the past that did not leave descendants. Successful reproducers are the only individuals who pass on genes to the next generation.

EVOLUTIONARY PSYCHOLOGY

It is important to note that adaptations are not restricted to physiological characteristics, such as the heart and lungs. They can also include psychological characteristics, such as specific preferences, desires, motivations, emotions, and ways of thinking about the world. These psychological adaptations evolved because they guide organisms' behaviors in directions that led to greater reproductive success for our ancestors, *on average*, than did the characteristics possessed by others who left fewer or no descendants. The study of psychological adaptations is known as *evolutionary psychology*.

You will notice that the words "on average" are in italics in the second to the last sentence of the previous paragraph. We want to draw your attention to these words because they are extraordinarily important in understanding the process of evolution by natural selection. A characteristic does not have to be successful in solving a problem and contributing to reproductive success every time in every individual who possesses it in order for the process of natural selection to favor it. Selection will favor any characteristic that leads to better average reproductive success, across all individuals who possess it.

An evolutionary psychological perspective can be a valuable tool to help predict, in advance, the kinds of functional psychological adaptations that people possess. In a general sense, evolutionary psychologists hypothesize that psychological adaptations should ultimately have functioned to promote reproductive success in our ancestors. This provides a powerful framework through which evolutionary psychologists can explore the design of the human mind.

This is exactly what Randy Thornhill and Steven W. Gangestad (1999) did in a study they conducted at the University of New Mexico. These two researchers have a long history of generating hypotheses using evolutionary theory and then evaluating their hypotheses with research. One hypothesis they proposed is that people should find cues to health attractive in members of the opposite sex (Gangestad, Thornhill, & Yeo, 1994). A powerful cue to health in a person is symmetry. Bilateral symmetry refers to how similar the left side of a person's body is to the right side of the person's body.

FLUCTUATING ASYMMETRY

Thornhill and Gangestad (1994) hypothesized that high levels of bilateral symmetry (thus low fluctuating asymmetry or low FA for short) is the result of *developmental stability*. Developmental errors can occur in the process of growing a person. Genetic mutations and too much or too little of particular hormones at certain points in development can make the process go haywire. To complicate matters, as people develop from children into adults, they face a number of hardships, such as infectious diseases, lack of nutrients, injuries, and other environmental stresses. Any or all of these events can derail the development of a perfectly symmetrical human, leading to, for example, one ear that is slightly longer than the other or one nostril that is slightly wider than the other. People whose developmental process is more resistant to the environmental perturbations that could waylay normal development have lower FAs than do people with less stable developmental processes. As such, low FA (high symmetry) is a cue to developmental stability. Healthier people are less likely to have deleterious genetic mutations and are better able to fight off diseases and deal with other environmental challenges like food shortages. Low FA turns out to be a reliable indicator of both developmental stability and health.

Thornhill and Gangestad (1994) hypothesized that if low FA was a recurrent cue to health over human evolutionary history, then people may have evolved to find more symmetrical people to be more attractive. Individuals in the past who preferred to mate with more symmetrical members of the opposite sex would have passed on the same genes that led to developmental stability and good health in their mates to their mutual offspring. The offspring of parents with low FA would have had an advantage, on average, over the offspring of parents who did not exhibit a preference for symmetry. The offspring of parents with high FA would have had genes that were, on average, more prone to mutation or less effective at dealing with environmental insults and, as a result, would have been less healthy.

Gangestad, et al. (1994) tested their hypothesis and found that people rate members of the opposite sex who were lower in FA to be more attractive than those who were higher in FA. The researchers also wondered if FA affected actual mating behavior. They hypothesized that, if more symmetrical men were more attractive than less symmetrical men, then there should be a positive correlation between symmetry and number of sexual partners. This is precisely what they found. Men with low FA reported significantly more sex partners in their lifetime than men with high FA.

Some of you may be wondering why the researchers did not expect to find the same results for women. Why did they not predict that women who were low in FA would have more sex partners than women who were high in FA? The answer to this question can be found in another important evolutionary theory, the parental investment theory (Trivers, 1972).

Parental investment theory is based on the observation that women often invest more in reproduction than men do. If you consider the minimum amount of investment that women and men are biologically obliged to make in order to reproduce, women must invest a minimum of nine months in a pregnancy. Men can invest as little as an evening to conceive a child with a woman. This represents a huge discrepancy in parental investment between women and men. All available evidence suggests that this difference between women's and men's minimum obligatory parental investment has been a recurrent part of our species' evolutionary history for millions of years.

Robert Trivers (1972) hypothesized that this biological difference between women and men may have led to the evolution of differences in the way that they think about sex, particularly in short-term sexual relationships. Specifically, he proposed that women should be choosier than men when selecting mates because the costs of a poor mate choice are greater for women—they have to live with their mate choice for at least nine months. Trivers proposed that men should be less choosy when selecting mates because they can invest so little in reproduction. Men can have sex, conceive a child, and then leave. To put it another way, short-term sex is expensive for women, so they evolved psychological adaptations to ensure that they make good choices. For men, short-term sex is relatively cheap, so they evolved different psychological adaptations that lead them to be less choosy than women.

Women's greater investment in reproduction also means that women cannot benefit from having multiple different sex partners in the same way that men can. Short-term sex with multiple partners can lead to additional offspring for men. Once a woman is pregnant, in contrast, additional sex partners will not lead her to have additional offspring. Trivers' (1972) parental investment theory provides the answer to why Gangestad et al. (1994) did not predict that women with lower FA would report more sex partners in their lifetime—women do not desire as many different sex partners as men do.

The explanation that parental investment theory provides about sex differences in the benefits of short-term sex may lead some readers to think that women cannot benefit from short-term sexual relationships. Parental investment theory, however, does not suggest this. It only points out that ancestral women did not benefit from *multiple* short-term partners in the same way that men did. Ancestral women may, however, have benefited from short-term sexual relationships for other reasons. Specifically, short-term sexual relationships may have given ancestral women access to partners with good genes.

Thornhill and Gangestad (1999) knew that women and men find members of the opposite sex with lower FA to *look* more attractive than those with higher FA. Because low FA is a cue to good developmental stability, they wondered if men and women with low FA would *smell* better to members of the opposite sex as well. They hypothesized that, if women's preferences for low FA men evolved to help women choose male partners with the healthiest genes, then women's preferences for the smell of low FA men should be greatest when they are most likely to conceive—when they are ovulating and the days immediately preceding ovulation.

Participants

To find out, the researchers enlisted the help of 80 male and 82 female research participants. The men ranged in age from 17 to 33 years old, with a mean age of 20.4 years. The women ranged in age from 17 to 53 years old, with a mean age of 22.3 years. In exchange for their participation in the research, participants received research credits for the introductory psychology class they were taking. A range of ethnicities was represented by the participants. More than half of male and female participants were Caucasian, about 30 percent were Hispanic, 8 percent of men and 7 percent of women were African American, 4 percent of men and 2 percent of women were Asian, and 4 percent of men and 7 percent of women were Native American. Recruitment posters for the study specifically asked for women who were not taking the pill or other hormone-based birth control. However, some of the women who reported to participate in the research indicated that they actually were taking hormone-based contraceptives.

The researchers tried to exclude women who were taking contraceptives for an important reason. The pill and other hormone-based contraceptives are recent inventions. Women did not have access to them for the vast majority of their evolutionary history. These contraceptives work by altering women's physiology, some by tricking women's bodies' into believing that they are pregnant and preventing them from ovulating. There is reason to believe that women taking contraceptives might experience cues important to mate choice differently than women who do not take them.

Methods

Participants reported to the lab in same sex groups of about four people. They filled out a demographic questionnaire that asked them for information like their age, height, weight, ethnicity, and lifetime number of sex partners. Participants were then taken one at a time into another room where their bilateral symmetry was measured. This was accomplished by measuring a number of characteristics on both the right and left sides of the participants' bodies. Measurements were made with a digital caliper, which yields highly precise measurements that are sensitive to 0.01 mm. Each characteristic was measured twice to help assess the reliability of the measurements. The characteristics that were measured were ear length and width; elbow, wrist, and ankle width; foot breadth, and the lengths of all fingers with the exception of the thumb. These characteristics were chosen because previous research demonstrated that behavioral factors, such as being right or left handed, tended not to affect the measurements. In addition to the measurements, a high-quality, color photograph was taken of each participant's face in front of a plain background from about two and a half feet away.

Thornhill and Gangestad wanted to focus their research only on asymmetry produced by aberrations in normal development caused by genetic effects, hormone irregularities, or disease. They did not want to include asymmetries caused by injuries because it is unlikely that these sources of asymmetry would be associated with the way that the participants smelled. Symmetry measurements of parts of the body that had been broken or sprained were not factored into subsequent analyses.

The measurements of asymmetry were combined in order to generate a single, overall asymmetry score. The score was calculated by dividing the difference between measurements on the right and left sides of the body by the average of the two measurements. Each of the 10 scores was then summed to produce an overall FA score.

After being photographed, each participant was given a white, cotton T-shirt. The T-shirt was new, clean, and had not been worn previously. Participants were told to wear the shirts while they slept for two nights. Before wearing the T-shirts to bed, participants were instructed to wash their bed sheets with unscented detergent that was provided by the experimenters. This helped prevent scents previously in participants' beds from contaminating the T-shirt. Participants were also provided with unscented soap to use during the period when they were to wear the T-shirts. In addition, participants were instructed to refrain from activities that might alter their individual natural body smell during the period when they wore the T-shirt to bed. The prohibited activities were (1) using any product with a fragrance on their body or hair, including cologne, perfume, and scented soaps; (2) eating foods that were spicy or had strong flavors, such as onions, garlic, pepperoni, cabbage, asparagus, and lamb; (3) drinking alcohol or using other drugs; (4) smoking; (5) having sex; and (6) sleeping with someone else. Participants were instructed to place their T-shirts in a plastic bag during the day when they were not being worn. They returned the T-shirts to the researchers in the same bag at 9:00 A.M. after wearing them for the second night. Ninety-two percent (74) of male and 95 percent (78) of female participants returned their T-shirts. When they returned their shirts, the researchers used a questionnaire to ask the participants if they had violated any of the research guidelines during the time they had worn them. Participants were informed that there was no penalty for violations. The experimenters only wanted to use shirts that were not contaminated by scents other than natural body odors.

The smell of fragrances, soaps, or smoke was present on some of the shirts that were returned. Fifteen of the shirts returned by women smelled like either some kind of fragrance or smoke. Six of the shirts that men returned also had nonhuman odors. These shirts were excluded from being rated.

Smelling T-shirts.   At about 10:00 A.M. on the same morning that the T-shirts were returned to the researchers, the same participants who wore them began reporting to the lab to rate the scent of the shirts worn by members of the oppo-site sex. The shirts were separated and put into boxes of about ten shirts per box.

Male and female raters were asked to lift each bag holding a shirt, open the bag, and smell the shirt without touching it. Raters evaluated each shirt on three dimensions. First, they rated how pleasant the shirt smelled on a scale from 1, indicating a very unpleasant-smelling shirt, to 10, indicating a very pleasant-smelling shirt. Using similar 10-point scales, the raters also indicated how sexy and how intense each shirt smelled. On completing their ratings of a shirt, the raters were instructed to close the bag and put it back in the box before rating another shirt.

Four male and two female raters indicated that their sexual orientation was either homosexual or bisexual. Because the focus of the study was heterosexual evaluations of FA, the ratings of these participants were not included in subse-quent analyses.

Out of the 72 heterosexual women who rated the scent of the T-shirts, 16 were taking some kind of hormone-based contraceptive, one had recently taken a morning-after pill to avoid an unwanted pregnancy, two did not experience normal menstrual cycles due to medical reasons, two had already gone through menopause, and one was pregnant. An additional two women did not complete the rating sheet. Fertility risk (likelihood of becoming pregnant) was estimated for the 48 female raters who remained based on their day in their menstrual cycle. The researchers used medical literature to estimate their fertility risk. On average, women ovulate about 15 days before the end of their typical menstrual cycle. Fertility risk is highest on days 6 through 14 of women's cycles. Thirteen of the women who rated the scent of the T-shirts were in this range. The rest of the women were outside this range and were considered to be a low fertility risk.

Thornhill and Gangestad pointed out that estimating the day of ovulation from information about the beginning of women's last periods and the typical length of their cycles can be problematic. It does not provide as precise a meas-ure of ovulation as other techniques. However, those other techniques are much more intrusive. The researchers suggested that this lack of precision does not weaken their results. If anything, errors in the estimates of raters' ovulation dates should lead to underestimates of how strong the relationships between the vari-ables are.

All researchers who presented T-shirts to the raters were unaware of the symmetry measurements of the men and women who wore the shirts. Partici-pants were also unaware of the symmetry measurements of the people who wore the shirts. As you will remember from Chapter 1, this is called a double blind procedure because both the researchers and the participants did not know the symmetry measurements. This kind of procedure is useful because it prevents the researchers from inadvertently influencing participants' ratings. It also deprives participants of information that might affect their ratings.

After completing their ratings, female participants were given a brief ques-tionnaire that assessed whether they were currently using hormone-based contraceptives, the first day of the women's most recent menstrual period, and the number of days that their menstrual period typically lasted. The latter two items were used to calculate whether the female participants were currently or close to ovulating.

Facial Attractiveness.   Fourteen women and 15 men who did not participate in the other parts of the study were recruited to rate the facial attractiveness of participants who wore the T-shirts. They made their ratings based on the photographs that were taken of the participants on the day their symmetry was measured and they picked up the shirts. The ratings were made on a 1 to 10 scale, where 1 was least attractive and 10 was most attractive. The raters were instructed that they should not rate the attractiveness of anyone they recognized. The opposite sex ratings were averaged in order to generate a mean facial attractiveness rating for each photograph.

Results

Women's Ratings.   Many of the research findings in this study are expressed in the form of correlations between variables. If you need a refresher on correlations, refer to Chapter 3.

The authors found that FA was a moderately good predictor of lifetime number of sex partners for men, $r = -.34$, but not for women, $r = 0$. This represents a replication of findings from the researchers' previous work (Thornhill & Gangestad, 1994) and suggests that the finding is the result of a real relationship between the variables rather than some form of error.

When the researchers looked at the correlation between participants' ratings of the pleasantness and the sexiness of the way shirts smelled, they found that the correlation between the ratings was quite high (.85 for women and .82 for men). To simplify data presentation, the researchers combined these measures in subsequent analyses.

Researchers also noticed that the scent of shirts worn by men who showered more frequently were rated as more attractive than the shirts worn by men who did not bathe as often. The correlation between frequency of bathing and the attractiveness of the scent of shirts was a strong $r = .42$. As a result, the researchers statistically controlled for the frequency of bathing in the other statistical analyses they performed. They did this to get a clearer estimate of how the FA of the men was related to ratings of the attractiveness of their scent.

As illustrated by Figure 5.1, women's ratings of the attractiveness of the scent of shirts worn by all men did not significantly differ depending on the women's estimated fertility risk. The average scent rating for high fertility women was 4.99, and the average for low fertility women was 4.81.

Men's FA was found to be a significant predictor of the attractiveness ratings of the smell of shirts among high fertility women, $r = -.33$, but not

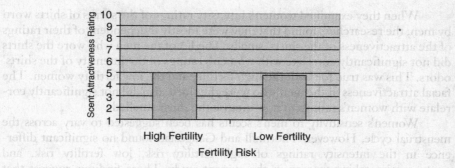

FIGURE 5.1 Average Attractiveness Ratings of the Scent of T-Shirts by High Fertility and Low Fertility Women

low fertility risk women, $r = -.09$. Subsequent comparisons of these correlation values revealed that these correlations significantly differed from each other.

The researchers conducted another analysis in which they examined the relationship between women's ratings of the attractiveness of shirt scents and the independent ratings of the facial attractiveness of the male participants. They found that both the high fertility and low fertility women exhibited a slight preference for the scent of shirts worn by men who were lower in FA. There was, however, no difference in the preferences of the two groups of women.

Thornhill and Gangestad performed some additional analyses in which they examined the relationship between fertility risk across the women in their sample and preferences for the scents of shirts worn by the men. They found a statistically significant correlation between fertility risk and women's preference for the scent of symmetrical men, $r = .49$. As women's fertility risk increased, so did their preference for the scent of shirts worn by more symmetrical men. The researchers found a similar result when they examined the relationship between women's fertility risk and the facial attractiveness of the male participants. As women's fertility risk increased, so did their preference for more facially attractive men, $r = .29$.

Even though they did not plan to include women raters who were taking hormone-based contraceptives, some of the participants were using them. The researchers examined whether these contraceptive-taking women exhibited any of the preferences that the high fertility risk women did. They found that women who were taking hormonal contraceptives did not exhibit any preferences for the smell of men who were lower in FA or for the smell of men who were higher in facial attractiveness.

When they examined women's intensity ratings of the scents of shirts worn by men, the researchers found that they were mostly independent of their ratings of the attractiveness of the shirts' smells. The FA of the men who wore the shirts did not significantly correlate with women's ratings of the intensity of the shirts' odors. This was true for both the high fertility and the low fertility women. The facial attractiveness of the men who wore the shirts also did not significantly correlate with women's ratings of how intense the shirts smelled.

Women's sensitivity to men's scents has been suggested to vary across the menstrual cycle. However, Thornhill and Gangestad found no significant difference in the intensity ratings of high fertility risk, low fertility risk, and contraceptive-taking women in the current study. These findings suggest that the relationship between women's fertility risk and their preference for the scent of more symmetrical men is independent of any general increased sensitivity to smells during their fertile period.

Men's Ratings.   Men's average rating of the attractiveness of the scent of T-shirts worn by women was 4.8. This did not differ significantly from the ratings given by women in the high or low fertility groups of the attractiveness of men's shirts.

Men's ratings of the attractiveness of the scent of women's shirts also did not correlate with the FA of the women who wore them, the facial attractiveness of the women, or the women's age. When only women who did not use any form of fragrance during the time they wore the T-shirts were considered, the attractiveness of their scent was significantly correlated with their facial attractiveness, $r = .31$. However, women's FA and age were still not significantly correlated with the attractiveness of women's scent, $r - .03$ and $r = -.03$.

Men rated more attractive female scents as being more intense, $r = .15$. However, this correlation is quite small. Men's ratings of the intensity of the scent of women's T-shirts was not significantly correlated with women's FA ($r = -.06$), age ($r = .01$), or facial attractiveness ($r = -.07$).

DISCUSSION

The results of this study suggest a difference in men's and women's detection of the relationship between the attractiveness of body odor and FA. Noncontraceptive-taking women in the fertile phase of their cycles found the scent of more symmetrical men to be more attractive than the scent of less symmetrical men. During times of low fertility, women did not exhibit this preference. Women who were taking contraceptives also did not exhibit this preference. There is no evidence that men found the scent of more symmetrical women to be more attractive than the scent of less symmetrical women. These findings may help explain why women in other research have indicated that the scent of their partner is central to deciding who to choose as a mate and their experience of sexual desire (Herz & Cahill, 1997).

Although this study provides evidence that high fertility women prefer the scent of men who have greater developmental stability, it did not isolate the substance that more symmetrical men produce (or fail to produce) that makes them smell better. To obtain definitive evidence that such a substance exists would require carefully controlled experiments that asked participants to rate the attractiveness of the substance in isolation, as well as other scented substances produced by men.

Research has demonstrated that women's sexual desire peaks at the fertile period in their menstrual cycle (Regan, 1996). Other research has documented that women in nightclubs and on university campuses wear clothes that expose more skin when they are in the fertile phase of their cycle (Grammer & Jutte, 1997). Taken together, the results of these studies and the findings of the research discussed in this chapter suggest that fertile women's preference for the scent of more symmetrical men may function to motivate them to conceive children with men of high genetic quality. Thornhill and Gangestad argue that the motivation to obtain good genes for offspring may sometimes supersede women's desire to find or be faithful to a loving, investing male partner.

Thornhill and Gangestad used the logic of evolutionary theories proposed by Darwin (1859) and Trivers (1972) to generate hypotheses about how aspects of women's sexual preferences and desires were likely to function. They then conducted careful research and found strong support for their hypotheses that is consistent with research done by others on a range of similar topics. The evidence suggests that high fertility women's preference for the smell of more symmetrical men is an adaptation that evolved because it led to greater reproductive success for our female ancestors compared to other females who did not have the preference. This study is a good example of how a strong theory can lead to new discoveries in the field of psychology.

The findings of this study suggest something else that is important to consider—people's decisions and behaviors are likely influenced by processes that occur outside their conscious awareness. The high fertility women in this study did not know that they had a preference for the scent of more symmetrical men. They did not know that the preference would disappear when they moved into the low fertility phase of their cycle. These preferences, however, are real and may influence women's decisions and behaviors in important ways.

REFERENCES

Darwin, C. (1859). *On the origin of species*. London: John Murray.

Gangestad, S. W., Thornhill, R., & Yeo, R. A. (1994). Facial attractiveness, developmental stability, and fluctuating asymmetry. *Ethology and Sociobiology, 15*, 73–85.

Grammer, K., & Jutte, A. (1997). The war of odors: Importance of pheromones for human reproduction. *Gynakologisch-geburtshilfliche Rundschau, 37,* 150–153.

Herz, R. S., & Cahill, E. D. (1997). Differential use of sensory information in sexual behavior as a function of gender. *Human Nature, 8,* 275–286.

Regan, P. C. (1996). Rhythms of desire: The association between menstrual cycle phases and female sexual desire. *Canadian Journal of Human Sexuality, 5,* 145–156.

Thornhill, R., & Gangestad, S. W. (1994). Fluctuating asymmetry and human sexual behavior. *Psychological Science, 5,* 297–302.

Thornhill, R., & Gangestad, S. W. (1999). The scent of symmetry: A human sex pheromone that signals fitness? *Evolution and Human Behavior, 20,* 175–201.

Trivers, R. L. (1972). Parental investment and sexual selection. In B. Campbell (Ed.), *Sexual selection and the descent of man* (pp. 136–179). Chicago: Aldine.

CHAPTER 6

BEING SICK OF THE HOSPITAL

Usually, people go to the hospital when they are ill. This chapter considers the reverse: the learning process through which the hospital, and the treatment associated with it, can make people sick. When you first consider a hospital making people sick, you may be tempted to focus on the food, which is stereotypically considered to be bad. In defense of the food, it is not like Mommy makes, but it is exactly what Mommy *would* make if she had to feed 1,000 or more people, many of whom are on highly specialized diets.

Because we are not referring to the food, what is it about a hospital that can make people sick? First, we need to be clear about what we mean by "sick." We mean *sick*, physically sick, sick in a way that can be measured using the kinds of assessments available to contemporary medicine. It is important to be precise. We are talking about the kind of illness that is technically called *somatoform* illness. Sometimes the older label for this disorder, *psychosomatic illness*, is used in popular media to mean an imaginary illness, one that has no physical basis. That is not correct. In a somatoform illness, a person has observable symptoms, but, unlike other illnesses, the cause is not an obvious disease organism, such as a virus or bacterium. This is not to suggest that the causes of somatoform illness are mystical or unknowable. In fact, the causes are just as concrete as viruses and bacteria. In the case to be discussed here, no one would argue about the concreteness of the causes: the hospital was made of concrete. We are doing more than playing with words. The research to be discussed has shown that a hospital, in all its concrete and glass glory, can make people sick.

To understand how this can occur, we have to follow a path that connects the hospital to the illness through a process of learning. The special kind of learning that has been implicated in this example is called classical conditioning, or Pavlovian conditioning, after its discoverer, Ivan Pavlov (1849–1936). We will briefly consider Pavlov's work before returning to the illustration of somatoform

Incorporating the research of D. H. Bovbjerg, W. H. Redd, L. A. Maier, J. C. Holland, L. M. Lesko, D. Niwdzwiecki, S. Rubin, and T. B. Hakes, "Anticipatory immune suppression and Nausea in Women Receiving Cyclic Chemotherapy for Ovarian Cancer," 1990, *Journal of Counseling and Clinical Psychology, 59*, pp. 153–157.

illness. There are at least two reasons for this detour. First, you should know a few things about Pavlov. Although we try to focus on contemporary psychology in this book, there are a few examples of psychological phenomena that are so well known that they are familiar to any educated person. Pavlov's work is one of these. It is an important model, or way of thinking, about certain types of events in psychology. These models are sometimes called paradigms (pronounced *pair-ah-dimes*). A second and perhaps more compelling reason is that some somatoform illnesses, and many other examples from life, cannot be understood without a clear understanding of the Pavlovian paradigm.

GOING TO THE DOGS

Initially, Pavlov did not seek to find out about somatoform illness, or even about learning. Pavlov lived and worked in Russia, and was educated as a physiologist. He studied at the University of St. Petersburg, a center of intellectual life in a largely agrarian country that otherwise had high levels of illiteracy. In this setting, Pavlov was aware of the privilege afforded by a university education. As a young man, he was very much influenced by the study of reflexes. Reflexes were considered to be automatic responses to stimuli; responses that did not require any conscious thought or planning. With some slight refinement, this basic definition is still used today. The physiologists of Pavlov's student days considered reflexes to be the basic building blocks of behavior. Complex behaviors were presumed to be made of reflexes, in the same way that a brick wall is made of bricks. In particular, Pavlov was greatly impressed by the work of Sechenov, a professor of physiology in St. Petersburg. Sechenov believed that all physical acts were reflexes and that the study of reflexes would move psychology away from philosophy and "the deceitful voice of consciousness [to] positive facts or points of departure that can be verified at any time by experiment" (Frolov, 1938, p. 6). Clearly, the scientific establishment of the time felt some uncertainty about the emerging field of psychology and wanted its approach and content to be more like that of other sciences. So do we.

Pavlov worked for many years studying digestive physiology. He approached digestion by observing it in animals who were alive and who were functioning as normally as possible. He developed masterful surgical techniques for collecting and studying saliva and gastric juices from the stomach. Pavlov even augmented his meager research budget by selling gastric juice from dogs to the general public as a supposed aid for stomach problems (Babkin, 1949). This stuff did not turn out to be a miracle cure and probably tasted just as you might imagine it would. If anything, its sales bring credit to Pavlov's ability to sell his ideas to others.

In 1904, Pavlov was awarded the Nobel Prize for his research on digestion. Pavlov's formal speech on the occasion of the award spoke little about digestion but, rather, presented some other observations that he made while doing the digestion research. The observations he recounted took him to the forefront of psychology. He retains this position today, over 100 years later.

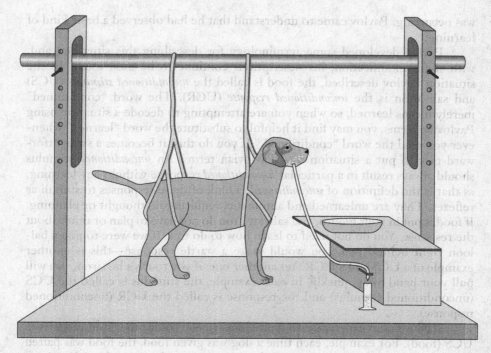

FIGURE 6.1   Classical Conditioning Apparatus Similar to That Used by Pavlov

In his work on the digestive processes of dogs, Pavlov perfected a little operation in which a cut was made in the dog's cheek, allowing a tube to be introduced through the cheek and into the salivary duct. A glass vial at the end of this tube collected and measured the saliva produced in response to various stimuli (Figure 6.1).

AN UNEXPECTED OBSERVATION

Pavlov was interested in studying the amount and timing of saliva production in response to various foods. Salivation was clearly a reflex because it did not have to be consciously turned on or off; it was an automatic response to food being placed in the dogs' mouths. However, Pavlov noticed that dogs often salivated before the food was in their mouths. The dogs salivated when they saw food, when they saw a food bowl, or even when they heard the footsteps of laboratory personnel at feeding time. At first, these responses were considered no more than nuisances that interfered with the study of digestion (Anokhin, 1971). Over time, Pavlov and his coworkers came to realize that they had observed something very important. Because the stimulus for these salivary responses was not the usual stimulus, food in the mouth, something unusual was occurring. Pavlov came to understand that he had observed a basic kind of learning.

Pavlov developed some terminology for describing this situation, and, with slight modification, his descriptions continue to be used today. In the situation Pavlov described, the food is called the *unconditioned stimulus* (UCS) and salivation is the *unconditioned response* (UCR). The word "conditioned" merely means learned, so when you are attempting to decode a situation using Pavlovian terms, you may find it helpful to substitute the word "learned" whenever you read the word "conditioned." If you do this, it becomes a straightforward task to put a situation into Pavlovian terms. An *unconditioned* stimulus should always result in a particular *unconditioned* response without any learning, as that is the definition of *unconditioned*. Think of these responses to stimuli as reflexes. They are unlearned and automatic, requiring no thought or planning. If food is put in your mouth, you salivate. You do not have to plan or think about the response. You do not need to learn how to do this. If we were to pop a balloon right behind you, you would make a startle response—this is another example of a UCS and a UCR. Yet another one: if you touch a hot iron, you will pull your hand away quickly. In each example, the stimulus is called the UCS (unconditioned stimulus) and the response is called the UCR (unconditioned response).

Pavlov's dogs experienced a repeated pairing of some other stimuli with the UCS (food). For example, each time a dog was given food, the food was paired with the footsteps of a laboratory worker bringing it. After a number of pairings, the dogs learned that footsteps signaled the approach of food. Once this was learned, the saliva would begin to flow in response to the sound of the footsteps. In this new pairing of stimulus and response, the footsteps and the saliva were called, respectively the *conditioned stimulus* (CS) and the *conditioned response* (CR). They were called the CS and the CR because they were learned: the dog learned to make this response to a new stimulus. One way to diagrammatically represent this learning can be found in Figure 6.2.

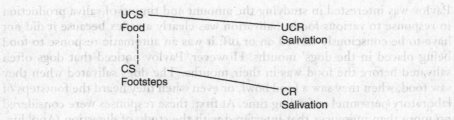

FIGURE 6.2 Pavlovian Analysis of Salivation

When you are trying to analyze a Pavlovian or classical conditioning situation into its elements, you can use four guidelines to check your analysis:

1. The UCR and the CR will be responses—something that the organism does. The UCS and the CS will be stimuli, usually something in the environment that elicits the responses, such as food or footsteps.
2. The UCR will be the organism's reflexive response, one that requires no learning. If the response has to be learned, it is not a UCR. By this logic, you should expect the same UCR to follow the same UCS in all the members of a particular species.
3. The stimulus that will become the CS should not lead to a response until it has been repeatedly paired with the UCS. Footsteps only resulted in salivation when repeatedly paired with the UCS, the food. Sometimes many pairings are required for classical conditioning, sometimes a smaller number are sufficient.
4. The UCR and the CR will appear to be the same behavior. The difference between the UCR and the CR is how behavior came to be produced by a stimulus. In one instance, the response is not learned (UCR), and in the other case, the response is learned (CR).

If you survey a number of sources that discuss classical conditioning, you may be surprised at how many give examples that contain errors because they do not pass these little tests. Probably the fourth guideline, similarity of UCR and CR, is the most often violated.

As a footnote to Pavlov's work, popular culture usually remembers the CS as a bell, not footsteps. Pavlov's early work on conditioning used a variety of stimuli for the CS, including footsteps, a metronome, a variety of tones, and some visual stimuli.

Although Pavlovian conditioning is a form of learning, it is not what most people have in mind when the topic of learning is discussed. People intuitively tend to think of learning as involving conscious concentration on information in order to remember it. Classical conditioning is not like this. Learning a new association between a CS and a CR occurs outside conscious awareness. In addition, the CR can be physiological activity like salivation. These aspects of classical conditioning have two important implications. First, classical conditioning can lead individuals to learn associations and not be aware that any learning has taken place. Second, individuals may not be aware that a particular physiological change is the result of classical conditioning.

Not all learning involves Pavlovian conditioning. Despite the importance of the Pavlovian paradigm, it is quite restricted because it requires an unlearned association as the basis for subsequent learning. Although subsequent studies identified so-called higher-order conditioning in which an additional stimulus is paired with an already established CS, classical conditioning has to start with an unlearned association. Once you understand the components of the Pavlovian paradigm, you should quickly be able to determine if classical conditioning is at work in behavior you observe. Learning to play basketball, for example, has little if anything to do with classical conditioning. It is much better explained by the imitation of behavior and the resulting rewards, such as the ball going through the hoop or the cheers of others.

Probably the only way for you to thoroughly understand classical conditioning is for you to use the terms we have described and to try to apply them to new examples. When you can do this for novel examples, you will own this concept. To give you a start, try to do a Pavlovian analysis, identifying the UCS, UCR, CS, and CR, in the following situation:

> Imagine that you live in an old building with problematic plumbing. If you are in the shower and someone in the bathroom next door flushes the toilet, the cold water disappears from your shower. You feel the water temperature go from pleasantly warm to scalding, and you jump out of the shower. After a few experiences with this situation, you jump out when you hear the next-door toilet flush. Once you have assigned classical conditioning terms, you can check your Pavlovian analysis against Figure 6.3.

So much for dogs and toilets. You should now have a sufficient grasp of the concepts of classical conditioning to allow us to discuss the work of Dana Bovbjerg et al. (1990) about hospitals making people sick. It has been known since the 1980s that cancer patients who receive chemotherapy often experience two side effects of the treatment: nausea and suppression of the immune system (DeVita, Hellman, & Rosenberg, 1985). These outcomes were first noticed shortly after the treatment. However, some patients showed more puzzling symptoms of nausea or vomiting *before* each treatment. This was called anticipatory nausea and vomiting, or ANV. Between one-quarter and three-quarters of patients were troubled by ANV. ANV seemed to be triggered by things as diverse as the sight of the clinic, the sound of a nurse's voice, or even the mere thought of treatment.

A number of clinical studies investigated ANV, and the conclusions pointed to classical conditioning (Redd, 1989). If you want to test your ability to

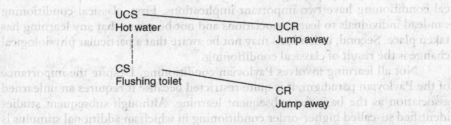

FIGURE 6.3   **Pavlovian Analysis of Jumping Away from Hot Water**

analyze this example in Pavlovian terms, stop here, look away, and do so before we give you the answer. The toxic drugs that are used in chemotherapy (UCS) make people feel nauseated (UCR). The hospital (CS) is constantly paired with the drug treatment (UCS) until the hospital (CS) itself makes people feel nauseated (CR). This is diagrammed in Figure 6.4.

The effects of this classical conditioning are so powerful that hospitals can still nauseate some former patients years after chemotherapy has ended (Cella, Pratt, & Holland, 1986). This fits with other research that has shown that for many animals, classical conditioning has long-lasting effects when feeling ill was the CR (see, for example, Gustafson, Garcia, Hawkins, & Rusinak, 1974).

The study by Bovbjerg et al. (1990) further investigated ANV and, in addition, sought evidence that anticipatory immune suppression (AIS) was also occurring in cancer patients. Immune suppression is the name given to a number of physiological responses that result in depressed functioning of the immune system. The immune system is the body's way of recognizing and dealing with disease organisms. When immune system function decreases before some event, in this case chemotherapy, it is called anticipatory immune suppression, or AIS. AIS has been the subject of a number of other research studies because of its importance to clinical medicine (see, for example, Kiecolt-Glaser & Glaser, 1988).

Participants

Thirty-six patients who had all undergone surgical treatment for ovarian cancer were identified. These women also met other criteria for being participants, including: they had not been treated with chemotherapy for any prior illness, their treatment plan called for chemotherapy, they had already received at least three treatments, and they lived within a two-hour driving time of the hospital where the chemotherapy was being given. Twenty-seven of the original 36

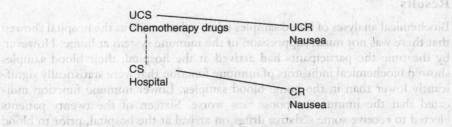

FIGURE 6.4   Pavlovian Analysis of ANV

eligible women agreed to be in the study. Of these 27, seven had to be dropped for a variety of reasons, including eventual change of their chemotherapy treatment and difficulty in drawing blood from their veins.

Procedures

During the course of the study, an appointment was made for a home visit at least three days before chemotherapy treatments. Blood was drawn for later analysis in order to assess immune system functioning. During the home visits, an experienced research technician administered some rating instruments called *scales*. On the scales, patients were asked to rate their current level of nausea. They rated this by choosing a number from a visual scale in which numbers were arranged as if they were numbers on a thermometer. This is called a visual analog scale, or VAS. The VAS is a useful tool for the quantification of feelings. Turning subjective states into numbers makes it possible to deal with the data quantitatively by computing averages and drawing graphs. The amount of anxiety being experienced was recorded on a questionnaire, the Spielberger State-Trait Anxiety Inventory, or STAI, as well as by asking for a single assessment of anxiety on another VAS. These two different measures of anxiety were used so that one could be a reliability check for the other. Measures of anxiety can be imprecise and having more than one was a way of boosting confidence in the results of the study.

Later, when participants arrived at the hospital, the anxiety measures were repeated. Participants were asked to recall and rate past feelings of nausea at three times before chemotherapy: the previous evening, on awakening the morning of chemotherapy, and immediately before chemotherapy was administered. Another sample of blood was drawn just before chemotherapy. The independent variable in this part of the study was the setting: home or hospital. The dependent measures were the ratings of anxiety, nausea, and analysis of immune functioning. This part of the study is a so-called *within-subjects* design. It is an experiment, but unlike some other experiments, the participants are their own control group. The same participants are exposed to two different situations, in this case, home and hospital.

Results

Biochemical analyses of blood samples taken at home and at the hospital showed that there was not much suppression of the immune system at home. However, by the time the participants had arrived at the hospital, their blood samples showed biochemical indicators of immune function that were statistically significantly lower than in the home blood samples. Lower immune function indicated that the immune response was worse. Sixteen of the twenty patients elected to receive some sedative drugs on arrival at the hospital, prior to blood drawing. To ensure that these sedatives were not responsible for immune suppression, a separate statistical analysis was performed on the patients who did not want to have any sedatives. The patients who had no sedatives also showed immune suppression, suggesting that sedatives were not suppressing the immune system. Although the researchers might have preferred to have no sedatives given to any of the participants in the study, it is important to understand that these "participants" were also people. In older studies, the participants were usually referred to as *subjects*. This terminology is still used in phrases such as *within-subjects design*, where no reference is made to specific people. The American Psychological Association (2001) now suggests that authors avoid the impersonal term *subjects* in the preparation of research reports. The word *subjects* is sterile and might lead us to forget that these participants were women, each recovering from surgical treatment for a frightening disease. It speaks well of them that they were willing to participate in research and to tolerate additional procedures in the home and hospital in order to help advance our understanding of immune supression.

The measures of anxiety, the STAI and the VAS, both indicated higher levels of anxiety in the hospital than at home. In addition, the visual scale for nausea indicated that anticipatory nausea was a greater problem in the hospital than at home (Figure 6.5).

In Figure 9.5, levels of all three symptoms were statistically significantly lower at home than in the hospital.

Although, as a group, the women showed immune suppression in the hospital, five individuals within the group did not. An additional analysis of the data was performed in which these five women were considered as one group and the other women were placed in another group. In this additional analysis, immune suppression was the variable that was being investigated by comparing the

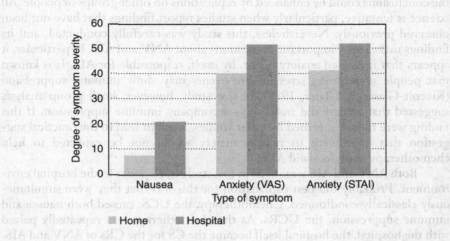

FIGURE 6.5 Degree of Symptoms Reported by Chemotherapy Patients at Home and in the Hospital

groups; one group had it, and one group did not. Nausea and anxiety continued to be outcome measures. The finding was that there were no significant differences between the anxiety measures when the AIS group was compared to the non-AIS group. Both groups were anxious in the hospital. This can be interpreted as meaning that the subjective feelings of anxiety were not always linked to immune suppression. This was important because it indicated that anxiety was not a cause of immune suppression. It follows that finding ways to lower the anxiety felt by these women would not be expected to also help them with immune suppression. Anxiety and immune suppression are separate responses to the situation.

In contrast, in this analysis, the patients who had immune suppression also reported higher levels of nausea in the hospital than those who had no immune suppression. In this case, it seems possible that, because these symptoms are linked, dealing with one of them might help treat the other. The discovery of a link of some sort can point the way to future research that may find causal links.

DISCUSSION

Bovbjerg et al. (1990) acknowledge their debt to studies of laboratory animals that pointed the way to this research. Lab animals can be used in studies that would not be ethically acceptable for human participants. It might be interesting to know what other types of stimuli, other than hospitals, can serve as conditioned stimuli for immune suppression, but ethics rightly limit research manipulations that can be performed on humans.

The sample in the Bovbjerg et al. (1990) study is small, and the validity of the conclusions could be enhanced by replications on other groups of people. All science is tentative, particularly when studies report findings that have not been observed previously. Nevertheless, this study was carefully conducted, and its findings make some important suggestions about ANV and AIS. In particular, it appears that increased anxiety is not, by itself, responsible for AIS. It is known that people undergoing stressful life events may show immune suppression (Kiecolt-Glaser & Glaser, 1988). In this study, however, small group analysis suggested that anxiety did not always accompany immune suppression. If this finding were to be confirmed by other studies, it might lead to the practical suggestion that counseling to relieve anxiety would not be expected to help chemotherapy patients avoid AIS.

Both ANV and AIS were seen in this study in response to the hospital environment. Probably the best explanation for this was that they were simultaneously classically conditioned. Chemotherapy, the UCS, caused both nausea and immune suppression, the UCRs. As the chemotherapy was repeatedly paired with the hospital, the hospital itself became the CS for the CRs of ANV and AIS. This seems like alphabet soup, but when you can read this and understand it, you are getting a grasp of classical conditioning.

The importance of the research can be illustrated by one case. Among the group of women studied by Bovbjerg et al. (1990), one person showed a dramatic 50 percent decrease in one of the measures of immune function. A person who is immunocompromised to this extent, even before the chemotherapy has been administered, is at considerable risk for contracting other diseases. Despite sanitation procedures, hospitals are, after all, full of diseases lurking around waiting for people to come by. For people with AIS, the hospital might not merely nauseate them, it might play a role in making them severely ill because of their poor immune function.

Even though this 1990 study by Bovbjerg et al. is more than 15 years old, it has stood the test of time. One of the powerful things about the research is the use of multiple dependent measures. This requires extra work on the part of the researchers, but pays off by allowing them to be more confident in their results.

Other studies have provided additional evidence and insights into how classical conditioning can affect patients' responses to treatments for cancer. For example, researchers have demonstrated that stimuli in the environment that do not by themselves lead participants to experience nausea and vomiting can have this effect if they are repeatedly paired with treatments that do cause nausea and vomiting (Klosterhalfen et al., 2005). These researchers demonstrated the process by which previously neutral elements of the environment can become conditioned stimuli. The findings of another study suggest that patients who receive stronger chemotherapy treatments have a greater risk of experiencing ANV (Morrow, 1982). To put it in terms of classical conditioning, a stronger UCR leads to a stronger pairing between the CS and the CR. Another study found that patients who experience the greatest feelings of nausea after chemotherapy are at a much greater risk for experiencing ANV (Stockhorst, Steingruber, Enck, & Klosterhalfen, 1993). A study conducted by Bovbjerg et al. (1992) demonstrated that reexposure to the CS that was paired with chemotherapy lead to anticipatory nausea even outside a medical setting and on a day when chemotherapy was not scheduled. Many chemotherapy patients report that the CSs that led them to experience ANV during chemotherapy continue to make them feel nauseous years after their treatment ended (Cameron et al., 2001).

Additional research has examined the role of classical conditioning on the severity of the side effects that occur after chemotherapy. For example, research conducted by Bovbjerg (2006) found evidence that classical conditioning may contribute to post chemotherapy nausea and vomiting. Additional research demonstrated that post chemotherapy fatigue may also be influenced by classical conditioning (Bovbjerg, Montgomery, & Raptis, 2005).

Understanding is the first step toward finding a remedy. Other classically conditioned responses, such as unreasonable fears—called *phobias*—have been successfully treated by programs designed to gradually expose the participant to the fear-producing object. It is not clear that this process of systematic desensitization would help chemotherapy patients, but it is an illustration that understanding classical conditioning can lead to treatment. Perhaps further work in this area will assure that, in the future, there is no need for the hospital to make people any sicker than they are already.

REFERENCES

American Psychological Association. (2001). *Publication manual of the American Psychological Association* (5th ed.). Washington, DC: Author.

Anokhin, P. K. (1971). Three giants of Soviet psychology. *Psychology Today, March*, 43–78.

Babkin, B. P. (1949). *Pavlov: A biography*. Chicago: The University of Chicago Press.

Bovbjerg, D. H. (2006). The continuing problem of post chemotherapy nausea and vomiting: Contributions of classical conditioning. *Autonomic Neuroscience: Basic and Clinicial, 129*, 92–98.

Bovbjerg, D. H., Montgomery, G. G., & Raptis, G. (2005). Evidence for classically conditioned fatigue responses in patients receiving chemotherapy treatment for breast cancer. *Journal of Behavioral Medicine, 28*, 231–237.

Bovbjerg, D. H., Redd, W. H., Jacobsen, P. B., Manne, S. L., Taylor, K. L., Surboke, A., Norton, L., Gilewski, T. A., Hudis, C. A., et al. (1992). An experimental analysis of classically conditioned nausea during cancer chemotherapy. *Psychosomatic Medicine, 54*, 623–637.

Bovbjerg, D. H., Redd, W. H., Maier, L. A., Holland, J. C., Lesko, L. M., Niwdzwiecki, D., Rubin, S., & Hakes, T. B. (1990). Anticipatory immune suppression and nausea in women receiving cyclic chemotherapy for ovarian cancer. *Journal of Counseling and Clinical Psychology, 59*, 153–157.

Cameron, C. L., Cella, D., Herndon, J. E., Kornblith, A. B., Zuckerman, E., Henderson, E., Weiss, R. B., Cooper, M. R., Silver, R. T., Leone, L., Canellos, G. P., Peterson, B. A., & Holland, J. C. (2001). Persistent symptoms among survivors of Hodgkin's disease: An explanatory model based on classical conditioning. *Health Psychology, 20*, 71–75.

Cella, D. F., Pratt, A., & Holland, J. C. (1986). Persistent anticipatory nausea, vomiting and anxiety in cured Hodgkin's disease patients after completion of chemotherapy. *American Journal of Psychiatry, 143*, 641–643.

DeVita, V. T., Hellman, S., & Rosenberg, S. A. (1985). *Cancer: Principles and practice of oncology*. Philadelphia: Lippincott.

Frolov, Y. P. (1938). *Pavlov and his school*. London: Kegan, Paul, Tench, Trubner.

Gustafson, C. R., Garcia, J., Hawkins, W., & Rusinak, K. (1974). Coyote predation control by aversive conditioning. *Science, 184*, 581–583.

Kiecolt-Glaser, J. K., & Glaser, R. (1988). Psychological influences on immunity: Implications for AIDS. *American Psychologist, 43*, 892–898.

Klosterhalfen, S., Kellermann, S., Stockhorst, U., Wolf, J., Kirschbaum, C., Hall, G., & Enck, P. (2005). Latent inhibition of rotation chair-induced nausea in healthy male and female volunteers. *Psychosomatic Medicine, 67*, 335–340.

Morrow, G. R. (1982). Prevalence and correlates of anticipatory nausea and vomiting in chemotherapy patients. *Journal of the National Cancer Institute, 68*, 484–488.

Redd, W. H. (1989). Anticipatory nausea and vomiting and their management. In J. Holland & J. Rowland (Eds.), *Psychooncology* (pp. 423–433). New York: Oxford University Press.

Stockhorst, U., Steingruber, H., Enck, P., & Klosterhalfen, S. (2006). Pavlovian conditioning of nausea and vomiting. *Autonomic Neuroscience: Basic and Clinical, 129*, 50–57.

CHAPTER 7

YOKING SMOKING

B. F. Skinner (1904–1990) started his academic life wanting to be a writer with an academic major in English. By the time his career was over, he was the best-known empirical psychologist of his time. He was a confirmed behaviorist and had little use for things inside the body, including mental events. He believed that mental characteristics were unobservable and, therefore, beyond the reach of science. For Skinner, proper scientific psychology should center its attention on the manipulation and measurement of the frequency of behavior. A great deal of Skinnerian psychology, also known as *operant conditioning*, can be summarized by the statement, *behavior is maintained by its consequences*. Skinner believed that the events that followed a behavior played a significant role in the subsequent frequency of the behavior. If pleasant stimuli followed a behavior, the behavior would increase in frequency. In contrast, if unpleasant events followed the behavior, its frequency would decrease. If the behavior actually produced the consequences, Skinner would say that the consequences were *contingent* on the behavior.

PULLING HABITS OUT OF A RAT

Skinner believed that control over consequences would mean control over behavior. Many of his studies were carried out in an apparatus that he called an *operant chamber*, but almost everyone else calls it a *Skinner box*. The steps in the development of this device were amusingly described by Skinner (1956) in a well-known article entitled "A Case History in Scientific Method."

The Skinner box was a chamber tailored to the size of the organism under study. For example, a typical Skinner box for a rat might have dimensions of a little less than one foot on a side. The walls and lid were usually made of clear plastic to facilitate observation of the animal. The floor was a series of closely spaced

Incorporating the research of J. M. Roll, S. T. Higgins, and G. J. Badger, "An Experimental Comparison of Three Different Schedules of Reinforcement of Drug Abstinence Using Cigarette Smoking as an Exemplar," 1996, *Journal of Applied Behavior Analysis*, 29, pp. 495–505.

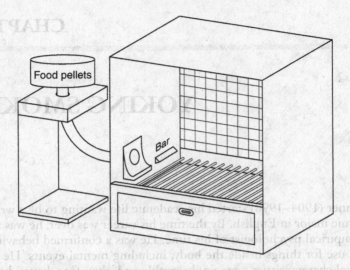

FIGURE 7.1   Skinner Box. An example of the sort of Skinner box that might be used in studies of learning with rats.

metal bars. Usually one wall of the box was a control panel with a device variously called a *bar* or *lever* protruding from it. This smooth metal object was the correct height so that a rat could push it down. The wall with the control panel also typically included an automatic food or water dispenser, which could be programmed to deliver water or food rewards to the animal in a manner controlled by the researcher (Figure 7.1).

The researcher was able to program the Skinner box creating a contingency, or causal link, between a behavior (pressing the bar down) and a pleasant event (receiving food or water). Skinner devised operant chambers for many different types of organisms. Although design of the device might be different, the point would be the same: to alter the frequency of behavior by changing consequences. A Skinner box for pigeons might have a little window that the pigeon could peck and a feeder that delivered birdseed, but the idea, and the resulting behavior, were not much different from a rat in a Skinner box.

In a typical Skinnerian training situation, the researcher would watch a hungry rat and, using a handheld switch, reward it for small movements, thereby coercing it nearer to the bar. At first, the researcher might reward the rat for turning toward the bar. Each time the rat turned that way, it would be rewarded. The effect of this contingent consequence was that the rat would begin to turn toward the bar more frequently. Next, the experimenter would reward only steps in the direction of the bar. The rat would move successively nearer the bar. Following this, the criteria would be restricted, and only a lift of the paw in the direction of the bar would be rewarded. Next, the rat would have to touch the bar for a reward, and finally it would have to push the bar down to get food. This procedure of training a rat to press the bar by rewarding successive approximations to the desired behavior is called *shaping*. In the space of two or three shaping sessions in a Skinner box, a hungry rat can learn to press the bar and feed itself. Skinner was not merely interested in teaching rats to feed themselves. He wanted to predict and control behavior. He found that changing the consequences of behavior rapidly changed the behavior itself.

REINFORCEMENTS AND PUNISHMENTS

Skinner believed that for humans, the world was like a big Skinner box. We usually experience consequences following behavior, and he expected that the nature of those consequences would determine the frequency of our behavior. Consequences that increased the frequency of behavior were called *reinforcements*, and those that decreased behavior frequency were called *punishments*. An additional complication is introduced by saying that both reward and punishment can be administered in one of two ways: a stimulus can be added to the situation, or it can be taken away. When the consequences following a behavior involve adding a stimulus, we say that the reinforcement or punishment is *positive*. When the consequences involve removing a stimulus, we speak of negative reinforcement or negative punishment being applied to the behavior. Notice that the words *positive* and *negative* do not mean good or bad; they are only technical labels telling us that a stimulus has been added or removed.

This is best understood with a little patience and a few examples. In *positive reinforcement* there are two components: *positive* means that a stimulus is being added, *reinforcement* means that the frequency of the behavior is going to increase. If you mow someone's lawn and they give you $20, you have been positively reinforced. The consequences of the behavior were that a stimulus was added ($20) and the behavior frequency was likely to increase (you will do this again if you can). Here's another one: you are watching television and a particularly annoying commercial comes on with loud music of a sort you hate. You press the mute button on the remote control and find the silence to be a relief. You find that you do this more often when this commercial comes on. You have been negatively reinforced. A stimulus has been removed (annoying music), and the frequency of the behavior (pushing mute button) increases. It is likely that the stimulus that is removed in negative reinforcement is something aversive or irritating. The removal of this unpleasant event is likely to increase the frequency of the behavior. People sometimes use the term *negative reinforcement* when they are really referring to *punishment*. This is a common error, and you should learn to discriminate between these two operant situations. Imagine that you catch your finger in the car door as you slam it. It hurts. It hurts a lot. You do not do that again. This is positive punishment. A stimulus (pain) has been added following the door-slamming behavior. The frequency of the behavior decreases.

Negative punishment may be a bit difficult to picture, although there are a few common examples of it (Cautela & Kearney, 1986). Probably one of the best is the application of so called "time-out" to reduce various undesirable behaviors in children. It may help you see this as negative punishment if we tell you that the original name of this procedure was *time-out from reinforcement*. A child does not get his or her way and throws a tantrum. The child is taken to some quiet place and told that he or she can return to the family when the crying stops. This is punishment because the goal is to decrease the frequency of the behavior (tantrum). It is negative punishment because a stimulus has been removed (interaction with family and toys). This will be easier to see if you understand that the child is being placed into a neutral environment that has few, if any, sources of reward or reinforcement. Schools sometimes have a room designed to be a time-out environment. It is quiet and ordinary, perhaps carpeted with a chair or two, but it has no other source of entertainment or reinforcement. Because most kids prefer to be around other people, toys, and things to do, removing these things decreases the frequency of the behavior. This is negative punishment. In recent years, negative punishment has largely replaced positive punishment in the management of child behavior. Positive punishment required adding a stimulus, generally a painful one. Spankings and other physical forms of positive punishment have been associated with undesirable outcomes, such as increased aggressive behavior toward others (Strassberg, Dodge, Pettit, & Bates, 1994). The four operant learning situations described previously are diagrammed in Figure 7.2.

In trying to analyze behavior in Skinnerian or operant terms, it is important to remember that the consequences must follow the behavior and must be seen to have a contingency with the behavior in order for reinforcement or punishment to be effective in behavior change.

To do an operant analysis of behavior, you must answer two questions. Is behavior going to increase or decrease following consequences (reinforcement or punishment)? Is a stimulus being added or taken away as a consequence of behavior (positive or negative)? Operant analysis of behavior into these four categories can be challenging and calls for precision. The target behavior and target

	Behavior frequency increases	Behavior frequency decreases
Add stimulus	Positive reinforcement	Positive punishment
Take stimulus away	Negative reinforcement	Negative punishment

FIGURE 7.2   Positive and Negative Types of Reinforcement and Punishment

organism must be clearly specified before this analysis can take place. For example, a child in a grocery store checkout line starts screaming because he or she wants some candy that is displayed next to the cash register. The parent eventually gives in and buys some candy. To do an operant analysis of this situation, we first have to decide who is the target: parent or child. If it is the parent, then the situation is negative reinforcement. Immediately following candy buying, a stimulus (screaming) is removed. The parent is more likely to make this response in the future because it works. If the target organism is the child, then the situation is positive reinforcement. The response (screaming) is rewarded with candy. The screaming behavior is more likely to occur in the future. In this case, both individuals in the setting are receiving reinforcement, so it is easy to imagine more screaming and candy buying in their future.

SCHEDULES OF REINFORCEMENT

Skinner discovered quite early in his career that it was not necessary to reinforce every single response in order to maintain a high level of responding. There are a variety of ways to manipulate the frequency of rewarded responses. Collectively, these methods are called *intermittent* or *partial reinforcement*. Procedures of partial reinforcement can be seen to belong to one of four basic categories. In thinking about these, it is important to remember that reinforcement is an event that follows a response: the response must come first in operant conditioning. It is possible to issue reinforcements in some ratio to the number of responses. For example, every third response might be reinforced. This is what would happen if a rat in a Skinner box was given a food reward following three bar presses. This is partial reinforcement because not every response is reinforced. The first two presses would not be followed by reinforcement, but the third would be. Correspondingly, the next two presses would not be rewarded, but the third would, and so on. This kind of schedule is called a *fixed ratio* schedule because every third response is rewarded. The ratio between responses and rewards does not change. Contrast this with a long operant session in which, *on the average*, one response in three is rewarded. Sometimes reinforcements occur close together, sometimes they do not, but, over time, the ratio *averages* to one in three. This is a type of partial reinforcement called a *variable ratio* schedule. The rat must make responses in order to receive reinforcements, but it is impossible for the rat to predict which particular response will be followed by food reward. A shorthand used for this situation is VR 3, or variable ratio three.

Instead for reinforcing on a ratio schedule, it is, alternatively, possible to reinforce responses after a particular *time* interval has passed. Partial reinforcement schedules that work this way are called *interval schedules*. If we continue to use a Skinner box example, the important thing to remember is that the rat in the Skinner box must still make a response. In an interval schedule the time interval since the last reward is what matters, not the number of responses the rat makes.

	Payoff	
	Predictable or regular	Unpredictable or irregular
Time	Fixed interval	Variable interval
Reinforcement only after:		
Responses	Fixed ratio	Variable ratio

FIGURE 7.3   Four Schedules of Reinforcement

In a *fixed interval* schedule, the first response after some period of time, for example, two minutes, will be rewarded. The rat can do anything it likes during the interval, but only the first bar press after every two-minute interval will be reinforced. The rat must make a response. Simply sitting and waiting will not be reinforced. However, only one response is required, and that has to occur at least two minutes after the previous reinforcement. This would be called an FI 2 schedule, meaning that there is a fixed interval of two minutes before another reinforcement can be obtained. After some experience of FI 2 schedules, rats will respond with few bar presses until the two-minute interval approaches. There will be a burst of responses around the end of the interval until the reinforcement is delivered. Responding is then likely to decrease until the end of the interval again draws near. The last of the basic schedules is the variable interval schedule. In this schedule, over a long session the rat is rewarded after an *average* time interval, for example, two minutes. The Skinner box would be programmed to pay off after a series of time periods that over the course of a long session would average to two minutes. In this situation, the rat cannot figure out the length of the interval. Merely sitting and waiting will not be reinforced, the rat must continue to respond and, when one of the programmed variable intervals passes, the next response will be rewarded. As you will have guessed, this schedule would be called a VI 2, indicating a variable interval averaging overall to two minutes. These schedules are diagrammed in Figure 7.3.

We have chosen three responses and two minutes for use in describing the ratio and interval schedules. Be aware that these were arbitrary choices for the purposes of example, and either schedule might have any reasonable number attached to it.

THE HUMAN SIDE OF REINFORCEMENT SCHEDULES

Skinner firmly believed that these schedules of reinforcement were part of everyday life. We have used Skinner box situations as examples, but we would not want you to think that these phenomena are restricted to rats in operant chambers. For example, imagine that a class you are in meets on Mondays, Wednesdays, and Fridays and has a quiz every Friday. You do well on the quizzes, and this reinforces your studying and hard work. You are on a fixed interval schedule. This is an interval schedule because the reinforcement is issued only after a period of time (one week) passes. It is not dependent on your responses. In contrast, another Monday, Wednesday, Friday class has pop quizzes that can be given any time, during any day of class. The instructor has decided that the average frequency will be two each week, but you do not know when they will be given. There may be four of them the first week and none the second week. You are on a variable interval schedule. If you are like many students, these two schedules would influence your study patterns. The fixed interval schedule tends to make you put off studying until it is almost time for class on Friday. The variable interval schedule tends to result in more continual study patterns. These frequency differences in your behavior are similar to those that would be seen in a rat responding in a Skinner box. Skinner believed that the schedule would determine the behavior frequency, and the species of organism did not much matter. If you were to work in a car salesroom where you were given a bonus for every five cars you sold, you would be operating on a fixed ratio schedule. You get the bonus after five sales. Time does not matter. If you sell five cars in a morning, you get the same bonus you would get by selling five cars in two weeks. A variable ratio schedule is illustrated by a slot machine. It is programmed to pay off at some average low frequency but only after a varying number of responses. Time does not matter to a slot machine. It is not operating on an interval schedule, so waiting around does not make it more likely to pay off.

CHANGING THE FREQUENCY OF BEHAVIOR

The rather simple notions of reinforcement and punishment and the schedules of reinforcement have been shown to be powerful means of changing behavior. For many psychologists, Skinner's radical behaviorism has been tempered by cognitive approaches, yet it continues to provide a useful technology for implementing behavior change. John M. Roll, Stephen T. Higgins, and Gary J. Badger (1996) investigated the use of schedules of reinforcement to promote and sustain abstinence from cigarette smoking. Their study was not intended to be a treatment for people who wanted to quit smoking. Instead, they studied people who did not want to quit smoking in order to demonstrate the power of reinforcers to increase abstinence. Because none of the participants wanted to quit or was trying to quit, any cessation of smoking among the participants was probably a result of reinforcements, not other factors. Roll and his colleagues pointed out that use of addictive drugs is a kind of operant behavior. It is maintained by the reinforcing consequences of the drug effects. The researchers believed that alternate nondrug reinforcers should be able to increase drug abstinence if they were sufficiently attractive to the participants and if the reinforcers were delivered on an optimum schedule. The schedules of reinforcement used in this study were more complex than the basic examples we have described, but they are not difficult to understand once you have mastered the basics.

Participants

The participants were 60 adult smokers who responded to descriptions of the study in newspaper advertisements or flyers posted on bulletin boards. Twenty-one of them were females and 39 were males. The mean age was 30 years, and the mean number of years they had smoked was 13. On the average, they smoked 26 cigarettes per day, with a range from 10 to 50. The extent of their addiction was measured with a scale called the Fagerstrom Tolerance Questionnaire (Fagerstrom & Schneider, 1989). The Fagerstrom Tolerance Questionnaire is scored from 0 to 11, with higher numbers representing more nicotine dependence. The participants had a mean Fagerstrom score of 6.5, with a range of 4 to 9. To be eligible for the study, participants had to be older than 18 years and appear for the initial meeting with an initial exhaled carbon monoxide (CO) reading of at least 18 parts per million (ppm). This was assessed with a CO meter that measured exhaled CO. Smokers have high levels of CO in their lungs, so this was one way of assessing whether a person was a smoker. To be included, participants also had to answer "no" to the question, "Are you currently trying to, or do you want to, quit smoking?" Last, people were allowed to participate only if they showed no signs of physical or psychiatric problems. Questionnaires were administered that collected information on drug use, as well as medical and psychiatric history. Following this initial interview, the study took five days to complete.

Procedure

All participants agreed to either visit the laboratory or to be visited by the researchers at a prearranged place three times a day for the duration of the study. These visits occurred between 9:00 and 11:00 A.M., 3:00 and 5:00 P.M., and 8:00 and 11:00 P.M. The first visit of the study took place on a Monday morning. Participants were told that they should stop smoking by the previous Friday night. On each visit, a CO level was taken to assess whether the participant had remained abstinent from smoking. Abstinence was defined as having a CO level equal to, or less than, 11 ppm. Participants were given immediate feedback about their CO level at each visit. They were also offered a supply of their own brand of cigarettes at each visit. Presumably, this was to ensure that abstinence was a result of the reinforcement schedule, not merely lack of access to cigarettes.

Participants were randomly assigned to one of three reinforcement schedules:

PROGRESSIVE REINFORCEMENT GROUP

The first time the CO level indicated abstinence, the participant received $3.00. On each subsequent consecutive measurement indicating abstinence, the amount of money was increased by $.50. In addition, every third consecutive abstinent visit was rewarded with an extra $10.00 bonus. A participant in this group who remained abstinent for four visits would earn for those four visits, respectively, $3.00, $3.50, $14.00 ($4.00 + $10.00 bonus), and $4.50. If a participant was over the 11 ppm level, indicating that smoking had taken place, payment was withheld for that visit. On the next visit in which abstinence was demonstrated, the reinforcement was reset to the initial $3.00 level. If the participant had three abstinent visits following a reset, the reinforcement level was restored to the high value that had been received before the reset occurred. It was believed that this would support efforts to achieve abstinence again following a reset because the early gains made in level of reinforcement would be given back to the participant after three abstinent visits.

FIXED REINFORCEMENT GROUP

Participants were paid $9.80 each time they made an abstinent visit to the researchers. There was no bonus money, and there were no resets. The reason why the amount $9.80 was chosen was that this made it possible for a completely abstinent individual in this group to earn the same amount of money overall as a completely abstinent participant in the progressive reinforcement group.

CONTROL GROUP

Payments to control participants were yoked to the average of payments to the first 10 participants to be assigned to the progressive reinforcement group. Yoking was described in Chapter 1, where a control group was fed the same quantity of food as an experimental group. In the smoking study, the concept was the same: the control group received the same payment as another group; however, the payment was not contingent on the control group's behavior. The control group was paid no matter what CO level they had at any given visit. They were told to try to achieve a CO level at or below 11 ppm, but there were no reward contingencies attached to this request.

Each participant received a detailed oral and written explanation of his or her reinforcement schedule. It was made clear to them exactly what they would have to do in order to receive payment. Money was paid in cash immediately following each CO assessment. In addition, participants were given an additional $50.00 on completion of the study. This encouraged them to finish the study, even if they were having problems achieving abstinence.

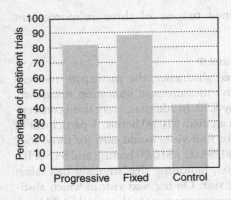

FIGURE 7.4   **Abstinence by Group.** Mean percentage of CO readings at 15 trials at which participants were abstinent during the course of the 5-day study.

Results

Reinforcement contingencies were found to make a difference in abstinence as measured by the mean percentage of visits with CO readings at or below 11 ppm. These data are shown in Figure 7.4.

Mean abstinence levels in the progressive and fixed group differed significantly from the control group ($p < .05$), but not from each other. This measure showed that contingent reinforcement could lead to abstinence from smoking. The control group showed that even noncontingent reinforcement had some effect, but less than with other groups. Using other measures, we can see a difference between the progressive and the fixed schedules. An immediate difference could be seen between the groups in their ability to achieve an initial period of abstinence indicated by three consecutive visits with CO levels under 11 ppm. These data are shown in Figure 7.5.

The control group is significantly lower on this measure than the other two groups ($p < .01$). The fixed group appears to be a little higher in abstinence on this measure, although not statistically significantly so. The percentage of participants from each group who resumed smoking during any part of the study following an initial period of three abstinent visits is shown in Figure 7.6.

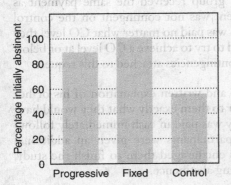

FIGURE 7.5   **Achievement of Initial Abstinence.** Percentage of participants from each group who achieved initial abstinence as defined by having the first three visits show levels of CO at or below 11 ppm.

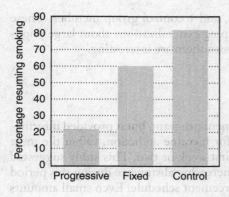

FIGURE 7.6   Resumption of Smoking. Percentage of participants in each group who, following an initial period of abstinence, resumed smoking.

The progressive group had significantly fewer individuals resuming smoking than in the fixed or control groups ($p < .02$ and $p < .01$, respectively). Although they appear to be different in Figure 7.6, the fixed and control groups were not statistically significantly different on this measure. A last interesting measure was the percentage of individuals who remained abstinent through the entire course of the study. These data are shown in Figure 7.7.

The first thing to notice here is that the scale on the y-axis has changed. To think critically about data, it is important to look at the scales on graphs. Whereas on the previous figures, a bar reaching almost to the top would indicate 100 percent, on this graph it only indicates 60 percent. This does not diminish the importance of the findings shown in Figure 7.7, but it illustrates the importance of paying attention to the scaling. The progressive and fixed groups were each statistically significantly different from the control group ($p < .01$ and $p < .04$, respectively), but not from each other. Another question you might ask at this point is "How many people are we talking about?" Percentages do not, by themselves, tell you how many individuals are presented in each bar of the graph. Remembering that there were 20 participants in each group, you can figure out that the numbers abstaining throughout the entire study were 10 progressive

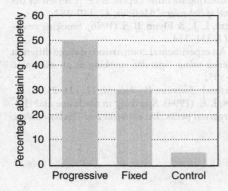

FIGURE 7.7   Abstaining throughout Study. Percentage of participants in each group who were abstinent on all 15 visits during the course of the five-day study.

group members, 6 fixed group members, and 1 control group member. These numbers are quite small for making sweeping generalizations about large populations, nevertheless, the differences between them are interesting.

DISCUSSION

This study was not intended to be a treatment program, but it provided information that might be useful in treatments for nicotine addiction. Often the most difficult part of quitting smoking is the first week or two. This study suggested that monetary rewards were effective in increasing abstinence during this period of time, at least with a progressive reinforcement schedule. Even small amounts of tobacco use during attempts to quit have been found to be a significant predictor of long-term failure to remain abstinent (Chornock, Stitzer, Gross, & Leischow, 1992; Hughes, Gulliver, Fenwick, Valliere, & Flynn, 1986). Progressive reinforcement might help people remain abstinent, improving their chances of long-term abstinence. You might argue that this was an expensive program, costing about $150 per participant in reward money for only 5 days. This has to be put in the context that a two-pack-a-day smoker may be spending over $2,000 a year on cigarettes. In this context, the money required to get through initial weeks of quitting is small. Although the study did not address this issue, it is also possible that people who want to quit would be more amenable to abstinence than the participants in this study and might find it easier to achieve and maintain. Further study will be required if the hopeful outcomes reported here are to become part of attempts to treat drug addictions.

REFERENCES

Cautela, J. R., & Kearney, J. A. (1986). *The covert conditioning handbook.* New York: Springer.

Chornock, W. M., Stitzer, M. L., Gross, J., & Leischow, S. (1992). Experimental model of smoking re-exposure: Effects on relapse. *Psychopharmacology, 108,* 495–500.

Fagerstrom, K. O., & Schneider, N. G. (1989). Measuring nicotine dependence: A review of the Fagerstrom Tolerance Questionnaire. *Journal of Behavioral Medicine, 12,* 159–182.

Hughes, J. R., Gulliver, S. B., Fenwick, J. W., Valliere, L. J., & Flynn, B. S. (1986). Smoking cessation among self-quitters. *Health Psychology, 11,* 331–334.

Roll, J. M., Higgins, S. T., & Badger, G. J. (1996). An experimental comparison of three different schedules of reinforcement of drug abstinence using cigarette smoking as an exemplar. *Journal of Applied Behavior Analysis, 29,* 495–505.

Skinner, B. F. (1956). A case history in scientific method. *American Psychologist, 11,* 221–233.

Strassberg, Z., Dodge, K. A., Pettit, G. S., & Bates, J. E. (1994). Spanking in the home and children's subsequent aggression toward kindergarten peers. *Development and Psychopathology, 6,* 445–461.

CHAPTER 8

I DO!

Previous chapters have described two kinds of learning: *classical* (Pavlovian) conditioning and *operant* (Skinnerian) conditioning. A third broad category of learning, *social learning*, or *imitation*, will be described in this chapter. Although many behaviors owe their existence to classical conditioning or to operant conditioning, it is apparent that these two types of learning do not account for everything we do. Imagine trying to teach someone to hit a baseball with a bat using these techniques. It is difficult to imagine any significant role for classical conditioning: batting is not a reflex, and classical conditioning must begin with a reflexive response. Operant conditioning could certainly play a role: the consequences of a successful hit, or a strikeout, probably have the effect of increasing the frequency of hits and decreasing strikeouts. Even though operant conditioning plays a role, it is not the only process involved in learning to bat. It would take a long time to teach someone to hit a baseball if we had to depend entirely on operant processes. We would have to wait for the person to emit behaviors and then reinforce or punish them to alter the behavior frequency. If a person had never seen baseball being played, it could take a long time before any of the appropriate behaviors were emitted spontaneously.

SOCIAL LEARNING

We can learn a great deal by watching others. If a person had a chance to watch other people playing baseball for a while, that person would probably be able to make a credible start at playing the game. Many of the behaviors could be learned, at least in rudimentary form, by watching others. Of course, additional practice and operant consequences would further shape the behavior, but the basics could be learned by imitating others. This process is called *social learning*, and it is responsible for much of our behavior.

Incorporating the research of P. W. Dowrick and J. M. Raeburn, "Self-Modeling: Rapid Skill Training for Children with Physical Disabilities," 1995, *Journal of Developmental and Physical Disabilities*, 7, pp. 25–37.

The most widely known early studies of social learning were conducted by psychologist Albert Bandura and his colleagues (Bandura, Ross, & Ross, 1961). Since Bandura's early research, hundreds of studies have been done showing the wide applicability of the principles of social learning (Bandura, 1986). The classic research demonstration of social learning by Bandura et al. (1961) is sometimes known as the Bobo doll study because some of the best-known findings involved one of these dolls. The Bobo doll was a child-size inflatable plastic doll, painted to resemble a clown. It had a rounded weighted base so that it would fall over and stand back up when it was punched in the face. Punching it in the face was the most common response to this toy. In this study and subsequent literature, people demonstrating behavior to be imitated are called *models*. In this classic investigation, children were given the opportunity to observe adults performing unusual acts of aggression directed at the Bobo doll. The adult models pushed the Bobo on its side and punched it in the face while holding it down. The models also struck the Bobo with a mallet that was lying around. These behaviors were not typically observed in children playing with a Bobo until after the children had observed others doing these unusual acts of aggression. Bandura et al. (1961) found that children readily learned novel acts of aggression by watching adult models.

In the research that followed this study, a body of thought developed that is called social learning theory (Bandura, 1977, 1986). Its findings helped delineate the characteristics that increased the probability of social learning. Models were shown to be readily imitated if they were *attractive* (Loken & Howard-Pitney, 1988), *powerful* (Bandura, Ross, & Ross, 1963), *personally warm* (LaVoie & Adams, 1978), *celebrities* (McCracken, 1989), or *enviable* (Hosford & Krumboltz, 1969). Another of the principles established empirically by social learning research was that when there were greater similarities between model and observer, the power of the model to elicit behavior change through imitation was enhanced (Kazdin, 1974).

THE SELF AS A MODEL

If similarity of model to observer is important, then it follows that one of the best models for any of us would be ourselves. The appearance of home videotape technology enabled researchers to study the effects of individuals being their own models. In 1983, Peter Dowrick defined self-modeling as "the behavioral change which results from observation of oneself in videotapes that only show desired behaviors (p.81)." For example, Bray and Kehle (1996) made videotapes of children who stuttered. All episodes of stuttering were edited out, so that the children could see and hear themselves speaking fluently. This study showed that using these tapes, children could be powerful models for themselves. This medium showed children images of themselves functioning at a superior level of performance, a level that they had not yet attained. They saw what they would look like at a point in the future when they might have mastered the behavior. Dowrick (1983) called this *feedforward*, making an analogy with a technique called *feedback* in which children merely watched videotapes of unedited current performance to show them how well or poorly they had done in the past. In feed-forward, children are shown how they would be able to perform in the future, once the behavior has been learned.

In the time since this formulation, video self-modeling, or *VSM*, has become a powerful tool for treatment of some kinds of behavior disorders. For example, Woltersdorf (1992) used VSM to treat some problem classroom behaviors associated with children who had Attention-Deficit Hyperactivity Disorder. These kids tended to play with pencils and pens instead of working, they talked and made noises when they were supposed to be quiet, and they were easily distracted. Children were taped, problem behaviors were edited out, and children were shown the tapes. In this instance, VSM was successful as a treatment for behaviors that interfered with classroom learning.

The standard treatment for childhood physical disability is training from physical and occupational therapists using verbal instruction, adult demonstration, and guided practice in which problems with behavior patterns are singled out for additional work. The outcomes of this standard form of treatment have been only modestly successful when evaluated empirically (see, for example, Batshaw & Perret, 1992). Peter W. Dowrick and John M. Raeburn (1995) used VSM to treat children with disabilities. They argued that particularly with these children, self-modeling might be more effective than other social learning approaches. One social learning approach might be to get other, able-bodied children to serve as models for behavior. However, Dowrick and Raeburn believed that using nondisabled children as models might be less effective because it is difficult for disabled children to see able-bodied children as similar to themselves.

Participants

The participants were recruited by occupational therapists and physical therapists from facilities attended by children with disabilities, such as day programs, inpatient services at a pediatric hospital, and special classrooms for disabled children. The 18 children chosen for participation had to be available during the times required by the study. A summary description of the participants can be found in Table 8.1.

As you can see from Table 8.1, the children had a number of different disabilities. They were also diverse in terms of their cognitive capability, with IQs ranging from 45 to 95. At the lower end of the IQ range found in this study, cognitive impairment was sufficient to be associated with considerable problems in understanding and learning.

Procedure

A therapist who had been working with each child for at least two months selected two target skills. These skills were of approximately equal importance in daily life and in difficulty. Each skill was a behavior that normally would be fully

TABLE 8.1 Summary of Gender, Age, IQ, and Disability for Participants

NUMBER OF PARTICIPANTS	GENDER	MEAN AGE	MEAN IQ	DISABILITY
7	3F, 4M	7.7	74.8	Spina bifida[a]
6	4F, 2M	8.3	75.5	Cerebral palsy[b]
2	2M	8.5	75.5	Muscular dystrophy[c]
1	1F	7	90	Hemiplegia (acquired)[d]
1	1F	8	89	Brainstem tumor[e]
1	1M	10	76	Multiple congenital abnormalities[f]

Notes:

[a]Spina bifida: developmental disability in which newborn has part of spinal cord exposed through a gap in the backbone. Outcomes may include paralysis of legs and mental retardation.

[b]Cerebral palsy: developmental abnormality of the brain caused by factors such as injury or lack of oxygen during birth and viral infections before birth. Outcomes may include weakness and lack of coordination in limbs.

[c]Muscular dystrophy: any one of a group of muscle diseases in which there is a pattern of genetic inheritance marked by a weakness or wasting of muscle tissue with associated problems in movement.

[d]Hemiplegia: disease of one hemisphere of the brain. Affects movements on the (opposite) side of the body, which are mediated by the diseased hemisphere.

[e]Brainstem tumor: tumor in the brainstem, the effects of which can include disability in fine motor coordination.

[f]Multiple congenital abnormalities: combinations of types of disabilities listed previously, perhaps including others.

developed in a child of the participant's age. The disabilities of the participants had slowed their behavior development, but the therapists and the researchers believed each target behavior was something the participant could learn to do. One of the two target behaviors was randomly assigned to be treated through self-modeling, the other target behavior was treated as a control. This random assignment was done to ensure that VSM was the only systematic difference between the group of target behaviors and the group of control behaviors. The target behaviors are shown in Table 8.2.

One way to set up experimental groups would be to assign some children to a self-modeling treatment and other children to a control group that did not experience self-modeling. In this study, each child served as its own control. For each child, amount of change in a behavior treated with VSM was compared to amount of change in another of that child's behaviors, one that was not being treated with VSM. As noted in Chapter 6, this kind of research design is called a *within-subjects design* because one behavior is compared with another within a single group of participants. If the experimental and control conditions consisted of different people, the research design would be called a *between-subjects design*.

TABLE 8.2   Target Behaviors for Each Participant

PARTICIPANT	SELF-MODELING	VIDEO TAKEN BUT NOT SHOWN
1	Exercises on floor	Manipulation of blocks
2	Ball skills, wheelchair	Attention to reading
3	Exercises on floor	Dressing outer clothes
4	Walking unaided	Dressing upper garments
5	Clapping to instruction	Drawing between dots
6	Clearing away	Playing concentration
7	Dressing outer clothes	Walking, prosthetics
8	Putting on shoes	Walking up steps
9	Walking unaided	Dressing upper garments
10	Walking with posture	Ball skills, standing
11	Ball skills, standing	Balance on one foot
12	Attending to writing	Dressing self
13	Maintaining posture	Feeding self with spoon
14	Dressing self	Writing from copy
15	Ball skills, wheelchair	Dismounting wheelchair
16	Ball skills, standing	Dressing upper garments
17	Trampoline skills	Exercises for feet
18	Trampoline skills	Ball skills, standing

Both target behaviors for each child were videotaped. During the taping, the children were encouraged to do their best. They were also helped to perform difficult maneuvers. For example, a girl who had difficulty stepping over a small obstacle was helped by holding a therapist's hand. The camera was aimed at the girl's feet, so that the therapist's assistance would not show in the final version that was used for self-modeling. About fifteen minutes of tape was recorded for each participant doing each task, and this was edited down to about two minutes for the self-modeling version. In this editing, any parts of the tape where the children performed poorly, or where assistance was evident, were edited out. The final version showed each child performing the task in a smooth and error-free manner. As noted previously, one of the behaviors was randomly chosen for treatment by self-modeling. The other behavior was taped, but the tape was never shown to the children. It was necessary to tape both behaviors because in an experiment an attempt is made to make the experiences of experimental condition, or group, as similar as possible to the control condition in every way except for the independent variable. Doing this helps ensure that differences in outcomes between the groups are the result of the independent variable, not unintended factors. In this study, if only one of the behaviors had been taped it would have been difficult to know whether behavior changes were the result of taping, VSM, or both. Although it may seem unlikely that a behavior will change because it is taped, it is possible that the close attention given to behavior performance during taping would result in changes in the behavior. This may sound far fetched, but it is known that people will sometimes change their behavior merely because psychologists are paying attention to it.

The classic example of this was a series of studies conducted at the Hawthorne plant of Western Electric Company in Cicero, Illinois. Psychologists studying worker productivity found that increased illumination in the factory was associated with higher work output. However, they also found that lower illumination boosted productivity. They gradually came to realize that it did not matter what they did. As long as they were studying the workers, productivity increased (Roethlisberger & Dickson, 1939). The *Hawthorne effect* is the name given to the phenomenon that behavior can change merely because participants know they are being studied. It is important to avoid Hawthorne effects in designing experimental studies, and one way to do this is to treat different groups or conditions of participants equally in all ways except for the independent variable.

The VSM treatment for the target behavior chosen consisted of participants watching the edited videotape of themselves, without any discussion, for two minutes on six occasions over a two-week period. Children received no discussion of the tape because Dowrick and Raeburn (1995) wanted to demonstrate the effects of self-modeling alone, without other factors being included. If discussion had been included with the tape, it would have been difficult to know which was responsible for behavior change: discussion or VSM. Although this could be the topic of another study, Dowrick and Raeburn chose to investigate only VSM as a variable. Previous observations of VSM suggested that six presentations over two weeks might be sufficient to result in behavior change, and so this was adopted as the treatment protocol in this study.

Data Collection

The observations that formed the basis for the data in this study were made by the therapists, mentioned previously, who worked with the children. Following the selection of two target behaviors, the therapists carefully observed each behavior and made detailed records of the child's performance. The therapists used standardized checklists that are common behavior assessments in occupational and physical therapy. The initial behavior assessment, before any intervention, was called a *baseline*. It was a measure of what the child could do before any treatment was undertaken. Next, each skilled therapist was asked to use his or her experience to make a prediction about the amount of progress expected for each behavior during the next three weeks. These estimates were based on the therapist's knowledge of the child and experience with the treatment of the particular disability. It is critical to understand that although the therapists had helped with the taping of the two target behaviors, they were not made aware of which of the two had been chosen for treatment by VSM. During the two weeks of self-modeling treatment, the therapists continued to work with the children, doing the usual occupational or physical therapy for a wide range of behavior problems, including both target behaviors. Therapist's predictions of change over the VSM period were based on their expectations from the usual occupational and physical therapy. They did not know which behavior received additional treatment from VSM, so their predictions could not include the effects of VSM.

During the next two weeks, one target behavior was treated with self-modeling. Following this, the therapists again made careful assessments of both target behaviors. These new assessments were compared with the baseline assessments made at the start of the study as a means of measuring improvements in either target behavior. If the improvement observed was at the level the therapists would have predicted after a three-week course of standard occupational or physical therapy, the behavior was rated 100 percent. If progress was different from the prediction, it was assigned a percentage based on how advanced or behind the current skill level was when compared to the initial prediction made by the therapist. For example, if the progress actually seen at three weeks was at the level that would usually be expected after six weeks, it was given a score of 200 percent. If progress observed at three weeks was similar to the progress normally predicted for a week and a half, the behavior would be scored 50 percent. The therapists gave a rating of "equal" to small amounts of change in a behavior that, although noticeable, represented a minimal change and, for practical or clinical purposes, an unimportant amount of change.

The reliability of the observations by therapists was checked by having other observers review videotapes of target behaviors made before and after the self-modeling intervention. The other observers were psychologists who did not know the children. They were shown the videotapes and, based on a number of specific evaluations, ultimately asked to make a choice of which of the two target skills for each child showed the greatest amount of improvement. There was 100 percent agreement between the ratings of "more progress," "less progress," and "equal" when these other psychologists' opinions were compared to the ratings of the therapists. Checking the accuracy of observations using multiple observers is a standard procedure in psychological research. It is a way of detecting bias or inaccuracy in the observations of a single observer, as we have noted before.

Results

The overall results suggested that VSM had been a successful treatment. Fourteen of the 18 participants showed more progress in the behavior that was self-modeled than in the behavior that was taped but never shown. For 3 children the differences were too slight to be considered important, or clinically significant. This is particularly striking when we remember that the VSM treatment only consisted of six viewings of a two-minute tape over a period of two weeks. The amount of improvement seen in VSM target behaviors and in control target behaviors, based on the ratings of the therapists, can be seen in Figure 8.1.

As you look at Figure 8.1, it is important to remember that a 100 percent improvement means that the behavior progressed exactly as expected using

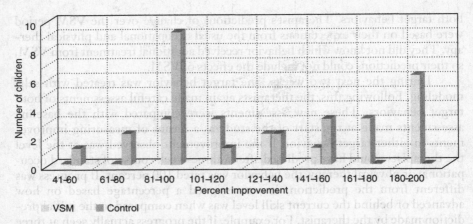

FIGURE 8.1   Improvement in Behavior. Percentage of improvement seen in VSM target behaviors compared to control target behaviors as rated by the therapists. One way to interpret this graph is to ask yourself which behaviors, the VSM or the control, appear to be more frequent above 120 percent? Which appear more frequent below 120 percent?

standard occupational and physical therapy. Behavior change that was higher than 100 percent exceeded the expectations of the therapists, while below 100 percent behavior change was less than expected. Figure 8.1 shows that the VSM behaviors more frequently exceeded the expectations of the therapists than did the behaviors assigned to the control conditions. One-third of the VSM behaviors fall in the highest category, 181 to 200 percent improvement, meaning that they showed progress almost twice as fast as would be expected in standard therapy, alone. In contrast, half of the control behaviors were near the expected level for standard therapy, in the category of 81 to 100 percent. The average for the controls was 106 percent, near enough to 100 percent to suggest that the therapists' estimates of progress with standard treatment were accurate.

Because the progress of some participants had been so great, the charts for 15 of the children were examined one year after the VSM treatment to see if these rather sudden behavior gains had been maintained. In all cases except a boy with the degenerative disease muscular dystrophy, the developmental gains were retained and, beyond that, the participants had continued to progress.

DISCUSSION

VSM treatment was shown to be successful for a variety of specific disabilities. The IQ of each child appeared to be unrelated to the success of VSM treatment. For example, the children with the lowest and the highest IQ scores were two of the four children who did not respond to VSM treatment. However, the children with the second-highest and second-lowest IQs did respond to VSM.

Only one child improved his nonmodeled behavior more than the one that was self-modeled. It was not known why this child showed behavior improvement in the nonmodeled skill but, certainly, the weight of evidence suggests that self-modeling is a useful therapy for problem behaviors of disabled children. Because people are so diverse and so many variables may influence behavior, the results of scientific psychology are probabilistic. Rarely, if ever, do all participants react in the same way to research manipulations. It is important to look carefully at the outcomes of any study and to make your own decision about the confidence you think you should have about the findings. Although you might be more confident of the value of self-modeling if all the children had shown benefits from this procedure, nevertheless, the success rate of the group as a whole was quite high. We believe that even the most cautious professionals would agree that a treatment that did not cost much money or take a long time, yet which helped almost 80 percent of the children, was worthwhile. There are no absolute guidelines for deciding when a therapeutic approach is effective. This has to be a decision for you to make, based on factors such as the expense, the success rate, and the confidence that you place in the research demonstrating success. When you make this decision and have some reasons why, you are thinking critically about psychology. As we have said in previous sections, this is our primary goal for you: to be able to evaluate assertions about behavior. We want you to be able to assess your confidence in assertions about behavior and to have reasons that you can use to convince others. This is a practical skill that will be very useful to you. Would we still believe that self-modeling was a worthwhile approach if 50 percent of the children had improved? Maybe. What if only one child had improved? Probably not, although it would be worth further investigation to try to discover why that child was helped and others were not.

Dowrick and Raeburn (1995) noted that their tapes were crudely edited using the quality of videotape recorders manufactured for household use. Nevertheless, their results suggest that relatively little exposure to these somewhat roughly edited tapes can dramatically improve the behavior of many disabled children. This certainly seems to be a useful and cost-effective approach to some behavior problems.

REFERENCES

Bandura, A. (1977). *Social learning theory*. Upper Saddle River, NJ: Prentice Hall.
Bandura, A. (1986). *Social foundations of thought and action: A social cognitive theory*. Upper Saddle River, NJ: Prentice Hall.
Bandura, A., Ross, D., & Ross, S. A. (1961). Transmission of aggression through imitation of aggressive models. *Journal of Abnormal and Social Psychology, 63*, 575–582.
Bandura, A., Ross, D., & Ross, S. A. (1963). Vicarious reinforcement and imitative learning. *Journal of Abnormal and Social Psychology, 67*, 601–607.
Batshaw, M. L., & Perret, Y. M. (1992). *Children with disabilities: A medical primer* (3rd ed.). Baltimore: Paul H. Brookes.

Bray, M. A., & Kehle, T. J. (1996). Self-modeling as an intervention for stuttering. *School Psychology Review, 25*, 358–369.

Dowrick. P. W. (1983). Video training of alternatives to cross-gender behaviors in a 4-year-old boy. *Child & Family Behavior Therapy, 5*, 59–65.

Dowrick, P. W., & Raeburn, J. M. (1995). Self-modeling: Rapid skill training for children with physical disabilities. *Journal of Developmental and Physical Disabilities, 7*, 25–37.

Hosford, R., & Krumboltz, J. (1969). Behavioral counseling: A contemporary overview. *The Counseling Psychologist, 1*, 1–33.

Kazdin, A. (1974). Covert modeling, model similarity, and reduction of avoidance behavior. *Behavior Therapy, 5*, 325–340.

LaVoie, J. C., & Adams, G. R. (1978). Physical and interpersonal attractiveness of the model and imitation in adults. *Journal of Social Psychology, 106*, 191–202.

Loken, B., & Howard-Pitney, B. (1988). Effectiveness of cigarette advertisements on women: An experimental study. *Journal of Applied Psychology, 73*, 378–382.

McCracken, G. (1989). Who is the celebrity endorser? Cultural foundations of the endorsement process. *Journal of Consumer Research, 16*, 310–321.

Roethlisberger, F. J., & Dickson, W. J. (1939). *Management and the worker: An account of a research program conducted by the Western Electric Company, Chicago.* Cambridge, MA: Harvard University Press.

Woltersdorf, M. A. (1992). Videotape self-modeling in the treatment of attention-deficit hyperactivity disorder. *Child & Family Behavior Therapy, 14*, 53–73.

■ ■ ■ ■ ■

CHAPTER 9

THE WOLF IN SHEEPDOG'S CLOTHING

The research in this chapter is an example of two more research methods, the *case study* and the *naturalistic observation*. A case study collects data or observations on one or a few individuals. It is often a rather weak method of investigation. In the research reported here, a case study was used to develop means of data collection about behavior and to support systematic observations on a new research question that might lead to testable hypotheses. Naturalistic observation qualifies for inclusion as a scientific method because it can be used as a means of hypothesis testing. This method is a sort of a maverick within the study of behavior. Some psychologists consider it to be the weakest possible approach to research, a last resort to be used only when all other methods have been ruled out. Others might celebrate this method because it examines real behavior in real settings. Opinions differ widely about the value of naturalistic observations because this label is used to describe a variety of actual research procedures. The common factor is the observation of behavior within a natural context. This description hinges on something difficult to define: a *natural context*. It is probably not productive to try to create a strict definition for this term, but usually natural contexts are considered to be the places where animals are typically found. For wild animals, it is the wild, but it might also be a zoo. The natural environment of a farm animal is, we suppose, a farm. For humans, it might be homes, workplaces, cars, recreational sites, and shopping areas. With humans, it is easier to say what a naturalistic observation is *not*: it is not a contrived lab setting in which people are randomly assigned to various experimental groups. It is not a survey, it is not an interview, and it is not a psychological test. Could a naturalistic observation of people be done in a lab? Maybe. If people were behaving without any particular instruction from the researcher, we might consider lab observations to be naturalistic. There are several examples like this in the chapters that follow. Even though they take place in labs, we believe they qualify as naturalistic observations. Naturalistic observations are sometimes

Incorporating previously unpublished observations of L. C. Shaffer and N. Tinbergen. Adapted from research presented in L. C. Shaffer, "Man Bites Dog," 1976, *Discovery*. Leeds, UK: Yorkshire Television.

used as one of the outcome measures in a study that employs other research methods as well.

At one extreme, naturalistic observations can be totally descriptive, producing only narrative text about behavior. Early studies of animal behavior were often like this: the animal was watched and actions were described (Lorenz, 1952). More recently, Dian Fossey's (1983) work on mountain gorillas was largely descriptive. However, it is also possible to produce numerical data from naturalistic observations, sometimes including making alterations in the natural environment and watching to see how behavior is affected. Early examples, which still make compelling reading, can be found in the work of Tinbergen (1958, 1974), who studied a wide variety of animals in outdoor settings. Although many people associate naturalistic observation with the study of nonhuman animals, sometimes it can be a good way of finding things out about people as well. Let us presume you wanted to know whether men or women drivers are more likely to wear seat belts. You could observe cars going underneath a highway overpass, while making recordings of sex of driver and seat belt wearing. We believe these data might be better than those you could collect in an interview or survey because surveys are susceptible to errors from faulty memories or purposeful attempts to misrepresent behavior. A published example of this method can be found in the work of Hoxie and Rubenstein (1994), who observed that traffic lights did not stay red long enough to allow elderly people to cross a busy street safely. An example from a different area of study can be found in the work of Martin and Ross (1996), who went to people's homes to make observations of parents responding to aggression in children.

A STUDY OF SHEEPDOGS

The researchers for this chapter, Lary Shaffer and Niko Tinbergen, worked in the north of England, near the Scottish border, making science documentaries for British television. In addition to being filmmakers, both of them had degrees in zoology, specializing in animal behavior. Indeed, during the course of the study to be described, Tinbergen was awarded a Nobel Prize for his enduring contributions to the study of animal behavior. While traveling in the rolling green farmland of northern England, they had numerous opportunities to observe border collie sheepdogs at work herding vast flocks of sheep. On distant hillsides, the white mass of sheep looked like a single organism, stretching out, bunching up, and forming into strings while being forced through gates in the stone walls. If Shaffer and Tinbergen looked carefully, they could sometimes see the single dog that was responsible for all this activity: a black and white speck, darting this way and that, rounding up errant branches of the flock. Thinking this behavior might be worthy of a research study, they asked a friend, Jimmy Rose, for help. Jimmy lived in the Pennine Hills, where there are many sheep farms, and he said he knew just the place to do a study of dogs. This was a lucky break for Shaffer and Tinbergen. They were fortunate to know someone who could make some introductions.

Two weeks later, Shaffer and Tinbergen, in the company of Jimmy, found themselves on their way to Dufton Village for an introduction to the Dargues, a family who had been farming the hills around Dufton for almost 1,000 years. The farms in that area were mostly family farms, staffed by sprawling extended families of parents, offspring, aunts, uncles, cousins, and grandparents, all living under one roof and all working, in some capacity, at the daily chores of the farm. Jimmy had known the Dargues for years, so, following the customs of the area, he drove up to the farmhouse and went right in without knocking. Shaffer and Tinbergen followed shyly behind. The Dargues were having their midday meal, seated around a big oak table covered with steaming mountains of food. After a one-sentence introduction from Jimmy, all three guests were invited to pull up to the table and "have a bit of dinner." No one paid any particular attention to the newly arrived guests, and food was shoveled down while the talk centered on cattle feed prices and the weather. Almost as an aside, Jimmy said, "Oh, by the way, Lary and Niko would like to hang about here in the next year or two, watch you work with your sheepdogs, and make a film about it." The head of the family, old John Dargue, slowly looked up from his plate. Chewing along without missing a beat he gazed first at Shaffer, then at Tinbergen, then at Shaffer again and softly said "Aye" between bites. That was all it took to seal the deal. Permission from "Boss" John Dargue meant that the whole farm would be at Shaffer and Tinbergen's disposal for as long as was necessary to complete the project. Shaffer shot a questioning glance at Tinbergen, who returned a meek little shrug and forked a roast potato into his mouth.

Jimmy Rose was correct in thinking that the Dargue's farm would be a good place to watch sheep and dogs. As with most of the farms in the area, their farm was too small to easily provide both food and pasture space for the number of sheep they owned. This fact necessitated a considerable amount of moving sheep from one place to another. Although the entire Dargue family would pitch in when needed, Edwin did most of the shepherding. At 50 years old, Edwin Dargue was short, stoutish, and strong as an ox. He had a quick wit and enjoyed the company afforded by Shaffer and Tinbergen on his rambles around the hills, shepherding his flock. At first, Shaffer and Tinbergen spent a great deal of time just watching the dogs. Sometimes naturalistic observations have a hypothesis immediately but, in this case, hypotheses grew out of weeks of initial observations. Tinbergen was one of the pioneers in the use of naturalistic observation, and he strongly believed that the way to approach a new research project was to "observe, observe, and observe again." As the researcher became acquainted with the behavior, questions would begin to appear. At first these might be small questions or puzzles, but, over numerous observations, they would gradually form into more specific and important questions. This research method required faith that sufficient observations of behavior in a natural setting could be counted on to lead to testable hypotheses. Naturalistic observations are also used by many scientists to suggest hypotheses that will later be tested by other research methods, such as experiments.

Although there were no specific and testable hypotheses at the start of the investigation, Shaffer and Tinbergen both believed that the spectacular performances of the sheepdogs were not merely a matter of training. Dogs are closely related to wolves, and good scientific studies of wolves were beginning to appear (Mech, 1970). Shaffer and Tinbergen suspected that much of the herding behavior was really thinly disguised pack hunting behavior. In the domestication of the dog, humans had created breeds by selective mating that emphasized different characteristics. In the sheepdog, Shaffer and Tinbergen believed that aspects of ancestral wolflike hunting behavior, which might have been useful in herding flock animals, had been retained through generations of selective breeding.

GETTING STARTED

Their first unsystematic observations seemed to confirm the idea that at times the dogs were behaving as a wolf pack. When groups of dogs worked together, a clear dominance hierarchy could be seen among the dogs. The same kinds of status arrangements are found in wolf packs. The dog who seemed to be in the role of the alpha male, or the head of the pack, was always out in front of the others as they trotted to the fields where they would work. If another dog tried to pass him, he would charge at it, chasing it back with the others. In particular, the lead dog spent a great deal of time rebuffing one particular challenger, who usually seemed to be in second place. The alpha male frequently urinated on rocks and tufts of grass. The number two dog would stop, sniff and urinate in the same places, followed by the other male dogs in a predictable order. Female dogs played no obvious part in this scent marking. One day, the dog who had been running second in the dog pack picked a fight with the lead male, which turned into a ferocious battle of flashing teeth and flying fur. The other dogs gathered around to watch. Shaffer and Tinbergen were surprised that Edwin did nothing to break up this fight, which looked as if it would certainly end in injury for both dogs, and maybe death for one. Edwin said, "If you let them fight, they will sort it out for themselves. If you break it up, they will be trying for a rematch every time they see each other. This way, both dogs may get hurt but when it is over they will know who is boss and will be able to work together without any more fighting." After a few minutes of fierce combat, the number two dog went squealing away from the fight. It was over, and the alpha male was still in charge. Edwin was correct about the reestablishment of order. Shaffer and Tinbergen saw no further fighting between these dogs. These observations further convinced Shaffer and Tinbergen that, at times, the dogs were behaving as a wolf pack.

After initial observations and discussions, Tinbergen returned to his busy professorship at Oxford University, reluctantly leaving much of the daily observation to Shaffer. At regular intervals, Tinbergen returned to Dufton to have some days among the dogs, discuss the work, generate new ideas, and debate interpretations.

Shaffer gradually got used to the routine of farm life. After a few weeks, he ceased to notice the smell of farm animals and hardly noticed when running sheep kicked up a spray of liquid manure, which flew in all directions, landing on his clothes and face. As Tinbergen predicted, he began to notice things about the dogs. For most ordinary work around the farm, Edwin used only one dog, a five-year-old male named Spot. Most border collies have large patches of black and white on their backs, but Spot was almost all black with a white nose, a white bib, and a white spot just behind his ears.

Shaffer marveled at how Spot seemed to know just what to do, requiring few commands from Edwin. They worked together like a well-rehearsed ballet when moving large flocks or isolating single sheep for specific purposes. When Shaffer asked Edwin about Spot's training, the response was, "They either have it in them, or they don't—you work them and they soon figure out what to do." As Shaffer observed, he was struck by the sorts of commands that Edwin was giving. There seemed to be many more commands telling Spot to *stop* doing some behavior than there were to tell him to *start* doing a particular behavior. Once Shaffer had this idea, it was easy to do the empirical checking. In his little note-book, Shaffer began to record the circumstances of Edwin's commands. The original intention had been to study the dogs, but Shaffer was coming to the realization that the dog behavior made no sense without some understanding of the shepherd and the sheep. For three weeks in ordinary work around the farm, Shaffer noted each of Edwin's commands and scored it as a command either to stop a behavior or start a behavior. Other utterances, such as "Good lad, Spot," were not scored because they did not tell the dog to do anything specific. The overall frequencies of these commands are shown in Figure 9.1.

Although the data here only involve one dog and one shepherd, Shaffer's hunch that most of the commands were *stop* commands was confirmed. Shaffer

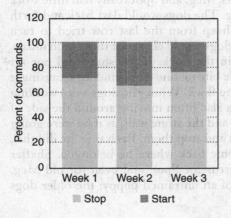

FIGURE 9.1 Frequency of Stop and Start Commands

was excited about this because it was the beginning of systematic observations and the start of an emerging story about sheepdog behavior. Although three weeks might seem to be a long time to spend confirming such a small point, at the same time Shaffer was beginning work on a documentary film about sheepdogs that was paying for the project, and the film work limited the amount of time each day that could be spent in unencumbered observation.

Having convinced himself that most commands were *stop* commands, the next question seemed to appear automatically: stop doing what? Another bout of research was launched with Edwin and Spot. Shaffer tried, over a series of days, to find a way to put Spot's behavior into meaningful categories. Initially, this proved to be a challenge. The behaviors of sheep and dog seemed chaotic at first. There seemed to be so many completely different kinds of situations in which Spot had to be stopped by a stream of shouted invective. Tinbergen gave Shaffer a lot of encouragement to keep watching, waiting, and thinking. Patience is more than a virtue in naturalistic observation; it has to be an obsession. Shaffer persevered and, rather suddenly, the clouds of confusion began to clear.

MISTAKES AND INSIGHTS

For a few days, Edwin and Spot had been moving sheep from one field to another, down a narrow road with high stone walls on both sides. Edwin's Uncle Joss was helping with this using his dog, Meg, as was Cousin John with a dog called Moss. Moss was just over a year old and was still a big, shaggy, good-natured pup. He would bound around, dividing his time between getting in trouble and working in useful ways. The high stone walls and gates on each side of the roadway focused the errors that a dog could make by squeezing the sheep from both sides. Unlike an open field, the sheep could only go forward or back. At some point, this constriction from the sides, combined with the large number of errors made by Moss, resulted in a flash of insight for Shaffer about the herding behavior of dogs. Moss, Meg, and Spot really had little work to do in order to keep the sheep moving. The dogs would dart back and forth behind the last row of sheep. If any sheep from the last row tried to turn around and run away from the flock the dogs would charge at these individuals, causing them to turn around and rejoin the flock. If the sheep did not act quickly enough, it was likely to get a little bite on one of its hind legs, causing it to launch into the air and land among the flock. While the dogs were working at this, it became obvious that Moss was also often moving around the side of the flock, pushing in between the sheep and the stone wall, as if he were going to work his way to the front of the flock and stop them. Each time he did this, John would yell at him to stop and come back where he belonged. Shaffer noticed that this was also a common error for Spot, and even for old Meg. These were more than random errors of an untrained puppy: the older dogs were doing the same thing.

Shaffer had been reading about the hunting of wolves and other pack-hunting carnivores, and the reading suggested a reason for this "error." The breakthrough came when Shaffer realized that the dog was acting as a social hunter, treating the shepherd as the head of the hunting pack. In a carnivore pack hunt, the hunters will try to isolate one or a few animals from a large flock. In the early phases, pack hunters split up and spread around the prey trying to make a grab for an individual.

Shaffer believed that this was the situation in which the dogs found themselves. They had moved in close to a small flock and if they were to use patterns of ancestral hunting behavior, the sensible thing to do first would be to spread out around the sheep. The farmers needed to have the sheep driven down the road. However, for a hunting pack, nothing is gained by endlessly driving prey in one direction with all the pack members close together. In the narrow lane, the dogs appeared to be reverting to an ancestral hunting strategy in the tendency to surround the sheep. To understand this, you have to remember that although the dogs had their own dominance hierarchy within the pack, they also treated the shepherd as the ultimate pack member.

Shaffer's head began to whirl as he tried to think about the other mistakes he had seen the dogs make. Had most or all of these "mistakes" really been pack-hunting maneuvers that happened to interfere with the dog's role as a sheepdog? Were the dogs depending on a pack-hunting ancestry in the mistakes they made as well as in their successes? Shaffer believed so, but he needed to confirm this hunch with new observations.

Much of sheepdog work involves handling sheep in close quarters in small fields. On other occasions, however, the dog has to run distances of a mile or more away from the shepherd to bring a distant flock back down to the shepherd. As Shaffer reflected on this, it occurred to him that there were four basic kinds of interactions involving shepherds, dogs, and sheep. These are shown in Figure 9.2a and b.

Figure 9.2 shows that there are two elements in the observed situations that closely resemble a pack hunt: pack members surrounding the sheep and pack members being close to the sheep. The plus and minus signs in Figure 9.2a became the hypothesis for further observations. The logic of the pack hunt is that it is important for the pack members, in this case shepherd and dogs, to surround the prey, preparatory to catching one of them. This is found in the upper left cell, and it has a double plus because Shaffer believed it was very like a pack-hunting situation and, therefore something the dogs should do well. Shepherds typically use this arrangement when it is necessary to surround and catch one sheep from a flock so that it can be given some medicine or other treatment.

Moving across the top of Figure 9.2, the upper right cell is the situation that the dogs had encountered in the narrow lane. "Pack members" were all near the sheep, but the shepherd wanted the sheep driven away from themselves and the dogs. This has a mixed sign because it is like the hunt in having pack members

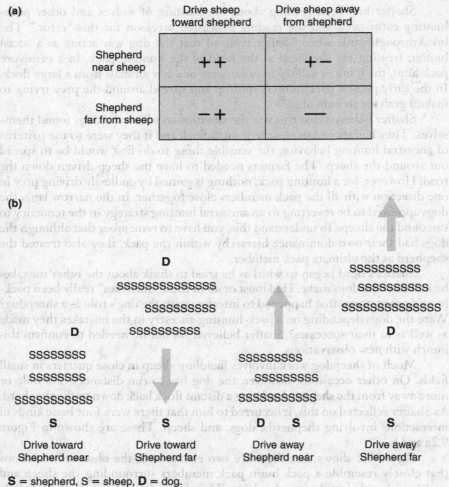

FIGURE 9.2   Categories of Sheepdog Behavior with Sheep and Shepherd.
(a) Shepherd, sheepdog, and sheep maneuvers reduced to basic examples. The plus signs indicate Shaffer's guess that the situation is something the dog would do readily based on hunting ancestry: driving toward the shepherd and being near the sheep. The minus signs suggest that a dog would be expected to have trouble performing well in the situation, as in driving sheep away and being far from the shepherd. Mixed signs predict mixed success. (b) Schematic representations of the maneuvers in (a).

near the sheep, but it also has the nonhunting element in that the goal is to drive the sheep away from the pack members.

The lower left cell has one hunting element: the pack has the sheep surrounded. The shepherd is a long way away from the dog and the sheep. In hunting terms, the head of the pack is too far away to help with the hunt. This is the situation that can occur when the dog is sent up a hillside to fetch sheep back to the shepherd.

The remaining cell in Figure 9.2 is an unlikely event in which the shepherd is far away from the flock and wants the dog to show itself and chase the sheep further away. Neither element of this, being far from the pack or chasing sheep farther from the pack, would have any obvious role in a pack hunt. As Shaffer worked out this theoretical scheme, he could not remember seeing any actual field situations that would fit in the lower right cell.

The next step was to go to the field and try to do observations that would support the model. The best times for getting observations of a number of different dogs was during the gathering days when sheep were brought down from the high moors where they shared common grazing during the summer. Because the sheep from many farms had been been grazing on hundreds of square miles of open moorland, gathering is a big job, requiring shepherds and dogs from all the farms in the area. Shaffer took this opportunity to observe behavior of several different dogs and to rate the overall success of each individual maneuver. The outcome was judged to be successful if fewer than 10 percent of commands given by the shepherd were attempts to get the dog to stop doing behaviors. This is a fairly high standard for success, and you should know that it was chosen somewhat arbitrarily. There are no established rules for observing and rating behavior. This leaves it up to the researcher to make a decision. Needless to say, Shaffer tried to avoid introducing bias into the data. Several different operational definitions of the successful maneuver did not produce very different patterns of results. The results of these observations are shown in Figure 9.3.

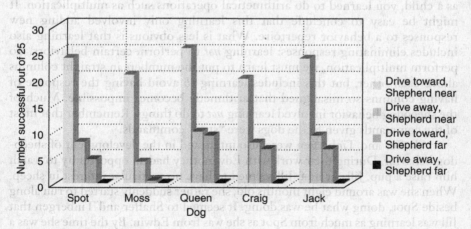

FIGURE 9.3   Success in Maneuvers for Several Dogs. Number of successful maneuvers of four different types by five different dogs. Success was defined as a herding event in which less than 10 percent of commands were telling the dog to *stop* a particular behavior.

The data offer some confirmation of the initial observation that closely surrounding the sheep, dog on one side of the sheep and shepherd on the other, was something that the dogs did readily and well. In this figure, the last column for each dog is the situation on the right of Figure 9.2b that rarely, if ever, occurred: the dog is sent by the shepherd to approach a distant flock and chase them further away. This had no application for a pack hunter and made little sense in sheepherding. Shaffer asked Edwin if he had ever done this and, after some thought, Edwin responded that occasionally he needed a dog to run at distant intruding neighbor sheep and move them out of the way in order to prevent mixing with his own flock. Zeros have been entered as data for this column in Figure 9.3, because Shaffer asked each of the shepherds to try to get their dogs to do it, and the result was a complete failure. The dogs refused to do this in spite of a barrage of commands from the red-faced, arm-waving shepherd. The dogs were practically incapable of this behavior.

It is important to make a distinction between these rough working farm dogs and the polished and trained dogs who perform in the spectator events called sheepdog trials. Dog trials are local and national competitions that are held to show off the peak achievements of herding dogs who have been meticulously taught to follow instructions. The training of these dogs is so intense and thorough that they appear to be radio controlled. The dogs trained for exhibition in sheepdog trials demonstrate that it is possible to teach these dogs to do exactly what the shepherd wants. For Shaffer and Tinbergen, however, the rough farm dogs provided a better window into the workings of canine behavior.

The observations described here illustrated an important, but rarely appreciated, aspect of learning. People sometimes think of learning as adding a new behavior to a list of behaviors that can already be performed. For example, as a child, you learned to do arithmetical operations such as multiplication. It might be easy to conclude that this learning only involved adding new responses to a behavior repertoire. What is less obvious is that learning also includes eliminating responses: learning *not* to perform certain behaviors. To perform multiplication, we must learn to put the numbers in straight columns above each other, but this includes learning to avoid having the response of having columns so misaligned that arithmetic becomes impossible. Much of the sheepdog behavior involved learning *not* to do things. Remember that most of the commands given to the dogs were "stop" commands.

Shaffer and Tinbergen were also interested in the development of sheepdog behavior. During their work with Edwin, they had an opportunity to watch him raise a pup, Jill. At first, Jill seemed to have no particular interest in sheep. When she was around eight months old, she rather suddenly started to run along beside Spot, doing what he was doing. It seemed to Shaffer and Tinbergen that Jill was learning as much from Spot as she was from Edwin. By the time she was a year and a half old, she was able to work on her own and be useful in herding the sheep. Years ago, Jill's behavior might have been described as a herding instinct, suggesting that it was caused by her genetic endowment. We now believe that this sort of label is too simple to be of any use. Herding behavior certainly has some genetic components. This becomes clear if, facetiously, we ask why *dogs* are used for herding? Why not cats? *Sheepcats?* Shaffer and Tinbergen believed that the dogs carried a genetic package that predisposed them to perform many of the behaviors needed by the farmer. These behaviors were thinly disguised hunting behaviors, and probably this genetic component had come to the dogs through ancestral lines. The spectacular levels of performance of the sheep dogs clearly showed that learning was involved. Much of this learning was the elimination of undesirable responses. Immediate situational components such as nutrition, time of day, and the behavior of other dogs also made a difference. One of the recurrent themes of contemporary psychological research is that a behavior does not have a single cause. All behaviors have genetic, biological, experiential, and situational components. As you will see in subsequent chapters, these components, and the interactions among them, are the primary topic for psychological investigations today.

People who know little about contemporary psychology may consider that most human behavior is learned: we use misleading phrases such as "the child learned to walk." Although learning is certainly a component of walking, other factors are also involved. For example, research by Esther Thelen (1992) has shown that the appearance of walking is delayed by the leg muscle strength of babies. The legs of young babies are so heavy that their underdeveloped muscles cannot move the legs in walking motions without assistance. Walking does not simply appear as the result of learning. Much as with the sheepdog behavior described in this chapter human walking has many components, not a single cause.

REFERENCES

Fossey, D. (1983). *Gorillas in the mist.* Boston: Houghton Mifflin.

Hoxie, R., & Rubenstein, L. (1994). Are older pedestrians allowed enough time to cross intersections safely? *Journal of the American Geriatrics Society, 42,* 241–244.

Lorenz, K. (1952). *King Solomon's ring.* London: Crowell.

Martin, J., & Ross, H. (1996). Do mitigating circumstances influence family reactions to physical aggression? *Child Development, 67,* 1455–1466.

Mech, L. D. (1970). *The wolf.* New York: Natural History Press.

Thelen, E. (1992). Development as a dynamic system. *Current Directions in Psychological Science, 1,* 189–193.

Tinbergen, N. (1958). *Curious naturalists.* London: Country Life.

Tinbergen, N. (1974). *Curious naturalists* (Rev. ed.). Amherst: University of Massachusetts Press.

CHAPTER 10

NOW YOU SEE IT, NOW YOU DON'T

Jean Piaget (1896–1980) was one of the founding fathers of modern developmental psychology. Most of his life's work involved studying the cognitive processes of children. Probably his most important discovery was that children think differently from adults. Piaget first noticed this while he was giving individually administered intelligence tests to children. Because this task involved having to ask the same questions over and over, he began to notice that different children independently and repeatedly came up with the same wrong answers to questions on the test. For example, children would repeatedly fail to understand the abstract point that objects can belong to two classes at once: a marble may be both red and round. Over time, Piaget came to see that these answers were only "wrong" from the adult perspective. Children think differently than adults do and, from the perspective of the children, their answers were right.

Later, Piaget (1954) did a number of classic demonstrations of childhood thought processes using his own children as participants. He recounted his interpretations of these demonstrations in his early and important books about cognitive development in children. Piaget's books were very influential because his work was a new approach to understanding the development of mental processes. Many researchers were soon working hard to find solid empirical confirmation for the charming observations he reported.

Piaget turned his observations into a theory of cognitive development in which a child progresses through a number of stages as childhood thinking comes to resemble adult thinking. In summary, this cognitive development consists of two major components: (1) the child being able to understand the viewpoints of others and (2) the child coming to deal with abstract ideas. One way to think about these abstract ideas is to contrast them with concrete ideas. *House* is a concrete word, *beauty* is an abstract word. Small children have difficulty grasping the meaning of ideas that are not tied to observable objects and events. The central idea of a stage theory is that the transition between stages is

Incorporating the research of Y. Luo, R. Baillargeon, L. Brueckner, and Y. Munakata, "Reasoning about a Hidden Object after a Delay: Evidence for Robust Representations in 5-Month-Old Infants," 2003, *Cognition*, *88*, pp 23–32.

quite rapid compared to the longer time spent within the stage. Much of the research on this topic attempted to evaluate the timetables Piaget proposed for the stages of development.

It may seem a bit strange, but part of the fun of science consists of taking on the established notions or theories of others and finding problems with them. This is an adult version of the giggle that a child might get when a feared authority figure gets a pie in the face. Although many textbooks correctly stress the value of science, few of them point out the fun. The most stolid scientists might not want to admit this, but it can be great fun, even for adults, to throw a pie at the establishment. The scientific way to do this is to conduct carefully designed research that contradicts long-held and widely believed notions. Often this involves redoing parts of earlier research, a process called *replication*. You can see one reason why science is self-correcting: a flawed theory is likely to be attacked from a number of directions. If these attacks find problems for the theory, then the theory is likely to be modified. In extreme cases, a theory may be found to be so badly flawed that it is discarded completely.

CONSERVATION

Although Piaget's entire theory is not exactly going down the drain, it has been successfully attacked by a number of contemporary researchers. These attacks have occurred on a number of Piagetian fronts. For example, Samuel and Bryant (1984) studied a well-known Piagetian task called *conservation*. The classic conservation task is designed to show that young children are unable to mentally manipulate ideas about concrete events. In the classic demonstration of conservation, a child is presented with two balls of clay that are identical in size and shape and asked if they are the same. The child responds that they are. Next, while the child watches, one of the balls is rolled into some obviously different shape, such as the shape of a pizza crust or a hot dog. Then the child is asked again whether the two objects still have the same amount of clay. Piaget found that children younger than about five years old tended to answer "no" to this question, indicating that one lump of clay or the other lump now contained more clay. He believed that the child could not grasp the transformation that the clay had undergone and was misled by the obvious visual difference between the two portions of clay.

Samuel and Bryant (1984) wondered if, perhaps, the children were also responding to being asked the same question twice in a row. Children learn that when they are asked a question twice, it is often because they are expected to change their answer. For example, if a child is being interrogated about some misdeed and the adult does not get an admission of guilt, the child is asked the same question again and is expected to change the answer. "Now I want you to tell me the truth, *did you scratch your initials in the side of the piano?*" Standard Piagetian conservation testing asked the same question twice and the "correct" outcome was to change the answer. Samuel and Bryant examined this by asking the question only once. The children were shown two objects that were equivalent and, without any questions being asked of them, watched while one was changed. Only then were they asked the question about equivalence. The children in this situation made fewer errors than children who were asked the question twice, in the usual Piagetian manner. This finding suggested that being asked the question twice played a role in children changing their answers.

Winer, Craig, and Weinbaum (1992) studied the classic conservation task with college students as participants and found that the wording of the question also played a role in correct responses. Many adults who were asked if they weighed more when they were standing up or sitting down, for example, chose one of the answers over the other rather than asserting a third and correct response that they weighed the same regardless of their body position. The findings suggest that asking forced-choice questions—questions in which participants are given limited responses to choose from, like true/false or multiple-choice exam questions—can lead participants to fail to consider other possible answers. Remember that Piaget expected children to be fully conservational by about six years old. He also expected that once people were fully conservational, they would stay that way. This is an important issue because the conservation task was considered by Piaget to be a hallmark achievement defining the boundary between two major stages of cognitive development. A stage theory suggests a one-way progression of development, and Piaget did not expect cognitive achievement to come and go depending on factors such as the number and nature of the questions being asked.

One of the more successful of the scientists leading commando raids into Piagetian territory has been Renée Baillargeon (pronounced "Bay-r-jon"). One of the focuses of her research has been the timing of another important cognitive achievement; this one is called *object permanence*.

OBJECT PERMANENCE

Object permanence is the name given to the ability of children to understand that objects continue to exist, or are permanent, even when they are out of sight. Piaget believed that children younger than about nine months did not yet have object permanence. His conclusions were based on observations of his young son and daughter. Piaget took an attractive toy away from his kids and hid it under a piece of cloth while they watched. At ages younger than nine months, they would make no effort to recover it. Piaget concluded that his kids did not try to recover the toy because they believed that it ceased to exist when it was out of sight (Piaget, 1954).

It is easy to jump to wrong conclusions based on simple observations where the researcher is emotionally involved with the observation. If you have ever tried to change a baby's diaper and had the infant use the instant of nakedness to urinate, you could probably convince yourself that the infant had planned this as a way to frustrate you. Your conclusion would have some of the same problems that Piaget's research had—you only made one observation, and you were part of the event that you were trying to observe. You might come to different conclusions if you were to observe a large number of caregivers diapering infants.

Sometimes students wonder why object permanence is given such prominence in the research literature. Much research energy has been devoted to object permanence because it is an early, clear, and important indication that a child is beginning to think the way an adult does. It is not possible to think rationally about the world if you believe that anything you cannot see no longer exists, and that when things reappear, they have suddenly started to exist again.

HABITUATION

It is always a problem to know what an infant has heard or seen. Inability to use language is a defining characteristic of infancy. One of the most common research methods for getting babies to show us what they know is a strategy called *habituation*. In habituation, a baby is exposed to the same stimulus—for example, a visual event—over and over until it shows significant decreases in responding to the stimulus. Although we do not know what the baby is actually thinking, if you were to watch a baby becoming habituated, it would be easy to conclude that the baby has just become bored with the repetitious event. Then the visual event is changed. Typically, when the baby first sees the change, strong responding will reappear. The return of responding indicates that the baby can tell something new has occurred. Several different infant responses have been used by researchers to indicate that a baby is reacting to a new event. These have included staring at the new visual stimulus, as well as more subtle measures such as pupil dilation or heart rate changes. As long as the baby does something different when the event is changed, we know that the baby has noticed the change.

Renée Baillargeon has published a number of articles that have questioned Piaget's notions about the age at which object permanence first appeared. Baillargeon and DeVos (1991), for example, used much more sophisticated methodology than Piaget. Unlike Piaget, they went to great lengths to ensure that their own beliefs and other uncontrolled factors were unlikely to bias their results. Baillargeon and DeVos believed that Piaget's observations may have misled him because the child was required to do at least two things at once in his demonstration. Piaget's children had to (1) understand that objects continued to exist when hidden *and* (2) be able to plan and execute a search for the objects. Planning a search involves knowing what to do first, what to do next, and so on. It is a fairly complex task that we, as adults, take for granted. A young child might know that an object continues to exist but may be unable to plan an orderly search for it—these are different tasks. Piaget's situation was even more complex because his kids had to plan the search as well as have the cognitive and motor skills to carry it out.

To disentangle object permanence from other cognitive and motor skills, a number of researchers have simplified the tasks that children must perform to demonstrate early object permanence. For example, infants have been given tests requiring only visual responses, which can be much easier for an infant than the crawling and reaching required by Piaget's tasks.

Baillargeon and DeVos (1991) studied object permanence with a habituation situation called, in the developmental psychology literature, the *possible event* and the *impossible event*. Special effects in the movies have trained us to think that no visual event is impossible. However, for a baby, disappearing and reappearing objects should be surprising anytime after object permanence develops. For example, imagine a simple visual test of object permanence in which a child watches while a toy car is rolled down a ramp. At one point, the car rolls behind a piece of cardboard that momentarily blocks the child's view of the car. On some trials, while the car is behind the cardboard screen, the researcher, unseen, grabs it off the ramp and hides it. Unaware of this, the infant continues to turn its eyes as if tracking the car behind the screen and then, perhaps, shows some surprise that the car has not reappeared on the other side of the cardboard screen, at the bottom of the hill. The little car failing to appear on the other side of the cardboard screen is called the *impossible event*. It is "impossible" because the car disappears into thin air. You should be able to figure out why showing surprise at this would be an indication of object permanence. The infants with object permanence show surprise because they are wondering, as we might, where the car has gone. In contrast, if these children did not have object permanence, if they believed objects ceased to exist when not visible, there would be no reason for them to show any particular surprise when a car vanished behind a screen and did not reappear: the car has ceased to exist.

You might make the argument that a disappearing and reappearing car is a surprising event in itself and that even children without object permanence would show surprise as cars come and go. This is why it is important to compare impossible event responses to those of a child watching the *possible event*: a car rolls down a ramp, behind a screen and out the other side. If a child did not have object permanence, the reaction to these events should be the same—cars here and there, coming and going. However, if the child has object permanence, then the reaction to the possible and impossible events should be different. The impossible event should be a surprise. The possible event, which does not contradict object permanence, should be less interesting, and maybe even boring. Because you have object permanence yourself (or you are going to have trouble in life), you can imagine the surprise of the impossible event compared to the ordinary nature of the possible event.

According to Baillargeon and her colleagues, the ability to know that an object continues to exist when you can no longer see it, touch it, smell it, or otherwise sense it requires that the brain create an internal representation of the object. The concept of *representation* is important in psychology. Baillargeon is interested in when infants first begin to form representations of the objects in their environment and how they use them to understand the world.

As we discussed previously, part of the fun in science is challenging the ideas of others. In the years since Baillargeon and her colleagues first began to conduct their pioneering research, they have met with a number of challenges from other researchers who have offered alternative explanations for Baillargeon's research findings. One such challenge proposes that, rather than representing hidden objects, infants form a prediction about the outcome of an event they are observing while the objects are still in view (Munakata, 2001). As an event unfolds, they check to see whether their prediction of the outcome of the object's movement was accurate. In the case of the toy car rolling down a hill, behind a screen, and re-emerging on the other side, this explanation argues that infants predict the future motion of the car while it is visible. The prediction is that the car will end up at the end of the track. This explanation does not require infants to continue to represent the car when it momentarily disappears behind a screen. As such, it does not require that infants possess object permanence.

Another explanation that has been proposed as an alternative to object permanence and the representation of objects by infants is that representations are not all or none. Instead, infants may gradually acquire or build a representation of an object over time after repeated experiences with the object. The more experience an infant has with an object, the stronger its representation of the object becomes. In the case of the toy car rolling down a hill, this account suggests that infants *did* represent the car when it rolled behind the screen. However, their representation was weak. It allowed them to react with surprise when the car did not appear on the other side of the screen, but it would not allow them to search for the hidden car or to remember it after a long delay.

In response to these challenges from competing hypotheses, Luo, Baillargeon, Brueckner, and Munakata (2003) conducted a new set of experiments designed to determine which explanation for Baillargeon's previous research findings was most plausible. The researchers presented a well-controlled series of experiments that used visual tasks similar to the one previously described to evaluate which among the competing hypotheses is most likely to be correct.

You may have noticed that the fourth author in the research we will explore is the same person who formulated the two alternative explanations for Baillargeon's previous research findings. It is not uncommon for scientists, even scientists who have different ideas about how the world works, to cooperate in order to move closer to the truth. Ultimately, this is what science is all about—understanding the nature of the world.

FAMILIARIZATION EXPERIMENT

The method used in the research to be discussed here is an *experiment*. Remember, although that word is often used loosely in everyday parlance, within psychology it refers to a specific set of operations that can lead to confident conclusions about cause and effect. In the most basic kind of experiment, there are experimental groups that get some particular kind of experience or treatment. There are also control groups that do not get the special experience. By comparing the outcomes of the different groups, we can see whether the special treatment had any effect. The experiment described here involved a between-subjects comparison similar to those described in previous chapters. Infants were randomly assigned to one of four experimental groups.

Participants

The participants were 24 healthy, full-term infants, 12 male and 12 female, ranging in age from 4 months, 18 days to 5 months, 18 days old (mean = 5 months, 4 days). Another eight infants were not included in the study because four were fussy, two were active, one was distracted, and one required a diaper change. Information about the participants who were excluded from the research may be important for our interpretation of the research findings. We should be skeptical of the methods of any study that exclude participants who have a relevant characteristic that may systematically affect the results. For example, if the researchers excluded all male infants without explanation, we should question whether including them would lead to different results. Previous research has shown that infant boys develop slightly slower than infant girls (Baillargeon & DeVos, 1991). In this study, there is nothing to indicate that the experimenters excluded infants who had relevant characteristics that would have altered the results.

Apparatus

Luo, et al. (2003) described the apparatus they used in great detail. This was done so that other researchers could replicate the study. Think of this apparatus as being like a small stage on which infants could observe events. It consisted of a wooden cubicle about 4 feet high, slightly more than 3 feet wide, and a little less than 1 foot deep. The floor of the apparatus was gray. The side walls were painted white, and the back wall was painted black. When the experimenters did not want the infants to view the apparatus, they covered the opening with a muslin-covered frame (see Figure 10.1).

There were two windows in the apparatus. At the bottom of the back wall was an opening slightly more than 2 inches tall that extended almost the entire length of the back wall and was filled with black fringe. In the left wall (from the infants' perspective), there was a window about 20 inches tall and almost 6 inches wide. This window was covered with muslin, a white-colored, cotton fabric. The experimenters, wearing long, white gloves, used this window to reach into the apparatus and manipulate the objects inside.

The experimenters used a rigid screen about 16 inches tall and almost 9 inches wide to hide some events from the infants during experimental trials. The screen was centered on the floor of the apparatus slightly less than 6 inches in front of the back wall. The front of the screen was covered with blue contact paper, and the back was the same color gray as the floor of the apparatus. This helped the screen blend in when it was lying flat on the floor of the apparatus. The bottom of the screen was attached to a dowel that extended through a hole in the right wall. The experimenter rotated the dowel to raise the screen and lower the screen during experimental trials.

The two boxes used in the experiment were covered with red and green striped contact paper. Each of the boxes was about 5 inches tall and almost 7 inches wide. The thicker box was about 5.5 inches thick. The thin box was less than half an inch thick.

Two cylinders that were about 12 inches tall and 3 inches in diameter were also used in the study. Both were made with white cardboard and covered with small blue dots. One of them was used in the last familiarization trial in which infants were habituated to the objects and the apparatus. The other cylinder was mounted on a hidden metal rod that extended through the black fringe at the bottom of the back wall of the apparatus. The metal rod was attached to a track that allowed the cylinder to be moved smoothly and silently across the apparatus without infants knowing that it was being controlled by the experimenter.

Procedure

The procedure used in this study involves a series of trials that occurred in a particular sequence. Each trial exposed the infants to a different element of the experiment. The infants were held on their parent's lap in front of the apparatus during the trials. Parents were asked to close their eyes and not to interact with their children during the experimental procedures. In this way, parents could not transmit their own reactions to their infants. The infants were watched by two observers looking through peepholes in cloth-covered frames on each side of the apparatus. The observers could not see each other nor, presumably, hear each other in any way. These arrangements prevented them from unknowingly biasing the data that each independently collected when they observed the infants in the study.

The observers' job was to watch each infant's gaze and keep track of how much time they looked at the apparatus in each trial. One of the observers used their measurements of gaze time to decide when each trial would end. At that point, they would cover the apparatus with the rigid, muslin-covered screen so the infants could not continue to study the apparatus between trials. Agreement in the infants' looking times collected by the observers averaged 93 percent or more, suggesting that they were both observing quite accurately. There is no minimum level of observer agreement that is universally accepted in psychology. However, it is not possible to place much confidence in results unless the agreement between observers is quite high. In practice, studies are published with agreements ranging upward from about 80 percent. If the event being observed is relatively unimportant to the main point of the study, one might accept slightly lower levels. If the event is central to the study, higher levels might be sought.

An outline of the steps of the different trials conducted in this research appears here. Use this outline to help guide you through the complete description of the trials that follow:

Familiarization Trial 1: Box Familiarization
1. The experimenter placed a box against back wall of the apparatus, centered behind the screen.
2. Half of the infants viewed a thick box, and the other half viewed a thin box.
3. The screen was in the down position, flat against the floor.
4. The muslin-covered frame was placed over the apparatus.

Familiarization Trial 2: Screen Familiarization
1. The screen was rotated upward, blocking infants' views of the box.
2. The muslin-covered frame was placed over the apparatus.

Familiarization Trial 3: Screen Familiarization
1. The screen was rotated upward, blocking infants' views of the box.
2. The muslin-covered frame was placed over the apparatus.

Familiarization Trial 4: Screen Familiarization
1. The screen was rotated upward, blocking infants' views of the box. The screen was left up for the remainder of the experiment.
2. The muslin-covered frame was placed over the apparatus.

Delay Begins—Half of the infants experienced a three-minute delay; the other half experienced a four-minute delay. Experimenters used the delay to secretly remove the box from behind the screen.

Familiarization Trial 5: Cylinder Familiarization—Conducted during the delay period
1. The cylinder was placed on the floor of the apparatus to the left of the screen, while the screen was upright, hiding the area behind the screen.
2. The muslin-covered frame was placed over the apparatus.
3. Parents play with infants for the remainder of the delay period.

Block 1 (three total trials) and Block 2 (three total trials) of the Test Trials—Each trial was identical, so a description of only one trial is provided.

1. The screen continued to be in an upright position, blocking infants' views of the area behind it.
2. The cylinder began in left side of apparatus and slowly passed behind the screen to the right side of the apparatus. The cylinder then moved in the opposite direction, passing behind the screen again to return to its starting point on the left side.
3. The muslin-covered frame was placed over the apparatus.

COMPLETE DESCRIPTION OF EXPERIMENTAL TRIALS

Familiarization Trials

Each infant received five familiarization trials. The purpose of the trials was to habituate the infants to the different stimuli used in the study. In the first trial, infants were familiarized to either the thick box or the thin box. The experimenter placed the box in the apparatus for the infant to view. The trial was ended by the experimenters when the infants (1) looked away for 2 consecutive seconds after looking at the box for at least 28 uninterrupted seconds or (2) looked at the box for a combined total of 40 seconds. The infants in the thin box trials and the thick box trials looked for about the same amount of time. These events were argued to be an indication that the infants had become habituated to the boxes. Images of the thin and thick box on the apparatus appear in Figure 10.1.

   In the two trials that followed, infants were familiarized with the screen being raised in front of the same box they had observed previously. Infants observed the static scene of the screen in front of the box until the trial ended. The experimenter ended the trial when the infants either (1) looked away for 2 consecutive seconds after viewing the screen for 16 straight seconds or (2) looked for a total of 40 seconds. Infants in both the thin box and the thick box

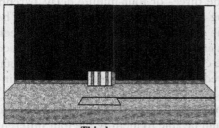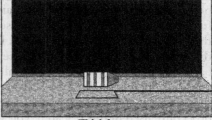

Thin box   Thick box

FIGURE 10.1   Apparatus as It Appeared with a Thin Box Placed on It and Apparatus with a Thick Box Placed on It

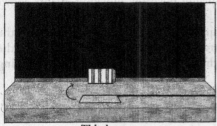
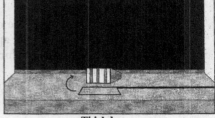

Thin box   Thick box

FIGURE 10.2 Direction the Screen Was Rotated Upward to Block Infants' Views of the Thin Box and the Thick Box

conditions looked for about the same amount of time. Images illustrating how the screen was rotated from a position flat on the floor to a vertical position using the dowel to which it was attached appear in Figure 10.2.

The fourth familiarization trial was identical in most ways to trials 2 and 3. The only difference was that, as the screen was rotated upward blocking infants' views of the box, the experimenters started a timer. Half of the infants were then exposed to a three-minute delay; the other half were exposed to a four-minute delay.

During the delay, infants completed the fifth familiarization trial in which they were habituated to the cylinder. In this trial, the screen remained upright. The cylinder was placed on the apparatus to the left side of the screen. The infants in both the thick box and the thin box conditions saw the same event. The trial was ended when infants (1) looked away from the apparatus for 2 seconds after looking at it for at least 16 seconds straight or (2) looked at the apparatus for a total of 40 seconds. As in the other trials, infants in both the thin and thick box conditions looked at the cylinder for roughly the same amount of time. An image illustrating the cylinder familiarization trial appears in Figure 10.3.

In the time that was left over in the three- or four-minute delay, parents played with their infants while remaining seated in front of the apparatus. The function of the delays was to increase the amount of time that elapsed between the last showing of the thin or thick box and the test trials. Experimenters used this time to remove the box and place the cylinder that was attached to the metal bar in the apparatus. The metal bar allowed the experimenters to move the cylinder back and forth behind the screen.

Now that you have read a description of the experimental methods and procedure used in this research, you should be able to identify the four different experimental groups. Infants were shown either a thin or a thick box and were exposed to either a three- or four-minute delay after the familiarization trials. An equal number of infants were randomly assigned to each group. The four experimental groups are shown in Table 10.1.

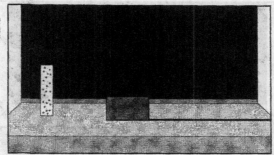

Cylinder familiarization

FIGURE 10.3   The Apparatus as It Appeared in the Cylinder Familiarization Trial

Test Trials

Infants in both the thin box group and the thick box group watched two blocks of three test trials, for a total of six trials. In each trial, infants in both groups saw the same event—the cylinder move back and forth behind the screen. The screen was in the up position for all trials so infants could not see the area behind it. The key to the test trials was that there was not enough room for the cylinder to pass behind the screen when the thick box was also behind the screen. In this kind of research, this is referred to as the impossible event. It is impossible because the cylinder either should be blocked by the thick box or push the box out of the way as it passed behind the screen. The thin box condition was the possible event because there was enough space for the cylinder to pass behind the screen in front of the thin box and move from one side of the apparatus to the other. The infants did not know that, prior to the test trials, the experimenters had removed the boxes from behind the screen to allow the cylinder to move unobstructed in both conditions. An image illustrating the movement of the cylinder appears in Figure 10.4.

Rationale of Experimental Methods

In the five familiarization trials, the box and cylinder were never visible at the same time. In the first of these trials, the box was placed flat on the floor of the

TABLE 10.1   Experimental Groups

Thin box; Three-minute delay	Thin box; Four-minute delay
Thick box; Three-minute delay	Thick box; Four-minute delay

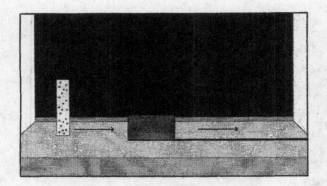

FIGURE 10.4   Position and Direction of Movement of the Cylinder in Each Test Trials
(Note that in the actual test trials the cylinder also moved back to its original position, following the same path behind the screen.)

apparatus. In the next three trials, the screen was rotated from a position flat against the floor to an upright position that blocked infants' views of the thick or thin box. At the beginning of the fourth trial, the screen was raised for a final time and remained in that position for the rest of the experiment. In the fifth and final familiarization trial, the cylinder was placed on the floor next to the screen.

All methods described here were devised in order to test the alternative hypotheses proposed by Munakata (2001). The first alternative hypothesis was that infants form a prediction about the outcome of an event they are observing while all relevant objects are still in view. As an event unfolds, they check to see whether their prediction of the outcome of the object's movement was accurate.

To address this alternative explanation, infants in this experiment did not see the cylinder and the box at the same time. The cylinder and its motion were not introduced until after the box was hidden from view. If this alternative hypothesis was correct, infants should not act surprised when they see the cylinder pass back and forth behind the screen where the thick box was placed previously because they have not formed a mental representation of the box and have not seen both objects at the same time. As a result, infants in both the thick box condition and the thin box condition should look at the movement of the cylinder behind the screen about equally.

The other alternative explanation was that representations are not all or none. Instead, infants may gradually acquire or build a representation of an object over time after repeated experiences with the object. The more experience an infant has with an object, the stronger its representation of the object becomes.

To address this alternative hypothesis, the experimenters inserted a timed delay before the test trials began. By the time the first test trial started, infants had not seen the box behind the small screen for either three or four minutes. Because this hypothesis argues that representations of objects are not all or none, experimenters reasoned that the time delay would weaken the strength of representations infants had of the hidden boxes or that their representations would not be strong enough to last through the delays. As a result, infants in both the thin box trial and the thick box trial should look at the cylinder moving behind the small screen for the same amount of time.

RESULTS

There were no sex differences in infants' looking times at the apparatus, so all subsequent statistical analyses were collapsed across sex. There were also no differences in the looking times of infants in the three-minute delay condition and infants in the four-minute delay condition, so data from these groups were also analyzed together.

As shown in Tables 10.2 and 10.3, all infants looked less at the apparatus as the experiment progressed across trials. These decreases in looking time are consistent with habituation. In the first block of the test trials, infants looked at the thick and thin box conditions for about the same amount of time, as shown in Table 10.1.

In Block 2 of the test trials, infants looked much longer at the thick box condition than the thin box condition in both the three-minute delay condition and the four-minute delay condition, as shown in Table 10.2.

TABLE 10.2   Block 1 of the Test Trials

	THICK BLOCK CONDITION	THIN BLOCK CONDITION
Trial 1 looking time	58 sec	57 sec
Trial 2 looking time	54 sec	50 sec
Trial 3 looking time	46 sec	54 sec

TABLE 10.3   Block 2 of the Test Trials

	THICK BLOCK CONDITION	THIN BLOCK CONDITION
Trial 4 looking time	50 sec	37 sec
Trial 5 looking time	48 sec	33 sec
Trial 6 looking time	42 sec	31 sec

DISCUSSION

The carefully planned and conducted experiment of Luo et al. (2003) demonstrates striking abilities in children as young as four months old. We doubt that many parents, even those having considerable experience with infants, would have predicted this level of reasoning in such young children.

In Block 1 of the test trials in which the cylinder moved back and forth behind the screen, infants in both the thin and thick block conditions looked at the cylinder moving behind the screen of the apparatus for similarly long periods of time. The researchers argue that this is likely due to the fact that none of the infants had previously seen the cylinder move. They were interested in observing an event that they had not seen before. Children as a group tend to be novelty seekers—they prefer to experience new things over alternatives with which they have substantial experience. This has been argued to be functional because it leads children to learn new things about the world (Bjorklund & Hernandez Blasi, 2005).

In Block 2 of the test trials, infants in the thick box condition looked at the apparatus longer than infants in the thin box condition. This was true of both infants in the three-minute delay condition and infants in the four-minute delay condition and for all the trials in Block 2. The results suggest that infants remembered that there was a thin box or a thick box behind the screen even after a three- or four-minute delay between test trials. The results also suggest that infants in the thin box condition knew that there was enough room for the cylinder to pass behind the screen without being blocked by the box (the possible event). Finally, the results indicate that the infants in the thick box condition were surprised when the cylinder was able to pass behind the screen rather than hitting the box (the impossible event), leading to their longer looking times.

These research findings challenge the alternative hypotheses proposed by Munakata (2001). The thick and thin boxes were hidden from infants after the fourth familiarization trial. The cylinder was not presented until the fifth familiarization trial and did not move back and forth behind the screen until the first test trial. If infants' understanding of the outcomes of events is based on predictions they make when they view all interacting items at the same time, then there should have been no looking time difference between infants in the thin box and thick box conditions. The fact that infants differed in their looking times suggests that they formed representations of the hidden boxes and used that information to deduce what would happen when the cylinder passed behind the screen. Infants as young as four months old appear to possess object permanence in the classic, Piagetian sense. In addition, there is no evidence that infants' representations of the thin and thick boxes were weak or short lived. Infants in this study continued to represent the boxes after a delay of a few minutes.

In this research, there is strong evidence that children knew that objects continued to exist when they were out of sight. They understood that objects retained their solidity and other physical properties when they were hidden.

They also knew that the interactions between physical objects did not change merely because they could not be seen. It seems likely that Piaget did not notice these things in young children because his methods were lacking in adequate experimental procedures and controls. Even though Luo et al. (2003) have revised Piaget's view of cognition in childhood, it must be remembered that Piaget's crude observations pointed the way to more sophisticated analyses of behavior. As a scientist, Piaget would probably have been well pleased with this outcome.

REFERENCES

Baillargeon, R., & DeVos, J. (1991). Object permanence in young infants: Further evidence. *Child Development, 62*, 1227–1246.

Bjorklund, D. F., & Hernandez Blasi, C. (2005). Evolutionary developmental psychology. In D. Buss (Ed.), *The handbook of evolutionary Psychology*. Hoboken, NJ: Wiley. (pp. 828–850)

Luo, Y., Baillargeon, R. Brueckner, L., & Munakata, Y. (2003). Reasoning about a hidden object after a delay: Evidence for robust representation in 5-month-old infants. *Condition, 88*, 23–32.

Munakata, Y. (2001). Task dependency in infant behavior: Toward an understanding of the processes underlying cognitive development. In F. Lacerda, C. von Hoften, & M. Heimann (Eds.), *Emerging cognitive abilities in early infancy* (pp. 29–52). Mahwah, NJ: Erlbaum.

Piaget, J. (1954). *The construction of reality in the child*. New York: Basic Books.

Samuel, J., & Bryant, P. (1984). Asking only one question in the conservation experiment. *Journal of Child Psychology and Psychiatry, 25*, 315–318.

Winer, G., Craig, R., & Weinbaum, E. (1992). Adults' failure on misleading weight-conservation tests: A developmental analysis. *Developmental Psychology, 28*, 109–120.

CHAPTER 11

ADOLESCENTS WILL
BE ADOLESCENTS

Researchers know that good parenting is important for the healthy development of children. There is disagreement, however, about who is qualified to administer good parenting. Does the sexual orientation of parents affect child development? If it does, how is development affected? The answers to these questions are important for legal proceedings and decisions about public policy involving child custody, adoption, and visitation privileges. This issue also has been introduced as important in discussions about whether gay marriage should be legalized or banned.

The question of whether parental sexual orientation affects child development is also important to the field of psychology and leads to related questions. Does healthy human development require that a child grow up in a home with one parent of each sex? How would the answer to this question inform our understanding of parent–child interactions? The results of studies conducted over the past 20 years have identified few associations between parental sexual orientation and children's well-being (Patterson, 2006). Instead, these studies suggest that processes within families that are independent of the sexual orientation and the sex of the parents are important influences on child outcomes (i.e., the quality of the relationships between children and their parents).

Most of the research that has been conducted on the effects of parenting by heterosexual, single, and lesbian and gay parents has examined young children. Adolescent outcomes of parenting also have been the focus of research, but primarily in families with heterosexual or single parents. Relatively little research has examined the adolescent children of lesbian or gay parents. It is inappropriate to generalize research findings on the developmental outcomes of the young children of lesbian and gay parents to adolescents. Children change rapidly as they get older. Adolescence is a time when children become aware of issues involving sexuality, which may lead to different outcomes for adolescents than for younger children (Perrin & The Committee on Psychosocial Aspects of

Incorporating the research of J. L. Wainright, and C. J. Patterson "Delinquency, Victimization, and Substance Use among Adolescents with Female Same-Sex Parents," 2006, *Journal of Family Psychology*, *20*, pp. 526–530.

Child and Family Health, 2002). The limited number of studies that have been done on the outcomes of adolescent children raised by lesbian parents found no differences compared to children raised by heterosexual parents in self-esteem, depression, anxiety, peer group hostility, grade point average, trouble in school, sexual behavior, or romantic relationships (Wainright, Russell, & Patterson, 2004).

Among heterosexual parents, an accepting and warm parenting style has been found to lead to good outcomes among adolescents. Setting fair but firm limits also can contribute to a good relationship between parent and adolescent, and can lead to fewer adolescent risk-taking behaviors (Matherne & Thomas, 2001). More original research on the adolescent outcomes of the children of lesbian and gay parents is needed to help validate previous findings and to examine other ways they might differ from the children of heterosexual parents. Wainright and Patterson (2006) conducted research to address precisely these issues.

PARTICIPANTS

The families that participated in the research were participants in a larger study called the National Longitudinal Study of Adolescent Health (Bearman, Jones, & Udry, 1997). This school-based research explored the health-related behaviors of adolescents in grades 7 to 12. A pair of schools in 80 different communities from across the United States were selected to participate in the study. Schools were specifically selected in order to make sure the sample of all schools was representative of the diversity of schools in the United States. The criteria used to make selections were area of the country, population density (urban or rural), school type, ethnicity, and school size. If any school chose not to participate, it was replaced with a school that had similar characteristics. Schools provided the names and grade levels of their students and most administered research instruments during class periods.

About 200 students were selected from the 80 pairs of schools yielding a total sample of 12,105 adolescents. The adolescents were interviewed by trained interviewers in their homes. Adolescents' responses to questions were entered directly into laptop computers. Interviewers asked questions directly about topics that the adolescents would not be reluctant to answer. For questions about sensitive issues, such as sexual activity, adolescents were asked to wear headphones through which they heard prerecorded questions. They entered responses to the questions themselves directly into the laptops.

A parent of the adolescents, usually the mother who resided with them, completed a questionnaire that asked about a range of issues, including parents' romantic relationships, the neighborhood in which they lived, involvement in local activities, behaviors that affected their health, educational and employment history, income, and the quality of the relationship the parent had with her adolescent child. Data were collected from children and their parents using a variety of measures, including questionnaires administered in school and at home, and interviews in the home.

The researchers do not describe the surveys used in their research in great detail. Instead, they refer readers to explore a description of these In Home Interview surveys in previous papers that used them as research instruments. Wainright and Patterson (2006) also refer us to the original research on the National Longitudinal Study of Adolescent Health (Bearman et al., 1997). It is not unusual for researchers to do this when they describe research that involves questionnaires that have been previously validated by other studies. Rather than explaining everything about the surveys, the study authors can simply refer interested readers to a more complete description available elsewhere. This does not mean that we should simply accept that the study measures are wonderful and flawless because they have been used in a number of different research projects. If we want to question the validity of the measures, we should track them down and examine them ourselves firsthand. In the case of this study, you can learn more about the questionnaires used by the researchers and the study design by visiting the National Longitudinal Study of Adolescent Health research website listed in the References section of this chapter.

The children of same-sex couples were identified within the sample by first looking for parents who indicated they were married or in a marriage-like relationship with a person of the same sex. Lesbian, gay, or bisexual parents who did not report such a relationship could not be identified and were not included in the final sample. Through this identification process, 44 adolescents being raised by lesbian parents were identified. Only six adolescents being raised by same-sex male parents were identified. Because of their small number, adequate data analyses could not be conducted on these adolescents, so they were not included in the study.

Of the 44 adolescents being raised by lesbian parents, 23 were girls and 21 were boys. The majority of them (68 percent) were White and slightly more than 31 percent indicated they were non-White or biracial. The adolescents ranged in age from 12 to 18. The average age of adolescents in the group was 15.1 years old. The average annual family income was $45,500.

Now that the researchers had identified a group of adolescents with lesbian parents to study, they needed a group of adolescents being raised by heterosexual parents to compare them to. The researchers did not want to compare the adolescents who had lesbian parents to just any other group of adolescents who had heterosexual parents. If they did, they would not have been able to know for sure if any differences they discovered between the two groups of adolescents were due to differences in the sexual orientation of their parents or other differences between the adolescents, such as differences between lesbian and heterosexual families' annual incomes, neighborhood characteristics, or something else. The large database provided by the National Longitudinal Study of Adolescent Health was used to match each adolescent who had lesbian parents with an adolescent who had heterosexual parents. The following characteristics of adolescents were matched: sex, age, ethnicity, adoption status, adolescent learning disabilities, family income, and parents' educational history. After matching, the final sample included 88 adolescents, 44 with same-sex, lesbian parents and 44 with heterosexual parents.

Even though the researchers carefully matched their sample of adolescents who had lesbian parents with other adolescents who had heterosexual parents, they were concerned that the characteristics of their sample might not be accurately representative of the entire sample of adolescents, which included 12,105 young adults. To find out, the researchers compared the characteristics of adolescents in their sample to the characteristics of the adolescents in the larger sample. They did not find any significant differences in any of the characteristics. This encouraged the researchers that their sample was still adequately representative of the demographic characteristics of adolescents in the United States.

DEPENDENT MEASURES

Wainright and Patterson (2006) assessed substance use, physical problems due to substance use, how substance use affected sexual activity, delinquent behavior, and victimization among the adolescents. They did this by assigning numerical ratings to the research participants' responses to questions about each topic. Many of the questions that the researchers asked were open ended. This means that the participants were not constrained in the kind of response they could give. An example of an open-ended question is, "What did you do yesterday?" People who are asked this question can respond in a variety of different ways, depending on what information they want to express. Closed-ended questions, in contrast, limit the range of responses that a research participant can make. For example, the question, "Did you eat breakfast yesterday?" prompts people to respond with either "yes" or "no." To give other examples, an essay question on an exam is open ended, while a multiple-choice question is closed ended.

Coding research participants' responses to open-ended questions can present a challenge to researchers. A large part of the challenge is converting participants' responses into numbers that can be statistically analyzed. This requires the development of specific criteria for assigning different numerical values to different responses. The next step is to carefully read through participants' responses and assign appropriate numerical values to them. The data coding procedure used in this study is the topic we turn to next.

TOBACCO

Use of tobacco was examined using a brief survey. Based on their responses to the survey, adolescents' tobacco use was classified at one of the following levels:

1 = has never smoked

3 = is currently smoking between 1 and 2 cigarettes each day

5 = is currently smoking between 6 and 10 cigarettes each day

7 = is currently smoking more than 20 cigarettes each day

Tobacco use by the friends of the adolescents was also assessed by asking how many among the adolescents' three best friends smoked at least one cigarette each day?

ALCOHOL

The adolescents' alcohol use was also surveyed. They were told not to include "a sip or taste of someone else's drink" in estimates of their alcohol consumption. Responses were classified according to the following scale:

1 = has had between two and three drinks in entire lifetime

3 = has consumed alcohol on one or two days in the past 12 months

5 = has had alcohol on two or three days per month over the past 12 months

7 = has had alcohol between three and five times per week over the past 12 months

8 = has had alcohol almost every day or every day over the past 12 months

Other items assessed how frequently the adolescents binged on alcohol, which was operationally defined as consuming five or more drinks in a row. They were also asked how many times they had gotten drunk. These items were classified on a scale that ranged from 1 (almost never) to 7 (every day or almost every day).

MARIJUANA

Marijuana use by the adolescents was surveyed and classified using a method similar to tobacco and alcohol use. The classification scheme appears as follows:

1 = have never used marijuana

3 = have used marijuana more than three times, but not in the past 30 days

5 = have used marijuana between two and three times in the past 30 days

7 = have used marijuana more than five times in the past 30 days

RISK TAKING

The number of risky behaviors that adolescents reported engaging in while using alcohol or other drugs—including driving a car, going to school, getting into a fight, and carrying a weapon—were summed to produce an index value out of a possible score of 8.

HEALTH AND RELATIONSHIP PROBLEMS

Problems adolescents had with their physical health or in their relationships as a result of their use of alcohol in the past 12 months were assessed with survey items that included questions about how frequently the adolescents were hung over, sick, in fights, regretted events in their lives, were in trouble with parents or at school, and had disagreements with their friends or dates. The average across all items rated on a scale ranging from 0 (never) to 4 (five or more times) was used as an index of the frequency of alcohol-related problems.

SUBSTANCE USE AND SEXUALITY

The co-occurrence of substance use (alcohol or other drugs) and sexual activity was assessed by asking adolescents whether they had used alcohol, drugs, or been drunk the first time they had sex or the last time they had sex. An index score for sexual behaviors while under the influence was computed by summing adolescents' affirmative responses to the six survey items. Higher values indicated more frequent sexual behaviors under the influence.

DELINQUENCY

Delinquent behavior was assessed by asking adolescents how frequently they engaged in a variety of delinquent acts, including damaging property, shoplifting, and getting into fights during the past 12 months. An index score for delinquent behavior was computed by summing adolescents' affirmative responses to these 10 survey items. Higher values indicated more delinquent behaviors.

VICTIMIZATION

The assessment of victimization included survey items that examined how often the adolescents had been victimized and how often they had witnessed violence occurring. The survey items included questions about how often the adolescents had a gun fired at them, had been intentionally cut by someone else with a sharp object, had been jumped, had a weapon pulled on them, or had seen someone else get shot or stabbed. An index score for victimization was computed by summing the affirmative responses adolescents gave to the five survey items, with higher scores representing greater victimization.

RELATIONSHIPS WITH FAMILY AND OTHERS

An index score for how much adolescents believed their parents, teachers, and friends cared about them was created by averaging the ratings they made on a scale with values from 1 (not at all) to 5 (very much). Ratings were made for each relationship type. Higher scores were indicative of higher levels of caring. Parents' perceptions of the quality of their relationships with their children were also assessed using survey measures. Parents rated the amount of trust, understanding, communication, and quality in their relationships with their adolescent children. Closer relationships were indicated by higher average scores on a 1 to 5 scale.

RESULTS

Taken as a group, the adolescents reported having positive life outcomes. Their use of cigarettes and alcohol was moderate. Only 25 percent of the participants indicated that they had ever smoked on a regular basis. Forty-four percent of the adolescents indicated that they had consumed alcohol while not in the presence of their parents. As illustrated by Figure 11.1, adolescents' frequency of alcohol and tobacco use were low, as were their reports of alcohol abuse, binge drinking, and getting drunk. Adolescents' reports of physical and relationship problems resulting from alcohol use were also low. In fact, there were low levels or low frequencies of all problem behaviors, including the risky use of alcohol and drugs, the co-occurrence of drug or alcohol use and sexual activity, delinquent behavior, and victimization.

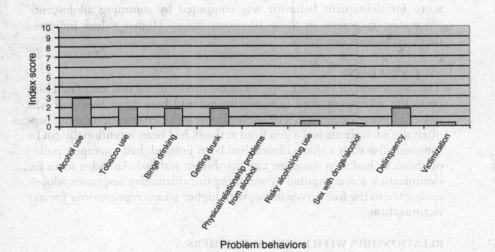

FIGURE 11.1   Assessments of Problem Behaviors Across All Adolescents in the Sample

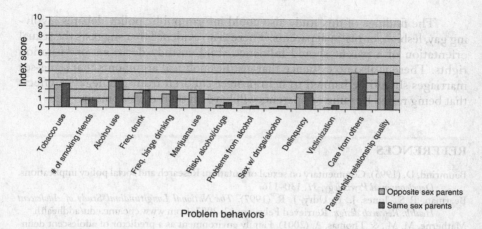

FIGURE 11.2   Comparison of Adolescents Raised by Lesbian Parents and Those Raised by Heterosexual Parents

When Wainright and Patterson (2006) compared the adolescents raised by lesbian parents with those raised by heterosexual parents, they found no significant differences between the groups for any of the issues they assessed. The findings are illustrated by Figure 11.2.

DISCUSSION

There were no differences between the adolescent children of lesbian parents and the adolescent children of heterosexual parents across a range of different measures of adolescent adjustment. The results of this study suggest that the quality of the relationship between adolescents and their parents matters more than the sexual orientation of parents in contributing to this outcome. Other studies have led researchers to draw similar conclusions. Research by Wainright et al. (2004), for example, found no differences between the adolescent children of lesbian parents and the adolescent children of heterosexual parents in their psychosocial adjustment, school outcomes, or romantic relationships.

According to some theories of human development, children raised by same sex parents should be expected to encounter adjustment difficulties, especially when they are adolescents (Baumrind, 1995). The results of this study and findings from other studies that have examined the outcomes of children raised by same sex parents (Patterson, 2006; Wainright et al., 2004) suggest that the importance of having a parent of each sex in the home in order for normal development to take place may need to be reevaluated.

The findings of this study also could inform public policy debates involving gay, lesbian, or bisexual parents. There is no evidence that suggests the sexual orientation of a parent should influence child custody decisions or visitation rights. There is also no evidence that justifies political arguments that same-sex marriages should be banned to help protect children from the negative effects that being raised by same-sex parents will have on their development.

REFERENCES

Baumrind, D. (1995). Commentary on sexual orientation: Research and social policy implications. *Developmental Psychology, 31,* 130–136.

Bearman, P. S., Jones, J., & Udry, J. R. (1997). *The National Longitudinal Study of Adolescent Health: Research design.* Retrieved February 12, 2007, from www.cpc.unc.edu/addhealth

Matherne, M. M., & Thomas, A. (2001). Family environment as a predictor of adolescent delinquency. *Adolescence, 36,* 655–664.

Patterson, C. J. (2006). Children of lesbian and gay parents. *Current Directions in Psychological Science, 15,* 241–244.

Perrin, E., & The Committee on Psychosocial Aspects of Child and Family Health. (2002). Coparent or second-parent adoption by same-sex partners [Policy statement]. *Pediatrics, 109,* 339–340.

Wainright, J. L., & Patterson, C. J. (2006). Delinquency, victimization, and substance use among adolescents with female same-sex parents. *Journal of Family Psychology, 20,* 526–530.

Wainright, J. L., Russell, S. T., & Patterson, C. J. (2004). Psychosocial adjustment, school outcomes, and romantic attractions of adolescents with same-sex parents. *Child Development, 75,* 1886–1898.

CHAPTER 12

KIDS SAY THE DARNDEST THINGS

Memory was a topic of research within psychology before the beginning of scientific psychology over 100 years ago. One of the most surprising findings of recent decades is the extent to which memories can be modified by events that happen subsequently. You will have some hint of this if you have ever heard a friend relating a past incident that included you as a participant. As you listen to your friend's account, you find yourself thinking, "That isn't what happened; that's not the way I remember it."

RECALLING AN ACCIDENT

One of the most formative classic pieces of research about the manipulation of memory was done by Loftus and Palmer (1974). This study demonstrated that memory was unlike a video recorder; it was not a faithful or objective record of what happened. Instead, they found that memory was reconstructive: some aspects of our memory were shown to be accurate, but later events were merged with some existing memories, changing their content.

In an experiment, Loftus and Palmer (1974) showed adults a film of a car accident. Following this, participants wrote a description of what they had seen and answered some questions about it. One key question was: "About how fast were the cars going when they *contacted* each other?" Different groups of participants were given different versions of this question. Although some were asked the question with *contacted* as the verb, for other participants this word was replaced with one of the following: *hit, bumped, collided,* or *smashed.* The speed estimates given by the participants as answers to the question were a dependent variable. These estimates varied depending on the word that had been used in the question. Participants who were asked about the speed as the cars *contacted* each other gave an average speed estimate of 32 miles per hour (mph). Other

Incorporating the research of M. D. Leichtman and S. J. Ceci, "The Effects of Stereotypes and Suggestions on Preschoolers' Reports," 1995, *Developmental Psychology, 31,* pp. 568–578.

words resulted in successively faster estimates, culminating in *smashed*, which resulted in a 41 mph average estimate.

A week later, participants were asked to recall the film and to answer another group of questions. Memory was operationally defined as the responses that participants made to questions about past events. One of the questions asked was, "Did you see any broken glass?" There was no broken glass in the film, but most participants who had heard the word *smashed* in the initial phase of the study also remembered broken glass that was not really there. This nicely illustrates what is meant by reconstructive memory. When we refer back to memories of past events, what we retrieve is a patchwork composed of things that really happened, things that have been changed a bit, and things that were added later. Memory is not like a photograph, unchanged in storage across time. Rather, it is a project constantly under reconstruction.

PRESUPPOSITIONS

In a subsequent study, Loftus (1975) further investigated memory reconstruction as a function of additional information tucked into questions. This extra information was called a presupposition. For example, in the sentence "Did it hurt when the vicious dog bit you?" the question is "*Did it hurt?*" but there is also a presupposition that the dog was vicious. You are not being *asked* if the dog was vicious, you are being *told* this. You are asked about being hurt. Loftus showed participants a film involving a car hitting a baby carriage. Some participants were asked if they had seen a barn, although there was no barn in the film. Other participants were asked if there was a station wagon parked in front of the barn. In this latter case, the question asked directly about a station wagon and the barn was a presupposition: these participants were not asked about the barn—they were told about it.

When asked a week later, 29.2 percent of the participants who were given false presuppositions, such as the barn, claimed that they actually remembered the nonexistent object. In comparison, surprisingly, only 15.6 percent of people who had false objects introduced as direct questions—for example, "Did you see a barn?"—remembered false objects. Lastly, only 8.7 percent of a control group, which had not been given any false information, remembered false objects. The wider implications of these findings ought to be of great interest to a society that depends on testimony from memory.

These are among many clear research demonstrations of the reconstructive nature of memory. We observe events, but the memory we have of them includes more than perfectly stored observations. Even completely false information can be included merely because it happened to be available around the time of the event. We all believe that there are some things we *know*; things that we remember so clearly that we have no doubt about the objectivity or truthfulness of our memory. The studies of Loftus and others indicate that we should not be so sure of ourselves. What does this say about objectivity? If we accept these research findings as having external validity, it becomes nonsense to instruct someone to "be objective" about past events, as if objectivity were something that could be turned on or off at will. The studies of memory suggest quite different conclusions: the memories in which we put so much stock are mosaics of real and false information.

These observations ought to undermine some of our confidence in the truth of our memories. Usually this does not matter very much. Who cares if we remember that there was potato salad at the family picnic last summer when, in fact, it was a fruit salad? Aunt Mildred may care when you rave about the potato salad she never made. The worst-case scenario might have you remembering a salad as good when it was not, and, as a result, Aunt Mildred makes it "especially for you" every time there is a family gathering.

Setting the salads aside, there are cases where memory and confidence in memory can be a matter of life or death. When we take account of research findings, this becomes a scary proposition. Courts of law often consider that eyewitness testimony is a truthful account of events, particularly if it holds up under grueling cross-examination. In the time since the memory studies of the 1970s, psychologists have increasingly questioned this assumption. In the studies discussed previously, the participants were adults. However, in the past decade there have been a number of high-profile cases in which the recollections of children have played a pivotal role. If the accuracy of adult memory is questionable, what about the memories of children? The research literature in this area shows, unsurprisingly, that memories of younger kids are even more vulnerable to false information than those of older kids (see Ceci & Bruck, 1993, for a review of the literature).

Michelle D. Leichtman and Stephen J. Ceci (1995) identified two classes of reasons for false memories in children: cognitive factors and social factors. Children have difficulty in distinguishing the sources of their stored memories. Younger children are particularly likely to remember performing an act when, in reality, they only repeatedly imagined performing it. This is called *source misattribution*, and it is an example of a cognitive factor. Social factors include bribes, threats, or feeling pressured to respond in ways that will please certain adults. When children are required to testify in court, both cognitive and social influences may be present, setting the stage for false memories. Cognitive factors will operate in court, where it is routine that children are questioned in detail and at great length. It is easy to imagine that some of the questions will contain presuppositions or will be leading questions. Repeated leading questions can make particular scenarios so familiar to children that they become incorporated into the child's memory. In one case involving child sexual abuse, a mother indicated that her daughter had been interviewed between 30 and 50 times by county officials (Humphrey, 1985). It is also easy to imagine a role for social factors: a child might figure out which responses please the adults. The child may give those responses at higher frequencies. A key child witness in a Texas murder case changed her testimony saying, "Originally I think I told police just what I saw. But the more questions I was asked, the more confused I became. I answered questions I wasn't certain about because I wanted to help the adults" (quoted in Leichtman & Ceci, 1995).

Leichtman and Ceci (1995) conducted an experiment in which they studied the recollections of children about a prearranged event. This has become known as the *Sam Stone Study* because an enactment was staged for the children in which a man called Sam Stone visited their day care center.

Participants

The participants were 176 preschool children who were enrolled in private day care centers. The children represented a wide range of socioeconomic status and ethnic groups. The children belonged to one of two age groups: early preschoolers (three- and four-year-olds) and later preschoolers (five- and six-year-olds). They spent their days in classrooms consisting of eight children each. Whole classrooms, not individual children, were randomly assigned to an experimental condition. This was done to prevent children within a single class from talking with each other and discovering that different things were going on for different children.

Procedures

There were eight different groups of kids in the study. There was a control group and three experimental groups for the young preschoolers and the same four groups for the older preschoolers. The procedure for the actual visit of Sam Stone was repeated in each of the eight classrooms. A confederate acted the role of Sam. *Confederate*, in this context, means someone who works for the researcher as an actor, pretending to be someone else. You will see this again in later chapters where, for example, confederates pretend to be additional participants in studies. These confederates are sometimes making behavior observations of the real participants. By pretending to be participants themselves, they are able to do so without the awareness of the real participants. In this study the confederate, Sam, was not collecting data, but was playing the role of a classroom visitor. Sam entered the classroom during a story reading session and said hello to the adult in charge. He was introduced to the children. He commented on the story being read by saying, "I know that story; it's one of my favorites!" He walked around the perimeter of the room, waved to the children, and left. His visit lasted about two minutes.

Neither the young nor the older control group had prior knowledge of Sam Stone's visit. Following the visit, they were interviewed once a week for four weeks. In these interviews, they were asked questions about what Sam had done during the visit to their school, but they were given no suggestions or additional information about Sam or his visit.

The *stereotype* experimental groups, one younger and one older, were told about Sam Stone before his visit in a manner designed to create a stereotype of Sam's personality. A research assistant went to these groups once a week for a month before the visit and, while playing with the children, told three different scripted stories about Sam. Over the course of the four visits, these children heard 12 stories that presented a consistent stereotype of Sam. In each story Sam was shown to be a kind person, but somewhat accident prone. In one of these stories, for example, the children were told that Sam Stone had visited the research assistant the previous night and asked to borrow a Barbie doll. On the way down the stairs he tripped and broke the doll, but he was having it fixed. In other versions of the story, Sam did other things. They were told he lost a borrowed pen and replaced it, spilled soda on the research assistant but cleaned it up, and accidentally took some board game pieces home but brought them back. After four weeks of stereotype building, this group had a two-minute visit from Sam Stone in which he behaved as he did in all groups: he walked around doing nothing remarkable. Following Sam Stone's visit, this group was treated like the control group in being asked neutral, suggestion-free questions at one-week intervals for four weeks.

For the *suggestion* experimental groups, no attempt was made to create a stereotype of Sam Stone in the month before his visit. Instead, following the visit, at one-week intervals, the children were asked questions that contained two false suggestions about Sam Stone's visit: that he had ripped a book and that he had gotten dirt on a teddy bear. Children were asked, for example, "When Sam got the bear dirty, did he do it on purpose or was it an accident?" and "Was Sam Stone happy or sad that he got the bear dirty?"

The children in the remaining experimental condition received both the stereotyping information about Sam's clumsiness before his visit and the leading questions once a week after the event. They were called the *stereotype-plus-suggestion* groups. These children were exposed to a stereotypical expectation about Sam for the month before the visit as well as misinformation planted in the month following the visit.

At the completion of the experimental conditions described above, all children were exposed to a final interview conducted by a new person who was not present during Sam's visit or the experimental procedures. The quality of their memory for events was operationally defined as the accuracy of their responses to interview questions. In this interview, the same questions were asked of all children. In this test of memory, the children were first asked to describe, in their own words, the happenings on the day of Sam's visit to their class. Once this free narrative was done, children were asked specific probing questions about whether they had "heard something" about the book or the teddy bear or had seen Sam dealing with either of these objects. If children indicated that they had seen Sam do something, which, in fact, he had not done, other questions were asked to test the strength of belief in the memory, such as "You didn't really see him do this, did you?"

Results

The final interviews were videotaped, and data were produced by having the children's responses coded. The coders were people who did not know which condition the children had been in. Twenty percent of the tapes were randomly selected and recoded by another rater to check for rater reliability. Agreement between raters was found to be 90 percent, certainly high enough to indicate that raters were sufficiently reliable. The coders were looking to see if individual children made false statements either during free narrative or pointed questioning.

As can be seen from Figure 12.1, there were striking differences in the extent to which children made false allegations in their unguided recall about what happened during Sam Stone's visit.

No children from the control group or from the stereotype group made any false statements about the visit in free recall. However, the group that had been given after-the-fact suggestions about tearing the book and soiling the teddy bear did include these events in their free narrative. It is important to remember that these suggestions were presuppositions inserted in questions that were, ostensibly, asking about something else. A stereotype was established for two groups in which Sam was clumsy, likely to spill and break things. It is interesting that the stereotype alone was not enough to result in false events being reported in free recall. Yet, Figure 12.1 shows that in the *stereotype-plus-suggestion* group, it had an additive effect: levels of false allegations were higher than in the *suggestion-only* group. The stereotype procedure did not have an effect on its own, but it made a difference when combined with subsequent suggestions. In

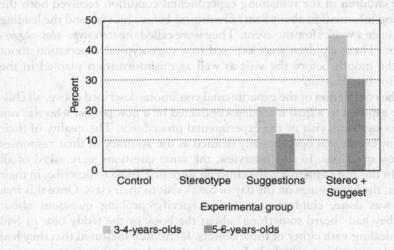

FIGURE 12.1 Percentage of Children Making False Allegations. Statements were made during the free recall narrative at the beginning of the fifth interview.

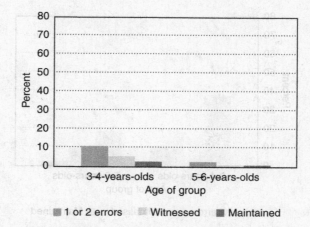

FIGURE 12.2   Erroneous Answers Given by Control Group (No Stereotype; No Suggestions). *1 or 2 errors* indicates that the child asserted that a false event really happened. *Witnessed* indicates that the child claimed to have observed the false event. *Maintained* indicates that the child insisted on having observed the event, despite the attempt at dissuading: "You didn't really see him do this, did you?"

these latter two groups, there was also a difference between the younger and the older children, with the younger ones being more likely to include false stories in their narratives.

Figure 12.2 shows the control group outcomes for the procedures that followed free narratives in the final interview. These were responses to probing questions about (1) whether the child believed that the book or the teddy bear incidents had occurred, (2) whether they had seen either of them, and (3) whether they would insist on the reality of the events. Because the control group had been given no formal exposure to any of the false events, the expectation was that they would not make false assertions, even when pointed questions were asked. As expected, only a few such responses were seen in this group. Although these children had not been previously exposed to false information about the book and the teddy bear, a few of them were prepared to say they remembered these false events. They had first heard about the book and the bear minutes before, in final interview questions.

Even though the stereotype group did not mention false events during free recall, Figure 12.3 shows that they became likely to assert the reality of false events under pointed questioning. As in all these data, there is an age trend favoring better memory for the older children.

In the suggestion group the levels were even higher as shown in Figure 12.4. More than half of the three- and four-year-olds reported one or two false

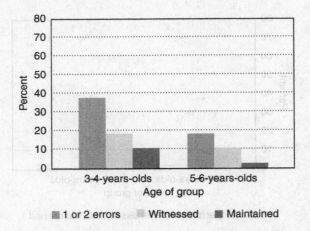

FIGURE 12.3   Erroneous Answers Given by Stereotype Group (Stereotype; No Suggestions). *1 or 2 errors* indicates that the child asserted that a false event really happened. *Witnessed* indicates that the child claimed to have observed the false event. *Maintained* indicates that the child insisted on having observed the event, despite the attempt at dissuading: "You didn't really see him do this, did you?"

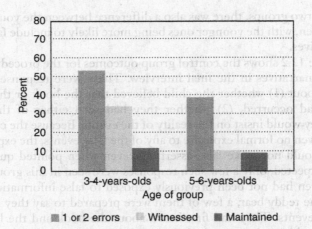

FIGURE 12.4   Erroneous Answers Given by Suggestion Group (No Stereotype; Suggestions). *1 or 2 errors* indicates that the child asserted that a false event really happened. *Witnessed* indicates that the child claimed to have observed the false event. *Maintained* indicates that the child insisted on having observed the event, despite the attempt at dissuading: "You didn't really see him do this, did you?"

memories under pointed questioning, and there was a noticeable increase in the percentage of younger children who claimed to have witnessed a false event.

Last, Figure 12.5 shows the effects of having some training in a stereotype about Sam's personality and then, over time, having a number of embedded suggestions made that are congruent with the stereotype. As in the other groups, there is an age trend when the two age groups are compared. Particularly in the younger children, there are strikingly high levels of reporting false beliefs, claiming to have witnessed the event, and maintaining this stance under gentle, but adverse, questioning.

These are important findings. We know, from earlier studies, that even adult memory can be influenced by presuppositions, but this study presents clear evidence that the memory of a child, particularly a young child, can be greatly influenced especially when previously held stereotypes are supported by subsequent suggestions. The design of the study is clever in being able to create stereotypes about a person previously unknown to the children and in being able to follow this up with congruent suggestions. These findings are not only important for what they tell us about reconstructive memory, they also bear directly on the issue of children testifying in courtrooms. Children quickly pick up stereotypes. Imagine a child who witnesses a crime committed by a person of an ethnic group different from the child itself. Further imagine that the child has grown up in a home where there is substantial prejudice against other ethnic

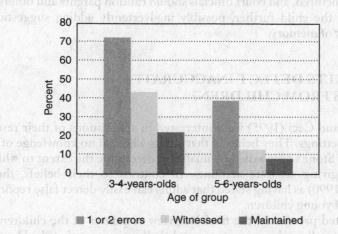

FIGURE 12.5 Erroneous Answers Given by Stereotype Plus Suggestion Group (Stereotype; Suggestions). *1 or 2 errors* indicates that the child asserted that a false event really happened. *Witnessed* indicates that the child claimed to have observed the false event. *Maintained* indicates that the child insisted on having observed the event, despite the attempt at dissuading: "You didn't really see him do this, did you?"

groups. In addition, imagine that, following the crime, the child is repeatedly questioned by all sorts of people: parents, police, and prosecuting attorneys. Unless these interrogators are extraordinarily careful in the wording of questions, it would be easy for them to unknowingly make presuppositions or suggestions such as, "Did the long-haired man with the knife yell at the store clerk?" In this question, there are presuppositions about the man having long hair and a knife, yet the child has not been asked about either of these. It takes little imagination to apply the findings of the Leichtman and Ceci (1995) research to the real world. It creates a chilling picture.

This research suggests what should be avoided with child witnesses, but it also suggests what should be done to maximize the value of their recollections. As can be seen in Figure 12.1, the free narratives of children in the stereotype group are factually accurate, in spite of experience with stereotypical information. Although the stereotype in this study may be weaker than real-life stereotypes embedded by repeated expression in a child's daily environment, the data here indicated that stereotypes play no role in false allegations during free narrative. The problems begin to occur when suggestions are made. A conclusion that might be drawn by police and prosecutors is that evidence from the free narrative might be more accurate than evidence under pointed questioning. Free narratives of child witnesses should be solicited and carefully recorded at the earliest possible time following a crime. At the least, any additional questions should be carefully structured, and court officials should caution parents and others against questioning the child further, possibly inadvertently adding suggestions that become part of memory.

CAN ADULTS DETECT INACCURATE REPORTS FROM CHILDREN?

Leichtman and Ceci (1995) were interested in applications of their research to real-world settings. They believed that adults who had no knowledge of the history of Sam Stone's visit would be unable to determine the extent to which children were giving accurate accounts. In contrast to their beliefs, they cited Goodman (1990) as having stated that adults can easily detect false reports in the narratives of young children.

As noted previously, the final interview responses of the children experiencing free recall, probing questions, and challenging questions had been videotaped. Leichtman and Ceci (1995) showed some of these tapes to adults, asking them to try to detect false statements. The videos chosen were of a three-year-old, a four-year-old, and a five-year-old. Each of these children was selected from the *stereotype-plus-suggestion* group. The particular children were chosen because they were coherent and seemed engaged by the interviewer. On the tape, the three-year-old spontaneously asserted that Sam had done the false acts. The four-year-old was a soft-spoken child who made no false allegations in her

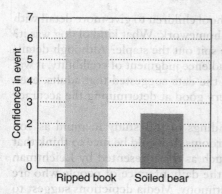

FIGURE 12.6 Mean Confidence Levels That Events Occurred. Confidence ratings of professional adults that events occurred, based on videotapes of children (1 = sure it didn't, 7 = sure it did).

narrative or in subsequent prompting. The five-year-old included no false acts in his narrative, but assented to false memories under prompted questioning.

At a conference, these tapes were shown to 119 researchers and clinicians who worked in the area of children's testimony. This audience was only told that each child had witnessed the same visit by Sam Stone. Based on the three videotapes, the audience was asked to rate their confidence about which events really happened. They were also asked to rate their confidence in the overall account given by each child. These ratings were made on a 7-point scale, where 7 represented the most confidence and 1 represented least confidence. The data are presented in Figures 12.6 and 12.7. Figure 12.6 shows that although the adults tended not to believe that Sam soiled the bear, they had considerable confidence that he ripped the book. This showed that even skilled professionals who are interested in children's testimony could come to have confidence in some false memories reported by children.

Interestingly, Figure 12.7 shows that the adults had the least confidence in the reports of the four-year-old, even though she was the only child giving accurate reports. One of the reasons for this may have been that the three-year-old child provided the most detail in her story. A story rich in detail may seem more

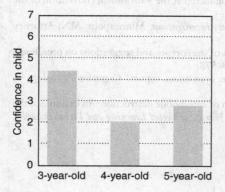

FIGURE 12.7 Mean Confidence Levels in Accounts Given. Confidence ratings of professional adults in the accounts given by three children.

credible. If this is so, it may be useful for school children to give more detail with the old excuse about how the dog ate their homework. What kind of dog was it? How long did it take him to eat it? Did he spit out the staple? Although details may not have formed the entire basis for audience judgment of credibility, it was probably part of it. Whatever the reason, the data suggested that adults, even interested and motivated adults, are not very good at determining the accuracy of reports by children.

We hope that you will bear the findings of this study in mind as you watch media accounts of children in courtrooms. It would be nice to think that results of carefully conducted research, such as that presented by Leichtman and Ceci (1995), will find their way into the daily practice of people who are professionally involved with children's testimony. Media depictions suggest to us that the scientific studies concerning eyewitness testimony have not yet resulted in standardized procedures for dealing with eyewitness accounts. Maybe the general public, even members of the educated general public such as police, judges, and lawyers, do not understand research about behavior. *Psychology* means many things to different people, but few people associate it with a cautious, empirical approach to understanding behavior. In reading these articles, you are coming to see that no research study is perfect. Those who are ignorant about psychological research may use this fact to conclude that psychology is useless and meaningless. It is our contention that a person with adequate skills in understanding psychological research can assess and evaluate studies, making decisions about when and how results can be applied to daily life. We believe that this is the point of learning about psychology. We hope that you agree.

REFERENCES

Ceci, S. J., & Bruck, M. (1993). Suggestibility of the child witness: A historical review and synthesis. *Psychological Bulletin, 113,* 403–439.

Goodman, G. S. (1990). Media effects and children's testimony. In D. Singer (Chair), *The impact of the media on the judicial system.* Symposium conducted at the 98th annual convention of the American Psychological Association, Boston.

Humphrey, H. H., III. (1985). *Report on Scott County investigations.* Minneapolis, MN: Attorney General's Office.

Leichtman, M. D., & Ceci, S. J. (1995). The effects of stereotypes and suggestions on preschoolers' reports. *Developmental Psychology, 31,* 568–578.

Loftus, E. F. (1975). Leading questions and the eyewitness report. *Cognitive Psychology, 7,* 560–572.

Loftus, E. F., & Palmer, J. C. (1974). Reconstruction of automobile destruction: An example of the interaction between language and memory. *Journal of Verbal Learning and Verbal Behavior, 13,* 585–589.

CHAPTER 13

FLASH IN THE PAN

Quite a bit of day-to-day life depends on the things we remember. Our interactions with other people often depend on memories we share with them. We recall the first time we met someone else, happy times we had together, and countless small, ordinary occurrences. For the mundane operation of our lives, our memories seem to be adequate. Although we sometimes notice that our recollections of specific events are slightly different from the recollections of others, this is not usually much of a problem. We do not forget where we live, the names of friends and relatives, what time of day our classes are, or the thousands of big and little things that are required for daily functioning.

Nevertheless, psychological studies have found memories to be unreliable. Neisser and Harsch (1992) noted that psychologists have found it difficult to reconcile the fallibility of memories for some events with the dependability of others. Many studies have shown that remembering is a reconstructive process. Other information, which is unrelated to a remembered event, can find its way into memory. Memory seems to be a patchwork of events that really occurred and others that did not (Loftus, 1979).

In discussions of memory, psychologists use specific terminology to discuss different memory processes. Most of the terms they use are fairly intuitive. We now discuss some of the most common memory terms to help enhance your understanding of this chapter . . . as long as you remember them. Most psychologists argue that there are three general forms of memory: sensory store, short-term memory, and long-term memory. Information from the environment that makes it into sensory store lasts there for only a few seconds. For example, have you ever started daydreaming in the middle of a story that a friend was telling you? This can be problematic if the person unexpectedly asks you a question about something they just said. Often, all is not lost. The last few seconds of what our friend told us may be waiting for us in sensory store. If we focus our attention on our auditory sensory store, we may be able to play back those few

Incorporating the research of P. J. Lee, and N. R. Brown, "Delay Related Changes in Personal Memories for September 11, 2001," 2003, *Applied Cognitive Psychology*, 17, pp.1007–1015.

seconds of the conversation immediately preceding our friend's question and answer as though we had been paying attention the whole time.

The second kind of memory is short-term memory. Some psychologists also refer to this kind of memory as working memory or recent memory. Short-term memories can last for a period of several minutes before we forget them. If you have ever looked up a phone number and remembered it only long enough to dial the phone, you have experienced your short-term memory in action. Occasionally, people will repeat a piece of information that is in their short-term memory to themselves over and over again. Eventually, that information might be transferred or *encoded* into their long-term memory. Information that makes it into long-term memory may eventually be forgotten or may be stored there indefinitely. Repeating information to yourself in order to get information from short-term memory into long-term memory is known as *rehearsal*. Studying for an exam can be considered a kind of rehearsal. The process of transferring information from short-term memory for storage in long-term memory is known as *encoding*. The process of remembering—getting information out of long-term memory is referred to as *retrieval*.

Lee and Brown (2003) studied a particular kind of memory called *flashbulb memory*. This term has been used to describe the recall of very specific images about a rare, striking, or significant event, personal or public. The word *flashbulb* is used because these memories are supposed to capture the action the way a camera flash does, creating an instant long-term memory that is permanent and rich in vivid detail. Weddings, graduations, and births, as well as personal tragedies, are the kinds of personal events that are supposed to be captured by flashbulb memories. Significant national events that have a large emotional impact are also supposed to be remembered in this way. The emotional content of these kinds of memories has been discussed within psychology for a long time. For example, researchers have suggested that the emotion that accompanies these memories may strengthen them (Brown & Kulik, 1977).

We are sure you have experienced events about which you have said, "I will *never* forget that. I remember everything so clearly." Among an earlier generation of Americans, many people believed they could remember exactly what they were doing at the moment they heard that President John F. Kennedy had been assassinated in 1963. People in younger age groups may remember details of what they were doing when they heard about the death of Princess Diana of Britain in 1997 or the bombings of two U.S. embassies in Africa in 1998.

Many Americans alive today have seemingly clear memories about what they were doing when they first heard about the events of September 11, 2001. Four passenger jets were hijacked by terrorists, who used them as missiles to attack the World Trade Center towers in New York City and the Pentagon in Washington, DC. The fourth plane was forced down by passengers and crashed in a field in Pennsylvania before it could be used as a missile against another target.

A common way that flashbulb memories are studied is called the "test–retest method." In this method, people are asked about their memories of an event very soon after it happens. This is the "test" part of the method. Later, the same people are asked the same questions about their memories of the same event. This is the "retest" part of the method. Researchers compare people's first reports of what they remember with the reports collected from them at a later date to determine how stable their memories were over time. This method is based on the assumption that people's earlier reports of their memories are accurate. It is also assumed that differences between people's initial reports and the reports collected later are due to forgetting some of the content of flashbulb memories over time. This presents a problem for researchers because there is always going to be some delay between the experience of a profoundly striking or significant event and the initial recordings of memories of the event. Research suggests that the average delay in this kind of research is three days (Winningham, Hyman, & Dinnel, 2000). This delay could be a problem because the range of experiences people have during the delay could distort the memories they encoded immediately after the event. This problem and others can make it difficult to interpret the results of flashbulb memory studies that use the test–retest method.

Lee and Brown (2003) addressed the problem of the delay between experiencing a significant event and recording people's flashbulb memories of the event. In their research, they recorded the memories of some people between 4 and 24 hours after the events of September 11, 2001 and the memories of other people 10 days after September 11. Their research focused on the amount of information people reported remembering, changes in the emotions people experienced when recalling the events of September 11, and the consistency between the memories people initially reported (within 24 hours or 10 days after September 11) and the memories they reported seven months later.

PARTICIPANTS AND PROCEDURE

Participants were given a comprehensive flashbulb memory questionnaire that was previously designed by another researcher. The initial participants were 1,481 undergraduate students from the University of Alberta. The 697 participants who made up the first group were given the questionnaire between 4 and 24 hours after the September 11 attacks. The second group was given the questionnaire 10 days after the September 11 attacks. Seven months later, in April of 2002, 142 participants were willing to complete the questionnaire again.

Going from 1,481 participants to 142 participants is quite a large attrition rate. Although no detailed information is available about the participants who did not continue in this study, it is common for researchers to present evidence about the similarity of participants who drop out compared to those who do not. In this study, for example, if many drop-outs had been people who were no longer at college because they forgot to do homework or forgot to register for classes, the resulting external validity of the study might be compromised.

The researchers who conducted this study had no reason to believe that the drop-outs differed in important ways from those who continued to participate in the study.

Participants were assigned to the different groups on an opportunity basis. This means that the students who were available between 4 and 24 hours after the September 11 attacks were assigned to the first group, and other students who were available 10 days later were assigned to the second group. This is far from the random assignment we would expect in a true experiment. If the results of this study show some difference between the first group and the second group of participants, we would have to question whether the difference was due to whether they were questioned within 24 hours or 10 days after the event, or if something else made people questioned 24 hours after the event different from people questioned 10 days after. The authors state that the two groups of participants did not significantly differ in age, sex, or nationality, suggesting that, overall, the two groups likely did not differ in ways that could bias the study's results.

The same questionnaire was administered to both groups of participants in a classroom setting. The first part of the questionnaire asked participants to describe the circumstances in which they first learned about the September 11 attacks. Participants were then asked a set of more specific questions about the people they were with, where they were, and what kinds of things they were doing when they learned of the attacks. Finally, participants were asked about their emotional arousal. To accomplish this, the researchers asked participants to rate how surprised, sad, shocked, and upset they were at the time they first learned of the attacks on a 5-point scale. The verbal anchors for this numerical scale ranged from no emotion (=1) to intense emotion (=5). At the end of the questionnaire, participants were asked if they could be contacted about a follow-up study. Those who agreed were administered the same questionnaire seven months later.

RESULTS AND DISCUSSION

Word Counts

Lee and Brown (2003) were interested in how much information people reported in response to the initial open-ended question on the questionnaire they completed, which asked them to describe the circumstances in which they first learned about the September 11, 2001 attacks. They achieved this by counting the number of words that participants used in their descriptions. For the purpose of their data analysis, the researchers excluded the responses of participants who did not write anything in response to the question or who wrote a great deal more than the median number of words written by the other participants. The responses of 45 out of the 1,481 participants were excluded for these reasons. Although the authors did not address the specific reasons for excluding them, the research participants who wrote nothing probably were left out of data analyses because the participants could have provided an answer, but chose not to. This is a common issue in survey research. It is also common for researchers to exclude extreme values or *outliers* from data analyses if they have some reason to believe that the extreme scores are the result of dishonesty, inaccurate responses by participants, mistakes in the process of collecting or entering data, or other factors that may have led to a biased or inaccurate response.

The researchers compared the number of words that participants wrote in response to the open-ended question that was presented to them first in September of 2001 and later again in April of 2002. As shown in Figure 13.1, they found that participants wrote significantly more words in September of 2001 than they did the following April. This finding was not a surprise to the researchers. It is consistent with the findings of many other studies of flashbulb memory that suggest the flashbulb memories degrade over time (e.g., Neisser & Harsch, 1992).

Lee and Brown (2003) also found that participants who completed the questionnaire 10 days after September 11 used significantly more words in their descriptions of the circumstances in which they learned of the attacks than participants who completed the questionnaire within 24 hours of the event. This finding puzzled the researchers. Why would participants who were farther away in time from the September 11 attacks provide lengthier descriptions than participants providing descriptions within 24 hours of the attacks? One explanation that was invoked is known as the Yerkes-Dodson's Law (Yerkes & Dodson, 1908). It proposes that high states of emotional arousal can prevent people from retrieving information from memory. The participants who completed the questionnaire within 24 hours of the attacks may have been experiencing such intense emotions that they remembered less than participants who completed the same survey 10 days later.

The researchers also discussed an alternative explanation for the finding. They argued that the participants who completed the questionnaire 10 days after the 9/11 attacks had more time to rehearse retrieving memories of the event and more cues to aid in memory retrieval as a result of discussions they had with others, reports of the event in the media, and even thinking about the event on

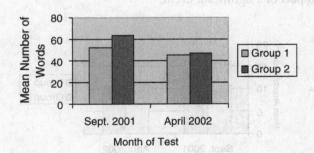

FIGURE 13.1   Mean Word Count for Groups 1 and 2 at Test and Retest

their own. This may have allowed them to remember details of the circumstances in which they learned of the attacks more easily and answer the open-ended question more quickly and with greater detail than the participants who completed the questionnaire within 24 hours of the attacks.

Lee and Brown (2003) admit that these explanations for their findings are speculative and that other explanations are also possible. This does not detract, however, from the important finding that memory reports for events that lead people to experience strong emotions could be influenced by both the quality of the initial encoding of the memories and factors that can impact access to memories after the event, such as rehearsal and a return to a less extreme emotional state.

Emotional Arousal

To calculate overall emotional arousal, the researchers summed all four of the participants' emotion ratings into a single score. A combined score of 0 was interpreted as meaning a participant had no emotional reaction to the events of 9/11. A combined score of 20 was interpreted as meaning a participant had a very intense emotional reaction to the events. As shown in Figure 13.2, participants in Group 1, who completed the questionnaire within 24 hours of the September 11 attacks, reported significantly higher levels of emotional arousal than participants who completed the same questionnaire 10 days later. In addition, participants in both groups who completed the questionnaire again in April of 2002 reported lower emotional arousal than when they initially completed the questionnaires in September of 2001. However, the difference between the emotional arousal in Group 1 and Group 2 disappeared when they were retested in April of 2002.

These findings illustrate that emotional arousal from events decreases rapidly, even for events that have a profound effect on people. An important lesson learned from this research is that it is important to collect information as soon as possible after a significant event occurs in order to obtain accurate data on the emotional impact of a significant event.

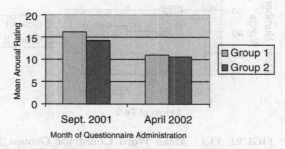

FIGURE 13.2 **Mean Emotional Arousal**

Consistency of Memories

Consistency between memories reported in September of 2001 and memories reported in April of 2002 were scored using a scale developed by Neisser and Harsch (1992). Only the 142 participants who completed a questionnaire in September of 2001 and April of 2002 were included in this analysis. Reports that were completely consistent were given a score of 2. Reports that were only partially consistent were given a score of 1. For example, the statement, "I was eating breakfast when I saw a news story on TV about the attacks," would be partially consistent with the statement, "I was ironing a shirt when I saw a news story on TV about the attacks." Reports that showed no consistency were given a score of zero. For example, the statement, "I was playing my guitar," is inconsistent with the statement, "I was in the shower."

There is no particular standard way to operationally define the accuracy of memories. Researchers involved in cutting-edge investigations often have to design an approach to the coding process that seems to most accurately translate qualitative descriptions into numbers. In so doing, researchers work to avoid the introduction of incidental bias into the data. In addition, researchers describe their methods as completely as possible in their research paper. This is done so that subsequent researchers working on similar questions can replicate the earlier work using the same operational definitions. Replications of research that produce the same results are one way of increasing confidence in the validity of research findings. If researchers use the same methods from previous research and get different results, we should question our confidence in the original research findings.

In Lee and Brown's (2003) research, the consistency of participants' memories was evaluated to be poor given that the delay between the initial test and the retest was only seven months. As shown in Table 13.1, more than 30 percent of participants inaccurately recalled who they were with when they learned of the 9/11 attacks. More than 10 percent of participants did not accurately remember where they were. About 30 percent of participants did not accurately recall what they were doing.

Lee and Brown (2003) created a composite score for the consistency of memories between the time they were initially reported in September of 2001

TABLE 13.1   Percentage of Scores Different Levels of Consistency for Each Category of Memory

CONSISTENCY	PEOPLE		LOCATION		ACTIVITY	
	GROUP 1	GROUP 2	GROUP 1	GROUP 2	GROUP 1	GROUP 2
Consistent	68	68	87	90	72	68
Partial	16	17	11	3	16	13
Inconsistent	16	15	1	7	13	19

and the time they were reported again seven months later. A composite score is created from the combination of a number of individual scores that all provide information about the same topic. This can be a useful data presentation strategy because people only have to consider a single value rather than having to sift through a number of different scores in order to draw a conclusion. The researchers created their composite scores by summing all of the measures of consistency for each participant. They used the composite scores to determine the percentage of memories that could truly be considered flashbulb memories. The lowest possible score was zero, indicating that there was no consistency in the responses on the first and second administrations of the questionnaire. The highest possible score was 6, indicating perfect consistency in responses on the initial questionnaire and the questionnaire completed seven months later. Participants who had a composite consistency score of 5 or higher were considered to demonstrate flashbulb memories. Those with scores lower than five were not. Using this method, the researchers found that 66.5 percent of participants exhibited flashbulb memories. Similar to the findings from previous research on flashbulb memories, this analysis shows poor consistency in responses from the initial test to the retest, especially given the short delay between the two questionnaire administrations. The evidence suggests that there may be no long-term memory encoding device that is consistent with the concept of flashbulb memory. The findings also suggest that delays up to a few days in length in the initial testing of participants in flashbulb memory studies that use the test–retest procedure will not have a large impact on study data that explore the consistency of recollections across time.

CONCLUSIONS

When confronted with an unpleasant turn of events, the late Jimmy Durante used to shake his nose (and the rest of his head), stare straight at the camera, and say, "What a revoltin' development dis is!" That is somewhat the way we feel about these results. It is not a comforting thought that our memories of important events may be wrong. It is further disconcerting that, oblivious to our erroneous recollections, we can be very confident that we remember events accurately (see Neisser & Harsch, 1992).

Lee and Brown's (2003) research has a good claim to external validity because the problem investigated was not an artificial laboratory creation. It should be remembered—even though we do not always remember accurately—that this study explored only one type of memory: flashbulb memory. Caution should be exercised in generalizing these findings to other kinds of memories. However, the conclusions of this research do support findings from a number of other studies that suggest our memories are not as accurate as we may believe them to be.

REFERENCES

Brown, R., & Kulik, J. (1977). Flashbulb memories. *Cognition, 5*, 73–99.

Lee, P. J., & Brown, N. R. (2003). Delay related changes in personal memories for September 11, 2001. *Applied Cognitive Psychology, 17*, 1007–1015.

Loftus, E. F. (1979). *Eyewitness testimony*. Cambridge, MA: Harvard University Press.

Neisser, U., & Harsch, N. (1992). Phantom flashbulbs: False recollections of hearing the news about Challenger. In: Eugene Winograd & Ulric Neisser (Eds.), Affect and accuracy in recall: Studies of "flashbulb" memories. New York: Cambridge University Press.

Winningham, R. G., Hyman, I. E., & Dinnel, D. L. (2000). Flashbulb memories? The effects of when the initial memory report was obtained. *Memory, 8*, 209–216.

Yerkes, R., & Dodson, J. (1908). The relation of strength of stimulus to rapidity of habit-information. *Journal of Comparative Neurology and Psychology, 18*, 459–482.

CHAPTER 14

THEY DON'T LOOK THE SAME TO ME

Have you ever found it more difficult to recognize people who are members of other groups (out-groups) than the people who are members of your own group (in-group)? If you have had this problem, you are not alone. Difficulty in recognizing the faces of members of other groups was well known before cognitive psychologists began to conduct research on the topic. Cognitive psychologists have proposed that a functional bias in the way that people think may be responsible for this phenomenon (Anthony, Copper, & Mullen, 1992). The amount of information that we encounter on a daily basis is far greater than our brain's ability to perceive and process the information (Todd, Hertwig, & Hoffrage, 2005). Simply put, there is too much information in our environments for us to take it all in. It would be adaptive if people's attention and cognitive effort were focused on elements of their surroundings that had the greatest probability of affecting them. The people we interact with are part of our surroundings. We interact with members of our own social group more frequently than with the members of other social groups. The members of our own social groups are more likely to influence our lives in important ways than the members of other social groups. Our family members and friends are the people we rely on and who rely on us. Our bias to perceive members of our own social group to be more variable and members of other social groups to be mostly the same is called the out-group homogeneity bias. It may function to help us adaptively allocate our limited perceptual and cognitive resources. We need to be sensitive to differences between members of our own social group (including being able to tell them apart) and changes in their characteristics in order to be able to interact with them appropriately. The out-group homogeneity bias that we experience may be the functional outcome of our brain doing the best it can with limited perceptual and cognitive resources (Sporer, 2001).

The out-group homogeneity bias is important because it has been argued to be related to stereotyping. Stereotypes are assumptions or generalizations that

Incorporating the research of J. M. Ackerman, J. R. Shapiro, S. L. Neuberg, D. T. Kenrick, D. V. Becker, V. Girskevicius, J. K. Maner, and M. Shcallner, "They All Look the Same to Me (Unless They're Angry): From Out-Group Homogeneity to Out-Group Heterogeneity," 2006, *Psychological Science*, 17, pp. 836–840.

people apply to all members of a group. Stereotypes can be positive or negative. An example of a positive stereotype is that Asian students tend to be better at math than other students. As we are sure you are aware, many stereotypes are negative. Any stereotype can be problematic when it leads people to make incorrect judgments about others. Stereotypes can lead people to treat others unfairly. Researchers often link stereotypes to discrimination. They argue that understanding that stereotypes are likely to be incorrect can help prevent discrimination.

Ackerman et al. (2006) wanted to explore the out-group homogeneity bias in greater detail. They wondered if the bias was present all the time, or if, under some circumstances, it might be eliminated or reversed. Specifically, they wondered if there were some circumstances that could make out-group members even more functionally important than members of a person's own social group.

Researchers have demonstrated one situation that leads people to pay greater attention to out-group members—when the out-group members are angry. Öhman et al. (2001), for example, demonstrated that people pay more attention to angry and happy facial expressions than they do to neutral facial expressions. This makes functional sense. Out-group members we encounter who look at us with neutral facial expressions have a lower probability of interacting with us than people who look at us with facial expressions indicative of a particular emotional state, which may be a cue that the person is motivated to interact with us.

People's facial expressions are often made in response to the nature of our interaction with them. When someone makes an angry face at us, it suggests that the person might intend to harm us. Even though the angry face may be short in duration, it can be an indication of a person's enduring disposition toward us. The person will likely continue to harbor anger even after their facial expression changes.

It is functional to pay attention to people who make angry faces at us because it may help us to avoid being the victims of their aggression. It is also functional to remember who the people are so we can be careful in our interactions with them in the future. There may, however, be a difference in how great a threat angry in-group members and angry out-group members pose to us. Members of our in-group are more likely to understand our point of view. They have a history with us. They know more about our lives. Members of our in-group are also more likely to have personal relationships with us. They are more likely to depend on us, our friends, or members of our families. These factors decrease the likelihood that an in-group member who was angry with us would pose an actual threat of harming us.

Interactions between members of two different groups, however, are typically more competitive. We do not have established relationships, partnerships, or friendships with people in out-groups. We do not know them at all. As a result, we may perceive anger expressed by an out-group member to be more threatening than the same expression of anger from an in-group member. Because angry out-group members pose a greater threat to us than angry in-group members, it would make sense that our cognitive system would recognize an angry out-group member more easily and remember characteristics of the angry out-group member more clearly than out-group members who were not expressing anger. We may also recognize and remember angry out-group members better than angry in-group members. This bias would function to allow us to avoid the more likely source of threat and harm. Based on this logic, the researchers hypothesized that when anger is perceived in both in-group and out-group members, there may actually be an out-group *heterogeneity* bias—people may be more sensitive to differences between out-group members than differences between in-group members.

Ackerman et al. conducted research to investigate the existence of an out-group heterogeneity bias for angry faces. Other studies have suggested that people's perceptual biases, like the out-group heterogeneity bias, can be magnified when it takes greater effort for people to perceive stimuli. We can only attend to and think about a small number of things at any one time (Maner et al., 2003). Some stimuli in the environment and problems are more complex than others. More complex stimuli and problems require greater cognitive resources. When greater effort is required to perceive something or to solve a cognitively demanding problem, it is called an increased cognitive load. When information processing is constrained by a high cognitive load, Ackerman et al. propose that people should selectively pay attention to stimuli in the environment that are the most important to their immediate well-being. Specifically, they hypothesize that people should pay particular attention to angry out-group members.

PARTICIPANTS

The participants in the study were 117 White male and 75 White female undergraduate students at Arizona State University who received course credit for their participation.

METHODS

Each participant was seated in front of a computer. The researchers then attached an electrode to the participant's arm. Participants were told that the electrode was going to be used to measure changes in their galvanic skin response. Galvanic skin response is a measure of the skin's ability to conduct electricity. When people sweat, their skin can more easily conduct electricity. In this study, however, the researchers were not really interested in galvanic skin response at all. They used the electrode to distract participants from the true purpose of the study.

Participants were then shown a series of stimulus images. There was a three-second delay between the presentations of each image. Participants were randomly assigned to one of two conditions. Those in the distractor-absent condition saw only faces. Other participants who were in the distractor-present condition saw images of the faces paired with grayscale abstract art that was similar in size to the faces. The distractor-present condition was used to try to increase the cognitive load of the research participants. The researchers hypothesized that the abstract image would distract participants from the face memory task enough to enhance the out-group heterogeneity bias.

There were 16 grayscale images of forward-facing male faces. The grayscale images looked like black-and-white photographs. Each image was about 5 inches tall and 3.5 inches wide. Four images were of White men with a neutral facial expression. Four images were of White men with an angry facial expression. Four images were of African American men with a neutral facial expression. Four images were of African American men with an angry facial expression. In total, the 16 images were equally divided between White and African American men who had neutral or angry expressions.

Participants watched the images of faces that served as stimuli in this study presented to them one at a time as a slide show on the computer screen. The order in which faces were presented to the participants was random. If all participants viewed faces in the same order, it is possible that something about the order in which the faces were presented would make some faces more memorable and others less memorable. This could introduce systematic trends in the research findings that are independent of the variables of interest to the researchers—facial expression and in-group, out-group membership. Randomizing the order in which faces were presented prevented any order effects from introducing these kinds of systematic errors that could influence the results of the study.

The researchers randomly assigned participants to view each image for different durations. One group of participants viewed each image for about half a second. The second group viewed each image for one second. The third group viewed each image for four seconds. The researchers presented the images to participants for different amounts of time as another method of varying the cognitive load of the face recognition task. The researchers hypothesized that participants who viewed each image for a shorter period of time would have a higher cognitive load than participants who viewed each image for longer periods of time. This greater cognitive load was hypothesized to enhance the out-group heterogeneity bias.

In the next part of the study, participants watched a film clip of landscapes for five minutes. The film clip had nothing to do with the study and was meant to distract the participants from thinking about the faces they had just seen. Without a distractor, it is possible that participants may have rehearsed the images of some of the faces in their minds, helping them recall the faces later. The distractor functioned to help prevent this kind of rehearsal from taking place.

Participants were then asked to look at 32 photographs of faces. They had seen 16 of the photographs previously in the slideshow they watched on the computer screen. The other 16 photographs were new to them. The new images were also equally divided between White and African American men with either neutral or angry expressions. Participants were asked to rate how much they recognized each of the faces on a six-point scale that ranged from definitely did not see (1) to definitely did see (6).

The researchers converted participants' face recognition ratings into binary yes/no responses so they could conduct special signal detection analyses on the data. Signal detection theory provides a framework for studying and understanding decision making and reasoning that takes place under conditions of uncertainty. When the participants in this study rated how much they recognized each of the photographs of faces, they were making decisions under conditions of uncertainty because they had only viewed half of the faces they were asked to rate and each image was viewed for four seconds or less, depending on the group to which participants were assigned.

The researchers in this study were specifically interested in evaluating participants' *sensitivity* to recognizing faces they had seen before. Sensitivity in this study provides information about how accurate participants were at recognizing the faces they had seen previously and how well they were able to differentiate those faces from the 16 new faces that were introduced in the recognition task.

The researchers were also interested in the presence of a *response bias* in the participants' face recognition ratings. A response bias refers to participants' threshold for indicating that they had seen one of the faces previously or had not seen one of the faces previously. A response bias occurs for previously viewed faces when one outcome is more probable than the other. Remember that the response bias the researchers hypothesized would occur in this study is an out-group heterogeneity bias for angry faces—in other words, out-group members with angry faces will be attended to more and will be better remembered than neutral out-group faces or the faces of in-group members.

The terms sensitivity and response bias deserve further exploration. These concepts come from signal detection theory. According to signal detection theory, our ability to perceive, remember, and respond to stimuli comes from a combination of sensitivity and bias. We are primarily interested in sensitivity. Sensitivity refers to detecting a signal against background noise or compared to another signal. In Ackerman et al.'s research, the signals were the images of faces that were shown to participants on the computer screen. The images that were not seen previously were noise, as were the abstract images that were paired with the faces presented on the computer screens of some research participants. In signal detection theory, bias refers to the inclination of research participants to respond one way or another. We need to account for bias because it can affect sensitivity.

This research involved four different manipulations. It is important to keep track of each manipulation as you consider the results. Each manipulation is

TABLE 14.1   Experimental Manipulations

MANIPULATION	LEVELS	WITHIN OR BETWEEN PARTICIPANTS
Race of face in image	African American or White	Within
Facial expression	Neutral or angry	Within
Abstract art distractor	Absent or present	Between
Presentation duration	0.5, 1, or 4 seconds	Between

listed, along with whether the manipulation was within or between participants, in Table 14.1. When an experiment has both within participants measures and between participants measures, it is referred to as a mixed research design.

RESULTS

Research findings about participants' hit rate (correctly identifying a previously viewed face) and false alarm rate (incorrectly indicated a previously unseen face was viewed before) are presented in Figure 14.1. To present the research findings in a format consistent with signal detection theory and for ease of interpretation, the researchers converted the findings to a proportion out of one. You can convert these proportions to the percentage of participants who made correct identifications and the percentage who incorrectly identified a face as appearing in the original sample. Because no sex differences were found for these measures, the results were collapsed across sex for subsequent analyses.

Figure 14.1 illustrates that participants' hit rates were highest for White, angry; African American, neutral; and African American, angry faces. The highest false alarm rate was for White, angry faces. The lowest false alarm rate was for White, neutral faces.

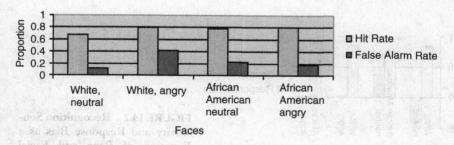

FIGURE 14.1   Recognition of Faces as a Function of Ethnicity and Facial Expression

The range of sensitivity scores was also presented as a proportion ranging from 0 to 1. Because participants who were guessing would have been expected to identify half of the faces correctly by chance, only values greater than 0.5 were believed to indicate correct identification; values less than 0.5 indicated a failure to correctly identify a photograph. A value of 0.5 indicated no sensitivity to whether a photograph was originally presented on the computer.

The researchers treated response bias differently than the other variables. Response biases ranged from − 1 to +1. Positive values indicate a bias toward falsely indicating that a face was seen before when it really was not. Negative values indicated participants had a bias that led them to falsely indicate a face was not presented previously when it really was. A value of zero indicated no response bias. Values farther from zero indicated a greater response bias.

Figure 14.2 shows participants' sensitivity and response biases to the different facial stimuli. Participants' response accuracy was better for neutral White faces than for neutral African American faces. This is evidence that the outgroup homogeneity bias was at work for faces that had a neutral expression. This is also indicated by the higher response bias for neutral African American faces than neutral White faces, indicating that participants tended to falsely indicate that they had seen the distractor African American faces on the computer screen previously. In contrast, participants were better at recognizing angry African American faces than at recognizing angry White faces. This is evidenced both by participants' greater sensitivity in detecting angry African American faces they had seen previously and their lower false alarm rate. Participants were also better at differentiating between angry African American faces than neutral African American faces. These findings provide support for the out-group heterogeneity bias for angry faces.

To evaluate the hypothesis that increasing participants' cognitive load would enhance the out-group heterogeneity bias, the researchers compared the condition with the least cognitive load (distractor absent, 4 seconds to view the image) to the condition with the greatest cognitive load (distractor present, 0.5 seconds to view the image). The researchers found a statistically significant difference between these two groups in the strength of their memories. A greater

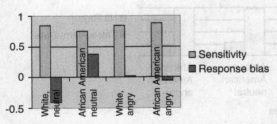

Sensitivity (.5=chance, 1=perfect accuracy);
Response bias (-1=did not see, +1=did see)

FIGURE 14.2   Recognition Sensitivity and Response Bias as a Function of Race and Facial Expression

out-group heterogeneity bias was evident in the group with the greater cognitive load.

DISCUSSION

People in all different ethnic groups report greater difficulty recognizing others they have encountered before from ethnic out-groups than in recognizing previously encountered others from their own ethnic group (Chance & Goldstein, 1996). The research by Ackerman et al. (2006) replicated these findings for neutral facial expressions. However, this out-group homogeneity bias disappeared for angry faces. African American angry faces were more likely to be recognized than White angry faces. When it comes to memory for angry faces, the evidence suggests the existence of an out-group heterogeneity bias.

The research findings are consistent with the proposal that an out-group heterogeneity bias for angry faces could be functional, helping people avoid others who may have violent intentions. Stereotypes that out-group members may be dangerous have also been shown to be activated more strongly when people are in situations that are perceived as more dangerous, such as being in the dark (Schaller, Park, & Mueller, 2003). Taken together, these findings suggest that stereotypes may not always be arbitrary. They may sometimes be linked to specific cognitive biases that can help individuals avoid dangerous situations.

REFERENCES

Ackerman, J. M., Shapiro, J. R., Neuberg, S. L., Kenrick, D. T., Becker, D. V., Girskevicius, V., Maner, J. K., & Shcallner M. (2006). They all look the same to me (unless they're angry): From out-group homogeneity to out-group heterogeneity. *Psychological Science*, *17*, 836–840.

Anthony, T., Copper, C., & Mullen, B. (1992). Cross-racial facial identification: A social cognitive integration. *Personality and Social Psychology Bulletin*, *18*, 296–301.

Chance, J. E., & Goldstein, A. G. (1996). The other-race effect and eyewitness identification. In S. L. Sporer & R. S. Malpass (Eds.), *Psychological issues in eyewitness identification* (pp. 153–176). Hillsdale, NJ: Erlbaum.

Maner, J. K., Kenrick, D. T., Becker, D. V., Delton, A. W., Hofer, B., Wilbur, C. J., & Neuberg, S. L. (2003). Sexually selective cognition: Beauty captures the mind of the beholder. *Journal of Personality and Social Psychology*, *85*, 1107–1120.

Öhman, A., Lundgvist, D., & Esteres, F. (2001). The face in the crowd revisited: A threat advantage with schematic stimuli. *Journal of Personality and Social Psychology*, *80*, 381–396.

Schaller, M., Park, J. H., & Mueller, A. (2003). Prehistoric dangers and contemporary prejudices. *European Review of Social Psychology*, *14*, 105–137.

Sporer, S. L. (2001). Recognizing faces of other ethnic groups: An integration of theories. *Psychology, Public Policy, and Law*, *7*, 36–97.

Todd, P. M., Hertwig, R., & Hoffrage, U. (2005). Evolutionary cognitive psychology. In D. M. Buss (Ed.), *The handbook of evolutionary psychology* (pp. 776–802). New York: Wiley.

CHAPTER 15

MAD ABOUT YOU

EVOLUTIONARY PSYCHOLOGY: AN INTRODUCTION

Quite recently, psychologists have begun to take notice of the explanatory power of evolutionary theory in understanding human behavior. Charles Darwin first proposed the contemporary version of evolutionary theory in 1859. It quickly became the basis for most thinking in biology because it explained many previously unexplained observations and unified data from many areas of biology. Although evolution is still called a "theory" and some details of what happened in the past are still considered to be controversial by some, we will adopt the same stance shared by the overwhelming majority of scientists: evolution is a fact. We are not so naive as to think that scientific facts are the truth. We understand that scientific facts can be modified by further research and that other factors (e.g., culture, learning, genetics) are also likely to play significant roles. We are confident that evolution occurred and continues to occur. Although we hope that you share this viewpoint, there is no way that we can force you to agree. To be critical consumers of information, it is important that all of us work to understand influential ideas such as evolutionary theory, even though we may not believe all of them. If we wanted to criticize some aspect of evolutionary theory, for example, people would take our criticisms more seriously if we demonstrated that we had strong knowledge of the topic. It is certainly possible to understand an explanation such as evolutionary theory, even if you do not believe it is correct. This is all that is required to understand the research in this area.

As we discussed in Chapter 5, evolutionary theory proposes that among the variation we observe in the physiological and mental structures, and the behaviors within populations of organisms, there are some variants that make certain individuals more likely to survive and reproduce than others. If there is a heritable basis for these characteristics and they are passed from parent to offspring, then the offspring of these individuals are also more likely to have surviving

Incorporating the research of D. M. Buss, R. J. Larsen, D. Westen, and J. Semmelroth, "Sex Differences in Jealousy: Evolution, Physiology, and Psychology," (1992) *Psychological Science*, 3, pp. 251–255.

offspring that reproduce themselves. In this way, the genes of the surviving and breeding individuals will, over generations, spread through the population and take over. Genes of organisms that do not survive to reproduce will disappear, which is also known as being selected out. Notice two important things about this description. First, some individuals are taking over the population with their genes, so the competition here is between members of the same species. This is the rabbits versus the rabbits, not the rabbits versus the foxes. Second, to be successful in this system, the individual must reproduce itself to a greater extent than other individuals—merely surviving or being healthy and strong are evolutionarily useless unless the individual also out-breeds its competitors. It is in this sense that the old catch phrase, *survival of the fittest*, is misleading. Survival of the fittest was a concept proposed by Herbert Spencer, not Charles Darwin.

The new thinking embodied in evolutionary psychology is that much of human cognition and behavior is the product of the process of evolution by natural selection. This process favored ancestral individuals possessing thoughts and behaviors that lead to their successful survival and reproduction. This is what we would expect because the humans who are alive today are the descendants of many generations of evolutionarily successful competitors who managed to outbreed their rivals. The people alive today are the result of this process of evolution by natural selection. We are not always aware of the evolutionary underpinnings of our behavior. For example, we are reluctant to eat food that smells bad. We would say, "That smells rotten, so I will not eat it." The rotten smell is the proximate or immediate reason, and it is usually the reason we give when we encounter food that has gone bad. The evolutionary or long-term reason, called the ultimate reason, is that individuals who ate rotten food in the past were likely to get ill, die, and therefore would not have reproduced. In the past, individuals who possessed genes for the development of olfactory and taste sensors that could not distinguish between rotten food and safe food were selected out. They did not leave any descendants. Only individuals who could distinguish between spoiled food and good food survived and reproduced. Those individuals are our ancestors.

Evolutionary psychologists stress that we often may be blissfully unaware of ultimate reasons for many of our thoughts and behaviors. This is often referred to as *instinct blindness*. Conscious awareness of the evolutionary reasons for our thoughts and behaviors do not matter for survival and reproduction. All that is required for a particular preference, desire, or motivation to evolve is that it contributes positively to reproductive success. For example, most adults have a desire for sexual contact with other adults. We are motivated to seek out others with certain characteristics as our sex partners. Our minds and bodies reward us with pleasurable sensations when we engage in consensual sex. We are also psychologically rewarded with an increased release of dopamine, a neurotransmitter that is a chemical messenger that signals pleasure between individual neurons in our brains. This is an *endogenous* motivation and reward system for sex. We do not need to learn that we should desire a mate or that sex feels good. These things have been built into our brains and bodies by the process of evolution by natural selection and occur automatically. Our conscious thoughts are blind to the ultimate or evolutionary origins of our mating motivations and sexual desires, unless we learn about the ultimate explanations for cognitive and behavioral phenomena provided by Darwin's theory of evolution by natural selection. Given this knowledge, human motivation to have sex and why sex feels good make perfect sense. Individuals in the evolutionary past who had similar mating motivations and enjoyed having sex would have had more sex than others, and thus would have left more descendants.

HUMAN MATING STRATEGY

Evolutionary psychologists note that the process of reproduction is biologically different for males and females. One difference is that females are always 100 percent certain that their offspring are genetically related to them because fertilization occurs internally within the female reproductive tract. Males, however, are always less than 100 percent certain that they are the parents of a mate's offspring. It is possible, for example, that a male's partner could have a secret sexual affair with someone else. This creates *paternity uncertainty* among males. The amount of paternity uncertainty males experience varies in proportion to how many cues to their partner's infidelity they perceive. For example, men with female partners who have always been faithful in the past, who do not express interest in other men, and who are not secretive about where and with whom they spend their time away from their partner would likely be high in paternity certainty. Conversely, men with female partners who have cheated in the past, who express an interest in other men, and who keep secrets about where and with whom they spend their time are likely to be low in paternity certainty.

Another biological difference between males and females was explained by Trivers' (1972) parental investment theory. Trivers noted that females are limited in the number of opportunities they have to reproduce and pass on their genes. Females must invest at least 9 to 10 months in reproduction. As a result, females have a limited number of pregnancy cycles during the fertile portion of their lifespan. Males, in contrast, are almost unlimited in the number of offspring they can produce. They must only invest a period of days, hours, or less in order to reproduce. Males are not physiologically limited in the number of offspring they can produce in their lifetime. Indeed, if dispensed door to door, the number of sperm in a single male ejaculate could fertilize all the women in the United States.

In terms of physiological investment in reproduction, women invest a great deal more than do men. However, this does not mean that men do not invest in relationships or in children. Although men's biology prevents them from physiologically investing in reproduction as much as women do, men can invest significant resources (food, shelter, protection) and time in their female partners and their children. Over evolutionary history, females and their children would have benefited greatly from their male partners' investment. Females with investing partners would have had healthier pregnancies, healthier children, and would have had a reproductive advantage over other females who lacked an investing partner. The problem for men is that, from an evolutionary standpoint, it is costly for males to lavish attention, time, and other resources on children who are not genetically related to them. Natural selection favors cognitive and physiological adaptations that contribute positively to individual reproductive success. It makes no evolutionary sense for a male to invest in children he did not father. In so doing, he would be increasing the reproductive success of some other man, while damaging his own reproductive success. As a result, the process of natural selection is argued to have shaped male psychological adaptations to help ensure paternity certainty and to avoid investing in other men's children. In sum, sexual infidelity by a partner posed a greater problem for men than it did for women because men could end up investing in children who were not genetically related to them.

Although women do not have any doubt about their genetic relatedness to their children, they are at risk of being abandoned by their partners, leaving them to support a pregnancy and raise a child alone. This is an adaptive problem that women but not men have faced recurrently throughout evolutionary history. A healthy pregnancy and successfully raising children depended in large part on male investment of resources, time, and protection. Men who became emotionally invested in a relationship with other women would have been more likely to divert some resources to their outside relationships. Doing so would have resulted in fewer resources for their partners and children, leading to a lower likelihood that those children would survive and reproduce. In sum, emotional infidelity by a partner posed a greater problem for women than it did for men because women are more dependent on partner investment to successfully raise children and ensure their own reproductive success.

JEALOUSY

As recently as 20 years ago, psychologists believed that jealousy was an immature emotion (Buss, 2000). They argued that it was the result of pathological thinking or a capitalist society that led people to treat each other like commodities. They also believed that jealousy was identical in men and women. Buss, Larsen, Westen, and Semmelroth (1992), in contrast, used evolutionary theory as a foundation to propose that jealousy is a functional emotion that evolved to help people solve the problem of their mate's infidelity. Buss et al. argue that jealousy is a negative emotion that is activated by events that indicate a relationship is being threatened by an outside party (i.e., cues that your partner might engage in sexual or emotional infidelity). The evolved function of jealousy is to prevent the partial or total loss of the relationship. Notice that jealousy is different from envy. Jealousy refers to a negative emotion in response to losing something you already have. Envy refers to a negative emotion in response to wanting something that someone else has.

The research described in this chapter attempts to answer an important question about jealousy—do men and women experience jealousy in a relationship in the same or in different ways? An evolutionary perspective recognizes that the consequences of infidelity and losing a romantic partner are similar for men and women in some ways, but different in others. Men and women are hypothesized to have similar psychologies of jealousy for those aspects of infidelity and partner loss that were similar over human evolutionary history. The sexes are hypothesized to differ in their psychologies of jealousy for the aspects of infidelity and partner loss that they experienced differently over human evolutionary history.

The article that is the focus of this chapter explores differences in men's and women's experience of jealousy. Although the article was published in 1992, it has proven to be a classic piece of research in the field. We will discuss more recent studies that have been built on the foundation of the research by Buss et al. (1992) at the end of the chapter.

Buss et al. (1992) differentiated between two forms of jealousy. If the cause of the jealousy was sexual infidelity, then it was termed sexual jealousy. If the cause was emotional infidelity, it was labeled emotional jealousy. As we discussed, the principle of paternity uncertainty and Parental Investment Theory, both of which are evolutionary theories, predict that men and women will respond differently to sexual and emotional threats to their relationships. It is important to note that the researchers hypothesized that both men and women would experience both forms of jealousy. It is in the best evolutionary interests of men and women to have partners who are emotionally and sexually faithful to them. However, because there were recurrently different costs of the different forms of infidelity for men and women over human evolutionary history, the researchers hypothesized that a partner's sexual infidelity would arouse more sexual jealousy in men than in women, whereas a partner's emotional infidelity would lead to more emotional jealousy in women than in men.

Study 1

Two hundred two undergraduates participated in Study 1. The study was designed to provide an initial test of the hypothesis that men and women would respond differently to different forms of infidelity. Participants were given the following instructions (Buss et al., 1992, p. 252)

Scenario 1
Please think of a serious committed romantic relationship that you have had in the past, that you currently have, or that you would like to have. Imagine that you discover that the person with whom you've been

seriously involved became interested in someone else. What would distress or upset you more?

    A. Imagining your partner forming a deep emotional attachment to that person.

    B. Imagining your partner enjoying passionate sexual intercourse with that other person.

Scenario 2

Please think of a serious committed romantic relationship that you have had in the past, that you currently have, or that you would like to have. Imagine that you discover that the person with whom you've been seriously involved became interested in someone else. What would distress or upset you more?

    A. Imagining your partner trying different sexual positions with that other person.

    B. Imagining your partner falling in love with that other person.

Between scenarios 1 and 2, participants were given other questions to consider that were not part of the data collection in the study. It was likely that the investigators were providing some distracting material between the two scored scenarios so that participants would not focus solely on the questions of interest. Using material that will not be scored is a common practice. It is done so that participants are not immediately aware of what the experimenters are studying. Such awareness could bias participants' responses.

In this study, the two scenarios that participants were presented were basically the same with slightly different forced-choice options. Because each participant responded to both questions, their responses to each should be in the same direction. In a sense, the two versions of the question are an internal reliability check. If Buss et al. (1992) obtained very different responses to each question within the male or female participant groups, the reliability of this questionnaire measure would be in doubt. The results from this study are graphically displayed in Figure 15.1

In response to the first scenario, which asked participants to choose whether they would be more upset by sexual infidelity or emotional infidelity, 60 percent of the men were found to be more upset by sexual infidelity, whereas only 17 percent of women felt that way. In contrast, 83 percent of women found it more upsetting for their partner to form a deep emotional relationship with someone else. The different response patterns for men and women were highly statistically significant ($p < .001$).

For the second scenario, which asked participants to indicate whether imagining the sexual infidelity or the love infidelity made them experience more distress, the same significant sex differences occurred ($p < .001$). Approximately 45 percent of males experienced more distress over sexual infidelity, while approximately 13 percent of females reported sexual infidelity to be more

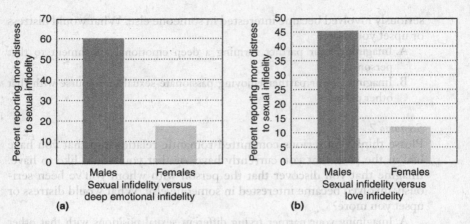

FIGURE 15.1   Distress Responses to Infidelity Jealousy Scenarios. Percentage of participants indicating more distress to sexual rather than (a) emotional and (b) love infidelity jealousy scenarios.

distressing. Women viewed emotional infidelity, in this case, "falling in love" as more distressing than purely sexual involvement.

Study 2

In the first study, participants' behavior was limited to forced-choice questionnaire responses. In the second investigation, the researchers used a number of physiological measures that assessed autonomic arousal to determine if the same emotional response (i.e., jealousy) found in the first study, could be measured in a person's physiological activity. Autonomic arousal refers to involuntary physiological reactions that are not under conscious, voluntary control. Therefore, assessment of autonomic responses serves as an additional and quite different source of information regarding jealousy than the forced-choice questionnaire responses.

When possible, it is always desirable to measure phenomena using a number of different methods. Convergent evidence from multiple different methods is more powerful than replications of data using the same or similar methods because similar methods share similar weaknesses. If the only studies conducted on jealousy, for example, used questionnaire measures, it is possible that the sex differences could be due to something about the questionnaire method that was used. However, if jealousy research using both questionnaire methods and physiological methods give the same results, it is more powerful evidence that the research findings are the result of real differences between men and women.

The following three different physiological arousal measures were used in the second study conducted by Buss et al. (1992):

ELECTRODERMAL ACTIVITY
Electrodes on the fingers of the right hand measured changes in amplitude of electrodermal activity. This is a measure of changes in electrical activity in the skin. Although it may seem to be an odd measure, increases in electrodermal activity indicate increased arousal.

PULSE RATE
Pulse rate in beats per minute was recorded from a device attached to participants' right thumb.

ELECTROMYOGRAPHIC ACTIVITY
The amplitude of electrical activity in a muscle in the brow area of the face associated with displays of negative emotion (i.e., furrowing of the brow).

Procedure

The participants in this study were 32 male and 23 female undergraduate students. The procedure involved "hooking up" the participants to the three physiological measures and asking them to relax in a comfortable reclining chair. They were told to relax for five minutes before the formal part of the research began. Participants were left alone in the room and were given instructions over an intercom. In addition, specific instructions for the upcoming imagery tasks were given to the participants in a written format.

Participants were asked to imagine three different situations. The first situation was neutral and was used to obtain a baseline measure of participants' arousal levels and to get them comfortable in the laboratory. In the neutral situation, participants were asked to imagine themselves walking to class while they were feeling neither good nor bad. Participants were told to signal the experimenter by pressing a button when they had the scenario clearly in mind. When participants pressed the button, physiological recordings on all measures were made for the next 20 seconds. The second and third situations used the same recording procedures but required the participants to imagine scenarios of sexual infidelity and emotional infidelity. Half of the participants were presented with the sexual infidelity scenario first, and half had the emotional infidelity scenario first. This procedure, called counterbalancing, reduces the probability that the order of the presentation of the situations will influence the results. Always giving the imaginary scenario involving sexual jealousy first and the emotional jealously scenario second might well create some problems in interpreting the data. It may be possible, for example, that the sexual infidelity scenario was so powerful that it colored participants' responses to the emotional infidelity scenario that followed it. As a researcher, it is important to make every attempt to ensure that your research findings are not a result of some incidental procedural practice.

To create the image of sexual infidelity in the minds of participants, they were given the following instructions:

> Please think of a serious romantic relationship that you have had in the past, that you currently have, or that you would like to have. Now imagine that the person with whom you're seriously involved becomes interested in someone else. *Imagine you find that your partner is having sexual intercourse with this person.* Try to feel the feelings you would have if this happened to you. (Buss et al., 1992, p. 253)

The instructions were exactly the same for the emotional jealousy scenario, except the instruction in italics was changed to "Imagine that your partner is falling in love and forming an emotional attachment to that person." Between each imagined scenario, participants were told to relax for 30 seconds. The dependent outcomes of this second study were the amount of physiological arousal indicated by the three physiological measures.

Making Sense of the Data

It is common for scientists to transform raw data into scores that both reflect what they are measuring and are in a form that is more appropriate for statistical analyses. Buss et al. (1992) transformed the raw data from three physiological measures using the following procedures:

ELECTRODERMAL ACTIVITY
The largest EDA amplitude found during the 20-second recording interval was used.

PULSE RATE
The average number of beats per minute during the 20-second interval was used.

ELECTROMYOGRAPHIC ACTIVITY
The average amplitude during the 20-second interval was used.

The next step in processing the data was to determine how different the physiological measures for the imagined sexual and emotional infidelity scenarios were from the baseline measure (in which participants imagined walking to class). These difference scores were used in subsequent data analyses.

The results of Study 2 are summarized in Table 15.1. As you can see, males showed more significant increases in EDA in response to imagining their partner's sexual infidelity than to imagining their partner's emotional infidelity. For women, the results were also significant but in the opposite direction. Women experienced significantly more EDA from imagining their partner's emotional infidelity than to imagining their partner's sexual infidelity. Males' PR findings

TABLE 15.1   Mean Difference Scores across Three Physiological Arousal Measures

AROUSAL MEASURE	IMAGERY SCENARIO	MEAN DIFFERENCE	SIGNIFICANT AT $p < .05$
MALES			
EDA	Sexual	1.30	YES
EDA	Emotional	−.11	
PR	Sexual	4.76	YES
PR	Emotional	3.00	
EMG	Sexual	6.75	NO
EMG	Emotional	1.16	
FEMALES			
EDA	Sexual	−.07	YES
EDA	Emotional	.21	
PR	Sexual	2.25	NO
PR	Emotional	2.57	
EMG	Sexual	3.03	NO
EMG	Emotional	8.12	

were similar to their EDA results (i.e., significantly higher PR in response to imagined sexual infidelity than to imagined emotional infidelity). Women exhibited higher PR for imagined emotional infidelity than for imagined sexual infidelity, but the difference was not statistically significant. The results for both men and women on the EMG measure were similar to the pattern of EDA and PR measures (i.e., males showed greater arousal for the sexual infidelity scenarios and females showed greater arousal for the emotional infidelity scenarios). However, the differences were not significant for both sexes. Even though some differences were not significant, all of the differences were in the predicted directions. Men were more upset by imagining partners' sexual infidelity than emotional infidelity. Women were more upset by imagining their partners' emotional infidelity than sexual infidelity.

Study 3

A third study was undertaken to evaluate whether having been in a long-term, committed relationship would impact participants' experience of jealousy. The investigators hypothesized that females who had been in committed relationships would experience greater emotional jealousy than females who had not. Similarly, they hypothesized that males who had been in a committed relationship would experience more sexual jealousy than males who had not. The researchers believed that the experience of being in a committed relationship would be a factor in activating psychological adaptations for emotional jealousy in women and sexual jealousy in men.

The participants were 133 men and 176 women who were undergraduate students. They were given the following instructions (Buss et al., 1992, p. 254):

> Please think of a serious or committed romantic relationship that you have had in the past, that you currently have, or that you would like to have. Imagine that you discover the person with whom you've been seriously involved became interested in someone else. What would distress or upset you more?
> A. Imagining your partner falling in love and forming a deep emotional attachment to that person.
> B. Imagining your partner having sexual intercourse with that other person.

The order of presentation of the two alternatives was counterbalanced. After selecting one of the previous options, the participants answered "yes" or "no" to two questions asking if they were ever in a serious or committed relationship. If they were, the participants were asked if it was a sexual relationship. The findings from this larger sample match closely with the results from the initial study and are presented in Figure 15.2.

A significantly larger percentage of men than women reported that they would be upset if their partner was sexually involved with another person than if

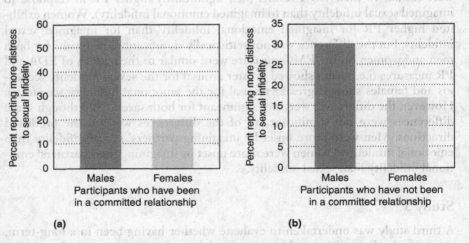

FIGURE 15.2 Distress Responses of Participants (a) with and (b) without Committed Relationship Experience. Percentage of participants indicating more distress to sexual rather than emotional jealousy.

their partner was emotionally involved with another person. The results for men who had previously been in a committed, sexual relationship were significantly different ($p < .001$) from the men who had not. Fifty-five percent of the men with experience in committed, sexual relationships reported they would be more upset by sexual rather than emotional infidelity. In the group of men who never had experienced a committed, sexual relationship only 29 percent felt this way. For women, the data do not indicate any significant difference between those who had experienced a committed, sexual relationship and those who had not. Both groups of women were upset more by emotional infidelity than sexual infidelity, but being in a committed, sexual relationship did not play the significant role that it did for men.

DISCUSSION

Three studies were conducted to test the evolutionary hypothesis that men and women experience jealousy in different ways. Study 1 found that men were significantly more distressed than women by imagining their partner's sexual infidelity. Women were more upset than men when imagining their partner's emotional infidelity.

The second study showed that physiological measures were able to detect changes in autonomic arousal associated with sexual and emotional jealousy. The electrodermal activity and pulse rate measures were especially sensitive in revealing greater arousal in men to imagining their partner's sexual infidelity than imagining their partner's emotional infidelity, and greater arousal in women resulting from imagining their partner's emotional infidelity than imagining their partner's sexual infidelity. The data from the physiological recordings provided an important source of supportive, converging evidence for the findings of Study 1. The close correspondence in the research findings using questionnaire methods and physiological measures suggests that the documented sex differences in jealousy are powerful enough to shine through different measurement methods.

Study 3 provided evidence supportive of the findings of Study 1. The results of Study 3 also suggest that men who have been in committed sexual relationships are particularly upset by sexual infidelity in their partners, more so than men who have not been in a committed sexual relationship. The three studies taken as a group provide support for the evolutionary hypothesis that the sexes experience jealousy in different ways. Men's and women's jealousy are well adapted to help them solve problems that were recurrent over human evolutionary history. For men, higher levels of sexual jealousy help them solve the problem of paternity uncertainty by motivating them to guard their partners and prevent their infidelity. For women, higher levels of emotional jealousy motivate them to engage in behaviors that prevent or curtail their partner's investment in other women.

Critics of the evolutionary approach have argued that the findings obtained in these investigations could be a result of cultural conditioning, and not the outcome of evolutionary processes. For the evolutionary viewpoint to respond to these critics, it is important to replicate their findings in a variety of different cultures. This is exactly what was done in two more recent studies (Buss et al., 1999; Buunk, Angleitner, Oubaid, & Buss, 1996). The first compared Japanese, Korean, and American participants. The second compared Dutch, German, and American participants. In both of these research replications that involved thousands of participants, evolutionary hypotheses for sex differences in jealousy were supported. This is usually seen as strong evidence against the "cultural conditioning" perspective because such conditioning is unlikely to be consistent across very different cultures. Evidence that psychological and behavioral phenomena are cross-culturally universal suggests that the phenomena are at least partially an expression of universal human nature founded on evolved psychological adaptations.

Buss et al.'s (1992) original research on jealousy focused on a small number of hypothesized evolved design features of jealousy. In the years since then, it has focused on many more. There are numerous outcomes of infidelity and losing a partner that are the same or similar for men and women. Similar outcomes of infidelity and partner loss would have selected for similarities in the way that men and women experience jealousy. Some examples of how jealousy is similar in men and women include (1) jealousy is a negative emotion that alerts people to the presence of a threat to their romantic relationship, (2) people feel jealousy when a more attractive same-sex rival expresses an interest in an individual's partner, and (3) jealousy is a mechanism that motivates people to engage in behaviors to prevent their partner's infidelity and to prevent their partner from leaving the relationship for someone else. In addition, both men and women are hypothesized to experience both forms of jealousy. Both sexual infidelity and emotional infidelity are cues to the loss of resources from a partner and may signal that a romantic partner is more likely to leave the relationship in the future. When one romantic partner is significantly more attractive to members of the opposite sex than the other, the less attractive partner will experience more jealousy. This is because the more attractive partner will have more opportunities to be unfaithful and may be more tempted to leave a relationship for a new partner who is more attractive.

Buss (2000) and various research colleagues have hypothesized a number of other differences in the way that men and women experience jealousy. All of them have been empirically supported. The first two differences were the focus of this chapter—men are more upset than women by sexual infidelity, and women are more upset than men by emotional infidelity. Other sex differences include the fact that women are particularly jealous of same-sex rivals who are physically attractive; men are particularly jealous of same-sex rivals who have more resources than they do; and when women are ovulating and therefore more likely to become pregnant, men will increase their jealous mate guarding behaviors to help prevent their partner's infidelity. In addition, men have a better memory for cues to sexual infidelity than for cues to emotional infidelity, and women have better memory for cues to emotional infidelity than they have for cues to sexual infidelity. Finally, on discovering a partner's sexual infidelity, men are less likely than women to forgive and are more likely to terminate a relationship than following a partner's emotional infidelity.

The findings in this series of investigations are consistent with evolutionary hypotheses about the origins of complex adaptive mechanisms such as jealousy. Evolutionary psychological research programs represent a good example of the process of using a scientific theory to generate empirically testable hypotheses. It is important to note that these findings do not preclude the influence of many other factors (including cultural, physiological, and sociological) from playing important roles in contributing to human behavior. However, the evidence from across studies in the field of evolutionary psychology is overwhelmingly supportive of the contention that much of the way that people think and behave is influenced by our evolutionary heritage.

REFERENCES

Buss, D. M. (2000). *The dangerous passion*. New York: Free Press.

Buss, D. M., Larsen, R. J., Westen D., & Semmelroth, J. (1992). Sex differences in jealousy: Evolution, physiology, and psychology. *Psychological Science, 3,* 251–255.

Buss, D. M., Shackelford, T. K., Kirkpatrick, L. A, Choe, J. C., Lim, H. K., Hasegawa, M., Hasegawa, T., & Bennett, K. (1999). Jealousy and the nature of beliefs about infidelity: Tests of competing hypotheses about sex differences in the United States, Korea, and Japan. *Personal Relationships, 6,* 125–150.

Buunk, B. P., Angleitner, A., Oubaid, V., & Buss, D. M. (1996). Sex differences in jealousy in evolutionary and cultural perspective: Tests from the Netherlands, Germany and the United States. *Psychological Science, 7,* 359–363.

Trivers, R. L. (1972). Parental investment and sexual selection. In B. Campbell (Ed.), *Sexual selection and the descent of man* (pp. 136–179). Chicago: Aldine.

CHAPTER 16

PANTS ON FIRE

Lives can depend on the ability to detect lies. Police and customs officers use this ability on a day-to-day basis. In most other occupations the detection of falsehoods may not be a life or death matter but, in one way or another, all of us hope that we are successful as lie detectors, particularly when it really matters. For example, we hope that we can tell when real estate agents, car dealers, and significant others are telling the truth.

As you might expect, this topic has drawn the attention of a number of psychological researchers. Most of the research in psychology has suggested that lie detection ability is not a stable trait. When we are in different situations or trying to detect lies from different people, our accuracy in lie detection may vary from good to poor (Kraut, 1978, 1980).

If a liar is under emotional strain, facial expressions of emotion might betray the lie. Paul Ekman and his coworkers have long been interested in the relationship between facial expression and emotions (Ekman & Friesen, 1971, 1975). In their 1971 study, they demonstrated that emotions could be recognized across cultures. In this study, pictures of facial emotions from Western societies were shown to people living in an isolated area of New Guinea. These people were asked to identify the emotion depicted. It was found that the research participants were usually more than 80 percent accurate in making these judgments, even though they had not had any extensive contact with Western people.

Ekman (1985) reasoned that so-called high-stake lies, where detection of the lie can result in major negative consequences for the liar, would be accompanied by facial expressions of emotion recognizable to many people. High-stake lies might, for example, be told by criminals attempting to avoid incarceration. If a jury believes the lie, a guilty person escapes penalties. The liar has a high stake in being believed, and Ekman expected the lie to be accompanied by signs of emotion on the face. Individuals who could detect these emotions through observation of facial expressions ought to be accurate high-stake lie detectors.

Incorporating the research of M. G. Frank and P. Ekman, "The Ability to Detect Deceit Generalizes across Different Types of High-Stake Lies," 1997, *Journal of Personality and Social Psychology*, 72, pp. 1429–1439.

Ekman further argued that people who are accurate high-stake lie detectors should be able to reliably detect lies across different situations, or different liars. This was expected because if an individual was good at detecting details of facial expressions, the emotions behind expressions should be noticeable whenever there were high-stake lies. Much of the previous research in psychology investigated the detection of trivial lies that made little or no real difference to the person who was lying. The liar was a confederate of the experimenter who had been told to lie about some small matter so that research participants could be presented with lies to detect. Ekman believed that these low-stake lies were less likely to be accompanied by strong emotion and, as a result, would be more difficult to detect. If this were correct, it would offer an explanation why past psychology studies had not found that lie detection generalized across situations. These trivial lies might be more likely to be detected through verbal behavior than facial expression of strong emotions. Ekman suspected that it is easier to lie with words than with genuine, strong emotions.

STIMULUS MATERIALS

Frank and Ekman (1997) performed carefully designed research to investigate these issues. The first step in this investigation was the construction of videotapes depicting some people telling high-stake lies and some people telling the truth. Much of the first part of this chapter involves the method for constructing the stimulus tapes. Usually the term *participant* is used to refer to the people whose behaviors provide the outcome data for the research. In this study, there were two sorts of participants: those involved in creating the stimulus materials and those whose responses were recorded as the data in the study. To avoid confusion, we will adopt the language of Frank and Ekman in calling the people who helped in the creation of stimulus materials *participants*. The people who viewed the stimulus tapes and made the ratings that became the outcome data, will be called *observers*. As will become obvious, the work in this study was divided into two parts: creation of stimulus videotapes and subsequent data collection using these tapes. Because Ekman believed that the facial expressions of emotion accompanying high-stake lies were difficult to fake, the creation of stimulus materials for the experiment required putting people in situations where they really wanted their lies to be believed. This required considerable human engineering.

Creation of the Stimulus Tapes

Twenty male participants ages 18 to 28 were involved in the creation of stimulus videotapes. They were recruited from the San Francisco area and were told that they would be paid $10 an hour for participation, but that they might be able to make more. A first engineered situation, called the *crime scenario*, involved a mock theft of money. The "crime" in which they might participate involved taking $50 from an envelope in a briefcase while they were alone in a lab room. They knew that it was not a real crime. They understood that the researchers planned to lose the money. They knew that the researchers expected some other participant to take the money if they did not. This "other participant" was a fictitious person only introduced because pilot testing had suggested that participants became very suspicious about the purpose of the entire procedure if they believed that they were the only "suspect." Although the actual instructions to these participants were fairly complex (see Frank & Ekman, 1997), for our purposes it is only important to know that there was a role-play theft in which some of the participants took the money and some did not. Participants believed that the researchers could not be sure if the "thief" was them or the "other participant."

All participants were instructed to deny they had taken the money. Participants were told that if they chose to take the money and were able to convince an interrogator that they had *not* done so, they could keep the $50. If a participant took the money and the interrogator detected the lie, the participant was told he or she would lose not only the "stolen" $50, but also the $10 per hour that was being paid for participating in the research. This created the high-stake situation—a successful lie could result in finishing participation with a tidy sum of money. Some participants chose not to take the $50. These participants were, of course, telling the truth when they were interrogated and denied taking the missing money. They were told that if their truthful denials were believed, they would get a $10 bonus in addition to the $10 per hour that they had been promised for being in the research. This was not as much money as the successful liars would get, but it was thought to be an easier task. However, if the interrogator did not believe their truthful denials, they were told they would not get the bonus and would lose their $10 hourly payment as well.

The same participants were also given a second situation in which they could lie or tell the truth. This one was called the *opinion scenario*. Participants were given a questionnaire that asked their opinion about various social issues and allowed them to rate their strength of feeling on the issue from 1 (strongly agree) to 7 (definitely disagree). The issues were things such as the death penalty and the banning of smoking in public places. The opinion that the participant felt most strongly about was selected as the one to be lied about or to be described truthfully. Participants could choose whether they would lie or tell the truth, and the reward structure was the same as in the crime scenario described previously. Truth tellers who were believed received a $10 bonus; liars who were believed received a $50 bonus. Liars or truth tellers who were disbelieved lost all money. All participants were instructed to claim that they were being honest in describing their beliefs.

All participants took part in the crime scenario first. They were told that the interrogator knew the money had been taken, but did not know who had taken it. After having the opportunity to take the money or not, they were taken to a small interrogation room. There were two chairs in that room: an uncomfortable metal one that was anchored to the floor and a comfortable padded chair. The participant was led to the metal chair and introduced to the interrogator, who had been described as an expert in deception. The interrogator did not know if the participant had taken the money. The participant was interrogated for five to seven minutes on a series of 20 questions from a printed list.

At this point, the interrogator left, and the researcher reentered and described the opinion scenario. The participant was told that he or she should choose whether he or she wanted to lie or tell the truth about the opinion. The participant was then told that he or she would have about two minutes to think about what he or she was going to say. After two minutes, the interrogator returned and asked another 20 scripted questions, similar to those asked in the crime interrogation. When this was complete, the participant was given a questionnaire that asked about his or her suspicions concerning the research, how good he or she felt about convincing the interrogator, and the extent to which he or she feared the consequences of being judged as a liar.

After this, the participants were told that their part in the research was over. They were informed of the interrogator's judgment concerning whether they had been lying about each scenario. Any bonus money that had been promised was paid. Those accurately judged as having lied were reminded they would not receive any bonus money, but, in contrast to expectations, all participants were paid the $10 per hour that they had been promised at the time they volunteered for the research. This was probably part of an effort to restore positive feelings about the research: the promise made during recruitment was kept. They were debriefed about the details of the research and dismissed.

Two videotapes were created, one containing men being interrogated about the crime scenario and one featuring men being interrogated about the opinion scenario. The tapes were assembled using the first six questions a participant answered. For the crime scenario, these were questions such as, "Describe exactly what happened, what you saw and did when you were in that room." "Did you take the money from the envelope?" and "Are you lying to me now?" For the opinion scenario, questions included, "What is your position on this current event issue?" "Is this your true opinion?" and "You didn't just make up this opinion a few minutes ago?" These tapes were edited down so that, in the end, each tape contained five men telling the truth and five men lying. No participant appeared more than once on each tape. For the opinion video, a few specific social issues were selected for inclusion, and equal numbers of men were lying and telling the truth about these issues.

Stakes Confirmation

Frank and Ekman believed that the threatened loss of $50 and the $10 hourly fee would be enough to induce strong emotions in the liars. To establish that this high-stake situation was associated with emotion, they had a person trained in scoring emotions look at both of the final edited videotapes. This rater scored the tapes using the Facial Action Coding System (FACS) (Ekman & Friesen, 1978). This is a standardized system that records all visible facial muscle movements, not just those presumed to be involved with emotion. Past research had established that each basic emotion was associated with particular patterns of muscle movements (Ekman, 1985). Based on these findings, it was predicted that the high-stake liars on these videos should show specific facial muscle movements associated with the emotions *fear* (of getting caught) and *disgust* (at oneself for lying). When scores of both videos were combined, the scorer found that 90 percent of the participants could be correctly identified as liars based on facial muscle movements associated with fear and disgust. Seventy percent of the truth tellers could be correctly identified by the absence of facial indicators of fear and disgust. A second FACS trained rater rescored 20 percent of the videos as a reliability check, and the agreement between them was 76 percent.

The presence or absence of facial expressions of emotion in the men confirmed two important things. First, it indicated that the liars were, indeed, in a high-stake situation because they displayed empirical evidence of strong emotions. Second, this finding indicated that there was an observable difference when the facial expressions of high-stake liars were compared to those of people telling the truth. The difference had been captured in the participants on the two videotapes. This enabled Frank and Ekman to proceed to their primary research question: how reliable are ordinary people—presumably responding to these differences—at detecting high-stake lies? Their hypothesis was that some people would be consistently better at high-stake lie detection than others. Frank and Ekman were also interested in the overall level of accuracy of lie detection, but made no particular prediction about this before the data were collected.

STUDY 1

The most important outcome measure was the observer's accuracy for each videotape. It might seem that whether the person was lying or not should be considered the independent variable. In a strict technical sense this is not an independent variable because the experimenter did not create it: people chose for themselves whether they were going to lie or tell the truth. Nevertheless it was an important variable and was associated with the most interesting findings in the study. As you know by now, the only reason why this is an issue is that one should be cautious about asserting a cause-and-effect relationship unless dealing with a real, randomly assigned, independent variable. To help you understand this, imagine that the people who chose to tell the truth were also personally more confident and secure than those who chose to lie. Observers watching the tapes might have responded to the display of confidence, not to the lie. Because this is possible, it is not correct to call lying or being truthful an independent variable in this study. The usual way to solve this in research design is to randomly assign some people to lie and some people to be truthful. Probably Frank and Ekman believed that they would get higher-quality performances if participants could choose to lie or be truthful. In designing the study the way they did, our confidence about cause-and-effect relationships was undermined. It is our judgment that this study should be considered a quasi experiment because of the lack of a real independent variable.

In this case, some compromise was necessitated because the participants' performance was the real priority. As we noted in Chapter 2, it may seem that we are worrying too much about a small matter, but we want you to be able to think critically and clearly about study outcomes. Researchers will sometimes consider, for example, gender to be an independent variable. Gender is not a characteristic that is randomly assigned by an experimenter and as a critical thinker you should exercise caution in drawing cause-and-effect conclusions when it is a variable in a study. Some statistical techniques routinely call one variable an *independent variable*, even though it is not really *independent*. For the purposes of this book, we have tried to be consistent, using this term only when the study is a true experiment. We are aware that this degree of caution is unusual, but we think it is important. We want you to be able to think clearly about research findings regardless of the terms that are used by a particular author.

The Judgment Procedure

Forty-nine observers were recruited, and they viewed the videotapes in an attempt to detect lies. They were 32 females and 17 males who were students at San Francisco State University. They received course credit for being observers. They watched the tapes in groups with seven to ten other observers. They were told that they would be seeing 10 men who were being interrogated about a crime and 10 men who were being interrogated about their opinion on a current event topic. Observers were given a form that permitted them to circle the word *truthful* or *lying* after viewing each participant's segment of the tape. Ability to detect lies was operationally defined as success on this task. The observers were told that between one fourth and three fourths of the men they would see were lying. This was done to prevent observers from merely assuming that all participants were either lying or truthful. Before and after the videotapes were viewed, observers were asked to rate their own ability to detect lying in other people. These ratings were done on a five point scale where $1 = very\ poor$ and $5 = very\ good$. One observer did not follow instructions and was dropped from the study.

Results of Study 1

Accuracy scores of observers were calculated by counting the number of correct judgments, out of 10 possible, for each video. To make the results easier to understand, data are presented as percentages. Each video had been constructed

TABLE 16.1   Number of Observers Scoring High and Low on Each of the Scenarios in Study 1

		OPINION SCENARIO SCORE	
		High	Low
CRIME SCENARIO SCORE	High	21	6
	Low	9	12

to contain five men who were lying and five who were telling the truth. Because there were two choices, lying or truth, an observer who only guessed would average 50 percent correct. Frank and Ekman divided the observers into two groups: high accuracy, those getting 60 percent or more correct, and low accuracy, those getting 50 percent or fewer correct. The number of high and low scorers for each scenario is shown in Table 16.1.

As Table 16.1 shows, people who scored high on the crime scenario were also likely to score high on the opinion scenario. Although less pronounced, the same trend can be seen for low scorers. You can see this by looking at the diagonally positioned cells on the table: the high/high cell in the upper left and the low/low cell in the lower right. In contrast, looking at the diagonal cells in the other direction—the high/low and low/high—there were not too many observers who scored high on one scenario and low on the other. Although it may take a bit of study to understand this table, it is worth your time to do so because this is a standard method for presenting data assessing two levels of behavior in two situations.

There were also some interesting correlational findings among the results. There was a significant positive correlation ($r = .48$, $p < .001$) between the performance of an observer on the crime scenario and on the opinion scenario. This indicated that many of those who performed well on one performed well on the other. Those who achieved about the chance level on one did about the same on the other, and those who were poor at lie detection on one videotape were also poor lie detectors when watching the other tape. These accuracy scores for individual observers ranged from 10 percent to 90 percent for the opinion video and from 10 percent to 80 percent for the crime video. These data can be used to illustrate the difference between the detection of ordinary and high-stake lies. In other psychology research, where lies were not high stake, it was unusual for any measured accuracy to surpass 60 percent (DePaulo, Zuckerman, & Rosenthal 1980). Neither the gender of the observer nor the order of videotape presentation had any effect on the results.

No relationship was found between observer's pretest or posttest ratings of *confidence* in their detection ability and their *actual* detection ability. People do not know how good or bad they have been, or are going to be, when it comes to actually detecting lies. Even though these assessments had no relationship to actual detection they did have a relationship to each other: observers who believed that they were good lie detectors before seeing the tapes continued to think they were good lie detectors after the tape, even though confidence was, in fact, unrelated to accuracy. This is a good example of a situation in which reliability is not evidence of validity.

STUDY 2

Study 2 was similar to Study 1, but it was also an attempt to directly demonstrate that observers who were good at recognizing facial expressions of emotions would also be good at detecting high-stake lies. In addition, Study 2 provided a replication of Study 1.

The observers in Study 2 were 13 male and 17 female undergraduates from San Jose State University who received course credit for taking part in the research. These observers saw the two deception videotapes developed for Study 1. As in Study 1, they were asked to rate pretest and posttest confidence in their ability to detect lying. Study 2 differed because after judging the videotapes, participants were all given a test of accuracy in judging facial expressions of emotion, called the *microexpression test*.

The 40-item microexpression test consisted of slides of facial expressions of emotions. The emotions depicted were anger, contempt, disgust, fear, happiness, sadness, and surprise. These slides were presented using an apparatus called a tachistoscope, which is essentially a slide projector with a shutterlike device that controls duration of presentation of the slide. In this case, the pictures of facial emotions were on the screen for one twenty-fifth of a second. Although this may not seem very long, it is easily long enough to see the facial expression. This slide show was videotaped for presentation to the observers. After each picture of an emotion was briefly flashed on the screen, the observer was given the opportunity to identify the emotion by circling the answer from a list of the seven emotions. Presenting the emotions for such a short period of time made the task more challenging and presumably helped separate those who were good at identifying emotions from those who were not.

As in Study 1, a hypothesis in this study was that observers who were good at finding liars in the crime tape would also be good at finding liars in the opinion tape. Frank and Ekman further predicted that there would be a positive correlation between performance on the microexpression test and the successful detection of lies in the crime and opinion scenarios. As in Study 1, they also expected to find no relationship between confidence in lie detection ability and accuracy at lie detection.

TABLE 16.2   Number of Observers Scoring High and Low on Each of the Scenarios in Study 2

		OPINION SCENARIO SCORE	
		High	*Low*
CRIME SCENARIO SCORE	*High*	15	4
	Low	4	7

Results of Study 2

As had been found in Study 1, neither the gender of the observer nor the order of videotape presentation had any effect on the results. As in Study 1, observers who were 60 percent accurate or higher were classified as high scorers and those 50 percent and below were considered to be low scorers. Table 16.2 shows the number of observers who were high and low scorers for each tape in Study 2.

A statistically significant positive correlation ($r = .31, p < .05$) was found between the detection of lies in the opinion video and the detection of lies in the crime video. There was a significant positive correlation ($r = .34, p < .04$) between the successful identification of emotions on the microexpression test and the successful detection of lies in the crime video. The relation between microexpression accuracy and opinion video accuracy was a positive correlation, but it was not statistically significant ($r = .20, p = .15$). It is not obvious why this happened, but unanticipated variation from one version of a study to another is not highly unusual. As in Study 1, observer's ratings of pretest and posttest confidence indicated, in Frank and Ekman's (1997) words, that "observers seem to have fairly reliable beliefs about their abilities to detect deception, independent of their actual ability" (p. 1436).

DISCUSSION

The results of these two studies suggest that the ability to detect high-stake lies may not vary much from one lie to the next, but may, instead, be a more general trait that some people possess and some people do not. The ability to accurately read emotions from facial expressions seems to be related to this ability and may well be an important component of it. This kind of cautious language is required here because the data were correlational, so although a relationship was established, there was no evidence for a cause-and-effect relationship between emotion recognition and lie detection. There may, of course, *be* a cause-and-effect relationship here, but a correlation is not sufficient evidence to confirm it.

Given the findings of these studies, it is possible to imagine a true experiment that might help determine if recognition of emotions is a cause of lie detection. An approach might be to identify a group of people who were not good at emotion recognition, randomly assign them to two groups and train one group to recognize emotions. This presumes that it is possible to train this skill, which, by itself, is another interesting question. Once training had been attempted, both groups could be given an appropriate lie detection task to see if the group that was taught the emotion detection skill would do better at lie detection. This design could be strengthened if these groups were given a lie detection assessment before training to assure that the groups were not different in lie detection before one group received training. It is easy to *imagine* further research, but we would not want the ease of this interesting activity to distract you from an appreciation of the vast amount of work involved in actually conducting such a study. Aside from the hard work involved in creating the stimulus videotapes, the study that we imagine would also involve a long-term commitment from observers through the training program.

Frank and Ekman showed appropriate caution in the interpretation of their results. Although they believed that the identification of emotions was a component of the detection of deceit, they also stated that lie detection probably involves a number of skills and abilities, some closely related to each other and some not. Because there is no one characteristic that is always present in people who are lying, there can be no one strategy that will always result in successful lie detection. It is highly probable that some people can tell lies, even high-stake lies, while exhibiting no outward evidence of emotional responses. It seems clear from this study, however, that many liars do give themselves away, at least to the skilled observer. The significant correlations in this study are of moderate strength, being in the range of .30 to the middle .40s. Although they have some predictive power, it is clear that other, unknown factors also play a role in lie detection.

Frank and Ekman noted that there are two rather different approaches that might be used in the application of these findings to professional high-stake lie detection in agencies. One approach would be to attempt training using facial emotion recognition. The other would be to identify those people within the organization who are already reliably good at lie detection and have these individuals take responsibility for this task, saving the investment that would be required for training programs. Either way, the future practical application of this important area of research is obvious.

REFERENCES

DePaulo, B. M., Zuckerman, M., & Rosenthal, R. (1980). Humans as lie detectors. *Journal of Communication, 30,* 129–139.

Ekman, P. (1985). *Telling lies: Clues to deceit in the marketplace, politics and marriage.* New York: Norton.

Ekman, P., & Friesen, W. V. (1971). Constants across cultures in the face and emotion. *Journal of Personality and Social Psychology, 17,* 124–129.

Ekman, P., & Friesen, W. V. (1975). *Unmasking the face: A guide to recognizing emotions from facial cues.* Upper Saddle River, NJ: Prentice Hall.

Ekman, P., & Friesen, W. V. (1978). *The Facial Action Coding System.* Palo Alto, CA: Consulting Psychologists Press.

Frank, M. G., & Ekman, P. (1997). The ability to detect deceit generalizes across different types of high-stake lies. *Journal of Personality and Social Psychology, 72,* 1429–1439.

Kraut, R. E. (1978). Verbal and nonverbal cues in the perception of lying. *Journal of Personality and Social Psychology, 36,* 380–391.

Kraut, R. E. (1980). Humans as lie detectors: Some second thoughts. *Journal of Communication, 30,* 209–216.

CHAPTER 17

AGGRESSION BREEDS AGGRESSION

Popular culture, self-help books, and pop psychology foster the belief that externalizing anger, hostility, or aggression is therapeutic. This process of catharsis or venting feelings, often on inanimate objects, is proposed as a healthy way to reduce the impact of negative emotions. Striking a pillow or hitting a punching bag are advocated as cathartic release techniques. Lee (1993), in a mass market self help book, advocates that "If you are angry at a particular person, imagine his or her face on the pillow or punching bag, and vent your rage physically and verbally . . . you are not hitting a person. You are hitting the ghost of that person— a ghost from the past, . . . that must be exorcised in a concrete, physical way" (p. 96). The catharsis hypothesis is endorsed widely and has led people to believe that venting anger is a positive, healthy strategy that will make you feel better. The research presented in this chapter focuses on the following questions: (1) can media endorsement of catharsis lead people to engage in cathartic activities such as venting anger? and (2) if people believe in the benefits of catharsis, will acting in an aggressive manner lead to reduced feelings of aggression?

WHAT IS CATHARSIS AND DOES IT HAVE SUPPORT?

Catharsis has a long history and has a great deal of contemporary mass media support. Aristotle advocated viewing tragic plays as a means of catharsis to cleanse personal emotional issues. Freud's views, which certainly dominated early twentieth-century thinking, suggest that the internal build-up of pent-up emotions is responsible for conversion and anxiety disorders. Freud's thinking is often referred to as the *plumbing or hydraulic model;* as negative emotions build up internally the "hydraulic" pressure inside the person increases, like water behind a dam.

Incorporating the research of B. J. Bushman, R. F. Baumeister, and A. Stack, "Catharsis, Aggression, and Persuasive Influence: Self-Fulfilling or Self-Defeating Prophecies?" 1999, *Journal of Personality and Social Psychology*, 76, pp. 367–376.

Because this pressure represents an uncomfortable state, an external release is proposed as being adaptive for the person (Geen & Quantry, 1977). The self-help book by Lee (1993) mentioned previously cites a number of ways to focus your hostilities on inanimate objects, including breaking glass, twisting a towel, and using a plastic baseball bat to strike a couch. Exploring the catharsis data from empirical studies, Tavris (1988) determined that there has been almost no research support for the value of catharsis in getting rid of negative feelings. However, it is very possible that venting anger through a cathartic process can lead to higher levels of feelings of aggression (Berkowitz, 1984; Tice & Baumeister, 1993). Despite this, catharsis continues to be seen in our culture as a remedy for anger and hostility, and the belief remains resistant to modification.

THE CURRENT SITUATION

POPULAR MEDIA

Endorses the catharsis hypothesis as truth and produces books, tapes, and articles in support. Because popular media is pervasive, the general public believes this view is fact.

SCIENTIFIC PSYCHOLOGY

Does not validate catharsis and supports just the opposite—acting in a violent manner leads to more violence.

SELF-FULFILLING AND SELF-DEFEATING PROPHECIES

In the first experiment, participants were evaluated to see if pro- or anticatharsis messages influenced their decision to select a method to cope with anger. The researchers hypothesized that participants exposed to procatharsis messages would elect to vent their anger by engaging in aggressive acts against inanimate objects. A second experiment explored the after effects of a participant's choice. Participants were exposed to one of three catharsis messages: procatharsis, anticatharsis, or a control message that said nothing about catharsis. After being encouraged to engage in aggression by striking a punching bag, they were given the chance to engage in aggressive behavior toward a person who has angered them. Would the prepunching message they received be a factor in determining later aggressive behavior? Bushman, Baumeister, and Stack (1999) suggested that a *self-fulfilling prophecy* viewpoint (a person's beliefs lead to outcomes consistent with expectations) would lead to low aggression after the participants engaged in the physical aggression of hitting the punching bag. In contrast, a *self-defeating prophecy* (a person's beliefs lead to outcomes opposite to expectations) would lead to higher levels of aggression after engaging in slugging the punching bag. This is not a socially desirable outcome.

First Experiment

The participants in this experiment were 180 male and 180 female introductory psychology students who volunteered and also received additional class credit. They were given a cover story that the investigators were studying people's perceptions in a variety of situations. Participants were assigned randomly to one of three message conditions: procatharsis, anticatharsis, and a control condition. The participants in all conditions were asked to write a brief essay on the topic of abortion, taking either a prochoice or prolife position. Half of the participant's essays were assigned to receive very negative evaluations regardless of the quality of the essay, and the other half were assigned to receive very positive evaluations. This was accomplished by comments such as "This is one of the worst essays I have read" in the negative condition or "No suggestions, great essay" in the positive condition. Previous research by Bushman and Baumeister (1998) supported the view that the previous manipulation does, in fact, create significantly more anger in the group receiving the negative evaluation than in the group receiving positive evaluations. Next the participants were given 10 activities to place in rank order based on their desire to engage in these activities later in the experiment. Activities in the rank ordering included reading, playing cards, playing computer games, and hitting a punching bag.

This research is an experiment with two independent variables, *media message* (procatharsis, anticatharsis, control), and *anger level* (angered or not angered by feedback). The dependent variable was the participants' preference ranking of "hitting a punching bag" among nine other activities.

Results of Experiment 1

The major results of this experiment are presented in Figure 17.1. Participants who were angry as a result of their essay evaluations and who received the procatharsis message ranked hitting the punching bag significantly higher than angry participants who received the anticatharsis message or those participants who were in the control condition. In the groups of participants that were not angered by the essay grading, the anticatharsis and procatharsis messages played no role in their rank of interest in hitting a punching bag. Overall, participants who received the anticatharsis message were significantly less likely to want to hit the punching bag than participants who received the procatharsis message ($p < .05$). Last, sex of participants played a role in wanting to hit the punching bag, with males participants having significantly higher rankings than females ($p < .05$). This experiment shows that messages from such popular media as self-help books, segments on the evening television news, and talk shows can impact an individual's choice to behave in an aggressive manner or not when provoked to anger. The researchers, Bushman et al. (1999) believed it was conceivable that demand characteristics found in the experiment may have been responsible for the findings. *Demand characteristics* are environmental or situational stimuli that guide our behavior. Small, seemingly insignificant messages and stimuli can play a major role in determining our behavior. For example, if you are led to believe

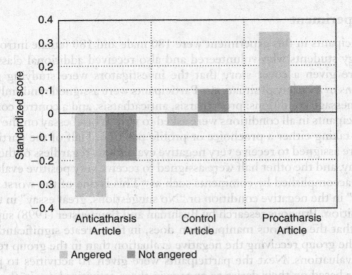

FIGURE 17.1 Bag Punching Preferences as a Function of Anger and Media Message. Preferences are displayed as standardized scores with positive scores indicating greater aggressive preferences and negative scores indicating lower preferences for aggressive action.

(even in the mildest way) that a course exam in college will be very difficult, it may affect your test-taking style and performance. This is true even if the exam is quite easy. Similarly, the sanctuary for a religious service contains demand characteristics for being quiet, reverent, and serious. An important interview in your senior year in college for a great job contains demand characteristic for formal dress and formal manners.

In their initial experiment, Bushman et al. (1999) believed it might be feasible that the participants' ranking of "bag punching" might have been affected by the specific mention of "bag punching" in the procatharsis message. Were the participants just giving the researchers what they believed the researchers wanted? In other words, did "bag punching" in the procatharsis message serve as a demand characteristic that affected their later ranking? Remember that only the procatharsis group had "bag punching" in their message. The researchers could not simply eliminate this possibility and so designed a second experiment to clarify what was happening.

Second Experiment

In this experiment, participants were given the chance to actually express anger toward an individual who had angered them. In the initial experiment, the outcome measure was a self-reported ranking; in this experiment, the outcome measure was behavioral. In addition, the researchers were able to determine how cathartic aggressive behavior might impact a person's anger level. Would such actions lower one's anger as the catharsis hypothesis suggests or not?

The participants were similar to the first experiment with 350 males and 357 females. Participants were evaluated individually and were told that the research project involved the accuracy of perceptions of people in various interactions. Participants were randomly assigned to one of three conditions; procatharsis, anticatharsis, or control condition with no relevancy to catharsis. The next step was similar to the first experiment, with participants writing a brief prolife or prochoice essay on abortion. Participants were led to believe that another participant would evaluate the essays. In fact, the essays were *all* given very poor assessments with comments describing poor organization, style, clarity, persuasiveness, and overall quality. As in the initial experiment there was a written comment stating that "This is one of the worst essays I have read." The same ranking procedure used in the initial experiment was used, with one of the 10 possible activities, "hitting a punching bag."

The next step was new to the procedure and involved participants actually hitting a punching bag. Participants were placed in a room with the punching bag, given boxing gloves, and encouraged to hit the bag for two minutes. After completing the punching bag exercise participants were asked to indicate their level of enjoyment in slugging the bag. The next step involved having participants engage in what they believed would be a competitive reaction time task. Participants were given instructions to press a button as quickly as they could in response to a signal because they were in competition with another participant. Some of the participants were told that their competitor was the person who evaluated their essay (remember all participants received very negative evaluations designed to induce anger), whereas other participants were informed that their competitor was unknown to them. The information about their competitor was transmitted to the participants before the bag punching exercise. This was done so that participants could "use" the bag punching exercise as a chance to "vent" their anger *or* to hold on to the anger and direct it against the person who made them angry by insulting them with a negative essay evaluation. The slowest of the pair in the competitive reaction time task would be subjected to a noise blast administered by the winner. The intensity of the noise could be set at one of 10 levels ranging from 60 decibels to 105 decibels. Participants could also select a no-noise condition. A second variable of the noise choice was the duration of the noise to the loser by the winner. The winner administered the noise by holding down a button. The longer the button was depressed the longer the noise was administered. Participants could therefore effectively "punish" other participants by selecting the level and duration of the aversive sound. In summary, the trial winner had control of a "noise gun" that could zap the other competitor. The competitive reaction time task had an initial trial followed by 24 succeeding trials. On the initial trial, the "real participant" always won, and on the succeeding 24 trials, the "real participant" won half the time. Because the experimental procedure is somewhat complex, the following procedural summary is provided:

- Participants randomly assigned to one of three conditions (procatharsis, anticatharsis, control)
- Participants write prolife or prochoice essays
- All essays given very negative written feedback to induce anger
- Ranking list of activities, which included punching a bag
- Some participants informed they would engage in competitive reaction task later with grader of their essay
- Participants engage in two-minute punching bag session with enjoyment level measured by self-rating
- Participants engage in competitive reaction task (competitor is believed to be essay grader or non–essay grader)
- Participants could inflict various levels of noise "pain" for various time duration

Results of Experiment 2

Sex of Participants.   Male participants showed a trend toward higher levels of aggressive behavior across all measures.

Angry Procatharsis Participants.   Participant rankings for the 10 activities were quite similar to Experiment 1, with participants who were made angry and exposed to the procatharsis message showing significantly more desire to hit the bag than participants made angry who were exposed to the anticatharsis message ($p <.05$). In addition, participants showed a trend to hit the punching bag more (but not significantly so) when they were aware they would be interacting later with the person who made them angry by evaluating their essay unfavorably ($p <.10$).

Zapping Your Competitor.   An additional component of Experiment 2 was to observe whether participants from various conditions, if given the opportunity, would show more hostility in punishing the person who made them angry. The dependent measures to determine this were level of noise intensity chosen and duration of exposure chosen. Both were seen as measures of anger toward the source or the aggression. Because these measures correlated significantly with each other a single *composite intensity* + *duration measure* was used to assess aggressive interpersonal behavior. The researchers thought that the initial trial (out of 25) represented the best test of aggressive behavior. They reasoned that on the next 24 trials the participant's aggressiveness response would be affected by how aggressive their competitor had been toward them. The results of aggressivity on Trial 1 showed a trend for participants who received the procatharsis message to be more aggressive than both the anticatharsis and control message groups

($p < .10$). On the remaining trials the procatharsis message group behaved in a significantly more aggressive manner than did the anticatharsis message group participants do ($p < .05$).

People Like to Punch.   Seventy-two percent of participants liked to hit the punching bag with no differences observed between message conditions. Male participants enjoyed slugging the bag more than females.

Does Hitting the Bag Lead to Catharsis?   Further analyses of procatharsis participants who hit the punching bag show higher aggressive levels in the *composite intensity + duration measure* than participants who did not hit the bag. These findings are contrary to the catharsis hypothesis.

These findings from Experiment 2 supported the results of the initial experiment. Hitting a punching bag does not appear to yield a cathartic effect. On the contrary, it increases aggressive behavior. Experiment 2 also provided a replication of the finding that desire to hit a punching bag ranked higher among the procatharsis participants than other groups.

This research shows that messages from the media can impact behavior. Most importantly it showed that interpersonal aggression is heightened by a procatharsis message even after participants have been given a chance to supposedly let off steam by hitting a punching bag. The findings support the viewpoint that a belief in catharsis appears to initiate a self-defeating prophecy.

DISCUSSION

The researchers in this experiment could not see any beneficial cathartic effect even when participants were given positive messages about its benefits. Catharsis leads to aggressivity rather than dampens it. Why then does the catharsis model retain its current popularity, prestige, and power? Bushman et al. (1999) suggested that the pop media endlessly promotes the catharsis as therapeutic, and people may believe it is a natural, normal process to lower one's anger level. In addition, because it has a long history, people may have come to believe it must be correct.

It is frequently the case that old ideas take a long time to die out, especially in psychology. The Rorschach inkblot technique for personality assessment and clinical diagnosis has consistently been found to have low validity and reliability when scored by traditional methods. However, it is still in wide usage among clinicians. The data from this research suggest that procatharsis actions are not effective in reducing aggressive behavior. In fact, catharsis promotes aggressive behavior and, therefore, is a hazard to personal, social, and community life. Alternatives to the catharsis hypothesis such as self-control and nonaggressive behavior should be promoted widely.

REFERENCES

Berkowitz, L. (1984). Some effects of thoughts on anti-social and pro-social influences of media effects: A cognitive-neoassociation analysis. *Psychological Bulletin, 95*, 410–427.

Bushman, B. J., & Baumeister, R. F. (1998). Threatened egotism, narcissism, self-esteem, and direct and displaced aggression: Does self-love or self-hate lead to violence? *Journal of Personality and Social Psychology, 75*, 219–229.

Bushman, B. J., Baumeister, R. F., & Stack, A. (1999). Catharsis, aggression, and persuasive influence: Self-fulfilling or self-defeating prophecies? *Journal of Personality and Social Psychology, 76*, 367–376.

Geen, R. G., & Quantry, M. B. (1977). The catharsis of aggression: An evaluation of a hypothesis. In L. Berkowitz (Ed.), *Advances in experimental social psychology* (Vol. 10, pp. 1–37). New York: Academic Press.

Lee, J. (1993). *Facing the fire: Experiencing and expressing anger appropriately.* New York: Bantam.

Tavris, C. (1988). Beyond cartoon killings: Comments on two overlooked effects of television. In S. Oskamp (Ed.), *Television as a social issue* (pp. 189–197). Newbury Park, CA: Sage.

Tice, D. M., & Baumeister, R. F. (1993). Controlling anger: Self-induced emotion change. In D. M. Wegner & J. W. Pennebaker (Eds.), *Handbook of mental control* (pp. 393–409). Upper Saddle River, NJ: Prentice Hall.

CHAPTER 18

SOME LIKE IT HOT

As you have learned from previous chapters, personality is an important area of study in the field of psychology. A personality trait, such as extroversion, is believed to remain stable across different situations. If someone is extroverted in the classroom, he or she will also be extroverted among a group of friends and at a party with a bunch of strangers. Physiological characteristics, such as eye color, are also stable across different situations. If your eyes are brown in class, they will also be brown among a group of your friends and at a party with a bunch of strangers.

At the same time that personality traits are argued to be stable across different situations, they also differ from person to person. For example, some people are very extroverted across the range of situations they encounter in their lives. Other people are very introverted in the same situations. The same is true of physiological characteristics. Some people have brown eyes, other people have blue eyes, and others have hazel eyes or green eyes.

There is another level of understanding personality that we have not discussed. Although individuals may differ in personality, they all possess the same set of cognitive mechanisms in their brains that produce personality traits. Everyone possesses cognitive mechanisms that can produce extroversion, for example. Some people may be so low in extroversion that we might refer to them as mostly introverted. Nonetheless, the cognitive mechanisms in their brains that give rise to personality traits are considered to be human universals. In other words, everyone has them. The same is true of physiological adaptations. Although people's eye color may differ, all normally developing humans have eyes. Eyes are a physiological human universal, just like hands and feet and hearts and lungs are universal to all humans. Brains are also universal to all humans. Because personality traits are housed in our brains, it should be no surprise that the brain mechanisms that produce personality are as universal as physiological traits. We can observe human universals and individual differences in physiological characteristics with our eyes. Without the help of equipment

Incorporating the research of L. A. Kirkpatrick, C. E. Waugh, A. Valencia, and G. D. Webster, "The Functional Domain Specificity of Self-Esteem and the Differential Prediction of Aggression," 2002, *Journal of Personality and Social Psychology, 82*, pp.756–767.

that allows us to examine a functioning brain, we can only observe universal psychological processes and individual differences in personality characteristics by how they affect people's behavior. In a real sense, by observing human universals and individual differences in the way that people behave, we are indirectly looking at similarities and differences in their brains.

Lee A. Kirkpatrick and his research colleagues at the College of William and Mary (Kirkpatrick, Waugh, Valencia, & Webster, 2002) conducted research to better understand the relationships between individual differences in some specific personality characteristics and individual differences in people's behaviors. Before we discuss the interesting research methods they used, we need to spend a few moments discussing the personality traits they investigated.

Self-esteem is one of the best known aspects of personality. It refers to a person's sense of self-value or self-worth. A great deal of research has been devoted to the topic of self-esteem. Psychologists generally argue that it is better for people to be higher in self-esteem than lower in self-esteem (e.g., Baumeister, Campbell, Krueger, & Vohs, 2003; Blascovich & Tomaka, 1991). Some psychologists have argued that one of the motivations of human behavior may be the pursuit of high self-esteem (e.g., Maslow, 1970). However, it turns out that self-esteem may be more complicated than this. Research suggests that self-esteem can propel different people's behavior in different directions. For example, men with higher self-esteem have a greater number of sex partners in their lifetimes than men with lower self-esteem. Women with higher self-esteem, in contrast, have fewer sex partners in their lifetimes than women with lower self-esteem (Walsh, 1991).

Other research suggests that high self-esteem may steer behavior in undesirable directions. Baumeister and Boden (1998), for example, argue that certain forms of high self-esteem can lead to increases in aggression. Specifically, they point out that some people's high self-esteem may be inflated and not justified. These people may believe that they are much smarter, more talented, stronger, or otherwise better than they actually are. If someone mocks, challenges, or otherwise threatens the inflated sense of self-value or self-worth that these people possess, they may feel threatened and aggress against the person who is the source of the threat.

Some people are more likely to have inflated views of themselves than others. People who are high in a personality trait called *narcissism* are arrogant, egotistical, and conceited. They are also less likely to care about the welfare of others. Narcissistic people have inflated self-esteem. Bushman and Baumeister (1998) found that people who were higher in narcissism were more likely to use aggression in competitive interactions with others, especially when they believed that their competitors had negatively evaluated them. Interestingly, global self-esteem was not a good predictor of aggression. Only narcissism was a good predictor of aggression in this situation.

Kirkpatrick et al. (2002) wondered why narcissism was a better predictor of aggression than self-esteem, especially because these two aspects of personality seemed to be related to each other. To find an answer, Kirkpatrick used a hypothesis he had proposed earlier with another researcher. According to Kirkpatrick and Ellis (2001), self-esteem should not be considered a single, unified personality trait. Instead, they proposed that self-esteem was comprised of a number of distinct, functional mechanisms. They proposed that we need to look at the distinct components of self-esteem individually in order to understand the relationship between self-esteem and aggression.

Based on Leary's sociometer theory (Leary & Baumeister, 2000), Kirkpatrick and Ellis (2001) argued that maintaining high self-esteem was not a function of our cognitive system. Instead, the function of self-esteem is to monitor where we rank in comparison to other people (e.g., attractiveness, being well liked), the quality of our relationships with others, and how valuable our relationships are to us. In a general sense, when we rank favorably in comparison to others and have good relationships with other people who we value, we should have high self-esteem. If we rank poorly in comparison to others and have poor relationships with people, our self-esteem should be lower. Kirkpatrick and Ellis point out that all relationships are not the same. Our relationships with our parents are different from our relationships with our romantic partners. Our relationships with our siblings are different than our relationships with our teachers or bosses. Rather than having one global self-esteem that captures all relationships, it makes more functional sense that we have multiple, different self-esteems for each different relationship. Kirkpatrick and Ellis also point out that not all of our relationships involve cooperation with other people. Sometimes we are in competition with others for resources, attention from parents, or affection from mates. In these competitions, the characteristics we possess may give us an advantage that leads us to experience increased self-esteem. Being the most attractive person at a party, for example, may lead someone to experience higher levels of self-esteem even though it does not strengthen the person's relationships with others.

According to Kirkpatrick and Ellis (2001), keeping track of where we stand in our relationships with others is functional. Information about our relationships with others influences the different components of our self-esteem, which, in turn, influences our behaviors. In sum, the different components of self-esteem are functional because they monitor our different relationships and motivate us to behave in ways that are adaptive for the relationships we have with others. For example, people who perceive themselves to be low in dominance should be motivated to avoid taking risks in their interactions with others in order to prevent potentially dangerous confrontations. Similarly, people who perceive their social group to be weak should be motivated to strengthen their social group or defect to another, stronger social group.

You may have noticed that we have not yet explicitly discussed what behaviors people use to achieve adaptive outcomes. In the study that is the focus of this chapter, Kirkpatrick et al. (2002) proposed that aggression may be one of the behaviors employed when people experience specific patterns of self-esteem in combination with specific situations. The next step in their research was to generate hypotheses about what combinations of self-esteem and situations lead to aggression.

Kirkpatrick et al. (2002) hypothesized that competition with other individuals within a person's social group was likely to lead to aggression. How people perceive aspects of themselves, such as their own attractiveness as a mate and social status, corresponds to specific components of self-esteem. These feelings of self-value and self-worth, in turn, influence how people will respond to competition with rivals. Those who are more attractive and higher in status—both of which contribute to higher self-esteem—will be more likely to use aggressive tactics. People who are less attractive or lower in status will be likely to avoid aggressive confrontations that they are unlikely to win. In sum, higher levels of the components of self-esteem associated with success at group competition were hypothesized to be predictive of aggression.

Another component of self-esteem is social inclusion, which refers to people's perceptions of how well liked and accepted they are by others in their group. People do not need to be better than the competition in order to be a trusted friend, a valued mate, or a good cooperator in a social group. Social inclusion is not characterized by competition. If a person is very well liked and accepted by other members of the group, behaving aggressively toward them can actually hurt the person. Other group members may distance themselves from the aggressive person in the group, damaging the person's social relationships. The person's degree of social inclusion and, consequently, self-esteem may decrease. As a result, Kirkpatrick et al. (2002) hypothesized that greater social inclusion should predict lower levels of aggression. However, people who are low in social inclusion have much less to lose by behaving aggressively. Low self-inclusion may predict a greater likelihood of aggression. In sum, higher levels of social inclusion, contributing to higher overall self-esteem, were hypothesized to be negatively related to aggression.

The arguments about self-esteem and aggression discussed in the previous paragraphs illustrate how ideas in the science of psychology can change over time. Researchers make new discoveries that lead them to ask new questions. To answer the questions, researchers generate new hypotheses. The next step is to test the hypotheses. Kirkpatrick et al. (2002) conducted two studies to examine the extent to which specific components of self-esteem—including self-perceived superiority and attractiveness as a mate (affecting within-group competition), and social inclusion (affecting within-group cooperation)—predicted aggression in a laboratory setting.

STUDY 1

Participants

The participants in the first study were 116 college students from a university in the southeastern United States. Fifty-five of the participants were men and 61 were women. They received course credit in exchange for participating in the research. The researchers excluded participants who were suspicious about the experimental methods that were used. In other words, they excluded some participants who were likely to have figured out what the experimenters were looking for. The experimenters also excluded participants who did not complete all of the research questionnaires that were designed to assess the participants' personalities. After these participants were excluded, the final sample consisted of 40 men and 48 women.

Personality Measures

The researchers prepared a packet of questionnaires for the participants to complete. The order of the measures completed by the participants was randomized so that no participants would complete the measures in the same sequence. They consisted of two measures of global self-esteem—the 10-item Rosenberg (1965) scale and the 40-item Narcissistic Personality Inventory (Raskin & Terry, 1988). They also contained some additional measures of the specific components of self-esteem that the researchers hypothesized would be predictive of aggression.

Perceptions of social inclusion were assessed using two scales. The first was the nine-item Inclusionary Status Scale (Spivey, 1990). Items from the scale include, "People often seek out my company," and "I often feel like an outsider in social gatherings." When researchers use scales like this, they typically add up each participant's ratings of the individual items. You probably noticed that a person who rated the first item highly would be likely to rate the second item lower. In this case, the second item would be *reverse scored*. This means that the researchers would reverse the sign of the participants' ratings of the second item from a negative value to a positive value. A rating of −3, for example, would be converted to a rating of +3. Using reverse scoring prevents the positive and negative values from cancelling each other out when they are added together.

The researchers also used the 10-item Interpersonal Support Evaluation List (Cohen, Mermelstein, Kamarck, & Hoberman, 1985) to measure social inclusion. The measure includes items such as "When I feel lonely, there are several people I could call to talk to," and "No one I know would throw a birthday party for me." As with the previous measure, the second item was reverse scored. You probably noticed that the items on these two measures of social inclusion seem to be quite similar. The researchers noticed this, too. They found in previous studies that the measures were very positively correlated with each other ($r = 0.75$). As a result, they combined the two into one, 19-item measure.

To measure the components of competitive within-group self-esteem, the researchers used the Self-Attributes Questionnaire developed by Pelham and Swann (1989). This questionnaire asked participants to rate themselves "relative to other college students their own age and sex" on 10 socially desirable characteristics. Examples of items include, "intellectual/academic ability," "social skills/social competency," and "sense of humor." Participants ratings were made on a 10-point scale that ranged from the bottom 5 percent relative to their same sex peers to the top 5 percent relative to their same sex peers. Kirkpatrick et al. (2001) believed that this would be a good measure of participants' self-perceived superiority to others.

The last measure the researchers included in the packet of questionnaires was a 12-item measure of attractiveness to potential mates, often referred to as mate value. This survey was developed by Williams (1999) and includes items such as "Members of the opposite sex seem to like me," and "In a social situation, I often find that persons of the opposite sex seem to act as if I'm not even there." The second of these two items was reversed scored. The researchers argued that this measure could provide information about participants' self-perceptions that would influence within-group competition for mates. It could also provide information about social inclusion in a romantic relationship.

Procedure

Participants were tested in small groups of three to five people at a time. They were separated into small cubicles that branched from a central room. The participants were brought to the cubicles quickly to try to prevent them from interacting with one another before the experiment. They were told that the experiment was going to examine "personality, attitudes, and taste preferences."

Participants were asked to read and sign an informed consent form. They then completed the questionnaire packet. Participants were then asked to write a short opinion essay about abortion. They were given five minutes to complete the essay and were instructed to support whichever position they preferred, for or against. After their essays were completed, they were collected by the researchers. The participants believed that their essays were going to be shown to a person of the same sex in another cubicle. The participants also were given an essay that they were told was written by a same-sex participant in another cubicle. In reality, the essay was prepared in advance by the experimenters. Half of the participants received an essay that agreed with their views on abortion. The other half of participants received an essay that did not agree with them. Participants were randomly assigned to one of these two conditions, called "position manipulation." Participants were asked to rate the essays that were given to them using scales provided by the researchers. They were told that their evaluations would be given back to the same-sex participants who wrote the essays.

After some time, the researchers returned comments to the participants that were supposedly written by another same-sex participant. Really, the comments were made by the experimenters. The experimenters indicated that the reason the feedback was being shared was that most participants were interested in knowing how another participant rated their essay. Half of the participants received negative evaluations of the organization, originality, writing style, and overall quality of their essays. At the bottom of the rating sheet was a handwritten note that stated, "This is one of the worst essays I've ever read." The other half of the participants received positive ratings and a handwritten note that stated, "No suggestions. Great essay!" The participants were told that they were to be randomly assigned to either the negative feedback group or the positive feedback group. The negative feedback condition was meant to attack the self-esteem of the participants in that group.

For the final part of the study, participants were instructed to taste and evaluate a sample of food. Participants were randomly assigned to either evaluate dry food or spicy food. Participants were told that the experimenters needed to be unaware of the type of food and the quantity of food that was being tasted, so participants would give food samples to each other.

Participants were instructed to complete a survey of their taste preferences for salty, spicy, dry, sweet, sour, and creamy foods. After participants completed the survey, the experimenter returned and informed each of them that they had been randomly assigned to the dry food condition. The experimenters took the completed food preference surveys and soon returned with a dry saltine cracker in a plain envelope. Participants were instructed to eat the entire cracker and then rate its taste on a scale from 1 (complete dislike) to 9 (extreme liking).

After a few minutes had passed, the experimenters returned. They brought with them the materials that participants would need to prepare a sample of hot sauce for another participant. These materials included hot sauce, plastic spoons, and Styrofoam bowls. Participants were told to prepare a sample of hot sauce for another participant, who they believed must have been randomly assigned to the spicy food condition. The participants were told that they would be preparing a sample of hot sauce for the person who gave them feedback on their essay in order to help the experimenters keep track of the participants. The experimenters also suggested that participants were often curious about the taste preferences of other participants, so they showed the participants the taste preference responses of the person who provided feedback on their essay. The responses indicated that the person disliked spicy foods.

The experimenters instructed participants to place a quantity of hot sauce in the Styrofoam bowl to be consumed by the person who rated their essay. To make certain that the participants knew how hot the sauce was, they were instructed to sample it using another spoon. Participants were told that they could put as little or as much hot sauce in the bowl as they wanted to. The experimenters made it clear that the person who received the bowl would have to consume all of the hot sauce it contained. Once the hot sauce samples had been placed into the bowls, participants were brought together into the same room and debriefed. The weight of the sauce allocations made by the participants was considered to be a measure of their aggression.

Debriefing research participants involves giving them complete information about the research in which they participated. In this study, the researchers needed to reveal to the participants that they were deceived about a number of aspects of the experiment. It is vital to adequately debrief research participants no matter what research methods are used. It gives the participants the chance to ask

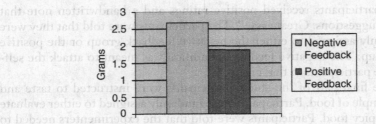

FIGURE 18.1 **Amount of Hot Sauce Allocated by Participants Receiving Negative Feedback and Positive Feedback in Study 1**

questions about the research and the researchers an opportunity to clear up any misconceptions the participants may have. It also gives researchers an opportunity to assist participants who might be upset as a result of their participation.

Results of Study 1

As the researchers predicted, the participants who received negative feedback on their essays allocated significantly larger amounts of hot sauce than the participants who received positive feedback. This is shown in Figure 18.1.

As shown in Figure 18.2, male participants allocated significantly more hot sauce than female participants did. Both of these findings are consistent with the findings of previous research conducted by others using similar experimental methods.

The position manipulation—whether participants received an essay to review that agreed with their views on abortion or disagreed with their views on abortion—did not significantly affect the amount of hot sauce allocated. However, two personality variables emerged as significant predictors of aggression measured by participants' hot sauce allocation. As the experimenters predicted, self-perceived superiority to others was found to be a positive predictor of aggression. Social

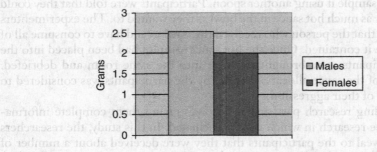

FIGURE 18.2 **Amount of Hot Sauce Allocated by Male and Female Participants in Study 1**

inclusion, in contrast, was found to be negatively related to aggression. In sum, people who were higher in self-perceived superiority tended to be more aggressive. People who were higher in social inclusion tended to be less aggressive.

The experimenters were also interested in whether people who were more narcissistic would also tend to be more aggressive. When the researchers explored this possibility, they found that narcissism did not predict aggression.

Discussion of Study 1

The results of Study 1 provide some support for the hypothesis that certain components of self-esteem are predictive of aggression. Self-perceived superiority was positively predictive of aggression. Greater social inclusion predicted lower levels of aggression. These results suggest that global self-esteem may not be the most useful personality trait to predict behaviors such as aggression. The two components of self-esteem examined in Study 1, superiority and social inclusion, were predictive of aggression in different directions. A single, global measure of self-esteem would have combined their effects, making them difficult or impossible to detect.

Kirkpatrick et al. (2002) were satisfied with their results, but worried that the emotionally charged nature of the abortion debate may have introduced factors unrelated to self-esteem that could have influenced aggression among the participants. To address this and other issues, the researchers designed a second study that targeted a single, specific component of self-esteem.

STUDY 2

Participants

Participants were selected from an original sample of 340 undergraduate psychology students, consisting of 168 men, 169 women, and 3 people who did not indicate their sex. Participants received course credit in exchange for their participation. Some participants were selected from the original sample to participate in the laboratory portion of the study if they (1) were not currently in a long-term relationship and (2) had not participated in Study 1. Seventy-five students from the original sample met these criteria and participated in the laboratory study. After one female participant was excluded because she was suspicious about the study, 35 male and 39 female participants were left in the final sample.

Materials

The questionnaire packet used for Study 2 was exactly the same as that used in Study 1. The order in which the individual questionnaires were presented was randomized by the experimenters so that no participants would complete the questionnaires exactly in exactly the same sequence.

The materials used to allocate hot sauce were also identical to those in Study 1. However, the researchers did change the taste preference scale to include more items, such as aroma, aftertaste, and texture, to help prevent participants from figuring out what the experimenters were really interested in. In the previous study, the taste preference scale only asked about spicy foods.

Procedure

The procedure for Study 2 was very similar to the procedure used in Study 1. However, there were some important differences. First, the self-esteem measures were administered to participants in a separate session that came before the laboratory session. This was done to try to prevent participants from inferring a connection between the two parts of the study.

The cover story and essay procedure for Study 2 also differed from those used in Study 1. The researchers told the participants that the study involved examining the relationship between food preferences and personality. Participants were told that the last part of the study was the food-tasting task. Participants were told that they would be competing with a same-sex rival for the chance to do the taste-test with a partner of the opposite sex who was also a participant in the study. Researchers told the participants that the taste test was "much more fun" that way than to complete it alone.

Participants were then instructed to write essays to the person who might be their opposite sex partner. The goal of the essay was to try to convince the person that they would be good partners for the food-tasting part of the experiment. The experimenters led the participants to believe that they would be evaluating their rival's essay. Participants were also told that the potential opposite-sex partner would use both the essays and the evaluations to choose a partner for the taste preference task.

Once they had completed their essays, participants were given an essay that they were told was written by their same-sex rival. They were also given an evaluation form to rate the essay. The essay was actually prepared in advance by the experimenters. It contained a number of very general statements that were not particularly interesting or compelling, including "I am an economics major and a psychology minor," and "I work at a restaurant." The statements on the essay were generic to try to prevent the participants from finding a reason to particularly like or dislike the person who they were told wrote it. All participants read the same essay.

After their ratings were completed, the experimenters collected them and showed the participants how their rival rated the essays they had written. The evaluation form used in Study 2 was slightly different from that used in Study 1. It was expanded to include scales of readability, originality, degree of attention grabbing, clarity, persuasiveness, and overall appeal. This was done to help make the evaluations seem more personal.

As in Study 1, the fake feedback that was given to the participants in their evaluations was prepared by the experimenters in advance. Feedback was either positive or negative just as it was in Study 1. The handwritten comments were different from Study 1 in order to better fit the new essays. The handwritten comments were also changed because the researchers believed that the negative comments in Study 1 might have been too extreme to be completely believable. In Study 2, the negative handwritten comment was, "This wasn't all that. Looks like I'll get to do the activity." The positive comment was, "Great job! He's [She's] going to have a tough choice!"

Participants were then instructed to participate in a preliminary taste test. They were told that the taste test was necessary to familiarize them with the foods and procedures used in the final taste preference task while the person of the opposite sex was deciding who to choose as a partner. The experimenters indicated that the participants had been randomly assigned to taste-test a cracker and instructed the participants to prepare a sample of hot sauce for their rival to consume. The procedural details for the rest of the study are identical to those used in Study 1.

Results of Study 2

The participants in Study 2 who received negative feedback allocated significantly more hot sauce than the participants who received positive feedback did, as shown in Figure 18.3. This finding is almost identical to what the experimenters found in Study 1.

As illustrated by Figure 18.4, the experimenters also found a significant sex difference in the amount of hot sauce allocated. As in Study 1, men allocated significantly more hot sauce than women did.

As predicted, self-perceived mate value was the strongest, single personality predictor of aggression. The higher a person's perception of their own mate value, the greater the amount of aggression they expressed. In this study, narcissism also emerged as predictive of aggression, but to a lesser extent than mate value. Global

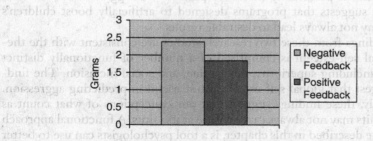

FIGURE 18.3   Amount of Hot Sauce Allocated by Participants Receiving Negative Feedback and Positive Feedback in Study 2

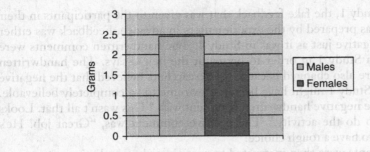

FIGURE 18.4   Amount of Hot Sauce Allocated by Male and Female Participants in Study 2

measures of self-esteem were not predictive of aggression. Superiority and social inclusion, the two components of self-esteem that were significantly related to aggression in Study 1, were not predictive of aggression in Study 2.

The experimenters' prediction that self-perceived mate value would be the strongest predictor of aggression in a context of mating competition was supported by the findings of Study 2. Self-perceived mate value was the only component of self-esteem to predict aggression in this context.

DISCUSSION

Kirkpatrick et al. (2002) point out that their research may help us better understand puzzling violent acts. On April 20, 1999, Eric Harris and Dylan Klebold entered their high school for the last time. On that day at Columbine High School in Colorado, the two teenagers murdered 12 of their classmates and one teacher before taking their own lives. An examination of the diaries and notebooks of the shooters indicated that Harris and Klebold felt superior to their fellow students, but low in social inclusion. This is the same pattern in the specific components of personality that were predictive of aggression in Study 1. This example suggests that programs designed to artificially boost children's self-esteem may not always lead to desirable results.

The findings from these two research studies are consistent with the theory that global self-esteem is comprised of a number of functionally distinct components, including superiority, mate value, and social inclusion. The findings also suggest that global self-esteem is not useful in predicting aggression. More generally, these findings suggest that our conceptions of what count as personality traits may not always carve nature at its joints. A functional approach such as the one described in this chapter, is a tool psychologists can use to better define personality traits. More accurate conceptions of personality traits give researchers greater power to accurately predict behavior.

REFERENCES

Baumeister, R. F., & Boden, J. M. (1998). Aggression and the self: High self-esteem, low self-control, and ego threat. In R. Geen & E. Donnerstein (Eds.), *Human aggression: Theories, research, and implications for social policy* (pp. 111–137). San Diego, CA: Academic Press.

Baumeister, R. F., Campbell, J. D., Krueger, J. I., & Vohs, K. D. (2003). Does high self-esteem cause better performance, interpersonal success, happiness or healthier lifestyles? *Psychological Science in the Public Interest, 4*, 1–44.

Blascovich, J., & Tomaka, J. (1991). Measures of self-esteem. In J. P. Robinson, P. R. Shaver, & L. S. Wrightsman (Eds.), *Measures of personality and social psychological attitudes.* (Vol. 1, pp. 115–160). San Diego, CA: Academic Press.

Bushman, B. J., & Baumeister, R. F. (1998). Threatened egotism, narcissism, self-esteem, and direct and displaced aggression: Does self-love or self-hate lead to violence? *Journal of Personality and Social Psychology, 75*, 219–229.

Cohen, S., Mermelstein, R., Kamarck, T., & Hoberman, H. (1985). Measuring the functional components of social support. In I. G. Sarason & B. R. Saraoson (Eds.), *Social support: Theory, research, and applications* (pp. 73–94). Dordrecht, The Netherlands: Martinus Nijhoff.

Kirkpatrick, L. A., & Ellis, B. J. (2001). Evolutionary perspectives on self-evaluation and self-esteem. In G. Fletcher & M. Clark (Eds.), *The Blackwell handbook of social psychology: Vol. 2: Interpersonal processes* (pp. 411–436). Oxford, UK: Blackwell.

Kirkpatrick, L. A., Waugh, C. E., Valencia, A., & Webster, G. D. (2002). The functional domain specificity of self-esteem and the differential production of aggression. *Journal of Personality and social psychology, 82*, 756–767.

Leary, M. R., & Baumeister, R. F. (2000). The nature and function of self-esteem: Sociometer theory. In M. Zanna (Ed.), *Advances in experimental social psychology* (pp. 1–62). San Diego, CA: Academic Press.

Maslow, A. (1970). *Motivation and personality.* New York: Harper & Row.

Pelham, B. W., & Swann, W. B., Jr. (1989). From self-conceptions to self-worth: On the sources and structure of global self-esteem. *Journal of Personality and Social Psychology, 54*, 672–680.

Raskin, R., & Terry, H. (1988). A principal-components analysis of the Narcissistic Personality Inventory and further evidence of its construct validity. *Journal of Personality and Social Psychology, 54*, 672–680.

Rosenberg, M. (1965). *Society and the adolescent self-image.* Princeton, NJ: Princeton University Press.

Spivey, E. (1990). *Social exclusion as a common factor in social anxiety, loneliness, jealousy, and social depression: Testing and integrative model.* Unpublished master's thesis, Wake Forest University, Winston-Salem, N C.

Walsh, A. (1991). Self-esteem and sexual behavior: Exploring gender differences. *Sex Roles, 25*, 441–450.

Williams, T. E. (1999) *Domain-specificity of self-esteem: An evolutionary approach.* Unpublished master's thesis, College of William & Mary.

CHAPTER 19

GOING TO POT

Jonathan Shedler and Jack Block (1990) studied personality traits in an extensive longitudinal study of adolescent drug use. A *longitudinal study* follows the same individuals over a period of time, collecting data on them at regular intervals. Usually this time period is no more than a few years because these studies can become expensive as they get longer. As a longitudinal study stretches out over time, it becomes more difficult to relocate the members of the original study. People move away and fail to keep in touch with the researchers. Others simply get tired of being studied and refuse to continue cooperating. Nevertheless, longitudinal studies are a powerful way of studying psychological factors across the life span.

Another research method, the *cross-sectional study*, overcomes some of the difficulties of the longitudinal study, but introduces a new problem. The cross-sectional study is of short duration. It selects people from different age groups and presumes these people are representative of those who have been, and will be, this age. Cross-sectional studies have been very useful in plotting the development of characteristics over a few years, usually the years of early childhood. A problem develops when cross-sectional studies are used to investigate changes occurring over large time periods across the life span. For example, imagine a study in which mathematical ability is being assessed. A cross-sectional approach might sample and test people who are currently 20 years old, 40 years old, 60 years old, and 80 years old. If the 80-year-olds perform more poorly than the others, it is not clear if this is because mathematical ability declines in old age or because this group had less formal schooling than the others. The 80-year-olds of today grew up during the Great Depression and World War II, when many people did not have the money to finish school or go to college, and when the material that was taught in school was much different than it is today.

This problem is called a *cohort effect*. A cohort is group of people who are about the same age. There is a cohort effect when one group has lived through

Incorporating the research of J. Shedler, and J. Block, "Adolescent Drug Use and Psychological Health: A Longitudinal Inquiry," 1990, *American Psychologist, 45*, pp. 612–630.

unique circumstances that have affected human development in some special way. In the previous example, the particular history of these 80-year-olds means that they may be substantially different in years of education from people who will become 80 in the future. They cannot be considered representative of the next few generations of 80-year-olds in some types of research because of their unique experiences.

A LONGITUDINAL STUDY OF PERSONALITY AND DRUG USE

Before the work of Shedler and Block (1990), few longitudinal studies of personality and drug use had been undertaken. These tended to follow adolescents for a few years, at best (Brook, Whiteman, Gordon, & Cohen, 1986; Smith & Fogg, 1978). A more typical approach to personality and drug use has been to assess the personalities of groups of adolescents who report drug use, comparing them to groups who say they do not use drugs (see Cox, 1985, for a review).

When cross-sectional or short-term studies are done that show personality traits to be correlates of drug use, it is still not clear which came first. As we have seen, this is the perennial problem with studies that are correlational: they cannot tell us which variable is the cause and which is the effect. Determination of cause and effect can only come from an experiment, and even with an experiment, one should be cautious. No experiment perfectly excludes every single imaginable factor that may influence the dependent variable in addition to the independent variable's influence. We believe that even cause-and-effect conclusions from experiments should be considered tentative. As is often the case with human issues, an experiment to study the effects of drug use can be designed, but could not be conducted. To determine if drug use causes certain personality traits, we would have to randomly assign one large group of kids to use drugs and another to abstain from drug use. This would be the independent variable. The dependent variable would be some subsequent measure of personality. Although this study could give us some important information, from a practical standpoint it is not going to be performed, and we believe that you can figure out why.

Although an experiment that might have settled the cause-and-effect question just went up in smoke for practical reasons, some information about this question can be gained by a thorough longitudinal study. A longitudinal study might demonstrate that stable personality traits develop early in life, well before drug use was an issue. If kids who already had a particular cluster of traits became drug users as teenagers, the case would be strengthened that personality causes drug use, not the other way around. This would be a very valuable step: one possible causal direction could be eliminated. However, even this longitudinal study could not tell us for sure that some third variable—for example, parenting style—was not a major cause of both personality and drug use.

Participants

The research findings on personality and drug use reported by Shedler and Block (1990) come from a broad longitudinal study of personality. The participants in this study were 101 18-year-olds. There were 49 males and 52 females. These kids were part of a group of 130 kids who were first studied when they were 3 years old. At that time, they were in one of two nursery schools in the San Francisco Bay area that were cooperating in recruitment of participants for a longitudinal personality study. The kids lived primarily in urban settings and were from a variety of socioeconomic groups. Their parents had a range of different levels of education. The group was about two-thirds White, one-quarter African American, and one-twelfth Asian American. The kids were given wide-ranging assessments of personality at ages 3, 4, 5, 7, 11, 14, and 18.

Procedure

At age 18, each participant had an individual interview with a skilled interviewer who questioned them about many aspects of their lives, including drug use. The interviews lasted approximately four hours and were videotaped. In the questions about drug use, the 18-year-olds were asked about their own frequency of using marijuana and other drugs. Were the kids honest in talking about their drug use? Shedler and Block (1990) argue that, at worst, drug use might be underreported in interview situations because kids might be reluctant to admit to using drugs. Shedler and Block further argue that there was every reason to believe that these kids answered honestly. The interviewers were skilled at gaining the confidence of kids. Moreover, it is important to remember these kids had been in this study since they were 3 years old. Over the years, they had always been assured that anything they said would be kept confidential. Unlike participants in most studies, these kids knew from a lifetime of experience that the researchers would keep their promise.

The personality assessment that was done at age 18 was broad in scope and took a long time to complete. It was consistent with the painstaking and thorough nature of the rest of this study. Each participant had a session with each of four psychologists who administered different sets of procedures designed to facilitate the observation of personality. These procedures included measurements of performance on perceptual tasks and puzzle solving. They were designed to be situations in which personality characteristics would be displayed. The psychologists who conducted the personality assessments were not the interviewers who had collected the earlier information about drug use. The psychologists were purposely not informed about the drug habits of the participants. When the sessions with the psychologists were over, each psychologist described the personality traits of each participant using the California Adult Q-sort or CQ. The CQ consists of 100 descriptive personality statements. The Q-sort task involves sorting a 100-item deck of cards with printed personality statements (e.g., *Is cheerful, Verbally fluent, Basically anxious, Generally fearful*) into nine separate piles ranging from "not characteristic" in pile 1 to "highly characteristic" in pile 9.

Essentially, the CQ is a device for turning observations of personality into numbers that can then be treated as quantitative data. One of the problems in the study of personality is the difficulty of turning qualitative observations—the ongoing stream of behavior—into valid quantitative data that are representations of the personality itself. Observations could be recorded merely by writing descriptions of personality, but these descriptions could not be handled statistically. Statistics are important because they enable good summaries to be made describing average behaviors of individuals in a group. The CQ has been frequently used for this task, and its validity has been demonstrated. Table 19.1 shows 10 of the CQ items to serve as examples of what was on the cards.

When a psychologist was finished interacting with a participant in this study, the psychologist would sort each card into one of nine piles, based on how well the description or trait on the card matched the personality of each participant. Each trait was given the numerical score of the pile in which it landed. Each participant received a score between 1 and 9 for each of the 100 personality characteristics.

All four psychologists rated the personality characteristics of each participant using the Q-sort technique. The scores were averaged to give a final score for that individual. Even though the psychologists met with each participant at a different time and observed them completing a different task, the CQ ratings of the psychologists were fairly similar. Inter-rater reliability ranged from 70 percent to 90 percent. This high level of reliability suggests that the personality measures may also be valid. For a measurement to be high in validity, it must also be high in reliability. The same is not true the other way around. Just because a measurement is reliable does not necessarily mean it is valid. It is possible, but unlikely, for all the psychologists to make similar ratings of a kid's personality and for all of them to be wrong. Imagine that the inner workings of your bathroom scale are a seized-up ball of rust that looks like the ship's scale from the

TABLE 19.1   Sample Items from the California Adult Q-Sort

Is critical, skeptical, not easily impressed
Favors conservative values in a variety of areas
Seeks reassurance from others
Gives up and withdraws in the face of adversity
Is moralistic
Is unpredictable and changeable in behavior, attitudes
Tends to be rebellious and nonconforming
Is sensitive to anything that can be construed as a demand
Feels cheated and victimized by life; self-pitying
Expresses hostile feelings directly

Titanic. If your scale is rusted tight at 126 lb, it will be highly reliable in weighing you or anyone else. It will always indicate that the person it is weighing is 126 lb. However, this weight measurement will not be valid, unless, of course, someone who is really 126 lb happens to weigh himself or herself on it. The rest of the time it will not be valid.

For the purposes of longitudinal comparison, these CQ personality rating scores were compared with scores obtained from the same kids, back when they were ages 7 and 11, using the California Child Q-sort, or CCQ. This is a version of the adult Q-Sort that was designed to assess the personality of children. The Q-sorts were conducted by entirely different sets of psychologists for each age group. This is important because it prevented any bias that a psychologist developed about a participant from being repeated in the data over successive years. The same procedures were used to administer the CCQ when the participants were children as were used when the Q-sort was administered at age 18. The only difference was that at age 7 three psychologists completed the CCQ and at age 11 five psychologists completed the CCQ. As with the CQ results of the 18-year-olds, the ratings of the psychologists who administered the CCQ were very reliable.

When the participants were 5 years old, they were brought to the lab and observed in one play session with their mothers and in a separate play session with their fathers. They were observed through a one-way mirror by a trained observer. They were also videotaped. They were given a variety of puzzles to solve that included arranging blocks and cut-out colored pieces into specific shapes, as well as finding a path through pencil-and-paper mazes. These tasks were constructed to be easy for the parents but challenging for the child. Observers used yet another Q-sort that contained descriptions of a range of ways that parents might interact with their kids. This Q-sort was completed by the trained observer and by a second observer who watched the videotape. This was a method of checking the reliability of the observations of the interactions between parents and their children. The Q-sort ratings of these two observers were combined to produce scores for parent interactions

Assignment to Groups

Among the 18-year-olds, 68 percent had tried marijuana, having increased from 51 percent when the sample was interviewed at age 14. Thirty-nine percent used it once a month or more, and 21 percent used it weekly or more than weekly. When compared to other national studies of drug use, these results seemed fairly typical. Because of the relatively high numbers of participants who had tried marijuana, Shedler and Block (1990) decided to focus on marijuana use in this study. Only one participant reported heroin use, so Shedler and Block's sample could not, for example, have yielded anything worth knowing about the use of this drug.

Shedler and Block (1990) made some additional decisions that affected the way in which the results would be presented. They decided to divide the

TABLE 19.2   Number of 18-Year-Old Males and Females in Each Drug Use Group

	MALES	FEMALES
Abstainers	14	15
Experimenters	16	20
Frequent users	11	9

participants into three groups. The requirements for assignment to these groups operationally defined drug use for the study. *Abstainers* were those who had never tried any drug. *Experimenters* were those who had used marijuana "once or twice," "a few times," or "once a month" *and* had used no more than one other drug. *Frequent users* used marijuana once a week or more *and*, in addition, had tried at least one other drug. Table 19.2 shows the number of teenagers in each group.

You can see from these data that even though the initial group was quite large, breaking them into three or six groups quickly reduced the number of people in each subgroup. Sixteen of the kids in the original longitudinal study could not be fit into any of the three groups and had to be dropped from the drug use study. These might be kids who had used marijuana once or twice but had also tried several other drugs. In most cases when participants are assigned to groups based on complex criteria, certain participants will not fit into any of the groups. Because so much other information was available about the kids from the ongoing longitudinal study of personality development, we can assume that every effort was made to include as many of them as possible in the study of drug use. Indeed, Shedler and Block (1990) stated that "broader and narrower definitions for the various groups" were considered. They were able to convince themselves that changes in the definitions of the groups did not affect the overall findings of the study.

Results

In presenting the results of the study, Shedler and Block (1990) chose to use the *experimenters* as the group to which the other groups would be compared. This was done because experimenting was most typical in national samples of adolescents. It is important to have one group as the comparison group because it allows us to better assess the outcomes in the other two groups. For example, the psychologists rated the Q-sort card that said "*Undercontrols needs and impulses; unable to delay gratification*" an average score of 3.7, on the 1 to 9 scale, for the *experimenters*. That does not tell us very much until we compare it to the rating of 2.9 that was given to the *abstainers* and the 4.4 that was given to the *frequent users.* Each difference is statistically significant and suggests that the *frequent users* are the most impulsive.

At age 18, the personalities of the *abstainers* and the *frequent users* were strikingly different. Compared to *experimenters, frequent users* did not have close friends and did not show emotions. It was obvious to those who interviewed them that they were unhappy. They did not seem to be able to control their behavior. They were described as "brittle," meaning that their feelings about themselves were fragile and they were not confident about their abilities. They were unable to delay gratification: to put off the fun things in their lives until the unpleasant or tedious things were done. They were not reliable or ethically consistent and were prone to express hostile feelings in a direct way. Compared to the *experimenters*, 18-year-old *abstainers* were able to delay gratification better and were more rational, fastidious, and conservative. Like the *frequent users*, they did not have close friends and lacked social skills. Unlike the *frequent users*, they were anxious, tense, and predictable.

Shedler and Block (1990) were able to look back at the data that had been collected when the participants were younger to examine whether these personality differences were recent developments or consistent with personality differences in the past. As the researchers did at age 18, each group was compared to the group who would later be labeled *experimenters*. In speaking of the three groups of kids in early childhood, we will use the labels that were given to them at age 18 based on their drug use. Of course, this is not meant to imply that drug use had already started at age 7.

Shedler and Block (1990) found that even in childhood the kids who later became *frequent users* showed signs of maladjustment. At age 7, the descriptions of them include not likely to think ahead, not trustworthy, unlikely to develop close relationships, not curious, and unable to identify with admired adults. Shedler and Block summarize the observations of the *frequent users* from ages 7 and 11 by saying, "The picture that emerges is of a child unable to form good relationships, who is insecure, and who shows numerous signs of emotional distress."

There were some similarities and some differences when the childhood personalities of the *abstainers* were compared to their personalities at age 18. At age 7, their personality descriptions included eager to please, inhibited, conventional in thought, neat and orderly, likely to think ahead, obedient, and noncreative. These traits showed considerable stability when the kids were observed again at age 11. Shedler and Block (1990) summarize by noting that *abstainers* present a picture of children who are overcontrolled, timid, fearful, and morose. We can also see what they are not: they are not warm and responsive, not curious and open to new experience, not active, not vital, and not cheerful.

At ages 7 and 11, we can see some of the central personality differences that were also found at age 18. Both *abstainers* and *frequent users* are not stars when it comes to personal relationships. Both seem to be emotionally withdrawn compared to the *experimenters*. At early ages, the *abstainers* already appear to be tense and overcontrolled, while the *frequent users* already seem unable to adequately control their impulses. Patterns of drug use among the participants are associated with personality differences, and these differences, have deep roots that extend back into childhood.

The differences found at age 18 may not have been a big surprise to you. Probably most people would guess that there might be personality differences between *experimenters*, *abstainers*, and *frequent users*. Many people believe that personality changes occur when kids are thrown into a drug-using peer culture. Some teenagers begin to hang out with the "wrong people" and become drug users. The teenage combination of peers and drugs is believed to account for teenage personality. The data presented by Shedler and Block (1990) suggest that this is a false picture.

THE ROOTS OF PERSONALITY

If personality has deep roots, where did the seed get planted? This wording probably can be taken literally: there is considerable evidence that individual babies are different in the way they react to the world from the time they are born. For example, some newborns react to small amounts of stimulation, and others require more before they react. Some babies react to stimuli for only a brief period of time, whereas others' reactions last much longer. Some babies are more likely to react to stimulation over and over in quick succession (Lewis, 1992). A baby might not show any of these reactions, a few of them, or all of them. These differences are called *temperament*. Temperament is different from personality. It is a general pattern of reacting to surroundings. Biological factors, such as the unique mix of neurochemicals in an individual infant's brain, are probably one major component of temperament. The amounts of various neurochemicals available can contribute to a style of behavior and mood that are consistent over time. Temperamental differences such as those found between inhibited and uninhibited kids have been shown to persist from the first year of infancy to the end of the second year and, in another study, from age 2 to age 8 (Kagan & Snidman, 1991).

These early generalized temperaments interact with their environments and grow into personality. It is important to understand that this is a true interaction. It is a two-way street. Personality changes can be a result of events such as conditioning, rewards, punishments, and social learning opportunities. In other words, personality can change as a result of the environment. Personality can also change the environment. We can change the environments we're in or choose new ones that are more consistent with our existing personalities.

For a child, the parent is usually the most important person in the environment. It seems likely that the parent is an important influence in shaping the child's temperament into personality. Shedler and Block (1990) observed the kids in this study interacting with their parents when the kids were five years old. There were interesting similarities between the mothers of the *abstainers* and *frequent users*. Both groups of mothers were seen as being cold and unresponsive. Solving the puzzles that were provided in the lab might have been a fun activity for mothers to do with their children. However, both sets of cold "momsicles" made it a grim and unpleasant task. They did not give their kids much encouragement to try to solve the puzzles. At the same time, they pressured them to successfully complete the puzzles. This situation is called a *double bind*. The kids are expected to do well but are not given the encouragement necessary for success. This double bind says to the child, "I want you to be successful, but don't bother me for help."

The fathers of the *frequent users* were similar to the fathers of the *experimenters* when they interacted with their 5-year-olds. The fathers of the *abstainers* were different. They wanted things done their way. These fathers were domineering and critical of their children and rejected their children's ideas and suggestions. They did not enjoy being with their kids and arranged the situation so that the children did not enjoy being with them. The fathers of the *frequent users* would not be able to rent a house in Mr. Rogers' neighborhood.

It is important to carefully consider the results presented here in order to appreciate the findings of this remarkable study. It is equally important to avoid jumping to conclusions. Although the behavior of these kids varied from one situation to the next, extensive personality screening over a long period of time showed considerable stability in their personality characteristics. This argues against an extreme situational view of personality in which personality varies from context to context and has no underlying stability. Someone might say, "Wait a minute, all these kids were assessed in a highly artificial situation. This situation must have played a major role in determining personality at the same time personality was being assessed. That is why personalities were so reliable from year to year." Although this might be true, it would not account for the stable personality *differences* that were found when *abstainers* and *frequent users* were compared to *experimenters*. A naive situational view would, instead, predict that all kids interacting with psychologists in a lab would have similar personalities in that situation. This is not what was found. Instead, these kids seemed to have relatively enduring personality traits.

It might be tempting to go tearing off with the assumption that the parents were the cause of the maladjusted personality of 18-year-old *abstainers* and *frequent users*. In doing so, one would be confusing correlation with causation. Shedler and Block's (1990) study found a correlation between parenting style and later drug use. Parenting style may well be a cause of the behavior, but the mere correlation of the two does not permit this conclusion to be drawn. Indeed, the opposite may be closer to the truth. It is possible that the cold parental style was a response to an unsocial, withdrawn child's personality. Either way, the correlation does indicate that a cold and unresponsive parenting style, which puts kids in a double bind, allows one to *predict* later maladjustment in personality. With a characteristic as complex as personality, the chances are remote that any single factor is the sole cause, even one as important as parenting style. It is much more likely that parenting accounts for some part of the differences Shedler and Block observed.

Because parenting styles were observed well before the kids started to frequently use or consciously abstain from drugs, we can rule out the notion that the parenting style was a reaction to the children's pattern of drug use. Although this may sound silly, it is sometimes alleged that parents become cold and unresponsive as a reaction to drug-using kids. The findings here suggest that this is a false conclusion. Parental coldness precedes drug-related behavior.

Given that at age 18 the *abstainers* and the *frequent users* were more maladjusted, does the finding here suggest that the way to overcome maladjustment is to be like the *experimenters* and smoke a little weed every now and again? To draw this conclusion would be to confuse correlation with causation again. There is a correlation between personality and drug use patterns, but this does not suggest that changing drug use patterns will result in personality changes. On the contrary, the longitudinal findings of this study suggest that personality traits are stable and resistant to change.

A few years ago, the U.S. government spent a great deal of money on a campaign to teach kids to "Just Say No" to drugs. Shedler and Block's (1990) study suggest that drug use is correlated with enduring personality traits, and therefore a small situational training program, such as "Just Say No," may have little effect. Recent research has demonstrated that "Just Say No" to drugs programs are not effective in preventing drug use (Spooner & Hall, 2002). For example, an average of $750 million is spent on the D.A.R.E. (Drug Abuse Resistance Education) program each year despite pervasive evidence that it does not work (West & O'Neal, 2004). Perhaps the money for these programs would have been better spent in training people to be supportive parents. As educated taxpayers, we should learn to "Just Say No" to programs that fly in the face of carefully conducted scientific studies.

REFERENCES

Brook, J. S., Whiteman, M., Gordon, A. S., & Cohen, P. (1986). Dynamics of childhood and adolescent personality traits and adolescent drug use. *Developmental Psychology, 22,* 403–414.

Cox, W. M. (1985). Personality correlates of substance abuse. In M. Galizio & S. A. Maisto (Eds.), *Determinants of substance abuse: Biological, Psychological, and environmental factors* (pp. 209–246). New York: Plenum.

Kagan, J., & Snidman, N. (1991). Temperamental factors in human development. *American Psychologist, 46,* 856–862.

Lewis, M. (1992). Individual differences in response to stress. *Pediatrics, 90,* 487–490.

Shedler, J., & Block, J., (1990). Adolescent drug use and psychological health: A longitudinal inquiry. *American Psychologist, 45,* 612–630.

Smith, G. M., & Fogg, C. P. (1978). Psychological predictors of early use, late use and nonuse of marijuana among teenage students. In D. B. Kandel (Ed.), *Longitudinal research on drug use* (pp. 101–113). New York: Wiley.

Spooner, C., & Hall, W. (2002). Preventing drug misuse by young people: We need to do more than 'just say no'. *Addiction, 97,* 478–481.

West, S. L., & O'Neal, K. K. (2004). Project D.A.R.E. outcome effectiveness revisited. *American Journal of Public Health, 94,* 1027–1029.

CHAPTER 20

TO CATCH A COLD

There is an increasing evidence that stress in life may contribute to the development of organic illness. The field of psychoneuroimmunology, a branch of behavioral medicine, deals with life and environmental stress, as well as psychological events that increase susceptibility to disease. Until recently, it was largely assumed that organic disease could only have organic origins. Current thinking is that excessive environmental stress, which exceeds the person's coping ability, can have negative physical consequences, such as disease (Lazarus & Folkman, 1984). It is believed that high stress may lead to negative cognitive and emotional reactions that, in turn, may alter the effectiveness of the immune system. The immune system can be adversely affected by autonomic and central nervous system activation (Felten & Olshchowka, 1987), release of hormones (Shavit, Lewis, Terman, Gale, & Liebeskind, 1984), and maladaptive lifestyle changes such as drug usage, smoking, or alcohol (Cohen & Williamson, 1991).

Although there is a belief that stress leads to illness, the research findings are not clear as to whether immune system breakdowns could be of such magnitude as to increase susceptibility to infection (Jemmott & Locke, 1984). Previous research on the current topic, catching a cold, is also unclear on the relationship between stress and the development of illness. The research reported in this chapter focuses on this question—can stress increase the likelihood of catching a cold? In the research described in this chapter, healthy participants were assessed on their level of stress, personality features, and health practices. They were then intentionally exposed to a cold virus or a placebo. Placebo groups are commonly used in research in order to create a control condition in which participants receive exactly the same treatment as the experimental condition, but do not receive the active ingredient under study. In a drug study, a placebo pill mimics the actual medication under investigation in size, color, taste, and even side effects, but the pill does not have the active therapeutic ingredient. In this study, the placebo group was treated identically to

Incorporating the research of S. Cohen, D. A. J. Tyrell, and A. P. Smith, "Negative Life Events, Perceived Stress, Negative Affect, and Susceptibility to the Common Cold," 1993, *Journal of Personality and Social Psychology*, 64, pp. 131–140.

the viral exposure group except that the solution the placebo groups received contained no cold virus, but rather a saline solution. The importance of having a placebo group is to determine if factors other than the variable under study, in this case cold viruses, had any impact on viral infection and disease. We are likely to respond to placebos due to prior learning. For example, if someone has a history of going to a physician and getting medication that relieves pain and symptoms, it is probable that he or she may develop pain and symptom relief by being exposed to talking to a physician. If this occurs, it is an example of classical conditioning in which the medication was the unconditioned stimulus and relief of pain and symptoms was the unconditioned response. Talking to the physician, without treatment, was the conditioned stimulus for the conditioned response of symptom relief. You can review the classical conditioning paradigm in Chapter 6.

PARTICIPANTS

The participants were 154 male and 266 female volunteers, with 394 randomly assigned to the virus infection group and 26 randomly assigned to the saline control group. The study was conducted at a medical research center in Salisbury, England. According to clinical evaluation and laboratory findings, all participants were judged to be in good health at the start of the investigation. Participants ranged in age from 18 to 54, with a mean age of 33.

PROCEDURE

The initial phase of the study consisted of a complete medical exam, administration of self-reported instruments including psychological stress, personality, and health practices questionnaires. Blood samples were obtained for immunity measurement and to check nicotine intake. Following these initial assessments participants were exposed to cold viruses using nasal drops. The placebo group was administered a saline solution.

For two days preceding the administration of nose drops and continuing for six days after exposure the participants were evaluated each day using a standard medical protocol. Protocol items included frequency of sneezing, eye tearing, nasal congestion, nasal blockage, postnasal discharge, sinus pain, sore throat, and coughing. In addition an objective count of number of paper tissues (e.g., Kleenex) used by the participants and twice-daily report of body temperature were made. Twenty-eight days after the viral exposure another blood sample was obtained. In all phases of this study, the researchers were purposely kept unaware as to the psychological status (based on the three measures used in the study) of participants and also whether they received a virus or were in the saline control group.

MEASURING PSYCHOLOGICAL STRESS

Psychological stress was assessed by these measures:

- Selected items from the *List of Recent Experiences* (Henderson, Byrne, & Duncan-Jones, 1981). The number of major stressful life events rated by the participants as having a negative impact.
- *10-Item Perceived Stress Scale* (Cohen & Williamson, 1988). This scale was used to measure the extent to which life circumstances are seen to be stressful. Items measured anxiety, sadness, anger, guilt, irritation, and related concepts.
- *Affect Intensity Measure*. A 5-point scale was used to assess affect (emotional) intensity experienced during the past week.

Previous research by Cohen, Tyrell, and Smith (1991) using the same measures suggested that the three scales were assessing a common underlying concept. Because these three measures are focusing on a single dimension, the researchers combined them into a single composite measure that was used to assess stress.

HOW WE CATCH A COLD

The growth and action of microorganisms is responsible for the development of the common cold. Infection results in the intensification of the attacking microorganism. It is possible for a person to be infected with the invading cold virus without developing clinical symptoms. In this investigation the researchers operationally defined whether a person was infected with a cold virus and also whether a person demonstrated clinical symptoms of a cold. Infection was determined by the presence of a virus found in fluid samples (cultures of nasal secretions) or a rise in cold virus specific antibodies found in blood samples. The presence of cold symptoms was determined by clinical rating on a 4-point scale ranging from complete absence of symptoms (0) to severe symptoms (3). A rating of a mild cold (2) or higher was operationally defined as a positive diagnosis of a clinical cold. In this study clinical diagnosis of colds agreed with participants' self-diagnosis in 94 percent of cases. Participants were operationally defined as having a cold if *both* infection and symptoms were detected. Thirty-eight percent (148 participants) of the total infected sample ($N = 394$) developed colds. In the saline control group, no participants became infected.

MEASURING BODY TEMPERATURE
AND MUCUS WEIGHTS

To obtain additional, objective measures of a cold, the investigators measured body temperature and mucus weights. These additional measurements provided objective assessments not influenced by how an individual participant presented symptoms or how a clinician completed a rating scale. Mucus weights were calculated by weighing the paper tissues used by participants. Body temperatures and mucus weights were taken on the day before "infection" and on each succeeding day.

HEALTH PRACTICES OF PARTICIPANTS

Participants' health practices are important to evaluate because they may serve as important connections between stress and susceptibility to infection. Therefore, smoking, alcohol consumption, exercise activity, sleep quality, and dietary habits were considered part of this study. Smoking was assessed objectively by reviewing cotinine levels in participants' blood samples. Cotinine is a biochemical indicator of nicotine intake that avoids the subjectivity of participants' self-report. However, in this study the correlation of self-reported smoking and cotinine levels was found to be $+.96$, indicating that both measures were assessing smoking behavior accurately. Alcohol consumption was measured by self-reports of the number of drinks per day with each drink (bottle of beer, glass of wine, shot of liquor) counting equally. Exercise was assessed by tabulating the self-reported frequency of engaging in walking, running, swimming, and other aerobic activities. Sleep was measured by a questionnaire tapping the various sleep qualities (e.g., feeling rested, difficulty falling asleep). Diet was measured by self-report items assessing participants' eating habits (e.g., dietary balance, eating vegetables and fruits).

PERSONALITY ASSESSMENT

Three personality dimensions were measured because the investigators believed it likely that psychological stress might be a result of more fundamental aspects of personality. Therefore they assessed self-esteem, personal control, and introversion-extroversion by using a variety of established scales. Self-esteem was discussed in Chapter 18. Personal control focuses on whether people believe that they control and are in charge of their lives and can determine outcomes. People with an internal personal control orientation feel in charge of their own destiny, whereas an external personal control would represent the view that things in life are a matter of chance and there is little personal control of how things turn out. Introversion represents a need for privacy and a lack of need for interpersonal relationships; extroverts are outgoing and social.

RESULTS

None of the saline control participants, the placebo group, became infected or developed colds and, therefore, the following data presented represent only the participants who were exposed to the genuine virus. For each of the four stress measure participants above the median score were considered high stress; those below the median were considered low stress. Table 20.1 presents the percentages of virally exposed participants in low and high groups on the four stress measures who became infected and of those who developed clinical colds.

As can be seen in Table 20.1, the rates of actual infection resulting from exposure are significantly higher for participants in the high groups for stress index (an overall composite score), perceived stress, and negative affect. The high stress group in the life events measure had greater levels of infection, but it was not statistically significant. In reviewing the data on those who actually developed a cold, the life events measure was the only assessment instrument to attain statistical significance between high- and low-stress participants. Therefore, while the life events measure did not differ significantly between high and low groups in determining infection, it did significantly differ for participants who actually became ill with a cold. Participants with high

TABLE 20.1   Percentages of Virally Exposed Participants in Low- and High-Stress Groups Who Became Infected and Developed Clinical Colds Symptoms

	% INFECTED (n = 394)	% DEVELOPING COLD SYMPTOMS AMONG THOSE INFECTED (n = 325)
COMBINED STRESS INDEX		
Low	78.7	43.2
High	86.3*	47.7
LIFE EVENTS		
Low	80.9	40.1
High	84.6	52.5*
PERCEIVED STRESS		
Low	78.4	44.2
High	86.7*	46.8
NEGATIVE AFFECT		
Low	76.9	45.8
High	88.2*	45.4

*$p < .05$ between low and high groups.

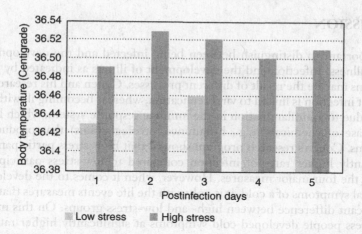

**FIGURE 20.1   Postinfection Body Temperature for High-
and Low-Stress Groups (Life Events Measure)**

numbers of negative life events had higher percentages of clinical colds than participants with low life events scores. This finding does suggest that the life events assessment is measuring something different from the other two measures (i.e., perceived stress and negative affect). The diagnosis of clinical cold in the data presented in Table 20.1 was made by clinical judgment. The data from the two other more objective sources of the presence of a cold, mucus weight in paper tissues and body temperature, provided mixed findings. Life events were not found to be associated with mucus weight changes in paper tissues (a good attempt at objective measurement that did not work). Participants with high numbers of life events did have correspondingly higher body temperature after infection than those participants with low numbers of life events. Figure 20.1 presents the average body temperature of high (more than two stressful events) and low (two or fewer stressful events) groups over the initial five days after being infected.

As you can see by the vertical axis scaling, the displayed centigrade temperature ranges from 36.4 to 36.55. The differences between high and low groups are quite small, but in all daily comparisons the high group always has a significantly higher body temperature than the low group ($p < .02$).

In analyzing the data among the three measured personality variables (self-esteem, personal control, and introversion-extroversion) and development of the common cold, no significant relationships were found. This suggests that these three broad personality measures had little to do with the development of the common cold. In addition, the data analysis did not find that the many health practices investigated played a role in the development of colds.

DISCUSSION

It is important to distinguish between being infected and the development of clinical illness. Infection and the development of illness as indicated by clinical symptoms may be the result of different processes. Cohen and his research team note that infection is linked to viral replication, whereas becoming ill with a cold may be due to an inflammation in the immune response system, which leads to the release of chemicals (e.g., histamines, prostaglandins) that produce cold symptoms. Cohen's research program showed that high-stress participants have significantly higher rates of infection compared to low-stress participants in three of the four major measures. However, when it comes to the development of clinical symptoms of a cold, it is only with the life events measures that we see a significant difference between high- and low-stress groups. On this measure, high-stress people developed cold symptoms at significantly higher rates than their low-stress counterparts.

This investigation provides evidence for a link between the psychological and environmental factors that play an important role in understanding a disease process. Simply focusing on organic, biochemical origins in understanding the development of illness may just reveal part of the picture. This research suggests that clinical medicine should focus attention on stress factors in understanding patient illness.

REFERENCES

Cohen, S., Tyrrell, D. A. J., & Smith, A. P. (1991). Psychological stress and susceptibility to the common cold. *New England Journal of Medicine, 325*, 606–612.

Cohen, S., Tyrrell, D. A. J., & Smith, A. P. (1993). Negative life events, perceived stress, negative affect, and susceptibility to the common cold. *Journal of Personality and Social Psychology, 64*, 131–140.

Cohen, S., & Williamson, G. (1988). Perceived stress in a probability sample of the United States. In S. Spacapan & S. Oskamp (Eds.), *The social psychology of health* (pp. 31–67). Newbury Park, CA: Sage.

Cohen, S., & Williamson, G. (1991). Stress and infectious disease in humans. *Psychological Bulletin, 109*, 5–24.

Felten, S. Y., & Olschowka, J. A. (1987). Noradrenergic sympathetic innervation of the spleen: II. Tyrosine hydroxylase (TH)-positive nerve terminals from synaptic-like contacts on lymphocytes in the splenic white pulp. *Journal of Neuroscience Research, 18*, 37–48.

Henderson, S., Byrne, D. G., & Duncan-Jones, P. (1981). *Neurosis and the social environment.* San Diego, CA: Academic Press.

Jemmott, J. B., III, & Locke, S. E. (1984). Psychosocial factors, immunologic mediation, and human susceptibility to infectious diseases: How much do we know? *Psychological Bulletin, 95*, 78–108.

Lazarus, R. S., & Folkman, S. (1984). *Stress, appraisal, and coping.* New York: Springer.

Shavit, Y., Lewis, J. W., Terman, G. S., Gale, R. P., & Liebeskind, J. C. (1984). Opioid peptides mediated the suppressive effect of stress on natural killer cell cytotoxicity. *Science, 223*, 188–190.

CHAPTER 21

SPACED OUT

Crowding. For most of us, living situations are likely to involve some crowding, now and in the future. Estimates vary, but it seems likely that the population of the world may double by the year 2040. Most of this increase is occurring in less-developed countries, but its effects will be felt everywhere. In more developed countries, the most noticeable increase in population density has been in the shift from rural areas to urban areas. However, even with population increases, you can still be by yourself if you want. In the United States, for example, there are 132 counties with fewer than two people per square mile. If that population density were applied to the five boroughs of New York City, only 600 people would live there, instead of 7.5 million (Duncan, 1993).

Psychologists who study population demographics make a distinction between the concepts of density and crowding. *Density* is an objective headcount; *crowding* is a subjective feeling. *Density* is the actual number of people living within a certain space. *Crowding* refers to the largely negative psychological feelings that can accompany living at high density. These feelings can range from generalized stress to specific feelings that other people are always in the way; that one never has a quiet moment to oneself. In some situations, architecture may be planned so that people can live at very high densities, yet not feel crowded. Nevertheless, some people feel crowded at very low densities.

This is one of the many areas in which it can be challenging to conduct meaningful studies on humans. One of the best-known early studies in this area involved laboratory rats (Calhoun, 1962). In this study, John Calhoun created a caged environment in which some rats ended up living at higher than usual densities. Calhoun observed a number of behaviors that appeared to be pathological when compared to the ordinary behavior of caged rats. There was more aggression among the rats at high density as well as failure to care for offspring. McCain, Cox, and Paulus (1976) studied prisons in which inmates lived at different densities. In the more dense living situations, there were higher rates of disciplinary problems, illness, suicide, and homicide. Making fair comparisons of different

Incorporating the research of A. Baum and G. E. Davis, "Reducing the Stress of High-Density Living: An Architectural Intervention," 1980, *Journal of Personality and Social Psychology, 38*, pp. 471–481.

prisons might be quite difficult because factors other than density probably play a role in the experience of crowding. It would be easy to imagine that through force of necessity corrections officers might act differently in more dense prisons than in less dense ones. If there were more prisoners per staff member in dense prisons, difficulties observed might be partially a result of staff ratios.

This situation in research is called a *confound*. A confound is some factor other than the variables under investigation that may make a difference in the dependent outcomes. In this situation, the outcomes—disciplinary problems, illness, suicide, and homicide—may be the result of density. However, density is also linked to, or confounded with, other factors, such as staff ratios. For example, assume that high density and poor staff ratios in prisons always occur together. If so, a study could not determine the individual influences of density and staffing because there would be no way to hold one constant while varying the other. In a real prison situation, this study would probably be too costly to undertake. As a general point, research has the most clear cut findings when one factor is varied and the others that might be important are held constant, or otherwise controlled. More complex research designs may have more than one independent variable. Even with these designs, a few things are systematically varied and everything else that is believed to be important is held as constant as possible.

An additional problem with prisons is that the people who are incarcerated are not representative of the rest of the population. It may be easy to study density and crowding in prisons where living situations are assigned, but this situation may not generalize to nonincarcerated groups. The question becomes, where can we find groups of nonincarcerated people living at high density and assigned to rooms . . . hmmmm . . . what about college students?

ALTERED STATES OF LIVING

Andrew Baum and Glenn Davis (1980) conducted an experiment in which the architecture of several college dormitories was manipulated in order to study the effects of crowding. As elsewhere in this book, we are being careful to use the word *experiment* to refer to a very specific kind of investigation. Three different kinds of living situations were compared, and they were the independent variable in this study. An older type of long-corridor dorm that housed 40 students was compared to a different building in which groups of 20 students lived in short-corridor arrangements. A third group of students lived on another floor of the long-corridor dorm, but this floor had undergone some architectural alterations. In the middle of the long corridor, three rooms that had been bedrooms were turned into lounges. Two sets of unlocked doors were installed adjacent to the lounges (Figure 21.1).

This arrangement had the effect of dividing the long corridor into two small corridors. The residency was reduced from 43 to 39 because two of the rooms that became lounges had been single occupancy and one had been double occupancy. Aside from this, the density on the floor was not changed. The doors and lounges tended to create two separate living units where once there had been only one.

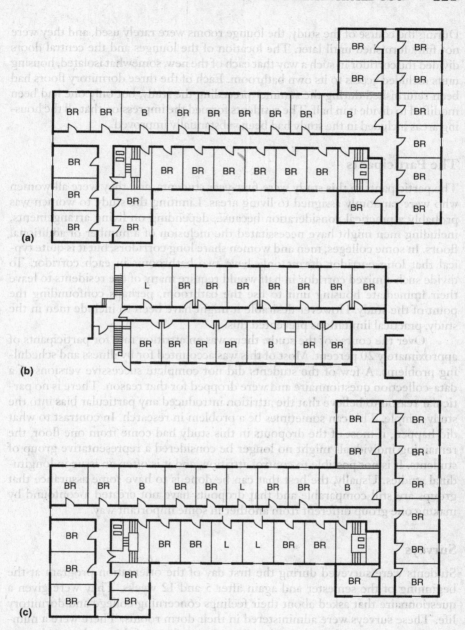

FIGURE 21.1 **Floor Plans of Dormitory Corridors.** (a) is the long-corridor arrangement, (b) is the short corridor, and (c) is the intervention floor—note lounge rooms and central doors in (c).

From "Reducing the Stress of High-Density Living: An Architectural Intervention," by A. Baum and G. Davis, 1980, *Journal of Personality and Social Psychology, 38*, p. 475. Copyright © 1980 by the American Psychological Association. Reprinted with permission.

During the course of the study, the lounge rooms were rarely used, and they were not fully furnished until later. The location of the lounges and the central doors divided the corridor in such a way that each of the new, somewhat isolated, housing units included access to its own bathroom. Each of the three dormitory floors had been refurbished during the summer preceding the study, but only one had been modified to divide it in half. The residents formed the impression that all the housing areas included in the study had been substantially improved.

The Participants

The participants in this study were first-year students, and they were all women who were randomly assigned to living areas. Limiting the study to women was probably a practical consideration because, depending on living arrangements, including men might have necessitated the inclusion of a number of additional floors. In some colleges, men and women share long corridors, but it is quite typical that long corridor dorms only have two bathrooms in each corridor. To divide such a mixed corridor in half would require many of the residents to leave their immediate housing unit to use the bathroom, perhaps confounding the point of the study. However desirable it might have been to include men in the study, practical limitations prevented this.

Over the course of the study, there was an attrition rate for participants of approximately 20 percent. Most of this was accounted for by illness and scheduling problems. A few of the students did not complete successive versions of a data-collection questionnaire and were dropped for that reason. There is no particular reason to believe that the attrition introduced any particular bias into the study sample. This can sometimes be a problem in research. In contrast to what did happen, if most of the dropouts in this study had come from one floor, the remaining individuals might no longer be considered a representative group of students. It is not possible to control attrition, and it is often an issue in longitudinal studies. Usually, the best that can be done is to have some assurance that groups are still comparable and that dropouts have not created a confound by making one group different from another in some important way.

Surveys

Students were surveyed during the first day of the orientation program at the beginning of the semester and again after 5 and 12 weeks. They were given a questionnaire that asked about their feelings concerning college and dormitory life. These surveys were administered in their dorm rooms. There were a number of questions on the surveys, but the primary focus of this study was the ratings about how crowded, hectic, and predictable students found dorm life. Students were also asked about expectations and success in maintaining control over social life and group formation. These survey responses served as operational definitions of the feeling of students about their living environments.

Naturalistic Observations

This study was unusual because it included some naturalistic observations among its dependent variables. Each floor was observed by a trained college-age male observer who was unaware of the hypothesis in the study. Three observations were made each week except for a few weeks that were abnormal (i.e., exam weeks or holidays). The observer moved through the three study sites recording the nature and location of social and nonsocial behavior, spending five minutes standing around in one end of the corridor then moving slowly to the other end and spending five minutes there. The observer also noted how many doors were open. Number of open doors was an operational definition of one type of sociability. The data were recorded covertly, and the success of this was illustrated by the fact that none of the residents were able to identify the observer when asked at the end of the semester.

Initial Laboratory Procedures

Eighteen students from each of the three groups were randomly selected for participation in the laboratory measures between the 5th and the 11th week of the investigation. Each of them arrived at the lab having been told that they were going to be in a study of "impression formation." On arrival, each participant was told that the study was running a few minutes late and was asked to wait in a waiting area. There were five chairs lined up against the wall, and a person was sitting in the first chair in the row. The participant was told that this was another participant for the lab study, but, in fact, this other person was a confederate of the experimenter. You will remember from previous chapters that a *confederate* in a psychological experiment is a person who is working for the experimenter and who behaves in some particular way as part of the setting of the experiment. The confederate in this study remained ready to respond, but did not make eye contact or initiate conversation.

The participant and the confederate were observed through a two-way mirror across from the chairs. The seat position of the participant was noted, and the number of seconds that the participant looked at the face of the confederate was recorded. The point of this was to assess the social behavior of the participants using the operational definition of visual attention to another person. It would have been possible to do this with some kind of questionnaire asking how each participant would interact with a stranger in a waiting room situation. Yet, what people say they would do and what they really do are sometimes different things. When people describe what they might do or think on a questionnaire, this is called a *soft measure* of behavior. When the actual behavior is observed, it is called a *hard measure*. This study had other hard measures that were taken in the naturalistic observation described previously. It would have been possible to ask residents how often they left their room door open—a soft measure, but in this case an observer recorded the door positions—a hard measure. Although it can be fairly easy to criticize the validity of soft measures, it is more difficult to do so for hard measures: the doors were open or they were not; faulty recollections or opinions could not corrupt the data.

A Measure of Persistence

After five minutes in the waiting room, the participant was given a questionnaire that asked, among other things, how comfortable the participant felt while waiting with the confederate in the laboratory. Next, the participant was ushered into a separate room and presented with 12 difficult, but solvable, anagrams. Each of these scrambled words was presented on a separate card. The participant was told that 20 seconds would be allowed to work on each one and that the work had to be done mentally, with no writing allowed. The participant was told that she could come back to any unsolved anagrams for additional trials as often as she wanted. This may seem a somewhat odd procedure, but it was really another hard measure, this time a behavioral measure of persistence. When the participant had either completed all the anagrams, or indicated that she did not want to continue, she was debriefed and thanked.

Survey Results

The dependent variables from the surveys showed some longitudinal trends on the floors. As the semester progressed, long-corridor residents reported more difficulty in being able to control their lives in the dormitories ($p < .001$). They reported that their lives were more hectic ($p < .01$). Another measure of this lack of control was the extent to which residents felt they could regulate their social contact. Over time, this measurement also indicated social problems on the long-corridor floor ($p < .001$), while the intervention floor residents appeared to have social attitudes similar to those on the short corridor. Figure 21.2 shows these results.

The actual numbers on the y-axis refer to a 5-point scale on which residents rated their agreement with statements about control and regulation of social contact.

Life on the long corridor also affected the friendships formed by residents. Survey data indicated that these students felt less successful at making friends and, as weeks went by, they felt they knew fewer other residents as friends. Although there were no differences in feelings of crowding among the three floors at orientation, by the 5th and 12th weeks the long-corridor residents felt more crowded than the others did.

A sinister trend toward learned helplessness also appeared among the long-corridor residents. In the psychological literature, learned helplessness refers to a pattern of behavior in which an individual no longer attempts to find remedies for aversive circumstances (Seligman, 1991; Seligman & Maier, 1967). Figure 21.3 contains survey responses that showed that long-corridor residents reported lower levels of motivation to gain some control over their housing situation ($p < .001$). In particular, they believed that it was not worth trying to structure social situations to improve social interactions with others ($p < .001$).

Naturalistic Observational Findings

The observational dependent measures tended to support the general impression that social activity decreased over the semester for the long-corridor

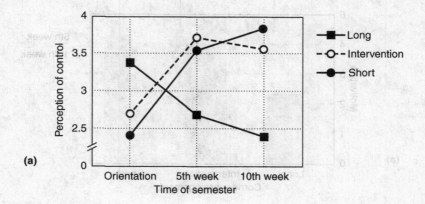

(a)

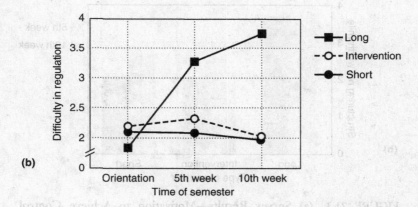

(b)

FIGURE 21.2 (a) **Survey Results—Perceived Control** (b) **Survey Results—Regulating Social Contact.** Survey results collected across the semester from residents in their dormitory rooms concerning (a) control of living situation and (b) ability to regulate their social contact.

residents when compared to the others. These data are presented in Figure 21.4.

The gaps in the data in Figure 21.4 are the weeks during which observations were not made. There are two measures displayed in this figure—the percentage of activity that was rated as social and the number of open doors. Open doors were chosen because Baum and Davis (1980) believed that they represented an aspect of social life: an indication that the residents of the room were open to social interaction. Although two different measures are shown in Figure 21.4, they both support the contention of decreased social activity in the long corridor. It is noteworthy that all groups appear to be similar at the beginning of the semester but not at the end. A statistical analysis of the data confirmed this.

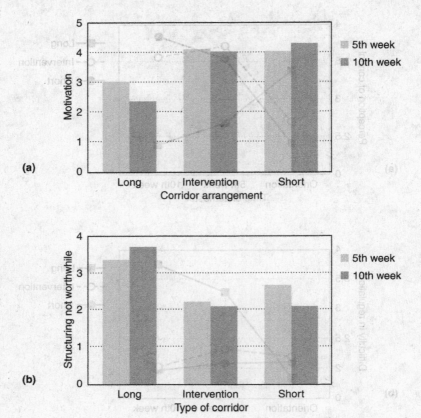

FIGURE 21.3   (a) Survey Results—Motivation to Achieve Control (b) Survey Results—Not Worth Structuring Sociality. Survey results collected across the semester from residents in their dormitory rooms concerning (a) motivation to achieve control over social interactions in the dormitory and (b) the worth of trying to structure situations to improve social interactions.

There were no significant differences among groups from the 3rd to the 9th week, but significant differences appeared in weeks 10 through 15 ($p < .001$).

In Figure 21.4, week 9 seems to show an increase in social activity on each of the floors. Baum and Davis (1980) believe that this was because week 8 was an open week, used by many students as a vacation. On returning in week 9, residents were more socially active as they reinvolved themselves in dormitory life. Although not expressed as a correlation coefficient, this point is based on correlational thinking. If you want to extrapolate this finding, you should be sure to tell your college administrators that dormitory life can be improved by having a vacation every week or two. We only make this suggestion to illustrate the care that should be exercised when correlational findings are assumed to be causal and applied to real situations.

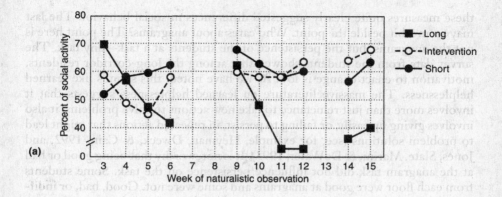

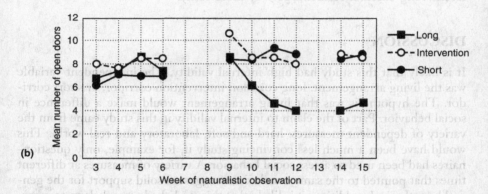

FIGURE 21.4   (a) Observed Percentage of Activity Rated as Social (b) Mean Open Doors during Observations. Data from covert observations in dormitories of percentage of activity that could be considered social (a) and number of open doors (b).

Laboratory Findings

The laboratory findings in this study consisted of both hard and soft measures. The hard measures were the number of seats left open between participant and confederate, the amount of time the participant spent looking at the confederate's face, and anagram performance. The soft measures included questionnaire ratings of discomfort, rated on a 7-point scale, while waiting for the anagram task to begin. The results of these assessments are presented in Table 21.1.

As with the other measures, the data presented in Table 21.1 support the hypothesis that long-corridor living has a detrimental effect on social behavior. Long-corridor residents chose to sit farther away from the confederate in the lab waiting area ($p < .05$), they spent less time looking at the confederate's face ($p < .05$), and they were more uncomfortable waiting for the lab procedure to begin ($p < .05$) (although, of course, for them it had already begun, but they did not know it). They also attempted fewer anagrams ($p < .01$). The first three of these measures quite clearly suggested differences in social behavior. The last may seem a bit beside the point. Who cares about anagrams? The point here is not the anagrams, but the persistence of the students at a task—any task. The survey data from the students showed that among the long-corridor residents, motivation to enact change is low. As we have noted, this sounds like learned helplessness. The massive literature on learned helplessness suggests that it involves more than just reluctance to take new actions to solve problems, it also involves giving up easily, or failing to persist, in repeated actions that might lead to problem solutions (see, for example, Heyman, Dweck, & Cain, 1992, and Jones, Slate, Marini, & DeWater, 1993). It is noteworthy that being good or bad at the anagram task did not influence persistence on the task. Some students from each floor were good at anagrams and some were not. Good, bad, or indifferent, long-corridor residents gave up more easily.

DISCUSSION

It is likely that this study had high internal validity. The independent variable was the living arrangement: long corridor, intervention corridor, or short corridor. The hypothesis was that living arrangement would make a difference in social behavior. Part of the claim to internal validity in this study came from the variety of dependent measures: hard and soft, laboratory and real world. This would have been a much less convincing study if, for example, only questionnaires had been used to assess social behavior. A variety of measures at different times that pointed to the same conclusions suggested solid support for the general hypothesis. In addition, it is likely that this study had a good claim to external validity. It is not known if men or upper-level students would have reacted

TABLE 21.1   Mean Responses in Laboratory Measures

	SEATS AWAY FROM CONFEDERATE	FACIAL REGARD FOR CONFEDERATE (SECS)	DISCOMFORT AFTER WAITING	NUMBER OF ANAGRAMS ATTEMPTED
Long corridor	2.6	18.2	4.3	15.8
Intervention corridor	1.9	50.3	2.8	21.8
Short corridor	2.0	52.2	2.7	20.6

Note: In each column, the long corridor score is statistically significantly different ($p < .05$) from the scores of residents from the other two corridors.

differently but, otherwise, there are many reasons to believe that subdivisions of long corridors would have positive social effects.

Baum and Davis (1980) pointed out that this kind of architectural intervention does not have to be very expensive. The actual changes to the building were minimal, and the largest cost to the college was the lost revenue from the three rooms that became lounges. The lounges themselves did not seem to be a necessary part of the intervention, but having them there as unoccupied space may have increased the perception that the intervention corridor was smaller.

For us, the most striking thing about the findings of this study was the extent to which a seemingly small intervention had persistent effects on the lives of the individuals involved. The real value of an experiment is that the results can be cautiously interpreted in cause-and-effect terms. The students were randomly assigned to the three floors, and there is no indication that the groups were different at the beginning of the study. Indeed, the data that were collected during orientation showed no significant differences among groups. The differences appeared as the semester unfolded. The effect of housing on social behavior in the dormitories was robustly demonstrated in this study. Perhaps the biggest surprise was the extent to which the influence of the housing unit seemed to permeate the lives of these students beyond the living unit. We might not have guessed that the social behavior of the long-corridor dwellers would be different in the laboratory setting.

The suggestions of helplessness that accompany crowding in this study imply that college housing should not be taken lightly. The beginning year of college is a time when it is very important for students to begin to take charge of their own lives. The frightening conclusion that might be drawn from this study is that those students who live in crowded environments become less likely to try to do something about situations that have made them unhappy. If this becomes a lifestyle trend, there is likely to be more unhappiness for them in the future.

REFERENCES

Baum, A., & Davis, G. E. (1980). Reducing the stress of high-density living: An architectural intervention. *Journal of Personality and Social Psychology, 38,* 471–481.

Calhoun, J. B. (1962). Population density and social pathology. *Scientific American, 206,* 139–148.

Duncan, D. (1993). *Miles from nowhere.* New York: Penguin.

Heyman, G., Dweck, C., & Cain, K. (1992). Young children's vulnerability to self-blame and helplessness: Relationship to beliefs about goodness. *Child Development, 63,* 401–415.

Jones, C., Slate, J., Marini, I., & DeWater, B. (1993). Academic skills and attitudes towards intelligence. *Journal of College Student Development, 34,* 422–424.

McCain, G., Cox, V., & Paulus, P. (1976). The relationship between illness, complaints, and degree of crowding in a prison environment. *Environment and Behavior, 8,* 283–290.

Seligman, M., & Maier, S. (1967). Failure to escape traumatic shock. *Journal of Experimental Psychology, 37B,* 1–21.

Seligman, M. E. P. (1991). *Learned optimism.* New York: Knopf.

■ ■ ■ ■ ■

CHAPTER 22

WEIGHT LOSS THAT WORKS

Obesity affects one-third of the population in the United States and represents a serious public health problem. It affects both physical and psychological health (Kuczmarski, Flegal, Campbell & Johnson, 1994). Obesity is a medical condition that refers to being severely overweight and is directly linked to diabetes, high blood pressure, and coronary heart diseases (Pi-Sunyer, 1994). Obesity affects how other people perceive and treat each other and even how you may view yourself. Ryckman, Robbins, Kaczor, and Gold (1989) reported that obese people are often stereotyped as slow, sloppy, and lazy.

For many years, behavioral approaches to weight management were the principal modes of treatment for obesity (Sbrocco, Nedergaard, Stone, & Lewis, 1998). Such programs, however, have been criticized for high relapse rates and for promoting a mentality of dieting (Brownell & Rodin, 1994; Garner & Wooley, 1991; Glenny, O'Meara, Melville, Sheldon, & Wilson, 1997).

In recent years, some newer treatments have emerged that do not stress dieting as the dominant strategy to permanent weight loss (Ciliska, 1990; Omichinski & Harrison, 1995). The idea behind these strategies is that discontinuing the diet orientation to food may be psychologically beneficial and may result in stable weight loss in the long term. Unfortunately, there have been only a few real empirical tests of these newer approaches to permanent weight management. The present research is designed to empirically examine the efficacy of a traditional behavior therapy (TBT) approach compared to a cognitive-behavioral approach (behavioral choice therapy; BCT), which emphasizes individual choices and minimizes *dieting*.

Incorporating the research of T. Sbrocco, C. Nedergaard, J. M. Stone, and E. L. Lewis, "Behavioral Choice Treatment Promotes Continuing Weight Loss: Preliminary Results of a Cognitive-Behavioral Decision-Based Treatment for Obesity," 1999, *Journal of Consulting and Clinical Psychology*, 67, pp. 260–266.

PRESENT STUDY

The BCT approach uses decision theory to relate eating behavior in certain situations to outcomes and goals (Sbrocco & Schlundt, 1998). People's goals regarding food choices go well beyond the need to satisfy hunger and extend to factors such as self-esteem and social acceptance. Research has shown that obese women were not aware of the positive reinforcers that served to maintain their maladaptive eating behaviors. Other research by Sbrocco and colleagues (Sbrocco et al., 1998; Sbrocco & Schlundt, 1998) indicate that obese women in traditional dieting programs failed to learn to eat in moderation and often overate or underate. In contrast, women with normal weight generally were moderate eaters. This research suggests that obese women would benefit from learning to eat in moderation and learning that they had choices and could make decisions about what to eat. It was hypothesized that a treatment plan centered on (1) learning to eat moderately, (2) learning to exercise moderately, and (3) disconnecting eating and self-evaluation (i.e., how you feel about yourself) might prove effective in promoting more permanent weight loss.

In the present study, it was expected that the TBT participants would achieve greater weight loss in the active treatment phase, but would gain back weight after the cessation of treatment. In contrast, it was hypothesized that the BCT participants would lose weight more gradually than the TBT participants during the active treatment phase, but would continue a gradual steady weight loss into the nontreatment follow-up phases. This assumption was based on the hypothesis that the BCT groups would learn a pattern of moderate eating and moderate exercise, whereas the TBT group would only be instructed to diet and reduce their caloric intake. It was also hypothesized that the BCT participants would experience an increase in self-esteem compared to the TBT group because the BCT participants would choose to eat in moderation, would gain an understanding of their eating behavior, and would be successful in controlling their weight.

METHOD

The participants in this study were women between the ages of 18 and 55 who were 30 percent to 60 percent above established body weight chart limits. The women responded to newspaper advertisements looking for participants for the study. All participants were in good health, were nonsmokers, and had medical clearance for participation. Participants paid a $150 fee to be part of the study, which was refunded to them at the end of the program. It is likely that the researchers imposed a fee to increase participant commitment to the program. Several participants paid a reduced fee because of their financial situation. All participants completed a two-week pretreatment phase during which they recorded their eating, weight, and other information. There were twenty-four women in the final participant pool. Half of them were randomly assigned to the BCT group and the other half to the TBT group.

Measures

PHYSICAL

Weight and body mass index (BMI) were calculated at pretreatment, at weekly meetings, at posttreatment, and at follow-up sessions. Height was determined at pretreatment. BMI was calculated using height and weight.

BEHAVIORAL COMMITMENT

The number of sessions attended and the number of self-monitored records that participants kept were used as indices of adherence and dedication to the treatment program.

EATING RECORDS

Participants were trained to use a Psion palmtop computer to record self-monitored behavior. The Comcard Compute-A-Diet Nutrient Balance System (1993) software facilitated the standardized recording of foods eaten and situational factors associated with eating behavior. The Comcard software contained a list of almost 4,000 foods. Participants were instructed to weigh all foods on a scale and to respond to six computer-generated questions regarding the context of their eating. Specifically, the participants were asked to record the following data about their eating: date, time, location, level of hunger, level of stress, and with whom they ate. From this data, immediate and weekly feedback, as well as individualized goals, were provided to the participants. The researchers monitored caloric intake as a measure of adherence to the caloric prescription that they set for the participants.

PSYCHOLOGICAL SELF-REPORT MEASURES

The following self-report measures were completed at pretreatment, midtreatment, posttreatment, three-month follow-up, and six-month follow-up:

- Eating Inventory-Restraint Scale   (Stunkard & Messick, 1988). This scale was employed to assess changes in dietary restraint.
- Eating Disorders Inventory-2   (EDI-2; Garner, 1991). This scale was used to measure behavioral and cognitive characteristics observed clinically in eating disorders. The following three subscales of the EDI-2 were used in the present research: Drive for Thinness, Bulimia, and Body Dissatisfaction.
- State Self-Esteem Scale   (SSES; Heatherton & Polivy, 1991). Designed to assess clinical changes in self-esteem.
- Beck Depression Inventory   (BDI; Beck, Ward, Mendelson, Mock, & Erbaugh, 1961). Designed to assess symptoms of depression.

Participants were scheduled to attend 13 weekly 1.5-hour behavioral weight management treatment sessions that were run by experienced professionals. The same professionals facilitated both the TBT and the BCT groups. Participants in both groups were given two-week meal plans, including recipe booklets. The only difference between the two groups was the amount of food that each was prescribed to eat. The TBT participants were given a 1,200 kcal/day (5,023 kJ) diet. The BCT participants were given a 1,800 kcal/day (7,534 kJ) diet. Both groups of participants were told to abide by the specific requirements of their plan and were offered encouragement. At weekly meetings, each participant's Psion diary data was downloaded and immediate feedback was provided, including graphic presentations of caloric intake, fat intake, a list of their highest-fat foods, and alternative low-fat food options. Participants were instructed to eat at a constant caloric rate to avoid overeating or overrestricting food intake. The two groups were treated exactly the same in terms of meeting topics, length of sessions, homework, contact with treatment leaders, self-monitoring of eating behavior, and exercise instructions. The prescribed exercise for both groups was home-based walking for 30 min/day, in a single session, 3 days each week. Participants maintained records of the exercise they completed.

Traditional Behavior Therapy (TBT) Plan. Schlundt's (1987) treatment model, consisting of 12 weeks of active treatment, has been shown to produce a short-term weight loss of approximately 12 lb (5.45 kg). This was the treatment given to the TBT group. The participants were informed that the goal of the program was to promote significant weight loss and to help them maintain the loss using behavioral approaches. Participants were taught three different techniques to assist in their weight loss program. The first was self-monitoring, which involves the systematic observation and recording of one's own behavior(s). Because people may have inaccurate ideas about how they behave, self-monitoring provides them (and their therapist) an objective profile of observed behavior(s). The second technique participants learned was stimulus control of behavior, which teaches people about how behaviors may be influenced by stimuli or environmental events in their lives. This technique allowed the participants to analyze, understand, and begin to modify their own eating behavior(s). Behavioral substitution was the third technique that participants learned to assist in their weight loss program. It involves the replacement of a maladaptive or problematic behavior (e.g., overeating) with a more adaptive behavior. Participants were encouraged to avoid high-calorie, high-fat foods and to keep their daily caloric intake to 1,200 kcal (5,023 kJ). Participants were instructed to explore their reasons for eating. If stress was a factor that led participants to eat, they were instructed to substitute another behavior in place of eating.

Behavioral Choice Treatment (BCT) Plan. The participants were informed that their treatment plan for weight loss was not based on dieting. In fact, participants in the BCT group were instructed *not* to diet. Part of their treatment was to view eating as a choice. They were also told that their weight loss would be slower than under traditional plans, but that permanent weight loss was the ultimate treatment goal. Concepts of healthy behavioral choices, appropriate food selection, exercise options, and developing healthy patterns of eating were stressed. Participants learned to identify their own choices and the consequences that controlled these decisions. Participants were helped to modify and restructure their thinking in order to enable them to select healthy foods. If a participant felt badly about eating a high-calorie or high-fat food, cognitive restructuring and behavioral modeling were used to enable the participant to eat a small amount of the "taboo" food and thereby develop the cognitive belief that she could handle such foods in moderation. Being able to eat in moderation and to eat small quantities of high calorie foods were seen as skills that could be learned. Three different learning techniques were used in the BCT group: cognitive restructuring, modeling, and homework assignments. Cognitive restructuring is the process of helping clients identify self-defeating or irrational thoughts and replacing them with more appropriate ones. Modeling is the learning strategy discussed in Chapter 8. This form of learning is based on observing how others act and imitating their behavior. Homework assignments are often used to take behaviors learned in treatment and apply or practice them in the "real world." Participants in the BCT group were told to eliminate the word *dieting* from their language and thinking, as well as the associated concepts of food restriction and rigid rules. They were encouraged to engage in pleasurable, positive activities not associated with eating and to participate in regular exercise. Finally, they were encouraged to accept themselves for who they were and lessen their concern about bodyweight and eating behavior. They were instructed to focus on the future and look toward their ultimate goal weight rather than focusing on dieting. Focusing on dieting leads people to believe that the goal is to lose as much weight as possible in the shortest amount of time.

RESULTS

Demographic data collected from the participants in the TBT and BCT groups showed that they did not differ significantly in age ($M = 43.1$, $M = 39.6$); weight ($M = 89.54$ kg, $M = 89.56$ kg); or caloric intake ($M = 9,964$ kj, $M = 10,654$ kj). A kilocalorie (kcal), what most of us call a calorie, can be converted to kilojoules (kJ) by multiplying by 4.184. Therefore, a person on a 2,000-kcal diet is on an 8,368-kJ diet.

Figure 22.1 shows the weight changes (in kilograms; 1 lb = .454 kg) for all treatment and follow-up assessments. The data analysis shows that the TBT groups had greater weight loss at the midtreatment assessment. The groups did not differ at the 3-month follow-up. There was, however, a difference between the groups at both the 6- and the 12-month follow-ups, at which times the BCT group achieved significantly greater weight loss than the TBT group.

Participants' commitment to treatment was reviewed by checking their self-reported diet adherence and exercise commitment. Daily caloric consumption

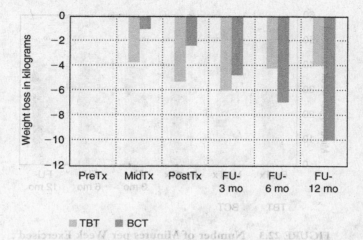

FIGURE 22.1   Weight Changes (in Kilograms) from Pre-treatment to 12-Month Follow-Up

differed significantly between the two groups. The TBT group consumed, on average, approximately 1,363 kcal, while the BCT group consumed, on average, approximately 1,674 kcal. This was not unexpected because the TBT group was instructed to consume 1,200 kcal/day and the BCT was instructed to consume 1,800 kcal/day. The data indicated that the TBT group was consuming more than instructed, while the BCT group was consuming less than instructed.

Figures 22.2 and 22.3 illustrate the frequency (days/week) and duration (minutes/week) of exercise from pretreatment until the 12-month follow-up

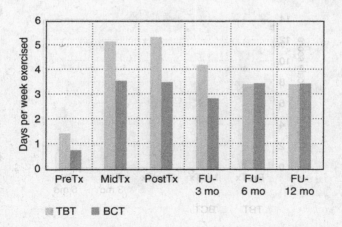

FIGURE 22.2   Number of Days per Week Exercised from Pretreatment to 12-Month Follow-Up

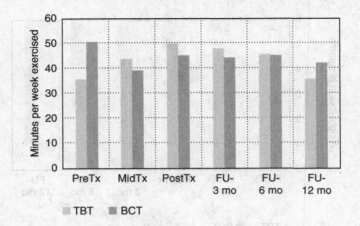

FIGURE 22.3   Number of Minutes per Week Exercised from Pretreatment to 12-Month Follow-Up

for both groups. Both groups significantly increased their frequency of exercise during the treatment phase of the study, with greater increases observed in the TBT group. The frequency of exercise for the BCT group tended to be constant from midtreatment to posttreatment. The TBT group tended to decrease exercise frequency from posttreatment to 12-month follow-up. Despite the reported differences at some points of assessment, there were no overall significant differences between groups in their exercise frequency at any of the three follow-ups.

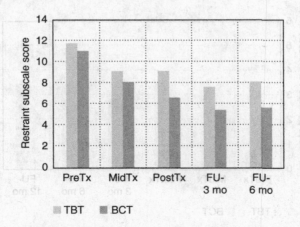

FIGURE 22.4   Restraint Subscale (Eating Inventory) from Pretreatment to 12-Month Follow-Up

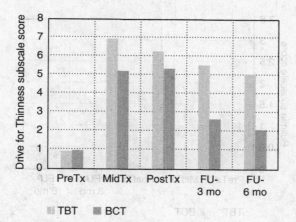

FIGURE 22.5 Drive for Thinness Subscale (Eating Inventory) from Pretreatment to 12-Month Follow-up

The self-report measures recorded by participants in both groups are displayed in Figures 22.4 through 22.9. The Restraint subscale of the Eating Inventory showed no significant differences between the BCT and TBT groups during active treatment. However, the groups did differ significantly in posttreatment follow-up, with the BCT group indicating lower Restraint scores. On the Drive for Thinness subscale of the EDI-2, there was no significant difference

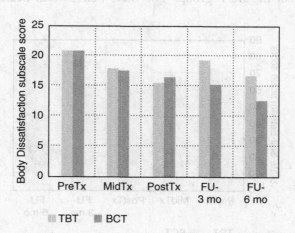

FIGURE 22.6 Body Dissatisfaction Subscale (Eating Disorders Inventory-2) from Pretreatment to 12-Month Follow-Up

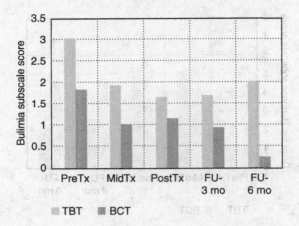

FIGURE 22.7   Bulimia Subscale (Eating Inventory) from Pretreatment to 12-Month Follow-Up

seen between the BCT and TBT groups. There was a trend on the EDI-2 Body Dissatisfaction subscale in which the BCT group showed less body dissatisfaction across the sessions and follow-ups, while the TBT group showed the opposite—more body dissatisfaction over time. The EDI-2 Bulimia scale did not suggest that either group evidenced clinical scores of bulimia, an eating disorder, nor were there any differences noted between the BCT and TBT groups. There was a trend, however, for the TBT group to have higher scores at all assessment checkpoints than the BCT group. The State Self-Esteem Scales showed no

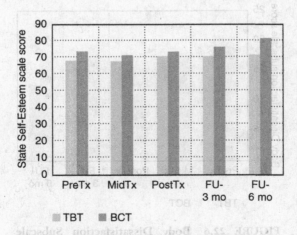

FIGURE 22.8 State Self-Esteem Scale from Pretreatment to 12-Month Follow-Up

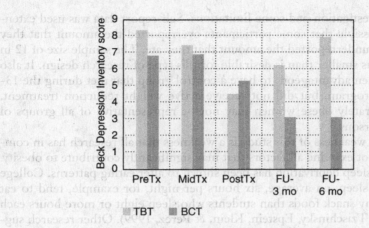

FIGURE 22.9 Beck Depression Inventory from Pretreatment to 12-Month Follow-Up

differences between groups at pretreatment with both BCT and TBT participants showing favorable levels of self-esteem. In both the BCT and the TBT groups, there was a trend of increased self-esteem during the course of treatment and follow-up. The Beck Depression Inventory showed no differences between groups at pretreatment and no significant differences over the course of the treatment. Neither group evidenced significant levels of depression. The depression scores of the BCT group continued to drop (i.e., lower levels of depression) in follow-up, while the scores of the TBT group increased to pretreatment levels over time.

DISCUSSION

This research is notable for the maintenance of weight loss by the BCT group up to one year after active treatment. Typically, traditional behavioral weight reduction programs have a pattern of weight regain after the cessation of ongoing treatment (Glenny et al., 1997). The exercise findings for the BCT participants were also encouraging because the group continued to exercise throughout the follow-up period. In contrast, the exercise pattern for the TBT participants started out with a bang and then tapered off. According to the guidelines of the National Heart, Lung and Blood Institute (1998), the typical BCT participant went from a BMI of 32.82 to a BMI of 29.13 after 15 months. This represents a diagnostic change from Obese to Overweight. The typical weight loss for the BCT was 11 percent. To calculate your own BMI, you can visit the BMI calculator at the The National Institutes of Health website: www.nhlbisupport.com/bmi/bmicalc.htm.

This investigation had some limitations. Self-report data was used extensively. It is possible that some participants overreported the amount that they exercised and underreported the amount that they ate. The sample size of 12 in each group was smaller than is desirable for this type of research design. It also might have been advantageous to have a control group that met during the 13-week active program, but did not receive active weight reduction treatment. Finally, moderately obese women may not be representative of all groups of overweight persons.

Another weakness of this study is a weakness that all research has in common—it did not examine all factors that may significantly contribute to obesity. For example, sleep deprivation has been shown to alter eating patterns. College students who sleep, on average, six hours per night, for example, tend to eat more unhealthy snack foods than students who sleep eight or more hours each night (Latzer, Tzischinsky, Epstein, Klein, & Perez, 1999). Other research suggests a link between stress, sleep deprivation, and the stress hormone cortisol.

Cortisol is a hormone that is secreted when people are under stress. When cortisol is secreted in response to sudden danger, it can be beneficial by helping mobilize the body's resources to deal with the source of the danger. When people are under persistent stress, however, cortisol levels can remain high for extended periods of time and begin to tax the body. Cortisol levels decrease when people sleep. When people are sleep deprived, their cortisol levels remain high. Sleep deprivation itself can be an additional source of stress, contributing to even higher cortisol levels. Research has found a positive association between cortisol levels and the amount of calories that people consume (Epel, Lapidus, McEwen, & Brownell, 2001). Taken together, these findings suggest that there may be a physiological basis for the relationship between stress and unhealthy eating.

Despite the drawbacks we have discussed, the research by Sbrocco et al., is an excellent example of how cognitive-behavioral, health-focused treatment can be used to manage an important public health problem. Cognitive-behavioral therapies have been demonstrated to be effective in treating other maladaptive behaviors as well, such as bulimia (Agras, Walsh, Fairburn, Wilson, & Kraemer, 2000) and social anxiety (Heimberg, 2002), and show great promise for addressing other behavioral problems.

REFERENCES

Agras, W. S., Walsh, B. T., Fairburn, C. G., Wilson, G. T., & Kraemer, H. C. (2000). A multicenter comparison of cognitive-behavioral therapy and interpersonal psychotherapy for Bulimia Nervosa. *Archives of General Psychiatry, 57,* 459–466.

Beck, A. T., Ward, C. H., Mendelson, M., Mock, J., & Erbaugh, J. (1961). An inventory for measuring depression. *Archives of General Psychiatry, 4,* 53–63.

Brownell, K. D., & Rodin J. (1994). The dieting maelstrom: Is it possible and advisable to lose weight? *American Psychologist, 49,* 781–791.

Ciliska, D. (1990). Beyond dieting: Psychoeducational interventions for chronically obese women. A non-dieting approach. In P. E. Garfinkel & D. M. Garner (Eds.), *Eating disorders* (Monograph series no. 5). New York: Brunner/Mazel.

Compute-A-Diet Nutrient Balance System [computer software]. (1993). Worcestershire, England: Comcard.

Epel, E., Lapidus, R., McEwen, B., & Brownell, K. (2001). Stress may add bite to appetite in women: A laboratory study of stress-induced cortisol and eating behavior. *Psychoneuroendocrinology, 26*, 37–49.

Garner, D. M. (1991). *The Eating Disorder Inventory—2 professional manual.* Odessa, FL: Psychological Assessment Resources.

Garner, D. M., & Wooley, S. C. (1991). Confronting the failure of behavioral and dietary treatments for obesity. *Clinical Psychology Review, 11*, 729–780.

Glenny, A. M., O'Meara, S., Melville, A., Sheldon, T. A., & Wilson, C. (1997). The treatment and prevention of obesity: A systematic review of the literature. *International Journal of Obesity, 21*, 715–737.

Heatherton, T. F., & Polivy, J. (1991). Development and validation of a scale for measuring state self-esteem. *Journal of Personality and Social Psychology, 60*, 895–910.

Heimberg, R. G. (2002). Cognitive-behavioral therapy for Social anxiety disorder: Current status and future directions. *Biological Psychiatry, 51*, 101–108.

Kuczmarski, R. J., Flegal, K. M., Campbell, S. M., & Johnson, C. L. (1994). Increasing prevalence of overweight among U.S. adults. *JAMA. 272*, 205–211.

Latzer, Y., Tzischinsky, O., Epstein, R., Klein, E., & Perez, L. (1999). Naturalistic sleep monitoring in women suffering from bulimia nervosa. *International Journal of Eating Disorders, 26*, 315–321.

National Heart, Lung and Blood Institute. (1998). *Clinical guidelines of the identification, evaluation, and treatment of overweight and obesity in adults.* Washington, DC: Author.

Omichinski, L., & Harrison, K. (1995). Reduction of dieting attitudes and practices after participation in a nondiet lifestyle program. *Journal of the Canadian Dietetic Association, 56*, 81–85.

Pi-Sunyer, F. X. (1994). The fattening of America. *JAMA, 272*(3), 238–239.

Ryckman, R. M., Robbins, M. A., Kaczor, L. M., & Gold, J. A. (1989). Male and female raters' stereotyping of male and female physiques. *Personality and Social Psychology Bulletin, 15*, 244–251.

Sbrocco, T., Nedergaard, R. C., Stone, J. M., & Lewis, E. L. (1998). *Differences in decision making patterns among obese and normal weight women.* Unpublished manuscript.

Sbrocco, T., Nedergaard, C., Stone, J. M., & Lewis, E. L. (1999). Behavioral choice treatment promotes continuing weight loss: Preliminary results of a cognitive-behavioral decision-based treatment for obesity. *Journal of Consulting and Clinical Psychology, 67*, 260–266.

Sbrocco, T., & Schlundt, D. G. (1998). *Applying decision theory to understand cognitive regulation in dieting: "Dysregulation" makes sense.* Manuscript submitted for publication.

Schlundt, D. G. (1987). *Helping others lose weight: A step-by-step program.* Nashville, TN: Author.

Stunkard, A. J., & Messick, S. (1988). *The Eating Inventory.* San Antonio, TX: Psychological Corporation.

■ ■ ■ ■ ■

CHAPTER 23

I THINK I CAN, I THINK I CAN

The way we think about our own abilities can have a serious impact on our performance. *Ability* is an interesting concept because it is often contrasted with another concept, *performance*. *Ability*, by definition, is supposed to refer to potential for behavior, whereas *performance* more often refers to the observed level of behavior. *Ability* is a somewhat slippery concept because it cannot be directly observed. Some psychologists believe that there are tests that can measure ability, but not all scientists agree (Cohen, 1998). Research in psychology has identified two different views that people might take concerning ability. The first of these, the *entity* view, is most in line with the standard definition: it treats ability as a fixed quantity that will not change. In this view, one possesses a certain amount of ability and that is all there is ever going to be. A person may not perform up to potential, but regardless of whether full potential is reached, it is limited. In contrast, the *incremental* view suggests that if a person wants more ability, it can be gained through hard work.

These two views of ability are closely related to another concept: *self-efficacy*. Self-efficacy refers to the judgments that individuals make about their capabilities to mobilize the motivation, cognitive resources, and courses of action needed to enable future performance on a specific task. If you have self-efficacy about some particular behavior, it means you believe you can perform the behavior, and, probably, you also believe that you are quite good at it. Just as with *The Little Engine That Could* in the children's story, research has shown that self-efficacious beliefs can lead to actual differences in performance.

SELF-EFFICACY IN JOB TRAINING

In contrast to the situation of earlier generations, it is now unrealistic to expect to enter the workforce and find lifetime employment with one company. The website of the California Trade and Commerce Agency sounds a contemporary warning: the average worker can expect to change jobs about six times, often as a

Incorporating the research of J. J. Martocchio, "Effects of Conceptions of Ability on Anxiety, Self-Efficacy, and Learning in Training," 1994, *Journal of Applied Psychology, 79*, pp. 819–825.

result of factors that go beyond personal dissatisfaction. Companies are frequently rearranged, moved, and downsized. Jobs within organizations can quickly cease to exist, being replaced by other positions requiring different skills. Because of financial pressures, workplaces are being transformed into high-performance sites where cost can be the single most important factor in personnel decisions. New jobs typically require rapidly changing skill sets that will require lifelong learning for all workers.

The federal government is spending considerable amounts of money on job training programs in an attempt to train or retrain workers of all ages. Most of this money is being distributed in the form of grants to states for the establishment of vocational training programs. Much of the research about job training has focused on learning specific skills (Gagné, 1962). However, as long ago as the 1940s, a program called job instruction training (JIT) recognized that putting the trainee "at ease" was an important part of job training programs (Gold, 1981). Unlike other approaches that merely gave instruction and manipulated rewards, this component of JIT recognized that workers' attitudes were an important part of learning. It may seem obvious that positive attitudes toward learning can result in better learning, but many job training programs have neglected cognitive states. Although putting a person at ease may involve physical arrangements such as having adequate light and sufficiently comfortable work surroundings, it could also include a variety of attitudes (Kraiger, Ford, & Salas, 1993). Some of the attitudes that have been found to increase the probability that an individual will benefit from training are realistic expectations about learning (Hicks & Klimoski, 1987), self-confidence (Tannenbaum, Cannon-Bowers, Salas, & Mathieu, 1993), and self-efficacy (Mitchell, Hopper, Daniels, George-Falvy, & James, 1994).

Martocchio (1994) studied the extent to which beliefs about self-efficacy and ability affected the performance of an adult population who was learning to use computers for the first time. If you have ever tried to teach computer skills to someone who has never used a computer at all, you will appreciate the complexity of this task. Many small routines are learned as part of computer literacy. Frequent computer users take these routines for granted. They are so commonplace to users that they may not be mentioned by instruction manuals. Consider the difference between the location of the cursor on a screen of word-processed material and of the mouse pointer on the screen. Anyone who has word processed very much will not confuse these two. Furthermore, people skilled in word processing will know that clicking the mouse will move the cursor to the mouse pointer's location on the screen, but that the mouse pointer will be "left behind" in that location by the cursor as soon as keyboarding starts adding new lines to the text. This is a difficult concept to fully describe in print. Instruction manuals are inclined to leave this out, assuming that people know it. If people are not aware of this convention, it may take a long time to learn. There are hundreds of other little procedures that enable experienced users to quickly figure out new software.

Adults who use computers for the first time may experience substantial fear of the machine. They have probably heard stories of computers "crashing" or "locking up," and they fear that some accidental combination of keystrokes will destroy the machine or, at least, result in loss of software or data. Nevertheless, adults who are looking for good jobs will probably have to learn some computer skills. Martocchio believed that individuals who had incremental ideas about ability, seeing ability as acquirable, might see computer training as an opportunity, not a threat. Martocchio designed a field study to examine this. It was probably an experiment, but the details of participant assignment to groups are not presented. When this happens you will have to exercise your own judgment about the research method. This field study was conducted in a real setting with real job trainees. These real-world setting factors give this study a greater claim to external validity than if the experiment had been conducted in a lab with college students pretending to be job trainees. The study offered three related hypotheses containing the following propositions:

HYPOTHESIS 1

People who were trained to believe that computer skills were an acquirable ability would experience lower levels of computer anxiety following training than they experienced before training. In contrast, trainees who experienced entity information about computer skills during training would have more computer anxiety after training than before it.

HYPOTHESIS 2

Trainees given the acquirable skill, or incremental, condition would show greater computer efficacy beliefs after training, compared to before. Trainees in the entity condition would report less computer efficacy following training.

HYPOTHESIS 3

Trainees' acquisition of declarative knowledge about computers would be influenced by computer anxiety and efficacy, as assessed by posttraining measures.

Participants

Seventy-six service and administrative employees of a large public university participated. Almost half of them were men, and the average age of the entire group was 42.2 years. A little more than 80 percent of these people had never used a computer before. The others indicated that coworkers had written down specific instructions about which keys to press, but the implication was that they had virtually no knowledge of the machine beyond a few specific instructions.

Procedure

Each participant was provided with an identification number that researchers used to link the measures of behavior taken before and after training. Participants were told, in advance, that this number would not be used to connect their performance in training with their name. This was a strategy for protecting these participants from thinking that their employer might have monitored their training. The goal was to avoid job-related threats of adverse outcomes for insufficient progress. Issuance of identification numbers to link various measures is a procedure often used when it is desirable that participants remain anonymous. Some voluntary medical tests, such as tests for HIV infection, use this as a way of linking blood samples to test results, allowing the identification of different pieces of data from the same person without the use of names.

The training program involved a 3-hour course that constituted an introduction to computing. A lecture was delivered, after which trainees used computers to practice the routines that were covered in the lecture. In the lecture, the researcher, who served as the instructor for the training, began the session with introductory remarks. Next, participants introduced themselves, and each stated the personal goal he or she had for the session. After this, each trainee filled out a questionnaire. At the end of the training session, another questionnaire was administered followed by a short multiple-choice test of computer knowledge. Finally, they were debriefed.

A number of measures were taken before any training began. The purpose of these was to provide assurance that the groups, which received different research manipulations, were equivalent at the beginning of the study. Demographic measures were collected to assess the equivalence of experimental groups before they received the training that included the independent variable. Age, sex, education, length of service with the university, occupation, and computer experience were recorded. Participants' expectations for training were also assessed. Participants rated the likelihood that using a computer would result in some "gain" and "benefits" in their work. They rated this on a 7-point scale ranging from 1 = *highly unlikely* to 7 = *highly likely*.

Participants were assigned to one of two conditions, or training manipulations: (a) information that computer ability is a fixed entity and (b) information that computer ability is a skill that can be acquired in increments. This information was integrated into the instructions for the computer skill learning exercises that trainees used. To avoid experimenter expectancy effects, defined in Chapter 1, instructions that contained the entity or incremental manipulation were all printed, and the researcher working with the participants was purposely kept unaware of the content. The following is an example of an incremental instruction from the study:

> [You should] Remember the old saying 'Practice makes perfect,' which holds true for computer skills. In acquiring your DOS [computer] skills, you will probably make some mistakes. That's normal. People who learn how to use microcomputers do not begin with faultless performance. Again, it is important to remember that the more practice you have, the more capable you will become. (Martocchio, 1994, p. 821)

In contrast, the following is an example of an entity instruction from the study:

> [You should] Remember the old saying 'Work smart, not hard,' which holds true for learning microcomputer skills. You will probably make mistakes during this DOS [computer] exercise. Such mistakes should serve as a useful reminder to work smart, not hard. Again, learning how to use microcomputers is based on skills that you already possess. Thus, I encourage you to work smart. (Martocchio, 1994, p. 821)

The differences seen in the previous statements were typical of the other passages found in the instructions, and this informational difference was the independent variable in this experiment.

There were a number of measures used as dependent outcomes in this study. Computer anxiety was measured on a 10-item self-report questionnaire, the Computer Anxiety Rating Scale (Heinssen, Glass, & Knight, 1987). This contained items such as "I feel apprehensive about using computers," which were rated by participants on a 7-point scale where 1 = *strongly disagree* and 7 = *strongly agree*. Total scores on this instrument could range from 10 to 70, high scores indicating greater reported anxiety about computers. Computer efficacy was measured using a 6-item scale adapted from Hollenbeck and Brief (1987). Items such as "Using microcomputers is probably something I will be good at" were rated on a 7-point scale from *strongly disagree* to *strongly agree*. Higher total scores represented higher computer efficacy. In addition, following the training session, participants took a test of what is called declarative knowledge. This test was the type of multiple-choice test that is often used in college classes to test knowledge of material that has been covered in a course. In this study, the test of declarative knowledge was a 10-question multiple-choice test that was designed to be fairly difficult so that it could *discriminate*, meaning show the difference, between those who learned the material and those who did not. If a test is too easy, everyone scores well and the test does not discriminate. This is called a *ceiling effect*, meaning that everyone scores at or near the top. If a test is too difficult, the reverse happens in scores: no one does well. This is called a *floor effect*. In both situations, a test does not identify those who have learned and those who have not. About half of the participants correctly answered each item on this test, showing that ceiling and floor effects had been avoided.

Two other questions were asked following the training session. These were included as a check to see if the manipulation in the study, the attempt to create particular attitudes about computer ability, was actually successful in changing attitudes. The two statements that formed the manipulation check were: "I can learn from the mistakes I make when learning how to use a microcomputer" and "Making errors reflects limits to my ability to learn microcomputers." These were rated on a 7-point scale from 1 = *strongly disagree* to 7 = *strongly agree*. Once participants had rated these, the answers to the second question were transposed, or reverse-scored, so that high scores indicated the conception of ability as an acquirable skill on both questions. The scores on these two statements were added together to give a final score assessing the effectiveness of the manipulation.

Results

No differences were found between the participants in the two experimental conditions on the pretraining measures of age, education, computer experience, length of service, computer efficacy, computer anxiety expectations, sex, or occupation. This is important because if there had been preexisting differences between groups in these variables, it would have been difficult to interpret the outcomes of the study. If, for example, one group had been higher in computer efficacy before training, it would not have been clear that the independent variable, the information about ability in the training session, had been responsible for differences in the dependent measures.

Following the training sessions, the two questions that were proposed as a check for the effectiveness of the manipulation yielded significant differences in the expected direction, as can be seen in Figure 23.1.

The mean for the entity group on this manipulation check was 10.49 and the mean for the acquirable skill group was 11.88. These means were statistically significantly different ($p < .05$).

Part of Hypothesis 1, that trainees in the acquirable condition would be less anxious about computers after training, was supported by the scores on the Computer Anxiety Rating Scale. The difference shown for the acquirable group before training compared to after training was statistically significant ($p < .001$). These data are shown in Figure 23.2.

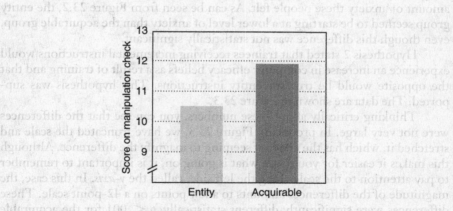

FIGURE 23.1   Scores on Manipulation Check for Both Groups. Scores from the manipulation check in which participants were asked two questions that assessed the extent to which mistakes indicated a permanent lack of ability. The scores for the two questions were combined in this figure. Higher scores indicated more self-efficacy.

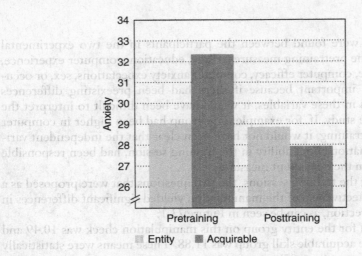

FIGURE 23.2   Computer Anxiety before and after Training

The other part of the hypothesis, that trainees in the entity condition would experience more anxiety as a result of training, was not supported. Apparently being reminded that ability is an unchanging quantity does not alter the amount of anxiety these people felt. As can be seen from Figure 23.2, the entity group seemed to be starting at a lower level of anxiety than the acquirable group, even though this difference was not statistically significant.

Hypothesis 2 stated that trainees receiving incremental instructions would experience an increase in computer efficacy beliefs as a result of training and that the opposite would be true for entity instructions. This hypothesis was supported. The data are shown in Figure 23.3.

Thinking critically about these numbers, you can see that the differences were not very large. In producing Figure 23.3, we have truncated the scale and stretched it, which has the effect of seeming to magnify the difference. Although this makes it easier for you to see what is going on, it is important to remember to pay attention to the scale along the left side, called the *y-axis*. In this case, the magnitude of the differences amounts to a few points on a 42-point scale. These differences were significantly different statistically, $p < .001$ for the acquirable skill condition and $p < .05$ for the entity condition. Nevertheless, the differences were small in magnitude. If you look back at Figure 23.2, you will notice that the situation was similar for those data: differences were small, considering that the scale could range from 10 to 70. We purposely did not mention this in our description of Figure 23.2 because we wanted to give you a chance to notice it for yourself. To critically evaluate data, it is important to pay attention to the size of the differences, regardless of how they are graphed and what the statistics say about them. We do not want you to think that scientific reports are purposely

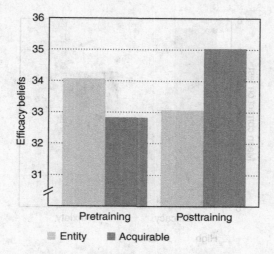

FIGURE 23.3   Self-Efficacy Beliefs before and after Training

untruthful; they are not. Scientists assume that their readers will pay attention to the data and arrive at their own assessment of the importance of the findings.

Perhaps surprisingly, the third hypothesis asserting that differences in declarative knowledge would result from differences in conception of ability, did not receive support in this study. However, computer efficacy and computer ability had some effects on declarative knowledge when data from all participants were combined, without regard to the experimental manipulation they had received. Participants were considered as new quasi-experimental groups of people high in computer anxiety or low in computer anxiety using the median, the middle score in the group, as a dividing point. The same was done for groups of people with high and low computer efficacy. Both variables used in this new group assignment, anxiety and efficacy, were measured *before* the experimental manipulation. Regardless of the experimental manipulation, people low in anxiety and people high in efficacy did better on the test of computer knowledge. The data for this quasi-experimental rearrangement of the participants can be seen in Figure 23.4.

The cautions we suggest for the other figures apply to this one as well. The knowledge test scores could range from 0 to 10 correct, and although the differences are statistically significant (*Anxiety: p < .05; Efficacy: p < .001*), the magnitudes of the differences found were somewhat small. Subsequent analyses of the data suggested that age of the participants was also important, particularly in predicting performance on the knowledge test. Age accounted for almost two thirds of the variance in test performance. The variance is a measure of the variability within a set of scores. Therefore, a considerable amount of that variability—people scoring high or people scoring low on a test—was attributable to their age. The relationship was inverse in that the younger people did better on the

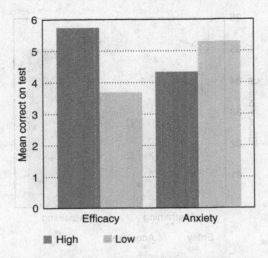

FIGURE 23.4 Declarative Knowledge Test Scores. Outcomes of the test of computer knowledge, which was given immediately following the training session.

test. Additional analysis also showed that in the acquirable ability condition, decreases in anxiety were greater among the older trainees. Within the entity condition, younger trainees did not experience any change in efficacy. They may have been sufficiently secure in their beliefs about what they could do so that a few instructions did not threaten them. However, among older trainees, the entity condition decreased computer efficacy. Among these older trainees, efficacy with computers was not very high before the training, and it was even lower after training. The instructions had undermined some of their beliefs about how successful they were likely to be in using computers. In summary, the primary outcomes on older people were that the acquirable condition had good effects in lowering anxiety, but the entity condition had adverse effects, decreasing self-efficacy.

DISCUSSION

We have said that the size of the outcomes in this study tended to be statistically significant but small. Yet, these findings are important because the manipulation was small, simple, and inexpensive. The treatment only involved inserting instructions of one sort or another into a training program. Given the simplicity of the manipulation, it may seem surprising that there were any differences in the outcome. These differences illustrate the power of a few words to change attitudes or behavior. It is likely that attitudes are easier to change in domains where the individual is uncertain about performance.

Age was found to be a very important variable in this study. Recently, there has been quite a bit of research on learning styles in adults. Probably some of this has been prompted by the large number of adult baby boomers in a rapidly changing workforce. Several studies have suggested that anxiety can interfere with memory in adults (Stigsdotter, Neely, & Backman, 1993; Yesavage, Lapp, & Sheikh, 1989). Martocchio's research demonstrated the effectiveness of cheap and easy incremental reminders in lowering anxiety in adults. The goal of applied psychological research is to help people function better in daily life, and this field experiment can be seen as a modest attempt to fulfill this goal. Attitudes about change are important in adult education programs, and creation of proper attitudes can be one step toward successful training.

REFERENCES

Cohen, M. N. (1998). *Culture of intolerance: Chauvinism, class and racism in the United States.* New Haven, CT: Yale University Press.

Gagné, R. M. (1962). Military training and principles of learning. *American Psychologist, 17,* 83–91.

Gold, L. (1981). Job instruction: Four steps to success. *Training and Development Journal, 35,* 28–32.

Heinssen, R., Glass, C., & Knight, L. (1987). Assessing computer anxiety: Developmental validation of the computer anxiety rating scale. *Computers in Human Behavior, 3,* 49–59.

Hicks, W. D., & Klimoski, R. J. (1987). Entry into training programs and its effects on training outcomes: A field experiment. *Academy of Management Journal, 30,* 542–552.

Hollenbeck, J. R., & Brief, A. P. (1987). The effects of individual differences and goal origin on goal setting and performance. *Organizational Behavior and Human Decision Processes, 40,* 392–414.

Kraiger, K., Ford, J. K., & Salas, E. (1993). Application of cognitive, skill-based and affective theories of learning to new methods of training evaluation. *Journal of Applied Psychology, 78,* 311–328.

Martocchio, J. J. (1994). Effects of conceptions of ability on anxiety, self-efficacy, and learning in training. *Journal of Applied Psychology, 79,* 819–825.

Mitchell, T. R., Hopper, H., Daniels, D., George-Falvy, J., & James, L. R. (1994). Predicting self-efficacy and performance during skill acquisition. *Journal of Applied Psychology, 79,* 506–517.

Stigsdotter, A., Neely, A., & Backman, L. (1993). Maintenance of gains following multifactorial and unifactorial memory training in late adulthood. *Educational Gerontology, 19,* 105–117.

Tannenbaum, S. I., Cannon-Bowers, J. A., Salas, E., & Mathieu, J. E. (1993). Factors that influence training effectiveness: A conceptual model and longitudinal analysis. *U.S. Naval Training Systems Center Technical Reports,* Technical Report 93-011.

Yesavage, J., Lapp, D., & Sheikh, J. A. (1989). Mnemonics as modified for use by the elderly. In L. W. Poon, D. Wilson, & B. Wilson (Eds.), *Everyday cognition in adulthood and late life* (pp. 598–611). Cambridge, England: Cambridge University Press.

• • • • •

CHAPTER 24

BETTING ON THE WINNERS

GAMBLING AS A PSYCHOLOGICAL DISORDER

Probably most of us, many times a week, offer to bet on something: "I bet it rains this afternoon; I bet we get a quiz in psychology today; I bet we end up being late for lunch. . . ." Most of our little wagers are not taken up by those around us and are forgotten. However, for some people, placing bets and other forms of gambling are a recognized psychological disorder. Starting in 1980, the *Diagnostic and Statistical Manual*, 3rd edition (*DSM-III*) (American Psychiatric Association, 1980) recognized a set of symptoms that defined pathological gambling. DSM is updated regularly, and it is taken by many to be the definitive list of disorders and symptoms within psychology, as well as in the medical specialty called psychiatry. This manual listed pathological gambling as "a chronic and progressive failure to resist impulses to gamble and gambling behavior that compromises, disrupts or damages personal, family or vocational pursuits." It is a preoccupation and urge that increases when people are stressed. The financial problems it creates lead to even more intense gambling. The debts incurred can also lead to various types of crime, such as embezzlement, theft, and knowingly writing bad checks. It includes the attitude that money is the cause of all one's problems; at the same time, money is the solution for all life's problems. People who have this disorder often lie to obtain more money. They are over-confident and energetic, but at times show signs of anxiety and depression. In males, it typically begins in adolescence, whereas in females, it appears later in life. It is esti-mated to be a problem for at least 2 to 3 percent of the adult population.

Notice that within the symptoms listed previously there are two different kinds of things: cognitive patterns and behavioral patterns. Concepts such as *urge*, *preoccupation*, and *attitude* refer to thoughts or cognitions, whereas *telling lies to obtain money* and *intense gambling* are behaviors. Often symptoms of psychological disorders include both thoughts and behaviors because disordered thinking is likely to be accompanied by problem actions.

Incorporating the research of C. Sylvain, R. Ladouceur, and J. M. Boisvert, "Cognitive and Behav-ioral Treatment of Pathological Gambling: A Controlled Study," 1997, *Journal of Consulting and Clinical Psychology*, 65, pp. 727–732.

APPROACHES TO TREATMENT OF PATHOLOGICAL GAMBLING

Various approaches have been tried as means of treating pathological gambling. For example, Dickerson and Weeks (1979) described a case study of a program that included *controlled gambling* in which an individual was allowed to make only small bets once a week. This manipulation was coupled with additional behavioral management and therapy. Behavior changes persisted over 15 months. This was a single-participant case study, and there was no control individual or group. Although it may serve as a pilot study suggesting treatment, caution should be exercised in generalizing the findings to other individuals. The case study is a weak research method for generalizing to large populations. Although psychological therapy is a common treatment, unfortunately it is fairly rare that some types of psychological therapies are evaluated to see if they are effective. One reason for this is that not all psychotherapists value science or have scientific training. Without an understanding of the power that a scientific approach has to evaluate new knowledge, assessment of therapeutic outcomes can be a matter of opinion. If treatment programs are to be evaluated successfully, they must be designed from the beginning with evaluation in mind. To be evaluated, treatment programs must make the assumption that psychological problems can be operationalized into measurable behavior. Participants should be randomly assigned into treatment and no-treatment control groups. Behavior problems should be assessed before treatment begins, after it has ended, and again after a longer period of time has passed.

A great deal of work and planning is required to design good research on efficacy of psychological treatment programs. Often the numbers of people being treated are small, and the treatment is not sufficiently standardized or quantified to permit numerical data to be collected. Probably one reason for this is that an individual therapist is unlikely to have a large number of clients with a single disorder, such as pathological gambling. In addition, unless the therapist is interested in scientific data collection, treatment of individuals is likely to be the only goal. To make matters more difficult, following treatment, people can be hard to find, disrupting assessment of long-term outcomes. In most studies of gambling previous to the one discussed in this chapter, the only outcome measured was the frequency of gambling behavior. This seems narrow, given the multiple symptoms described in *DSM-III*.

CONTROL GROUPS IN THERAPY EVALUATION

It is usual, but poor practice, to have no control groups in studies of treatment for pathological gambling (Lesieur & Blume, 1987). Having a control group that receives no treatment is important in studies of therapy because it is the only way to know that the treatment itself, and not mere passage of time, is making a difference. To do a scientific evaluation, ideally, a group of pathological gamblers would be randomly assigned either to the treatment group or to a no-treatment group. Following treatment, the two groups could be compared to determine the efficacy of the program. You may have some concern about the ethics of purposely withholding treatment from people identified as having a psychological disorder. One of the solutions to this ethical dilemma has been to put the no-treatment control group on a wait list, so that they are promised therapy eventually. They do not get it while the study is in progress, but it is given to them, at no charge, as soon as possible after the study has ended. Although this may help answer the ethical dilemma, it means that researchers have to assure themselves that wait-listed control participants do not seek therapy elsewhere while they are waiting.

THE GAMBLER'S FALLACY

Sylvain, Ladouceur, and Boisvert (1997) conducted a controlled study of a treatment program for compulsive gamblers. Sylvain and her colleagues argued that treatment should be based on cognitions as well as behaviors specific to gambling. These were specified in *DSM-III* and were the target of treatment. Ladouceur and Walker (1996) found that erroneous ideas about the concept of randomness were a primary cognitive component of the mistaken beliefs of gamblers. Gamblers believe and act as if they could predict, and maybe control, events that are not predictable or controllable. According to Ladouceur and Walker, even though gamblers may not expect to win any particular gamble, they have mistaken beliefs that lead to continued gambling. They believe that they have found, or can find, ways to predict events that are governed by chance. These researchers also noted that gambling is frequently associated with superstitious behaviors. Within psychology, this term refers to a mistaken belief that there is a real causal link, called a *contingency*, between two events, when, in reality, there is no contingency at all. Gamblers are likely to think their chance of winning is increased if they use their lucky dice, bet their birthday as a lottery number, or hold a gold coin in one hand while betting with the other. In actuality, of course, there is no contingency between any of these specific behaviors and winning. One of these erroneous ways of thinking is so common that it has become a technical term: *the gambler's fallacy*. One version of the gambler's fallacy is the idea that independent or random events are linked: if you lose a game of chance 30 times in a row, this means your number is about to come up, and you will win. In fact, your chances do not change. If you repeatedly toss an unbiased coin and, by chance, happen to toss 10 heads in a row, the probability of a head on the 11th toss is still 50 percent. The string of head tosses does not affect the next independent random event.

Participants

The participants in this study were gamblers who were seeking help for gambling problems. There were 56 men and 2 women among them. They were evaluated by a clinical psychologist who was experienced in working with people diagnosed as pathological gamblers. All participants met the criteria for pathological gambling found in *DSM-III-R* (American Psychiatric Association, 1987), which was the current edition of *DSM* at the time the study commenced. Their most common mode of gambling was playing video poker, but others bet on horse races or played casino games. Some were recruited for the study either through advertisements in the newspaper or announcements on radio or TV. Others were referred by a professional care provider such as a physician, psychologist, or social worker. The study was conducted in the Province of Quebec in Canada. All 58 potential participants underwent a preliminary evaluation, and 18 of them refused treatment following this evaluation. The remaining 40 individuals were randomly assigned to the treatment group or control group. Eight participants subsequently dropped out from the treatment group and 3 from the control group, leaving 29 individuals. These were reassigned so that 14 received treatment and 15 were left in the control group. Other studies of addictive behavior have shown similar proportions of participant attrition (Stark, 1992). This number of refusals and dropouts is high, but you should remember that these people are adults with complicated lives who were about to be involved in a rigorous program aimed at changing a problem behavior. They could not be required or coerced to remain in the study. The participants who completed treatment were significantly different from the dropouts and refusers on two variables: those completing the program began gambling at an older age ($p < .05$) and their *problem* gambling appeared later in life ($p < .05$). Does this invalidate the study as a whole? We do not believe so. Clearly, part of your skill in thinking critically about scientific studies includes careful consideration of problems such as the characteristics of participants who drop out. In this case, at worst, these differences might limit our ability to apply these study findings to problem gamblers who had gambling problems early in life. People who do not understand science may be more likely to categorically dismiss an entire study because of a limitation such as this. In contrast, an educated critical thinker knows that there will always be some imperfections in studies. The important thing is to evaluate their effect on whatever conclusions may be drawn. Scientific researchers do not try to hide the problems that appear in the course of research; they point out problems that can be seen in the design of the study or in the data and discuss them in their publications. If the problem is sufficiently large, the study will not be published. With smaller blemishes, researchers expect the reader to be critical. Researchers give their readers the information required to make a cautious, realistic interpretation of the results.

In the treatment group, the mean age was 37.6 years, and in the control group, it was 42.6 years. Half of the participants in each group were evaluated by a second clinician to check the reliability of the diagnosis. There was a 100 percent agreement between the evaluators. In other types of studies, the reliability of one rater is often checked by another observer who is unaware of the original ratings. You can appreciate that this was probably not possible here; clients who see a clinical psychologist do not expect the psychologist to be unaware of the problems they are having. In this case, the participants described these problems, and the nature of the reliability check was to see if the second clinician agreed that the symptoms indicated the same diagnosis.

Procedure

At the beginning of the study, all participants were made aware that because of random assignment to groups, some individuals would not be receiving treatment immediately. Once random assignment had taken place, participants in the control group were contacted and told that they would be on a waiting list. They were assured that they would receive treatment as soon as possible and that it was expected that all participants would receive treatment within four months. During this wait, they were phoned monthly as a way of keeping in contact with them. Two control participants believed that they could not wait any longer and were immediately assigned to the treatment group. None of the wait-listed patients reported receiving other therapy for this problem while they were waiting for treatment.

Cognitive-behavioral therapy was administered by two female psychologists who had, respectively, 4 and 5 years of clinical experience. They were supervised by Robert Ladouceur, a psychologist with 20 years of experience in cognitive-behavioral therapy. In the first session, treatment group participants were asked the question, "Are you willing to make an effort to reduce or stop gambling?" To continue in the study they had to answer in the affirmative. They also rated, on a scale of 1 to 10, their motivation to change the problem behavior.

The experience and training of the therapist are important to the success of cognitive-behavioral therapy, but we want to be clear that nothing magical or mystical is involved. By "nothing magical or mystical," we mean that the entire therapeutic process can be understood by ordinary people. It is a concrete teaching process in which a client learns to do new things and to think different thoughts. Unfortunately, popular media often depict psychological therapy as being a version of psychoanalysis, the approach developed 100 years ago by Sigmund Freud (see, for example, Freud, 1935). Freud believed that problems were rooted in unconscious desires and childhood problems. His therapy was supposed to dig deep into an unconscious mind using arcane and symbolic interpretations of the patient's verbal responses. Classically, the patient would lie on a couch and say anything that came into his or her head, while the therapist listened and attached florid interpretations to what was said. It was believed that as the contents of the unconscious came into the conscious mind, people could become aware of urges, often socially unacceptable urges, with sexual overtones.

The patient's growing awareness of the unconscious was believed to be part of the cure. This kind of therapy was an art, not a science.

We took this little aside to illustrate what cognitive-behavioral therapy is *not*: it is not psychoanalysis or anything particularly like it. It does require a therapist with sharp clinical skills, but the skills are used to discuss the client's conscious thoughts and viewpoints about the world. The client is made aware that changing patterns of thinking can help change behavior. The reverse is also important: changing one's behavior can change thinking. It is a rational and empirical approach that has no use for unconscious childhood trauma, hidden sexual urges, or couches. In some kinds of therapy, empirical evaluation is impossible, or nearly so. In contrast, the ultimate goal of cognitive-behavioral therapy is behavior change that can be observed and measured. As a result, cognitive-behavioral therapy can be evaluated through scientific means.

Cognitive-behavioral therapy was administered to the treatment group participants, or *clients*, in individual sessions. Sessions occurred once or twice a week and lasted between 60 and 90 minutes. This group received an average of 16.7 hours of treatment, with the maximum being 30 hours. They did not receive any additional therapy for this or other problems during the course of the study.

The cognitive-behavioral therapy had four main components. We describe these in some detail because we want you to understand the direct and sensible nature of this therapeutic approach. It has a strong empirical basis as well as a singular and determined goal to change behavior.

1. *Cognitive correction.*   This component was aimed at correcting the misunderstanding of randomness. It included direct teaching about the concept. Random, by definition, means *not predictable*. Control is impossible. Erroneous beliefs commonly held by gamblers, including the gambler's fallacy, were exposed as misconstruals and explained. A recording was made of the participant pretending to gamble. The participant reviewed this with the therapist, and the therapist offered detailed corrections of the faulty beliefs indicated by the participant's verbalizations. An example of one of these was "if I lose four times in a row, I will win for sure the next time."

2. *Problem-solving training.*   Participants were taught some specific strategies for dealing with problems in their lives. Obviously, the primary application of these tactics was to deal with some of the symptoms of gambling. They were taught to define the problems in unambiguous terms, collect information about the problems, generate alternative solutions listing the advantages and disadvantages of each, and implement the solution, subsequently evaluating their effectiveness. These are the same processes that most of us use daily in a somewhat haphazard way, but the participants were taught to go through the steps in a careful and rational way. An example of one of the problems that was approached in this way was the need to get better control over spending to pay off debts

incurred from past gambling. This was designed to help break the cycle of gambling to pay off debts.

3. *Social skills training.* Some of the individuals in the program suffered from links between poor social skills and gambling. For example, some of them needed assertiveness training because, even if they did not want to gamble, friends would persuade them to do so. These people needed to be taught how to resist social pressure from people they liked. Role-playing was an important part of this training. Through role-play, gamblers could practice and learn the communication skills necessary to steer them through social situations that might, otherwise, lead to gambling.

4. *Relapse prevention.* As part of the therapy, participants discussed the possibility of relapsing and described their past relapses. Risk factors for relapse were identified, and participants were taught specific ways to avoid the creation of high relapse-risk situations. For the gamblers, these included events such as carrying cash, loneliness, stress, and lack of alternate social activities.

DEPENDENT VARIABLES

The dependent variables, or outcome measures, included the number of *DSM-III-R* criteria for pathological gambling that still described the participant. If the program was successful, there would be a decrease in this variable. Another dependent variable, or *D.V.*, was the outcome of the South Oaks Gambling Screen (SOGS), a valid self-report instrument. A total score of 5 or more on SOGS interview questions has been found to be indicative of pathological gambling (Lesieur & Blume, 1987). Beyond this threshold, higher scores indicate more problems with gambling. As an additional measure, participants rated their perception of their own control over gambling on a scale from 1—*no control*, to 10—*all control*. They also rated their desire to gamble on a 1 to 10 scale. Several measures were taken of self-reported frequency of gambling, including the number of gambling sessions, the number of hours spent gambling, and the total amount of money spent on gambling during the previous week.

Pretreatment Scores

To assure themselves that the treatment and wait list control groups were not different with respect to some dimension of gambling, the dependent measures described previously were assessed on both groups before treatment began in order to obtain a pretreatment baseline. Because participants had been randomly assigned to the groups, there was no reason to think groups would be different, but, of course, by chance, it is possible for random assignment to produce groups that are different with respect to the primary characteristic under investigation: in this case, gambling. For example, if, by chance, the heaviest gamblers had ended up in the wait list control group, and no pretreatment measure had been taken, differences in dependent measures at the end of the study might suggest program success, when, in fact, the program had made little difference in changing behavior. For this reason, baseline measures were taken before any treatment began. No statistically significant differences were found between the groups in any of those measures of gambling.

Results

The changes between pretreatment and posttreatment for the treatment group and the same period of time for the wait list control group are found in Table 24.1. The control group received no treatment between these measures, so any changes in their scores must be a result of other things that were happening in

TABLE 24.1 Means of the Main Variables at Pretreatment, Posttreatment, and 6-Month Follow-Up Measurements for the Treatment Group and the (Wait List) Control Group

	PRETREATMENT	POSTTREATMENT	6-MONTH FOLLOW-UP*
DSM-III-R			
Treatment	7.3	1.1	1.3
Control	7.1	5.7	
PERCEPTION OF CONTROL			
Treatment	1.4	8.0	8.6
Control	2.7	3.6	
DESIRE TO GAMBLE			
Treatment	5.7	2.0	0.5
Control	6.3	6.1	
BELIEVE CAN RESIST GAMBLING			
Treatment	2.8	8.4	8.8
Control	3.4	3.7	
SOGS			
Treatment	12.6	2.7	2.7
Control	13.1	13.0	

Note: DSM-III-R refers to the number of diagnostic criteria found in the *Diagnostic and Statistical Manual* that were met, and SOGS refers to the scores obtained on the questionnaire.

*At 6-month follow-up, only 10 participants were included.

their lives. Statistical analysis showed that the treatment group and the control group were statistically significantly different at the posttreatment measure for each of the five dependent variables, all at $p < .01$. As a result of the therapy, the treatment group had fewer of the pathological gambling diagnostic criteria from *DSM-III-R*, reported less desire to gamble, and had a lower South Oaks Gambling Screen (SOGS) score. They reported a higher perception of control over gambling and a higher belief that they could refrain from gambling.

Table 24.2 shows the data for self-report frequency-of-gambling variables during pretreatment, posttreatment, and 6-month follow-up. Initially, it might seem that some of the numbers reported in Table 24.2 are going to make it difficult to interpret the findings of the study with respect to frequency of gambling. A glance at the means might suggest that, even though the groups were formed by random assignment, the unusual has happened: frequency of gambling appears to be quite a bit lower in the treatment group compared to the control group, even in the pretreatment measures. Arithmetic means can be misleading. There was a great deal of variability in these data, with a few individuals gambling either a great deal more than the mean or a great deal less. In this particular case, the mean is an inadequate one-number summary of the entire data set because there is so much variability. Probably the median, which is the middle score in the distribution, would be a better summary, but when scores are widely

TABLE 24.2   Means of the Three Frequency-of-Gambling Variables at Pretreatment, Posttreatment, and 6-Month Follow-Up Measurements for the Treatment Group and the (Wait List) Control Group When Asked About the Previous Week

	PRETREATMENT	POSTTREATMENT	6-MONTH FOLLOW-UP*
NO. OF GAMBLING SESSIONS			
Treatment	0.8	0.2	0
Control	1.5	1.7	
NO. HOURS SPENT GAMBLING			
Treatment	1.4	0.9	0
Control	3.3	4.6	
MONEY SPENT ON GAMBLING			
Treatment	23.29	8.57	0
Control	99.67	188.00	

*At 6-month follow-up, only 10 participants were included.

variable, no single number is likely to represent them very well. Remember, when the treatment and control group means for frequency of gambling were compared statistically before treatment began, there were no statistically significant differences.

As you think critically about this issue, you also need to see that the treatment groups and the control groups should be compared with themselves. The magnitude of group means is less important than the amount of change in them. If the program was effective, we should see a statistically significant decrease between pretreatment and posttreatment within the treatment group. We do. If we want to conclude that this change is a result of the therapy, not just time passing by, we should not see a significant decrease between pretreatment and posttreatment in the control group, as, indeed, we do not.

Six months after the end of therapy, measures were taken again on the 10 participants from the treatment group who were available. Four of the original participants were not included in the 6-month follow-up data. Three of them could not be located despite numerous attempts, and the other participant had probably relapsed. As can be seen from Table 24.1 and Table 24.2, 6 months later, the changes in gambling persisted among the 10 remaining participants. All pretreatment measures shown in Table 24.1 for the treatment group were significantly different from their 6-month follow-up scores ($p < .01$). Table 24.2 shows that at 6 months, those remaining in the study had no gambling activity.

Twelve months after the end of therapy, it was possible to reach 9 of the participants from the original treatment group either by telephone or in interview. For 8 of the 9, therapeutic gains persisted, and they were no longer considered pathological gamblers according to *DSM-III-R* criteria. One of these 9 had relapsed and was still considered a pathological gambler.

DISCUSSION

The results of this study suggest that cognitive-behavioral therapy can effectively treat pathological gambling for some individuals. Their attitudes changed and so did their behavior. The success of this program has to be evaluated in light of the initial dropouts and refusals. At this point, there is no evidence that this approach would work for everyone, even though it may have been successful for those who completed the program. In addition, it was a requirement that participants be willing to consider behavior change. There are probably many people who are classifiable under *DSM* criteria who are not willing to change their behavior. There is no therapy that is likely to be effective for people who make hard line refusals.

Part of the success of this program may have been a result of its multifaceted approach to the problem. These individuals received help in changing erroneous beliefs about gambling. This cognitive component was linked to problem solving and relapse prevention in this program, helping people develop the skills required to decrease or eliminate problem behavior. As we noted at the beginning of this chapter, the approach here was based on learning and, as you have seen, the therapy consisted of a variety of efforts to teach new skills, cognitive and behavioral. There was no hidden magic here. The therapy involved a skilled teacher, the therapist, working with a willing learner to change behavior. The process was not basically different from what might occur in learning to play tennis from an expert coach: behavior is changed. This was an important study because, although the final numbers were small, it was a careful and concerted attempt to evaluate the outcome of psychotherapy. If therapy had been seen as a probing of the unconscious in an attempt to repair primal forces, rather than an attempt to change behavior, there would be no outcome to measure. It is difficult for us to understand how a therapeutic approach can have any claim to success in the absence of observable and measurable outcomes.

REFERENCES

American Psychiatric Association. (1980). *The Diagnostic and statistical manual of mental disorders* (3rd ed.). Washington, DC: American Psychiatric Publishing, Inc.

American Psychiatric Association. (1987). *The Diagnostic and statistical manual of mental disorders* (3rd ed.). Revised. Washington, DC: American Psychiatric Publishing, Inc.

Dickerson, M. G., & Weeks, D. (1979). Controlled gambling as a therapeutic technique for compulsive gamblers. *Journal of Behavior Therapy and Experimental Psychiatry, 10*, 139–141.

Freud, S. (1935). *An autobiographical study.* New York: Norton.

Ladouceur, R., & Walker, M. (1996). A cognitive perspective on gambling. In P. M. Salkovskis (Ed.), *Trends in cognitive and behavioral therapies* (pp. 89–120). New York: Wiley.

Lesieur, H. R., & Blume, S. B. (1987). The South Oaks Gambling Screen (The SOGS): A new instrument for the identification of pathological gamblers. *American Journal of Psychiatry, 144*, 1184–1188.

Stark, M. J. (1992). Dropping out of substance abuse treatment: A clinically oriented review. *Clinical Psychology Review, 12*, 93–116.

Sylvain, C., Ladouceur, R., & Boisvert, J. M. (1997). Cognitive and behavioral treatment of pathological gambling: A controlled study. *Journal of Consulting and Clinical Psychology, 65*, 727–732.

CHAPTER 25

BEHAVIORAL TREATMENT TO CHANGE VOCALIZATION PATTERNS IN A PERSON WITH SCHIZOPHRENIA

Most of the chapters in this book are devoted to discussing research on normal psychological functioning. This is an accurate reflection of research conducted in the field of psychology. Most psychological research seeks to understand normal patterns of cognition and behavior. In some people, however, something goes wrong in their cognitive system, leading them to experience disordered mental processes and exhibit abnormal behaviors. A psychological disorder leads to cognitions and behaviors that are maladaptive for life functioning, cause personal discomfort, or both. In a general sense, psychological disorders prevent people from engaging in normal activities of daily living, like getting out of bed in the morning, dressing themselves, feeding themselves, going to school or work, and having comfortable social relationships with others.

Schizophrenia is a severe psychological disorder. Many people outside the social sciences and medicine use the word schizophrenic to refer to someone who seems to have multiple personalities or whose behavior is seemingly random and unpredictable. The psychological diagnosis of schizophrenia, however, is different. Schizophrenia refers to a group of psychotic disorders. Psychotic disorders are characterized by a loss of touch with reality manifested as disturbances in normal cognitive and behavioral functioning. Some of these disturbances can be quite severe. Some of the more debilitating symptoms of schizophrenia include:

- Delusions — possessing false beliefs. For example, a man believes that he was abducted by aliens and had a chip implanted in his brain that is used to

Incorporating the research of D. A. Wilder, A. Masuda, C. O'Connor, and M. Baham, "Brief Functional Analysis and Treatment of Bizarre Vocalizations in an Adult with Schizophrenia," 2001, *Journal of Applied Behavior Analysis, 34*, pp. 65–68.

monitor and control his thoughts. Delusions can be much more elaborate than this one.

- Hallucinations — perceiving things that are not really there. These false perceptions can be experienced through any sense modality, but are most commonly auditory (e.g., hearing voices or sounds). A woman who can hear verbal commands from aliens, for example, would be experiencing an auditory hallucination.
- Speech that shows incoherence or disorganization.
- Severely disorganized or catatonic (e.g., immobility, repeated movements) behavior.
- Symptoms such as flat affect (i.e., lack of emotions) or inappropriate affect (e.g., experiencing sadness or anger at funny events, or experiencing joy or laughing at upsetting events).

Schizophrenia is not a disorder that people have at birth. Although there are genetic links to some forms of schizophrenia, the environment also contributes to its development. The average age of onset of schizophrenia differs for men and women (Häfner, Maurer, & Loffler, 1998; Riecher-Rossler & Häfner, 2000). For men, it peaks at around age 20 to 25 years. The onset peak for women is later, at around age 25 to 30. There is also a second smaller peak in women after age 45. This means that most people with schizophrenia first lapse into the disorder in their college years or shortly thereafter.

Scientists do not know what causes schizophrenia, and there is no known cure for the disorder. However, the symptoms of schizophrenia can be treated. The ultimate goal of all treatments for schizophrenia is to help people with the disorder to live more normal lives. Treatments for schizophrenia do not eliminate symptoms of the disorder, but they do make them less debilitating. For example, if a person with schizophrenia was experiencing auditory hallucinations and delusions, medication might decrease the intensity of the symptoms, allowing a person with the disorder to more easily ignore them and engage in normal activities of daily living.

Other therapies also can be valuable in the treatment of schizophrenia. Counseling and psychotherapy can help people with schizophrenia better understand their disorder and provide strategies for overcoming irrational thoughts. These therapies also provide support and encouragement for people with schizophrenia and their families.

Behavioral therapy techniques take a different approach to the treatment of the symptoms of schizophrenia. Behavioral therapists recognize that hallucinatory speech (responding verbally to hallucinations, which are typically auditory), delusional speech (making obviously false statements), and perseverative speech (phrases that are frequently repeated and are not linked to conversation) are common features of schizophrenia. Rather than viewing these behaviors as symptoms of a psychological disorder, however, behavior analysts view them as *operants*. For behavior analysts, operants are voluntary behaviors that include most of the things we do or say every day. Consequences (reinforcement or punishment) follow operants and significantly influence the likelihood of the behavior occurring again under similar circumstances. This language should look familiar to you. We discussed operant conditioning in Chapter 7. Operant conditioning involves the selection of behavior by consequences. Those behaviors that are reinforced will increase in frequency. Behaviors that are punished will decrease in frequency. Behavioral techniques to decrease problem behaviors have been demonstrated to be effective for people who do not respond well to typical talking therapies because of psychological disorders or cognitive deficits due to mental retardation, autism, or traumatic brain injuries (Harris & Delmolino, 2002; Moran & Malott, 2004).

Wilder, Masuda, O'Connor, and Baham (2001) used principles of operant conditioning to treat bizarre vocalizations in a patient with schizophrenia. They noted that previous behavioral researchers had been successful in treating inappropriate vocalizations in patients with the disorder. These results suggested that the vocalizations in people with schizophrenia were either maintained by rewards and punishments from the social environment or sensitive to them. Examples might include receiving attention or being allowed to escape from an undesirable situation after vocalizing. To better understand how the social environment (relationships with other people) of patients with schizophrenia may inadvertently reinforce their inappropriate vocalizations, the researchers proposed it would be valuable to examine the social environments before beginning treatment. This is called pretreatment functional analysis.

There was only one participant in this research study. To protect his identity, the researchers referred to him as Jay. Because there was only one participant in the research, the method is a case study. In explicitly quantitative research that involves a large sample of research participants, the researchers rarely report specific information about any individual unless they are using that information to provide an example of typical results. In a case study, however, it is important for the researchers to provide relevant details about the individual case or cases they are describing. Other researchers need this information in order to evaluate how similar the case is to other cases, and ultimately to decide whether the techniques and results of the particular case study are likely to generalize to other cases.

Jay, the participant in this case, was a 43-year-old man. His diagnosis was chronic undifferentiated schizophrenia and an unspecified personality disorder. A *chronic* disorder is ongoing and long in duration. Many chronic disorders such as schizophrenia cannot be cured, but they can be treated. Disorders that are shorter in duration and sometimes severe, such as pneumonia, are referred to as being *acute*.

Jay's bizarre vocalizations included strange statements that were unrelated to the topic of conversation going on around him. Examples of the statements he made included, "Bruce Lee has a black belt in karate," and "I'm not going back to Margaret." Prior to his diagnosis, Jay had successfully completed the 10th grade. He lived in a residential treatment facility called a "board-and-care home." Board-and-care homes are assisted living facilities where residents receive 24-hour supervision and assistance from trained professionals.

Jay was taking the following medications during the study: Prolixin, Loxapine, and Seroquel. Prolixin is a drug that is prescribed to help decrease psychotic features such as paranoia and hallucinations. Loxapine is also an antipsychotic medication used to treat hallucinations, delusions, and hostility. Seroquel is a drug used to decrease the severity of symptoms of schizophrenia, including aggression. People who have schizophrenia often take a number of different drugs to help alleviate their symptoms. Because schizophrenia has different physiological bases in different people who have the disorder, the drugs prescribed to treat their symptoms can vary widely. Often, psychiatrists will try a number of treatment combinations before settling on one that works for a particular patient. Even then, treatments may decrease in their effectiveness over time, requiring additional changes.

The behavioral therapy conducted by Wilder et al. (2001) was in addition to the drug therapy Jay was receiving. The behavior therapy sessions were conducted in a room specifically designated for that purpose in a psychology clinic that was affiliated with a local university where the researchers worked. The room was equipped with a one-way mirror so the therapy sessions could be observed from an adjacent room. One-way mirrors are valuable research tools in psychology. They allow behaviors and therapy sessions to be observed, but do not allow the research participants to see the observers. This decreases the likelihood that the observers might inadvertently do something that would affect the participants' behavior or influence the treatment process.

DATA COLLECTION

The first step in using behavioral techniques to treat Jay's bizarre vocalizations was to create an *operational definition* of what they were. An operational definition is a description of something of interest to researchers. It provides information about techniques or processes that the researchers use to measure it. In this study, Wilder et al. (2001) defined bizarre vocalizations as phrases or sentences that either (1) "referred to stimuli not present or being discussed" or (2) "referred to one of five specific topics that Jay repeatedly discussed," such as karate, God, former girlfriends, drugs, and the FBI. Appropriate vocalizations were defined as any "statements or questions that did not meet the definition of bizarre vocalizations."

The researchers also operationally defined appropriate vocalizations, which included any spoken language that was not included in the definition of bizarre vocalizations. The researchers kept track of both bizarre and appropriate vocalizations during the treatment evaluation. Jay's vocalizations were recorded on laptop computers by two trained observers. A tally of vocalizations was made for every 10-second interval. The interobserver agreement averaged more than 85 percent for bizarre vocalizations and appropriate vocalizations.

The behavioral therapists in this research were a psychology professor and a master's-level graduate student. For each treatment session, the person who served as the therapist was randomly determined. All treatment sessions lasted for 10 minutes. Therapy sessions were held two or three days each week. Between two and four therapy sessions were conducted on each of these therapy days.

PROCEDURE FOR THE BRIEF FUNCTIONAL ANALYSIS PHASE

Wilder et al. (2001) believed that it was important to observe and evaluate Jay before beginning therapy with him. Specifically, the researchers were interested in determining whether any aspects of Jay's social environment (relationships with other people) contributed to his undesirable bizarre vocalizations. This is brief functional analysis. It refers to a specific procedure that is common among behavior analysts, therapists who use behavioral techniques to treat problem behaviors.

To conduct the brief functional analysis, the researchers alternated between four different functional analysis conditions. The first condition was called the demand condition. In this condition, the therapist asked Jay to perform a variety of tasks that are considered to be normal activities of daily living or normal job tasks, such as counting and sorting objects continuously for a period of 10 minutes. So the tasks would not seem artificial to Jay, the researchers told him that they were assessing his work skills. While Jay was engaging in the tasks, the therapist responded to each vocalization that Jay made. When the vocalizations were appropriate, the therapist would give brief one- to three-word responses. This was a mild form of positive reinforcement. When Jay made bizarre vocalizations, the therapist responded with the sentence, "Okay, this may be too stressful for you. Take a break." Jay was then instructed to take a 30-second break from the task he was working on. The break was a mild form of negative punishment. One could also argue that suggesting the task was stressful and instructing Jay to take a break was a form of positive punishment.

The second condition was called the "attention condition." Like the demand condition, each attention condition session lasted for 10 minutes. In this condition, the therapist sat across a table from Jay, but did not make eye contact with him. When Jay made appropriate vocalizations, he was given short responses, from one to three words, just as he had been given in the previous condition. Again, this was a mild form of positive reinforcement. When Jay made bizarre vocalizations, the therapist leaned forward in his chair, made direct eye contact with him, and made a statement prohibiting the specific bizarre vocalization Jay made. For example, the therapist might say, "You shouldn't talk about Bruce Lee so much." This was intended to be a form of positive punishment.

The third condition was referred to as the "alone condition." In this condition, Jay was in the observation room by himself for 10 minutes. He was not given any feedback for bizarre vocalizations or for appropriate vocalizations. As a result, there was no reinforcement or punishment in this condition. The researchers created this condition to see if Jay produced bizarre vocalizations when no one else was present. If he did not, it would be evidence that Jay's bizarre vocalizations were produced in order to influence the behavior of others.

The final condition was the control condition. In this condition, the therapist sat at a table directly across from Jay for 10 minutes. He asked Jay about appropriate conversation topics. When Jay answered with appropriate vocalizations, the therapist responded with complete sentences and full eye contact. This was positive reinforcement for appropriate vocalizations. When Jay answered with bizarre vocalizations, the therapist withdrew eye contact and did not speak to Jay again until his bizarre vocalizations had been over for 10 seconds. This was negative punishment for Jay's bizarre vocalizations. Each preceding condition was conducted twice over the course of the study.

RESULTS OF FUNCTIONAL ANALYSIS PHASE

Wilder et al. (2001) evaluated the percentage of the 10-second intervals in each brief functional analysis condition in which bizarre vocalizations occurred and the percentage in which appropriate vocalizations occurred. The most bizarre vocalizations occurred in the attention condition, occurring in 26 percent of the intervals. Bizarre vocalizations occurred only in 2 percent of the intervals in the demand condition, 5 percent of the intervals in the control condition, and in none of the intervals of the alone condition. These results are illustrated in Figure 25.1.

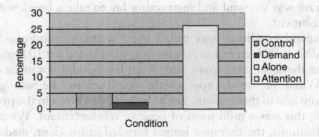

FIGURE 25.1   Percentage of 10-Second Intervals in Which Bizarre Vocalizations Occurred for Each Therapeutic Condition

PROCEDURE FOR TREATMENT PHASE

The researchers used the results from the brief functional analysis phase of the study to inform their therapeutic intervention. The researchers' goals for Jay's therapy were the reinforcement of his appropriate vocalizations and the extinction of his bizarre vocalizations. To evaluate the treatment, *a reversal design* was used. A reversal design is a single-subject design in which a pretreatment or baseline measurement is compared with a posttreatment measure. Then a second baseline measure is taken, followed by a second application of the treatment.

Baseline → Treatment → Baseline → Treatment

The baseline condition was identical to the attention condition of the brief functional analysis. In this condition, the therapist sat across a table from Jay, but did not make eye contact with him. When Jay made appropriate vocalizations, he was given short responses (mild positive reinforcement). When Jay made bizarre vocalizations, the therapist made direct eye contact with him and made a statement prohibiting the specific bizarre vocalization Jay made (positive punishment).

The therapeutic condition was the same as the control condition of the brief functional analysis. In the therapeutic condition, the therapist made eye contact with Jay and verbally responded to him when Jay made appropriate vocalizations (positive reinforcement). The therapist looked away and made no verbal statements when Jay made bizarre vocalizations until the bizarre vocalizations had stopped for 10 seconds (negative punishment).

RESULTS OF TREATMENT PHASE

There were fewer 10-second intervals with bizarre vocalizations during the therapy sessions than in the baseline sessions, as shown in Figure 25.2. Conversely, appropriate vocalizations were most frequent during the therapy sessions.

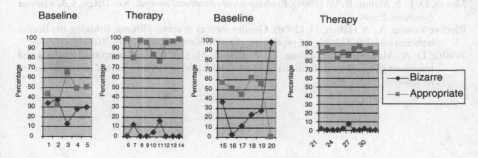

FIGURE 25.2   Percentage of Intervals in Which Bizarre and Appropriate Vocalizations Occurred in Baseline and Treatment Sessions

DISCUSSION

The results of this case study suggest that the bizarre vocalizations of an adult with schizophrenia can be successfully treated with behavior therapy techniques. The treatment in this study was successful both in decreasing bizarre vocalizations and increasing appropriate vocalizations. Jay's caregivers and others in his board-and-care home were encouraged to continue to use the therapeutic strategies after the therapy sessions ended to keep his bizarre vocalizations at a low frequency and his appropriate vocalizations at a high frequency. The researchers suggested that these behavioral techniques may also be effective in treating other symptoms of schizophrenia, such as inappropriate affect.

Jay's responsiveness to the behavioral therapeutic techniques provides evidence that his bizarre vocalizations were being inadvertently reinforced by his social environment. When he was positively reinforced (received a response with eye contact) for appropriate vocalizations and negatively punished (did not receive a response and eye contact was taken away) for bizarre vocalizations, Jay almost completely abandoned bizarre vocalizations in favor of appropriate ones.

It is important to note that the social influences that maintained Jay's bizarre vocalizations and the therapeutic interventions that proved successful in treating them were incredibly subtle. A behavioral perspective helps shed light on how our actions can influence the behavior of others. In some instances, we may not intend to influence others' behavior or even be aware that we are doing so. The outcomes of this influence, however, can be quite important.

REFERENCES

Häfner, H., Maurer, K., & Loffler, W. (1998). The ABC schizophrenia study: A preliminary overview of the results. Social *Psychiatry and Psychiatric Epidemiology, 33*, 380–386.

Harris, S. L. P., & Delmolino, L. P. (2002). Applied behavior analysis: Its application in the treatment of autism and related disorders in young children. *Infants and Young Children, 14*, 11–17.

Moran, D. J., & Malott, R. W. (2004). *Evidence-based educational methods.* San Diego, CA: Elsevier Academic Press.

Riecher-Rossler, A., & Häfner, H. (2000). Gender aspects in schizophrenia: Bridging the border between social and biological psychiatry. *Acta Psychiatrica Scandinavica, 102*, 58–62.

Wilder, D. A., Masuda, A., O'Connor, C., & Baham, M. (2001). Brief functional analysis and treatment of bizarre vocalizations in an adult with schizophrenia. *Journal of Applied Behavior Analysis, 34*, 65–68.

CHAPTER 26

TOKENS AGAINST AGGRESSION

Psychiatric hospitals are not places where most people want to spend their free time. Although they are valuable institutions for the treatment of psychological disorders, they are not always safe, even for the staff and the patients. Violence perpetrated by psychiatric patients can be a significant problem at inpatient psychiatric hospitals (Lehman, McCormick, & Kizer, 1999). Some studies have estimated that as many as 97 of every 100 patients will be involved in acts of aggression while admitted to psychiatric facilities (Cheung, Schweitzer, Tuckwell, & Crowley, 1996). Between 75 percent and 100 percent of the nursing staff in psychiatric hospitals report being assaulted by a patient during their careers (Wynn & Bratlid, 1998). Many of the assaults result in serious injury, time lost from work, or both (Hillbrand, Foster, & Spitz, 1996). This can lead to a significant loss of money for the institutions in terms of employee medical coverage, lost employee productivity, and the time employees cannot come to work.

The staff members who work with psychiatric patients face a unique challenge—curbing the violent behavior of people who can be extraordinarily difficult to reason with. Many people who are admitted to psychiatric treatment facilities are psychotic, which means they are not in touch with reality. The thinking of other patients may be distorted by other factors, including depression, the effects of psychoactive medications, and traumatic brain injuries. If you cannot reason with people, how can you change their behavior?

One strategy that has been shown to be useful in contributing to behavior change is known as a token economy. Token economies use principles of operant conditioning to shape behavior. Patients earn tokens when they perform desired behaviors. They can exchange the tokens they earn for items they desire, such as candy, gum, or magazines. In clinical settings, the desired behaviors are chosen by the treatment team. The behaviors may include cleaning rooms, attending anger management classes, not incorporating delusions into conversations, and taking prescribed medications. Previous research that studied token economies showed

Incorporating the research of J. P. LePage, K. DelBen, S. Pollard, M. McGhee, L. VanHorn, J. Murphy, P. Lewis, A. Aboraya, and N. Mogge, "Reducing Assaults on an Acute Psychiatric Unit Using a Token Economy: A 2-Year Follow-Up," 2003, *Behavioral Interventions, 18*, pp. 179–190.

them to be effective across a variety of patients, including long-term psychiatric patients, people with mental retardation, people addicted to drugs, and people with traumatic brain injuries (LePage, 1999). Despite the successes of token economies demonstrated by past studies, research exploring factors that increase and decrease their effectiveness have diminished in the past two decades.

LePage et al. (2003) conducted research to examine a modern implementation of a token economy in an inpatient psychiatric facility. To determine whether establishing a token economy in the facility contributed to decreased violence, the researchers measured the amount of aggression before it was implemented and measured aggression again in the two years that followed the start of the program. The authors predicted there would be a significant decrease in violence after the token economy program was established.

PARTICIPANTS

The participants in the study were housed for different periods of time in a 24-bed inpatient psychiatric unit. This unit was part of a larger 150-bed state psychiatric facility made up of six total units. Patients who were admitted to the unit had a variety of psychiatric diagnoses, including severe personality disorders and chronic mental illness. The unit where patients were studied was a general admission unit. Each of the six units in the facility also admitted patients younger than 18 years on a rotating basis.

In the year prior to the token economy being implemented in the facility, 316 patients were admitted to the psychiatric unit. Two hundred ninety of those patients were discharged during that year. An average of 26 new patients was admitted to the unit each month, and roughly 24 patients were released from the facility, on average, each month. Fifty-eight and a half percent of patients admitted to the hospital were male. The males admitted to the facility were an average of 32.8 years old. The average age of women admitted to the facility was 35.72 years. A typical male patient stayed in the facility for 18.77 days. A typical female patient stayed for 18.28 days. The number of patients in the facility on an average day was 26.

Starting two years after the token economy was established, the researchers examined patients in the unit for another year. During that time, 533 patients were admitted. Five hundred twenty-six of them were discharged during the year of observation. An average of 23 patients were admitted to the unit each month, and 22.2 patients were discharged. Of the new admits during the year, 55.5 percent were male. The average age of the males was 31.2 years and of females was 35.5 years old. Men stayed at the facility for an average of 22.03 days, and women's stays averaged 21.13 days. As they did during the first year that they studied the unit, the researchers did not include patients who stayed for longer than 100 days because such a long stay was not typical of most of the patients in the facility.

TOKEN ECONOMY

All patients who were admitted to the unit were given the option of enrolling in the token economy program. A staff member explained the token economy system to the new patients and gave them a patient handbook that described the program. Each patient who wanted to be included signed a form indicating their agreement to follow the program rules. On being admitted, some patients were too psychotic to understand the program. Those patients were still given a patient handbook and were allowed to enroll, but their program participation was more closely supervised and actively informed by the unit staff.

To conform with the request of mental health advocacy groups, the token economy program that was set up was voluntary for patients. They could opt out of the program at any time. Patients enrolled in the program who were not compliant with the rules, by, for example, failing to pay for the items they desired (reinforcers) with the tokens they earned, could be removed from the program by the researchers. Because the reinforcers were highly desired by the patients, more than 99 percent of new admits to the unit enrolled in the program. Those patients who were removed from the program by the researchers were typically out for only a day or two before requesting to be allowed back in.

The tokens in this study were called "credits." The researchers did not use the term "token" because there was a negative bias against its use at the time the research program was developed. The actual credits were small ink stamps of happy faces, dolphins, and the like that were made on a sheet of paper. An attempt was made for each clinician who worked with the patients to have a unique, identifiable stamp. This was done to help keep track of patient compliance and where patients were earning their credits. The sheets on which credits were recorded were standard sheets of typing paper with eight columns—one for each day of the week and a column for staff to record patients' participation in required programs. The sheets also had space to help patients keep track of meetings and other requirements of their hospitalization. Patients' sheets were collected at the end of the day on Sundays. Staff members prepared new credit sheets for each enrolled patient to use in the upcoming week. Unused credits from the previous week were rolled over to the next week. New credit sheets were given to patients on Monday morning. Some patients attempted to forge credits with stolen ink stamps or magic markers. Most of the forgeries were detected by staff members who noticed inconsistencies in the stamps or were not fooled by the drawings made with magic markers. Although they were not allowed to redeem them, the patients who forged credits were not punished for their first offense. Instead, the researchers viewed the forgeries as evidence that the credits were highly desired by the patients and had power to help influence the patients' behavior. Patients who forged credits twice, however, were temporarily removed from the program.

The credits in the study did not appeal to all patients for a variety of reasons. Some patients only responded to more tangible reinforcers, such as poker chips. Other patients required more frequent reinforcement to effectively influence their behavior. Giving these patients typical credits at a higher frequency would have left them with a large credit surplus that would have undermined the influence that desiring additional credits had on the patients' behavior. Instead, they were awarded poker chips and told that some number of the chips was equal to one credit.

Credits were awarded to patients for following rules that facilitated their treatment or engaged in behaviors that would be helpful to them when they reentered the community. Examples of these behaviors included showing up to meetings and activities on time, participating in group activities, staying for the duration of activities, attending recreational activities, bathing themselves and maintaining good hygiene, cleaning their rooms, and taking their medication without having to be reminded. Patients were given credits as soon after they engaged in the desired behaviors as individual situations would allow.

Some patients had more individualized behavior plans to help modify problem behaviors that were unique to them. Desired behavioral outcomes included increasing exercise and the consumption of food, spending more time practicing relaxation, and practicing social skills. For patients who engaged in extremely inappropriate behaviors, such as masturbating openly in the unit or intense foul language, credits could be deducted in combination with reinforcement for more appropriate, alternative behaviors. Credits could also be deducted for violations of safety rules, such as smoking in a room, or for violating laws by attacking or threatening someone else in the unit or destroying property. In the case of such severe violations, all tokens could be removed, depending on the severity of the offense. These patients could not redeem tokens for 24 hours, but could begin earning new tokens again immediately.

Credits awarded to the patients could be redeemed for additional privileges any day. These privileges included passes to leave the unit and go on the grounds, shopping trips, additional smoking breaks, and movie trips. Credits could also be redeemed at the token store, which was housed in the unit where the research was done. The token store was open for one hour on Saturday and on Sunday. Items available at the store included, drinks, snacks, and phone cards. Patients could also rent radios and tape players at the store.

All staff members in the unit received training about the token economy program. They were not asked to participate until they were comfortable with all of its aspects. New staff members received training and were supervised by senior staff for a period to ensure they understood the program. Some senior staff served as arbiters of disagreements about how credits were awarded and policies and procedures. When the program policies were violated by staff members, a meeting was held to discuss the violation, and all policies were subsequently reinstated and followed.

The token economy program was quite inexpensive. The training of new staff began with a brief meeting with the unit psychologist, but the bulk of it occurred on the job. There were some copying costs to duplicate training manuals, patient handbooks, and token sheets. However, the token sheets were also used to help evaluate patients' progress. The items used as reinforcers to help change the behavior of patients would have been available to them anyway. It was estimated by the researchers that the total cost of the program was about $10 per day.

METHODS

The levels of aggression that occurred during the year prior to the implementation of the token economy in the unit (3/15/96–3/14/97) were compared with the levels of aggression that occurred in the two years after it started (3/15/97–3/15/99). Outliers in the data were defined as those individuals whose levels of aggression were more than 3.08 standard deviations above the mean for the unit. A standard deviation refers to the average distance that scores are away from the mean of all the scores. To be considered an outlier in this study, patients' aggression score would have to be three times the average distance that scores were from the mean of all the scores. In this study, only the top 0.1 percent of patient scores were excluded. This technique for removing outliers led only one patient to be excluded from the final analysis.

As part of the facility's protocol, all injuries of patients and staff were reported on standard forms and sent to administrative personnel. The data were then transferred to central databases as part of state requirements. The data used in this study were extracted from these databases. If data were discovered to be missing, the researchers consulted patient files to fill in the gaps.

The researchers compared the number of assaults that occurred in the year before the token economy program to the number of assaults that occurred in the two years after the program started. Assaults could be perpetrated by patients against members of the staff or against other patients. Assaults were defined by producing injuries that required any form of medical attention, including everything from visual examinations of the injured area by medical personnel to emergency room visits.

RESULTS

Overall, the unit had significantly lower rates of injury after the token economy was established than before it existed. The rate of injury dropped by 33 percent. The researchers also examined changes in the rate of injuries involving different dyads and changes in self-injury. These findings are illustrated by Figure 26.1

There was a significant decrease in patient-to-patient injuries after the token economy was established in the unit. Although there was also a decrease in employee injuries and self-injury, these changes were not statistically significant. Despite the lack of significant change in employee injuries, there is evidence that the severity of their injuries decreased after the token economy was put into

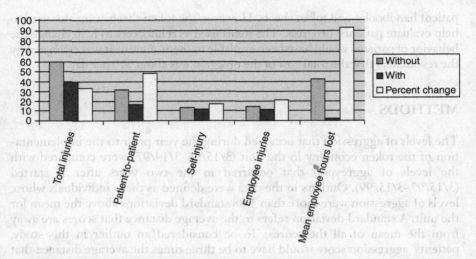

FIGURE 26.1 Comparison of Injuries and Injury-Related Events before and after the Token Economy

place. Evidence for this comes from the dramatic and significant decrease in the amount of time employees had to leave work to recover from their injuries, a 93 percent change after the implementation of the token economy.

The total decrease in lost time at work came to 146 hours. Assuming that the lost hours were restricted to the lowest paid employees who made $7.50 per hour, the total cost savings for not having to replace missing staff was $1,095. However, it is likely that the real savings were much greater because other employees were paid more money per hour. It should also be noted that overtime and the costs of medical treatments for injuries are not included in this amount. In addition, dealing with an injury typically takes about a half-hour of staff time. Fifty-five fewer injuries per year under the token economy translates into a savings of 27.5 hours. There were also savings as a result of needing less attention from psychiatrists, less prescription medication to treat aggression, fewer emergency room visits, and less administrative paperwork and follow through than is normally required when violent incidents occur.

DISCUSSION

This study by LePage et al. (2003) involved what is known as an AB research design. The A refers to the data collected before the implementation of the token economy. The B refers to the data collected after the token economy was established. Although the researchers argue that their findings provide important support for the efficacy of token economies for dealing with problem behaviors in institutional settings, they also acknowledge that other, more rigorous research designs would represent an improvement. For example, an ABA design—which would involve a period of no token economy, followed by a period with a token economy, followed by another period without a token economy—would demonstrate more conclusively that it was the token economy that led to changes in aggression rather than other potential sources of change, such as changes in the unit staff or changes in the characteristics of patients being admitted. An ABA design, however, would not have been practical. It would not have been in the best interests of the hospital staff or the patients to end a program that is likely to contribute to lower levels of aggression and injury.

Another factor that may have influenced the results of the experiment was the attitudes of the unit staff members toward the token economy. Some staff members were initially skeptical of the token economy program. However, as the program went on and staff members witnessed its benefits, they became more comfortable using the token economy as a regular part of their relationships with the patients.

The researchers point out that misconceptions about token economies may lead them to be underutilized in settings that have populations that could benefit from them. Critics of token economies have argued that they could discriminate against individuals who lack the self-control to earn tokens. They also have argued that token economies discourage individualized treatment or interventions and that their effects do not generalize to life outside institutions, where there are no longer tokens to reward desired behaviors. However, these concerns have not been evaluated by empirical research. LePage et al.'s (2003) findings suggest that token economies have great promise to positively change behavior.

REFERENCES

Cheung, P., Schweitzer, I., Tuckwell, V., & Crowley, K. C. (1996). A prospective study of aggression among psychiatric patients in rehabilitation wards. *Australian and New Zealand Journal of Psychiatry, 30,* 257–262.

Hillbrand, M., Foster, H. G., & Spitz, R. T. (1996). Characteristics and cost of staff injuries in a forensic hospital. *Psychiatric Services, 47,* 1123–1125.

Lehman, L. S., McCormick, R. A., & Kizer, K. W. (1999). A survey of assaultive behavior in Veterans Health Administration facilities. *Psychiatric Services, 50,* 941–944.

LePage, J. P. (1999). The impact of a token economy on injuries and negative events on an acute psychiatric unit. *Psychiatric Services, 50,* 941–944.

LePage, J. P., DelBen, K., Pollard, S., McGhee, M., VanHorn, L., Murphy, J., Lewis, P., Aboraya, A., & Mogge, N. (2003). Reducing assaults on an acute psychiatric unit using a token economy: A 2-year follow-up. *Behavioral Interventions, 18,* pp. 179–180.

Wynn, R., & Bratlid, T. (1998). Staff's experiences with patients' assaults in a Norwegian psychiatric university hospital: A pilot study. *Scandinavian Journal of Caring Sciences, 12,* 89–93.

CHAPTER 27

■ ■ ■ ■ ■

I CONFESS

We have all watched the police dramas in film and on TV in which the suspect is sitting in a small dimly lit room with bare walls. A few detectives who are eager to get him to confess to a crime are interrogating the suspect. In real criminal cases, as well as in popular media, a confession is viewed as powerful evidence in the prosecution of a case. The criminal justice system has constructed a number of safeguards to protect suspects from confessing to criminal acts that they did not commit. For example, suspects are read their Miranda rights and are given the opportunity to meet with an attorney. In addition, police may not coerce suspects with physical violence or threats to obtain a confession. Of course, police officers may attempt to use a variety of methods to gain confessions from suspects they believe were responsible for a crime. Saul Kassin and Katherine Kiechel, in introducing their research, refer to a popular police manual (Inbau, Reid, Buckley, & Jayne, 2004), now in its fourth edition, which guides police officers in a detailed nine-step strategy of techniques to elicit confessions. The approaches suggested use either a ploy of *minimization* or *maximization*. Minimization is a strategy that creates trust between the interrogator and the suspect by having the interrogator downplay the legal charges, place blame on the victim, state some reasons to soften the consequences of the crime, or provide the suspect with some excuses for the criminal behavior. In contrast, maximization refers to the use of procedures to frighten the suspect by magnifying and exaggerating the gravity of the crime and the strength of the evidence. Minimization can be typified as "good cop," whereas maximization can be typified as "bad cop" in the stereotype of detective stories. Kassin and Kiechel (1996) point out that although the American criminal justice system excludes confessions based on threats and false promises, courts have admitted coerced evidence under certain conditions.

However, research has continually shown that people believe it is unlikely that an individual would ever confess to a crime that they did not commit (Sukel

Incorporating the research of S. M. Kassin and K. L. Kiechel, "The Social Psychology of False Confessions: Compliance, Internalization, and Confabulation," 1996, *Psychological Science*, 7, pp. 125–128.

& Kassin, 1994). Kassin and Wrightsman (1985) outline three categories of false confessions. Remember, in each category, the person is admitting to a crime that he or she had not committed.

VOLUNTARY

This is the case in which a person confesses without external pressure. This may seem a little farfetched, but it does occur.

COERCED-COMPLIANT

This is the case in which a person admits to a crime in order to avoid a harsh interrogation, eliminate potential physical harm, or obtain a positive benefit.

COERCED-INTERNALIZED

This is the case in which a person develops the belief that he or she actually did commit the crime as a function of the process of interrogation.

It is this third type of false confession that is the focus of Kassin and Kiechel's (1996) research discussed in this chapter. It may seem like a very odd or unusual event for a person to come to believe they actually did commit a crime. However, there have been reported cases where police have used phony evidence to convince a vulnerable suspect that they actually committed a crime. Although not under study in the present research, it would be interesting to explore the factors that relate to vulnerability to this type of false confession. Kassin and Kiechel allude to participant's personality, level of stress, age, and mental status as potential factors related to vulnerability. Wright (1994) described the case of Paul Ingram, who was charged with satanic murders of newborn infants and rape. Although he initially denied the charges, while being interrogated under police custody for six months he was exposed to many crime scene details, including photographs. He was also informed that he was likely to be repressing (i.e., unconsciously forgetting) his criminal involvement. A clergyman and the police pressured him into making a confession. Eventually he began to "remember" how he came to commit the crimes, and he entered a plea of guilty and was imprisoned. In this case, there never was any physical evidence linking Ingram to the crime. A later review of this case indicated that Ingram was "brainwashed" into confessing to a crime he never committed.

Another line of contemporary research that tied directly to this sort of false confession is the research about memory. It is apparent that information occurring after an event has happened can significantly alter the recall of the event. The research reported in Chapter 12 is a very good case in point. The research described in that chapter suggests that young children were particularly at risk for "false memory." Loftus (1993) indicated that it is even possible to implant false memories of trauma, including child abuse, that presumably were long buried in the unconscious mind. This has raised an enormous amount of controversy, especially by questioning the authenticity of adults remembering "repressed" incidents of child abuse in their own childhoods. All of this leads us to the research questions for this chapter. Is it possible for crime suspects to accept guilt for crimes that they never committed? Can the memories of these suspects become altered so that they believe and substantiate their guilt?

THE CRIME

It is important for you to know that many important issues cannot be investigated in the environment in which they occur because of ethical concerns. In this study, like many others, the question was explored by setting up a laboratory simulation of the issue we want to investigate. Observations in labs are not automatically equivalent to what occurs in the actual setting. However, through careful laboratory investigations, a great deal can be learned that has significant implications for real-world events.

The participants in this experiment were 79 male and female undergraduate college students. The students participated for extra course credit and were drawn from a student body with a mean SAT of 1300 (a very bright group). The students believed they were going to be involved in an investigation of reaction time.

The procedure involved having two people (one was a participant and the other a female confederate) engage in a keyboarding assignment. The task involved the confederate reading a list of letters and the participant typing the letter on a computer keyboard. The roles were to be reversed after three minutes, but this never occurred because of the emergence of "the crime." Before the typing began, participants were informed specifically not to press the ALT key. If they pressed this key, it would induce the experimental program to terminate and data collected would be lost. It would end the experimental session. After a minute of the experimental procedure, while the confederate was reading letters and the participant was typing, the computer stopped functioning and an agitated, upset researcher accused the participant of having pressed the ALT key against specific directives not to do so. Participants in all four groups initially denied the accusation. After the experimenter fiddled with the keyboard and told the participant that data had been lost, he again asked if the participant touched the ALT key.

The participants were randomly assigned to one of the four following groups:
High vulnerability—False witness present
High vulnerability—False witness absent
Low vulnerability—False witness present
Low vulnerability—False witness absent
The first independent variable manipulated by the experimenters was vulnerability. Vulnerability referred to how certain each participant was concerning

his or her own status regarding "the crime." *High vulnerability* means that a person is not very certain about having committed the crime, whereas *Low vulnerability* means that a person is pretty certain of their innocence. Vulnerability was manipulated by varying the pace of the key-typing task. High rates of key typing (67 letters per minute) are equated to high vulnerability; low rates (43 letters per minute) of key typing are equated to low vulnerability. The assumption is that at low relaxed speeds you are very aware of your behavior and keying and are less likely to make errors due to rushing. At high keying speeds, you are moving at a feverish pace and are likely to miskey and not even be aware of making a mistake. The task for the participant was to key-type letters that were read by the confederate at either high or low speeds.

The second independent variable was whether there was falsely incriminating evidence available, in this case, the presence of a witness to "the crime." In this experiment, after the participant initially denied involvement in pressing the ALT key, the experimenter asked the confederate if she saw anything. In the *False witness present* condition, she confirmed that the participant did, indeed, press the ALT key. In the *False witness absent* condition, the confederate stated that she did not see what happened.

The experimenters used three dependent variables to assess different levels of the participant's response to being falsely accused. Remember that no participant in any of the four conditions ever touched the ALT key; all were falsely accused. The first dependent measure was *Compliance*, which was measured by whether participants agreed to sign the following "confession note" drafted by the experimenter:

I hit the ALT key and caused the program to crash. Data were lost.

To assess the participant's *Internalization*, the second dependent measure, recordings were made of the participant's behavior immediately on leaving the laboratory room. In a reception room, a confederate pretending to be the next participant, who overheard what transpired in the laboratory room, met the participant leaving the lab. The confederate asked the participant, "What happened?" The recording of participants' responses was coded for internalized guilt presence or absence by independent raters who did not know which of the four experimental conditions participants were in. The raters were unaware of the participant's group assignment so that this would not impact their ratings. The agreement between raters was 96 percent indicating excellent consensus on what was meant by the presence or absence of internalized guilt. An example of a response that demonstrated internalized guilt present response was "I hit the wrong button and ruined the program"; an example of the absence of internalized guilt was denial of any involvement in the "crime."

To determine the presence or absence of *Confabulation*, the third dependent variable, the experimenter brought the participant back into the lab room and reread the list of letters used in the experiment. The participant was asked to remember details of how or when they hit the ALT key. This investigation sought to determine if the participants would create specific details or evidence, in police terms, to account for the "crime" they were accused of committing. A positive confabulation response might be "I hit it with my hand after you asked me to type a Z." An absence of confabulation would be any failure to come up with a description of how they committed the "crime" of hitting the ALT key. Inter-rater assessment judging the presence or absence of confabulations achieved 100 percent agreement. In accordance with good research procedure, all participants were completely debriefed at the conclusion of the session.

RESULTS

Across all four groups, almost 70 percent of the participants signed the confession, 28 percent showed internalization, and 9 percent confabulated to include details of their research experience to show how they committed the "crime." The results, broken down by groups, are shown in Table 27.1.

The major hypothesis in this study was that high vulnerability with a witness would most likely lead to higher levels in the three dependent measures, and low vulnerability without a witness would favor lower levels in the dependent measures. The data confirm this hypothesis. Differences between these groups in statistical analyses were significant at $p < .001$ for compliance and internalization, and $p < .005$ for confabulation. As we have seen in other chapters, such levels of probability make it exceedingly unlikely (1 in a 1,000 or 5 in a 1,000) that the results were a result of chance alone. In looking further at the data, you can see that 35 percent of participants in the low vulnerability—witness absent group indicated compliance by signing the confession. However, none of these

TABLE 27.1 Percentage of Participants Showing Compliance, Internalization, and Confabulation

| | PERCENTAGE | | |
GROUP	Compliance	Internalization	Confabulation
High vulnerability—witness present	100	65	35
High vulnerability—witness absent	65	12	0
Low vulnerability—witness present	89	44	6
Low vulnerability—witness absent	35	0	0

participants showed any signs of internalization or confabulation. If you look at the groups that included the presence of a witness and had high vulnerability, you see how powerful these were, especially when combined, to affect all three dependent variables. This investigation provides strong support for the idea that increasing a suspect's vulnerability and providing a false witness can influence people to take the responsibility for acts they did not commit. These independent variables, vulnerability and witness present, are not unusual practices, but rather are common strategies used in the investigative process. The findings in this study suggest that caution should be employed by those in the criminal justice system because it is very possible, even likely, that an innocent suspect may sign a confession, internalize blame, and even confabulate details. Keep in mind that the outcomes seen in this study were obtained on participants who were intelligent, self-assured college students who were under minimal stress. If you compare these participants to actual crime suspects who are under high stress, often in jail, and separated from family and friends, you can imagine the effect obtained in this study may be magnified greatly in the real world.

REFERENCES

Inbau, F. E., Reid, J. E., Buckley, J. P. & Jayne (2004). *Criminal interrogation and confessions* (4th ed.). Baltimore: Williams & Wilkins.

Kassin, S. M., & Kiechel, K. L. (1996). The social psychology of false confessions: compliance, internalization, and confabulation. *Psychological Science, 7,* 125–128.

Kassin, S. M., & Wrightsman, L. S. (1985). Confession evidence. In S. M. Kassin & L. S. Wrightsman (Eds.), *The psychology of evidence and trial procedure* (pp. 67–94). Beverly Hills, CA: Sage.

Loftus, E. (1993). The reality of repressed memories. *American Psychologist, 48,* 518–537.

Sukel, H. L., & Kassin, S. M. (1994, March). *Coerced confessions and the jury: An experimental test of the "harmless error" rule.* Paper presented at the biennial meeting of the American Psychology-Law Society, Sante Fe, NM.

Wright, L. (1994). *Remembering Satan.* New York: Alfred A. Knopf.

CHAPTER 28

I'M OK, YOU'RE NOT

Prejudice, as the word is usually used, is an irrational attitude of hostility directed against an individual, group, or race. It is an ugly thing. It is also very common. When this irrational attitude is directed against the supposed characteristics of a group, it is a kind of prejudice called *stereotyping*. Prejudice has been studied for a long time in psychology (see, for example, Miller & Bugelski, 1948), and during the past decade, there have been many studies on this important issue (see Hilton & von Hippel, 1996, for a review).

It takes some courage to do these studies because in order to study prejudice and stereotypes, we have to admit that they exist. Moreover, the study of these attitudes often involves exposure to the distasteful details of prejudicial beliefs that may be held by those around us, maybe even by people we like, or love. This can make us uncomfortable, and rightly so. One reason why the study of prejudice is undertaken in psychology is because researchers are horrified by it. They believe that achieving understanding of prejudice may be one pathway to eliminating it. Sometimes the researchers themselves are members of the stereotyped group under study. You can imagine it is not easy for them to receive constant reminders of negative stereotypes about their own group.

We take the time to introduce this topic in this way because the study to be reviewed in this chapter examines stereotyping and other prejudice against two groups: young Jewish women and gay men. Some students are members of one of these groups, and many of you will have friends or family members included in these groups. It may upset you to read aspects of the stereotypes that are held about these people. It upsets us. Psychologists study many topics that are deeply and personally upsetting to some people, including such things as racism, sexuality, religious practices, social class, and child abuse. We believe it is better to study sensitive topics than to ignore them. Ignorance has always been a poor solution to human problems.

Incorporating the research of S. Fein and S. J. Spencer, "Prejudice as Self-Image Maintenance: Affirming the Self through Derogating Others," 1997, *Journal of Personality and Social Psychology*, 73, pp. 31–44.

Steven Fein and Steven Spencer (1997) did three related investigations to test different aspects of a hypothesis that prejudice is linked to a person's own self-image. As we have seen in previous chapters, it is not unusual that several small studies are reported in one journal article. If the studies are closely related, there is some economy for the reader. The introduction to the topic is likely to be the same for all of them, and the conclusions can summarize all the study findings at once. Fein and Spencer believed that, ironically, prejudice results from inherent attempts of people to maintain their own feelings of self-worth and self-integrity. People like to feel good about themselves. When something threatens positive feelings about the self, probably the best way to deal with the resulting discomfort is to confront the source. We do not always do that. If, for example, you have done something that later does not appear very smart—such as sitting on the plate of pizza (with extra toppings) that you left on a kitchen stool—you might rationalize it by saying that you were tired and not thinking too clearly. This permits you to remove the threatening idea that you were stupid, replacing it with the idea that you were merely tired. Your sense of self-worth and self-integrity has been maintained or restored.

Steel, Spencer, and Lynch (1993) pointed out that threats to self-worth do not always have to be addressed directly. Sometimes people will accept one set of negative implications about themselves and turn elsewhere to bolster some other aspect of their self-image, increasing their overall total sense of self-adequacy. For example, a person who believes that he is not particularly intelligent might accept and ignore that feeling, while taking particular pride in some other sort of personal achievement.

Unfortunately, making negative assessments of others is another tactic people use to feel better about themselves. Threats to a person's self-image can result in that person becoming more prejudiced. When people make disparagements in order to feel better, they avoid having to do anything about the sources of threat that lowered their self-image in the first place. The ability of prejudice to restore positive feelings about the self in prejudiced people has been called the *self-affirming* nature of prejudice. Self-affirmation is the name given to our own reassurance that we have overall personal worth and integrity.

STUDY 1

Fein and Spencer (1997) believed that increased self-affirmation ought to lead to decreased prejudice. A good way to think about this proposition is to imagine that each person needs to maintain a certain pool or supply of feelings of self-worth. Unfortunately, prejudice has been shown to boost self-worth and adds to this supply. If the self-worth supply is increased by having people do other, nonprejudicial, self-affirming things, self-worth levels will be high, and prejudice will be less necessary. Fein and Spencer set up a situation in which one group of people had the opportunity to review some aspect of their lives that they particularly valued and to remind themselves of the reasons why this value was important. This was the self-affirmation manipulation. Another group performed a task involving similar amounts of time, but did not engage in self-affirmation.

Participants and Procedure for Study 1

The participants in Study 1 were 54 students from an introductory psychology course at the University of Michigan who received course credit for being in the study.

They were told that they were going to be in two pieces of research. The first was described as a study of values and the second was supposed to be an investigation of how people evaluate job applicants. Really, the "values study" was a manipulation, or set of created conditions, within the investigation designed to create or boost self-affirmation in half the participants. *Self-affirmation* and *no affirmation* were operationally defined by the manipulation in the so-called values study. Half of the participants received the self-affirmation manipulation. The participants in the self-affirmation group were given a list of words such as *social life, business, pursuit of knowledge,* and *art.* They were asked to choose the topic from the list that had the most value to them and write a paragraph about why it was important. This was considered self-affirmation because it gave the participants a chance to feel good about their beliefs. In contrast, the participants in the no-affirmation control group were asked to choose a value that was least important to them and write a paragraph about why this value might be important to someone else. This no-affirmation procedure was conducted so both groups would have a somewhat parallel lab experience with the exception that one group was self-affirmed and one was not.

For the second part of Study 1, the participants were told their task was to evaluate a woman who was applying for a job as personnel manager in an organization. They were told to assess the fit between this individual and the job as accurately as possible. They were given a job description and a fictitious job application. The application was constructed by the researchers to make the candidate appear fairly well qualified for the position, but not an excellent match. There was a photograph on the application. After examining the application, the participants were asked to view an eight-minute videotape that showed an interview with the applicant. The woman playing the applicant put on an adequate performance, but was not outstandingly positive or negative.

All research participants saw the same videotape. The application materials shown to all participants were the same except a few modifications had been made to imply that the woman belonged to one of two different ethnic groups: Jewish or Italian. These groups were chosen because at that time on the Michigan campus there was a prejudicial stereotype that was widely held among the student body about young Jewish women. These women were the target of racist jokes about what was called the Jewish American Princess, or JAP, stereotype. This particular prejudice was chosen for study because many students openly believed it and seemed to see nothing racist in its endorsement. Italian ethnicity was chosen for comparison because pilot testing indicated that there was no widely held stereotype of any sort associated with Italian ethnicity on this campus.

To manipulate the ethnicity of the woman who was supposed to be the job candidate, some applications had different details than others. Half of the applications had the name Julie Goldberg, but on the others the name was Maria D'Agostino. Julie's application showed her volunteering for a Jewish organization and Maria's listed volunteer work for a Catholic organization. On the application, Julie belonged to a sorority that consisted predominantly of Jewish women, whereas Maria belonged to a sorority that had mainly non-Jewish women as members. All the other printed material was identical. The photograph was varied slightly so that Julie was wearing a Star of David necklace and Maria was wearing a cross. Julie had her hair clipped up with what was known on the campus as a "JAP clip," whereas Maria had her hair down. Because the participants viewed the same video, a sweater was arranged to cover the necklace, and the woman's hair was arranged to be intermediate between clipped up and let down.

Outcome Measures for Study 1

Participants rated the job applicants in terms of overall personality on a 7-point scale. Twenty-one specific traits were rated including *intelligent, friendly, trustworthy, arrogant, materialistic, cliquish, happy, warm, superficial,* and *vain*. The extent to which applicants were qualified for the job was also rated. *Prejudice* was operationally defined as high scores given on negative personality traits in this procedure.

Results of Study 1

Fein and Spencer (1997) predicted that participants who had not been self-affirmed and who believed that the job applicant was Jewish would be more negative toward her. The data are presented in Figure 28.1.

The prediction was supported; although there were no significant differences among the personality ratings from the two self-affirmed groups and the non–self-affirmed group who believed that the candidate was ethnically Italian, the nonaffirmed people who believed that she was Jewish rated her personality significantly more negatively ($p < .05$). As you can see in Figure 28.1, the same pattern was found for evaluation of the candidate's qualifications for the job. The data presented in Figure 28.1 consist of the total ratings given by each participant, averaged with the total ratings for all other participants. Because there were 21 traits rated, it appears that, most typically, participants rated traits around 3 or 4, using the middle of the 7-point rating scale. Ratings of about 3 or 4 on each of 21 traits would result in the kinds of totals found in Figure 28.1. We mention this because as part of your critical thinking, you should always try to discover what is being scaled when interpreting graphic material.

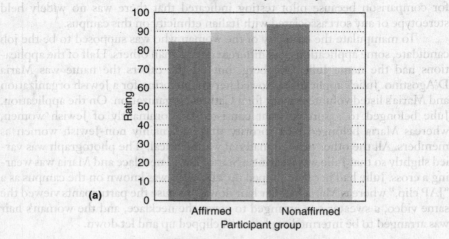

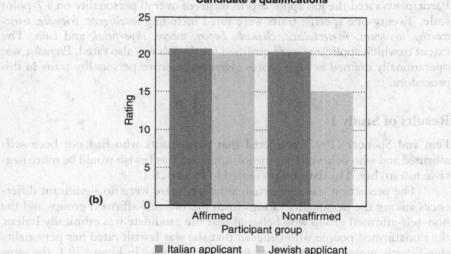

FIGURE 28.1 Ratings from Study 1. Affirmed and nonaffirmed participant's ratings of candidate's (a) personality and (b) qualifications for Italian and Jewish applicant conditions.

The nonaffirmed participants rated the Jewish woman as significantly less qualified ($p < .001$). The data shown for qualifications consisted of the average of the total ratings given by each participant on each of four statements, using a 7-point scale. An example of one these statements was "I feel this person would make an excellent candidate for the position in question."

STUDY 2

In Study 2, Fein and Spencer (1997) asked if posing a threat to self-image would make people more likely to use stereotypes to describe a member of a group. To return to the analogy of a pool or supply of self-worth discussed in Study 1, threatening self-worth ought to lower the supply, forcing people to behave in ways that would rebuild self-worth. In a way, this was the opposite question from that posed in Study 1: this second study set people up to feel negatively about themselves and predicted this would make them more likely to stereotype others. This was expected because, as was shown in Study 1, self-affirmation decreased prejudice. It would make sense, therefore, that a lowered self-affirmation would be associated with more prejudice, demonstrated in this case by increased stereotyping.

Participants and Procedure for Study 2

The participants were 61 male undergraduates from Williams College who were given either extra credit in their introductory psychology course or an opportunity to win money in a lottery. Allowing research participants to take part in a drawing for cash is one way to attract willing participants without having to spend as much money as would be required to pay each one of them a significant sum.

Half of the participants received a bogus intelligence test given on a desktop computer. They were told that this was "a new form of intelligence test that is given on the computer. It measures both verbal and reasoning abilities." They were told it was a valid way to measure intelligence. In fact, the fake test had been constructed so there were no possible correct answers to some questions, and the time limits given were so short that some items could not possibly be done in the time allotted. At the end of the test, the computer gave these participants a fake score for each part of the test. These scores ranged from the 56th percentile down to the 33rd percentile. The percentile rating of a score tells what percent of scores are typically found below the score in question. At best, these students were being told that they were barely in the top half of the population of people who had taken this intelligence test. Williams College is a very selective college, and these scores were disappointing to the experimental group participants, who were accustomed to doing well on other standardized tests, such as the SAT. The other half of the participants, the control group, were given the same test, but were told that it was a fake intelligence test. They were also told they were in the control group of a study and that although they should do the test, they should not work too hard because some of the questions were impossible. They were told not to worry about the phony scores that they would receive at the end. In short, they were told the truth about what was going on.

Following the testing experience, both groups were given what was described as a social judgment task. They were told they would be read some information about a man and then would make some judgments about him. The story they were told was of a man, Greg, who was trying to make it as an actor while living in the East Village in New York City. He got a part in a controversial play directed by a young director. He was eager to work with this particular director. The pronouns indicated that the director was a man. After some rehearsals, Greg asked the director if he wanted to get "a drink or something" so they could talk more about Greg's part in the play. There were more details in the story, but this was the substance. The intelligence test procedure had created two groups: those who were told the truth about the test (neutral self-image group) and those who thought the test was real (negative self-image group). These two groups were divided in half. Half of each group received an additional implication about Greg: that he was gay. The other half was led to believe that he was straight. This was accomplished by small changes to the story of Greg. In the *straight-implied condition*, participants were told that Greg had a girlfriend named Anne with whom he had been living for several years. She was mentioned several times in the story. In the *gay-implied condition*, participants were told Greg had "a partner," but no name or gender was specified. With these two variables: *IQ test feedback* and *Greg's implied sexual orientation*, four groups could be constructed:

> Neutral test feedback/Gay implied
> Neutral test feedback/Straight implied
> Negative test feedback/Gay implied
> Negative test feedback/Straight implied

Outcome Measures in Study 2

Following the story about Greg, participants were asked to rate Greg's personality on a number of measures using an 11-point scale ranging from 0—*not at all like Greg*, to 11—*extremely like Greg*. Three of the dimensions rated were not considered to be part of a gay stereotype: intelligent, funny, and boring. The stereotype-relevant traits included sensitive, assertive/aggressive, considerate, feminine, strong, creative, and passive. If participants endorsed the gay stereotype, they scored Greg high for some of these traits (e.g., sensitive, feminine) and low for others (e.g., assertive/aggressive, strong). This was done on purpose so that participants would pay attention to their ratings and not merely mark all traits high or low, without thinking about them.

Results for Study 2

The results of this study are shown in Figure 28.2. Remember that some individuals had been given a negative self-image through thinking that they had done

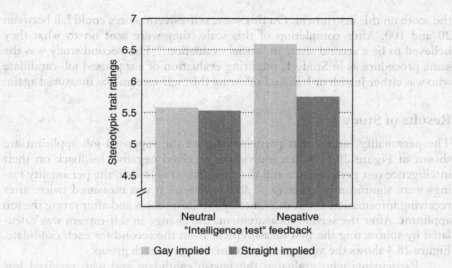

FIGURE 28.2   Findings from Study 2.
Amount of stereotypical gay trait ratings of Greg
by neutral and negative feedback participants in
the gay-implied and straight-implied groups.

poorly on a real intelligence test. Others had an experience that had little or no effect, called here *a neutral effect*, on self-image: they had taken a test that they had been told in advance was a fake.

As Fein and Spencer predicted, participants who had experienced an attack to their self-image on the intelligence test were significantly ($p < .001$) more likely to use stereotypically gay descriptions when their information implied that Greg was gay.

PARTICIPANTS AND PROCEDURE FOR STUDY 3

Study 3 combined some procedures of Study 1 and Study 2. Participants were 126 introductory psychology students from University of Michigan who participated as partial fulfillment of a requirement in an introductory psychology course. Seventeen students were excluded because they were Jewish and 7 because they were foreign students, unlikely to be familiar with the stereotype about Jewish American women. Two more were eliminated during participation because they refused to believe the false feedback about their supposed intelligence test.

All participants were given the bogus intelligence test used in Study 2. In this study, however, all participants were told that the intelligence test was real, but half of them were told they had done very well and half were told they had done poorly. Next, they were given a scale developed by Heatherton and Polivy (1991) that measured their self-esteem. *Self-esteem* was operationally defined as the score on this instrument. On this scale, self-esteem scores could fall between 20 and 100. After completion of this scale, they were sent on to what they believed to be a second study in "social evaluation." This second study was the same procedure as in Study 1, requiring evaluation of a supposed job candidate who was either Jewish or Italian. Following this, self-esteem was measured again.

Results of Study 3

The personality ratings that participants gave the supposed job applicant are shown in Figure 28.3. When individuals received negative feedback on their intelligence test performance and the candidate was Jewish, the personality ratings were significantly lower ($p < .01$). Self-esteem was measured twice: after receiving information about their intelligence test scores and after rating the job applicant. After the second measurement, the change in self-esteem was calculated by subtracting the first measurement from the second for each candidate. Figure 28.4 shows the average self-esteem change in each group.

Participants who evaluated the Jewish candidate and who received low scores on the fake intelligence test had a significantly greater increase in self-esteem ($p < .05$). There is a statistically significant difference, but it is not as dramatic as it may appear if you consider the scale on the *y*-axis of Figure 28.4. In this study, self-esteem could range from 20 to 100, and the maximum change seen here is a bit more than 3 points. In evaluating graphic presentations of data,

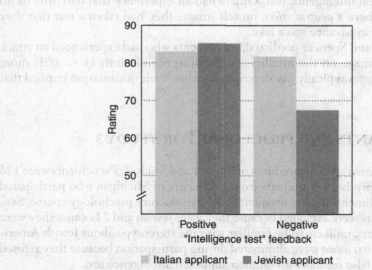

FIGURE 28.3 Results from Study 3. Ratings of candidate's personality from positive and negative feedback participants for Italian and Jewish applicant conditions.

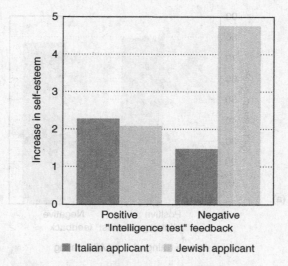

FIGURE 28.4   Increases in Reported Self-Esteem Following Ratings of Italian-Appearing or Jewish-Appearing Applicant for Negative and Positive Feedback Applicants

there is no substitute for being a careful consumer. It is important to look at the graph to discern the overall trends in the data, but it is also important to look carefully at the *y*-axis. Differences between groups can be made to appear striking if the data range is stretched out or if only part of the whole data range is shown. This is illustrated in Figure 28.5, using the self-esteem data from Figure 28.4 plotted in two different ways.

When part of the range is shown, the graph should indicate this with a "break line" that is either two little hash marks or a little squiggle in the otherwise straight vertical axis. The break line is there to help alert you that part of the data range is missing. In sources other than scientific journals, for example, in advertising, the *y*-axis is often distorted and break lines are missing in a deliberate attempt to mislead. Within scientific publications, the data presented in graphs are also described in the results, where you can find statistical tests that should support the graphic depictions of data. For example, even though the self-esteem differences in the study were small in absolute terms, the results indicated that the differences were statistically significant. Of course, Fein and Spencer (1997) pointed out the small but significant nature of these differences. As we have mentioned previously, we would not want you to think that reputable scientists purposely misrepresent data. Exaggeration of data is, however, common practice in the realm beyond reputable science. As a consumer of information, you should protect yourself by paying attention to important details, such as the ways in which data are presented.

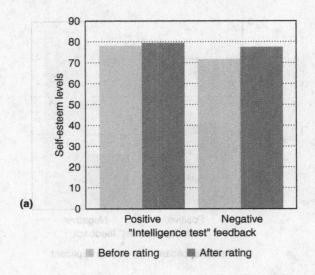

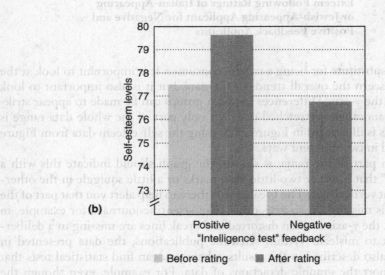

FIGURE 28.5   What a Difference a Scale Makes.
The (a) top and (b) bottom graph both show the same data taken from the Fein & Spencer study: the self-esteem levels before and after rating the Jewish applicant. Although the numbers are the same in both graphs, the y-axis of graph (b) on, a small section of the range was selected and stretched to make the differences appear to be bigger.

DISCUSSION

The results of this study supported the overall hypotheses of Fein and Spencer (1997). Study 1 showed that participants who were self-affirmed were less likely to be prejudiced than those who were in a neutral state. Study 2 showed that participants who had been given negative feedback were more likely to stereotype an individual than those in a neutral state. Study 3 showed that negative self-esteem not only leads to prejudice but also that prejudiced ratings, in turn, raised the self-esteem of the raters.

Aside from its important main findings, this study also illustrates the shallowness of stereotyping and other prejudice. Although prejudicial beliefs may be considered by bigots to be great truths and may be deeply held, it is noteworthy that this study showed how little was required in order for prejudice to be invoked resulting in negative ratings of other people. A necklace, hairstyle, and social group activities were enough to decrease ratings of job suitability for Julie. A residence in the East Village, living with a partner, as well as a few other non-specific descriptors, were adequate to make college men apply existing gay stereotypes to Greg. Clearly, it does not take anything substantial to unleash the mechanisms of prejudice.

It is important to notice that the prejudice displayed here, particularly following a lowering of self-esteem, was not broadly aimed, shotgun fashion, at anybody and everybody. If that were so, in Study 3, Maria would also have been rated lower in personality and job suitability by individuals who received negative feedback from the fake intelligence test. The prejudice seen here seems to be turned on in response to an attack to self-esteem, but only when participants believed that the applicant belonged to a group for which there was a preexisting negative stereotype. This research also casts doubt on the view that bigotry is a personality characteristic that is stable over time and across conditions. At least in this study, students were not as likely to act in a biased manner until their own self-esteem was threatened. Are there students who would not act prejudiced even in the face of severe threats to self-esteem? This is a question for future research.

This study is part of a traditional view within social psychology that sees behavior largely as the outcome of a particular context, rather than viewing it as a result of ingrained and stable personality traits as we have seen in other chapters. These two views are not really contradictory, and there is some evidence that both operate together. As you have seen in earlier chapters, situations can be powerful determinants of behavior but probably only within the limits set by more stable traits. The cautionary tale is that given a sufficiently powerful setting, many of us might become bigots. An understanding of what is going on here might help decrease prejudice. We hope most people would feel worse, not better, if they realized that they had disparaged another person only to raise their own feelings of self-worth. It is an empirical question.

REFERENCES

Fein, S., & Spencer, S. J. (1997). Prejudice as self-image maintenance: Affirming the self through derogating others. *Journal of Personality and Social Psychology, 73*, 31–44.

Heatherton, T. F., & Polivy, J. (1991). Development and validation of a scale for measuring state self-esteem. *Journal of Personality and Social Psychology, 60*, 895–910.

Hilton, J. L., & von Hippel, W. H. (1996). Stereotypes. *Annual Review of Psychology, 47*, 237–271.

Miller, N. E., & Bugelski, R. (1948). The influence of frustrations imposed by the in-group on attitude expressed toward the out-group. *Journal of Psychology, 25*, 437–442.

Steel, C. M., Spencer, S. J., & Lynch, M. (1993). Self-image resilience and dissonance: the role of affirmational resources. *Journal of Personality and Social Psychology, 64*, 885–896.

CHAPTER 29

IT'S IN THE BAG

COGNITIVE DISSONANCE

Cognitive dissonance, sometimes shortened to *dissonance*, is the name given to the unpleasant feelings that are experienced when there is a difference between our attitudes and our behavior (Festinger, 1957). In one of the classic research demonstrations of dissonance, Festinger and Carlsmith (1959) assigned college student participants to a few tasks designed to be boring and pointless. One of these involved a tray with 12 spools on it. Participants were told that their goal was to remove and replace the spools in the tray, over and over, for 30 minutes while being watched and timed by an experimenter. Next, they were presented with a board that had 48 square pegs in it. The task with these was to lift each peg out and give it a quarter of a turn clockwise before replacing it. This was continued one after another, over and over, for an additional 30 minutes. Next, they were told that another student was usually employed to describe the research as "enjoyable," "interesting," "intriguing," and "exciting" to a subsequent participant who was already waiting in another room to be in the study. The experimenter explained that the student who usually did this could not show up that day and asked if these participants who had just completed the task would be willing to help out by saying these positive things to the next participant. In short, they were asked to lie. Participants received one of two levels of payment for telling this lie. Half of them were told that the usual payment was $1, and half were told it was $20—a considerable sum of money in 1959, when the study was done.

Once they had completed the task and told their lies, they were interviewed about their real feelings concerning the spool placing and peg turning. In this interview, the group that had been paid $1 rated the tasks as being more enjoyable than the group that had been paid $20. The people who were paid $1 had been put in a situation where dissonance was created. They had lied about these boring tasks and only received $1 in payment. The easiest way to remove

Incorporating the research of J. Stone, E. Aronson, A. L. Crain, M. P. Winslow, and C. B. Fried, "Inducing Hypocrisy as a Means of Encouraging Young Adults to Use Condoms," 1994, *Personality and Social Psychology Bulletin, 20*, pp. 116–128.

the dissonance was to change their opinions. That is exactly what occurred: they began to think that the tasks were really quite interesting and enjoyable. It seems that they might have been thinking something like "It was boring. I said it was fun. Why did I say that for only $1? Wait a minute, I guess it wasn't so boring after all, it was kind of interesting." The $20 group showed no comparable shift in attitude. They knew the task was boring, but they had a reason why they would lie about it to someone else: they were well paid.

This study illustrated one of the more interesting aspects of cognitive dissonance: people were uncomfortable, and something had to be changed in order to reduce dissonance—attitudes or behavior. Dissonance motivated a change because of the discomfort associated with it. Particularly when attitudes and behavior are in conflict, it is often easier to change the attitude than to change the behavior. In Festinger and Carlsmith's (1959) study, it was not possible to change the behavior because it was in the past—the spools had been placed, and the pegs had been turned.

Even when the behavior can be changed, it is sometimes easier to change the attitudes. For example, it is likely that smokers are aware of the health risks associated with this addiction. This should create dissonance between the attitude, *smoking is dangerous*, and the behavior, *I smoke*. There are two ways a person could reduce dissonance. The behavior could be changed; that is, the individual could quit smoking. However, it is more likely that the attitude will be modified. The smoker might say, "Smoking is dangerous, but not for *me*. I feel fine. Anyway, I know someone who lived to be 96 and smoked two packs a day. . . ." Thinking critically about behavior includes being cautious about generalizing from anecdotes that begin "I know a person who. . . ."

There have been hundreds of studies of cognitive dissonance; some of them examined this concept from a theoretical standpoint. It is not unusual for studies of dissonance to suggest practical applications as well (Petty, Wegener, & Fabrigar, 1997). A research project by Stone, Aronson, Crain, Winslow, and Fried (1994) illustrated this point. Their original motivation was to apply the cognitive dissonance theory to the problem of HIV and AIDS prevention among sexually active young adults. According to the U.S. Centers for Disease Control and Prevention, the HIV epidemic, with its end-stage illness known as AIDS, is the leading cause of death of Americans ages 25 to 44. From the beginning, the HIV infection spread quickly: the first 100,000 cases of AIDS in the United States were diagnosed within the first 9 years of the epidemic. The next 100,000 cases were diagnosed within the following 18 months. More than 300,000 Americans have died of AIDS-related complications. It is estimated that between 800,000 and 1 million Americans are infected with HIV.

Stone et al. (1994) wanted to explore the extent to which cognitive dissonance could be used to encourage condom use in young adults, who comprise the population most at risk for HIV infection. Hypocrisy is a form of cognitive dissonance, and Stone and his colleagues believed that many college students had a prevailing hypocrisy about condom use. Hypocrites are people who have contradictions in their lives. They may say one thing and do another. They might be people who make themselves appear, through words or actions, to be better than they really are. Many people believe that they should systematically use condoms to prevent HIV infection, yet they do not behave according to this belief. On the surface, it might seem that this dissonant situation would be a motive for change with the result being more frequent use of condoms. There are, however, numerous studies on this topic showing that students are more likely to change their attitudes than their behavior (Hays & Hays, 1992; Netting, 1992; Roche & Ramsbey, 1993).

PARTICIPANTS

The participants were recruited from a pool of students in psychology classes. Extra course credit was available to reward them for participation in research. The study was advertised as being about "health and persuasion" and sought students 18 to 25 years old who had been heterosexually active within the previous three months. These criteria were used in order to include people who might be at risk for HIV infection and who might have some use for condoms. Students who were married were screened out, as were those who had taken a blood test for HIV. This latter group was excluded because part of the experimental manipulation included raising awareness of HIV, and it was believed that people who had been tested for HIV had probably already had their awareness raised by the circumstances of the test. The final ethnically diverse sample consisted of 32 males and 40 females between the ages of 18 and 25 ($M = 19.20$). In addition to course credit for one hour of participation, they were paid $4 and told that this was because the experiment "sometimes runs a little more than an hour."

PROCEDURE

When the participants arrived, a sign on the door led them to believe they were at the AIDS Research Program Office. They were told that they would be helping to develop an AIDS prevention and education program for high schools. They were further told that a goal of this program was to teach sexually active teenagers that "condoms are the easiest and most reliable way to prevent the transmission of AIDS during intercourse." The variables that defined the experimental groups in this study were *commitment/no commitment* and *mindful/unmindful*.

Commitment Manipulation

To operationally define *commitment*, participants were asked to develop a little persuasive speech about the role of sex in HIV and to deliver it to a video camera. They were told that the researcher believed that college students would be highly effective in communicating to high school kids because the college students were older and more experienced, yet otherwise not so different that they would lose credibility. They were given some fact sheets about HIV and asked to outline their speech on paper. Next, they were allowed to rehearse, and their speech was taped. After this, they filled out a short HIV/AIDS knowledge questionnaire. The researchers believed that giving the speech and having it taped would result in commitment. In the noncommitment condition, participants were told to develop a persuasive speech about HIV and AIDS. They did not have to give the speech and so no taping took place. They were told that the purpose of developing the speech was to see if there was a relationship between developing persuasive material and memory for material of similar content. After outlining the speech, the participants completed the HIV/AIDS knowledge questionnaire, ostensibly to test their memories for facts.

Mindfulness Manipulation

The other independent variable was mindfulness. Half of each group described previously received the *mindful* condition. The *mindful* participants were told that their task was to try to figure out why condoms are difficult for most people to use. They were told this information was going to be included in the prevention program for high school students to help them "deal more effectively with these situations." Participants were given a list of circumstances that might make it difficult to use condoms. The items on this list had come from an earlier study (Aronson, Fried, & Stone, 1991), but participants were not told this. Participants were asked to read the list and then to make a separate list of circumstances surrounding their own past failures to use condoms, including personal examples missing from the list they had been given. In this way, researchers believed that participants would become mindful of the problems they had experienced and, in addition, of their own failure to use condoms. As you can see, mindfulness was operationally defined as asking participants to reflect about problems with condoms. The other half of the participants received the *unmindful* condition. They went directly from the commitment or noncommitment procedure to the dependent measures, without any reference to their own past condom use.

Experimental Groups

Although they did not know it, all participants had been assigned randomly to one of four experimental groups before they arrived in the lab. The combination of the two manipulations described above created four different groups: (1) mindful and committed, also called the *hypocrisy* group, (2) commitment and unmindful, (3) mindful and noncommitted, and (4) unmindful and noncommitted, an *information-only* control group. This is a standard procedure for dealing with two independent variables. Four groups, arranged in this way, are adequate to assess the effects of each variable. It is common in psychological research that

**FIGURE 29.1   Design of this Study Showing Creation of
Four Groups from Two Pairs of Variables**

	Commitment	
	Yes	No
	Prepare talk	Prepare talk
	Make video	No video

Mindfulness		
Yes	Hypocrisy	Mindful only
Think about own past		
Difficulties with condoms		
No	Commitment only	Information only
No opportunity given to		
think about own past		
Difficulties with condoms		

two pairs of variables are used to create four groups. Indeed, we have seen this in Chapter 12. The design of this study is diagrammed in Figure 29.1.

Dependent Variables

Stone et al. (1994) used two sorts of dependent variables in this study: self-report and behavioral. In general, self-report measures are easier to collect. They are usually questionnaires, surveys, or interviews. As we have noted in previous chapters, the problem is that what people *say* may not be a good representation of what they *do*. Even in a carefully constructed study, if all the outcomes were self-reports about behavior, we might have reason to be cautious about the validity of the findings. This is not to say that questionnaires and interviews are necessarily lacking in validity, we are only suggesting that one might have a little less confidence in the validity of findings if they were entirely based on self-reports. In contrast, although behavioral measures may have more validity, they can be very difficult to construct.

In the study by Stone et al. (1994) the self-report dependent measures were two interview questions: one about frequency of past condom use and one about predicted future condom use. Both questions were answered by having participants rate the percentage of use on a scale from 0 percent to 100 percent. This scale consisted of a 17-cm horizontal line like this with 0 percent printed at one end and 100 percent at the other:

0% _____ 100%

The students were asked to make a mark somewhere along the line to represent the likelihood of condom use. For example, if their estimate was 50 percent, the mark would be made in the middle.

Given that the topic of the study was condom use, the construction of a behavioral measure presented more of a challenge. As Stone et al. (1994) pointed out "we cannot crawl into bed with our subjects [participants] during their love-making." As an admittedly less-direct behavioral measure, the participants were given the opportunity to purchase condoms. The researchers were aware that purchasing condoms and using them are not the same thing. Nevertheless, taking condoms might be one behavioral indication of intent to use them. The condom purchase was engineered to make it seem confidential because the researchers believed that, otherwise, factors such as social pressure to buy condoms might influence condom purchasing behavior more than personal convictions.

One of the reasons why participants were paid $4—ostensibly for their time—was to be sure that they had money to buy condoms when the opportunity was presented. After they were given the money, they were asked to fill out a receipt for the social science business office. But before they could begin the receipt they were given the following story:

> . . . the AIDS educators from the Health Center sent over some condoms and pam-
> phlets on AIDS when they heard about our prevention program. They wanted us to
> give our subjects [participants] the opportunity to buy condoms for the same price
> they are sold at the health center—10 cents—and this way you don't have to go
> across campus and stand in a long line. I need to go next door and prepare for the
> next subject, so go ahead and finish this receipt; you can leave it here on the table.
> And if you want to buy some condoms, just help yourself to anything on that desk;
> that dish has some spare coins so you can make change. OK? Thanks again for
> coming in today. (Stone et al., 1994 p. 119)

Next, the experimenter left the participant alone, closing the office door. There were 140 condoms, 10 each of 14 different brands, in a clear plastic container. A sign said that they were 10 cents each and change was available in a bowl next to the condoms. To assess the number of condoms taken by each participant, the container was recounted and refilled after each person left.

More Questions

As the participants were leaving, the experimenter appeared in the hallway, claiming to have forgotten to ask them to complete a questionnaire about their recent sexual behavior. Although this might have seemed a bit contrived, no one refused. The questionnaire asked the frequency of sexual intercourse during the past month and the past year, as well as the number of sexual partners during these time frames. Participants were also asked about frequency of condom use. Following this, they were debriefed.

As an attempt to measure the long-term effectiveness of the experimental treatments on subsequent sexual behavior, telephone interviews were conducted with the participants approximately 90 days after the experiment. The interviews were conducted by research assistants who were unaware of the experimental condition to which the participants had belonged. In the phone calls, researchers introduced themselves, reminded participants about the study, and asked if they could obtain some follow-up information about the participant's sexual behavior since the study ended. No participant refused to help with this request. The questions concerned frequency of sexual intercourse and condom use and were similar to those that had been asked at the end of the lab study.

Results and Discussion

The researchers believed that having participants make their speeches for the video camera followed by a reminder of their own problems with condoms and hit-or-miss condom use would induce classic cognitive dissonance, or hypocrisy. Attitudes about condom use would be at variance with behavior, and this would produce stronger dissonance in this group than in any of the other groups. The question was, would this dissonance provoke behavior changes? The primary measure of this was the condom purchasing behavior of participants in each of the four groups. Figure 29.2 shows that hypocrisy, or dissonance, represented by the commitment/mindful group did result in more people obtaining condoms when compared to the commitment-only group ($p < .003$), the mindful-only group ($p < .04$), and the information-only group ($p < .01$).

Although a higher percentage of the participants who were experiencing dissonance purchased condoms, the number of condoms purchased did not show this as clearly. Figure 29.3 presents these data.

Both commitment-only and mindful-only groups purchased significantly fewer condoms than the dissonant hypocrisy group ($p < .04$ and $p < .05$, respectively). The information-only group was not significantly different than the

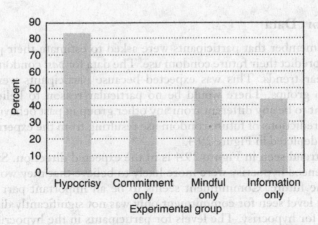

FIGURE 29.2 Percentage of Participants Who Obtained Condoms

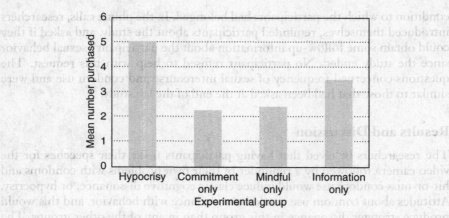

FIGURE 29.3   Number of Condoms Obtained

hypocrisy group ($p < .23$). There is no particular explanation for this nor does it support any particular hypothesis. The data concerning number of condoms purchased were, as researchers sometimes say, a bit fuzzy. The outcome was not as clear and obvious as it was for the percent of purchasers shown in Figure 29.2. The researchers presented the findings shown in Figure 29.3 so as to be completely honest about the outcomes and because it is possible that future research will uncover an explanation of why the number of condoms purchased did not present a clearer picture. Perhaps surprisingly, there were no gender differences on these measures: the purchasing behavior of males and females were not significantly different.

Self-Report Data

You will remember that participants were asked to estimate their past condom use and to predict their future condom use. The data for *past* condom use did not present clear trends. This was expected because participants were randomly assigned to groups. There would be no particular reason to believe that any group ought to be any different from any other group in past behavior. The participants' predictions of future condom use resulting from the experimental conditions are depicted in Figure 29.4.

The trend seen in Figure 29.4 is in the expected direction. Students who had experienced hypocrisy were more likely to believe that they would use condoms in the future. Commitment seems to be an important part of this and, indeed, the level seen for commitment only was not significantly different from that found for hypocrisy. The levels for participants in the hypocrisy condition were higher than those in the mindful-only ($p < .03$) and information-only ($p < .01$) conditions. You will remember that the data here were collected by

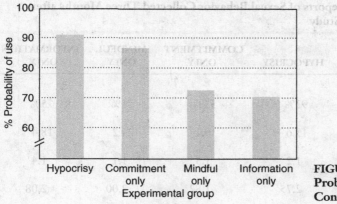

FIGURE 29.4   **Percent Probability of Future Condom Use**

asking students to respond to a scale line 17-cm long running from 0 percent to 100 percent.

Follow-Up Interviews

In telephone interviews conducted three months after the original study, researchers were able to reach 64 (89 percent) of the original 72 participants, and 52 (81 percent) of them reported having been sexually active since the study. Three of these participants were dropped from the interview data because they reported levels of sexual activity and condom use that were so high as to seem unlikely. Each individual claimed to have had sexual intercourse more than 90 times since the study and reported using condoms more than 90 times. In comparison, the highest group mean among other participants was 24 instances of sexual intercourse with an average of nine condoms used. It seems likely that the three participants who were dropped from the study had decided to have a bit of fun with the researchers in giving their answers. If this is what occurred, it is fortunate that they exaggerated to the extent that they were easy to detect. This incident raises a serious issue for interview and survey research in general. Setting aside the problems of faulty memory, discussed earlier in Chapters 12 and 13, if people willfully want to mislead researchers, it is sometimes fairly easy to do so. This further illustrates the value of behavioral measures that, depending on the research design, can be more difficult to falsify than mere verbal responses on surveys or interviews. If these three participants had wanted to disrupt the behavioral measure in this study, they could have taken handfuls of condoms, paying for them or not. They did not do this. Nevertheless, when they were phoned at home, with some distance between them and the researcher, they were comfortable in seemingly exaggerating their levels of sexual activity. This has been a common problem in self-report studies of sexuality (Catania, Gibson, Chitwood, & Cotes, 1990).

TABLE 29.1   Self-Reports of Sexual Behavior Collected Three Months after Participation in the Study

	HYPOCRISY	COMMITMENT ONLY	MINDFUL ONLY	INFORMATION ONLY
Percentage reporting condom use	92%	55%	71%	75%
Average amount of intercourse	13.6	9.1	24.2	18.4
Average number of sexual partners	1.2	1.5	1.1	1.4
Frequency of condom use	2.75	1.82	2.00	2.08
Number of condoms used	5.83	3.91	9.00	7.41
Percentage of times condoms used	63%	46%	44%	65%

Table 29.1 presents some of the data from the follow-up phone interview. Although, for example, the percentage of participants reporting condom use was higher in the hypocrisy group than in the commitment-only group, it was not significantly different from the mindful-only and information-only groups. A perusal of Table 29.1 suggests that the three-month follow-up interviews provided, in the words of Stone et al. (1994), "very little indication that the subjects [participants] in the hypocrisy condition were using condoms more regularly than subjects in the control conditions. . ." (p.125).

Does this study have a practical application? It is certainly a contribution to our understanding of behavior. Although long-term effects were muted, the creation of dissonance had some immediate effects on condom purchasing. It is probably unrealistic to hope that one short experience with dissonance would create permanent changes in behavior. Although it is a topic for future research, it is possible that a program that increased commitment and raised mindfulness at regular intervals would have more staying power. It is not easy to make permanent changes in behavior. Psychologists sometimes talk about a *behavior trajectory* in which behavior continues to develop in a single direction over quite long periods of time. We have seen these before in the personality development in Chapter 19. As we saw in Chapter 4, our genetic endowment may also contribute to the creation of stable modes of behavior. In contrast, some programs have been shown to result in behavior change, at least for selected groups of people. We have discussed this in several previous chapters. The discovery of ways to achieve positive, lasting behavior change has been an elusive goal, but it continues to be a major focus of some psychological research. We consider this to be a highly important endeavor.

REFERENCES

Aronson, E., Fried, C. B., & Stone, J. (1991). Overcoming denial and increasing the intention to use condoms through the induction of hypocrisy. *American Journal of Public Health, 81,* 1636–1638.

Catania, J. A., Gibson, D. R., Chitwood, D. D., & Cotes, T. J. (1990). Methodological problems in AIDS behavioral research: Influences on measurement error and participation bias in studies of sexual behavior. *Psychological Bulletin, 108,* 339–362.

Festinger, L. (1957). *A theory of cognitive dissonance.* Evanston, IL: Row, Peterson.

Festinger, L., & Carlsmith, J. M. (1959). Cognitive consequences of forced compliance. *Journal of Abnormal and Social Psychology, 58,* 203–210.

Hays, H., & Hays, J. (1992). Students knowledge of AIDS and sexual risk behavior. *Psychological Reports, 71,* 649–650.

Netting, N. (1992). Sexuality in youth culture: Identity and change. *Adolescence, 27,* 961–976.

Petty, R. E., Wegener, D. T., & Fabrigar, L. R. (1997). Attitudes and attitude change. *Annual Review of Psychology, 48,* 609–647.

Roche, J., & Ramsbey, T. (1993). Premarital sexuality: A five year follow-up study of attitudes and behavior by dating stage. *Adolescence, 28,* 67–80.

Stone, J., Aronson, E., Crain, A. L., Winslow, M. P., & Fried, C. B. (1994). Inducing hypocrisy as a means of encouraging young adults to use condoms. *Personality and Social Psychology Bulletin, 20,* 116–128.

. . . . .

CHAPTER 30

WHO'S AFRAID OF
THE BIG BAD AD?

In this book, we have tried to stress the side of psychological research that has some relevance to the real world. In doing so, we have avoided articles that are almost purely theoretical. If you were to go look in psychology journals, you would find some articles that seem to have no practical application. This basic research sometimes contributes to theories that have applications to daily life, sometimes not. We are not saying that basic research is without value, but it is our opinion that purely theoretical science may not be the best way to introduce psychology. At the other end of the continuum, there are studies whose applications were the main reason for their existence. The study of behavior to address practical questions is often called *applied psychology* because it applies psychology to the real world. This is a large field that includes advertising and marketing, as well as many other types of research aimed at solving problems in daily life.

A great deal of applied research is found in the area of consumer psychology. Consumer psychology is a large field that includes all aspects of consumer behavior including topics such as the effects of brand names, efficiency of distribution systems, preference for times of shopping, convenience of store locations, and responses to advertising. Vast sums of money are spent on attempts to persuade people to buy things. A minute-long TV advertisement during the Super Bowl costs a fortune. The purchase of goods is a type of behavior and, as you might expect, psychologists have long had an interest in understanding the power of advertising to convince people to buy products. One of the founders of the psychological viewpoint called *behaviorism*, John B. Watson, spent the last half of his career as an advertising executive. Psychologists who were behaviorists believed that the goal of psychology should be to measure and predict behavior, without any reference to mental states. Advertising welcomed Watson's practical approach to behavior. Ironically, in contrast to his views about the uselessness of considering internal states, Watson sometimes blatantly used the internal state *fear* in his attempts to sell products. One of his advertisement campaigns

Incorporating the research of M. S. LaTour, R. L. Snipes, and S. J. Bliss, "Don't Be Afraid to Use Fear Appeals: An Experimental Study," 1996, *Journal of Advertising Research*, 36, pp. 59–67.

featured a dramatic photograph of a surgical team at work in a hospital operating room with the caption "And the trouble began with harsh toilet tissue. . ." (Hothersall, 1990).

LaTour, Snipes, and Bliss (1996) conducted research into the use of fear appeals in advertising. Their research considered not only the effectiveness of fear, but also the ethics of using fear to persuade people to buy a product. One source of inspiration for their study came from a short-lived, but well-known, example of an ethical problem in fear advertising that stemmed from a commercial for a popular brand of athletic shoe. In this commercial, two individuals were bungee jumping. Only one of them was wearing shoes made by the advertiser. The jumper wearing the other brand of shoes plunged to his death as his feet came out of his shoes. As the camera focused on the loose shoes dangling in the bungee cords, the voice-over stated that the advertised brand "fits a little better than your ordinary athletic shoe" (Garfield, 1990). This joke about violent death was believed to be in bad taste by many consumers and was quickly discontinued in response to complaints. Many people would regard this ad as an obvious example of poor ethical judgment on the part of the shoe manufacturer and the advertising agency. It could be argued, in contrast, that this was a joke in bad taste, not a serious attempt to invoke fear. Nevertheless, there are many advertisements that do seriously attempt the induction of fear to motivate buying. Many health and hygiene products use this approach, ranging from pills that are depicted as keeping elderly people alive to threats concerning bad breath. The advertisement is often gentle, but the threat is there: elderly people who use this medication *will* be around to play with their grandchildren. Those who do not use it are taking their chances.

Advertisers are aware that stepping over the boundary in fear appeals can backfire. As Treise, Weigold, Conna, and Garrison (as cited in LaTour et al., 1996, p. 60) noted: "Consumer opinion that a specific advertising practice is unethical or immoral can lead to a number of unwanted outcomes, ranging from consumer indifference toward the advertised product to more serious actions such as boycotts or demands for government regulation."

Research on the effects of differing levels of fear in advertising has led to somewhat contradictory overall results. Some studies found that most persuasion occurs at low to moderate amounts of fear. However, other studies suggested that the relationship between fear and persuasion is linear: more fear resulted in more persuasion. One reason for this variability may be that the thought processes involved in fear are different for some people (Rotfeld, 1989). Although some people may respond strongly to a particular fear stimulus, others may not. Some people may be kept awake for many nights by the notion that seeing one insect in a house means that there are more, many more, crawling around in the walls. Other people might not be bothered by this idea. If most of the participants in a research study about an ad campaign for insecticide were from one or the other of these groups, they might react quite differently to fear messages threatening teeming hoards of household insects.

LaTour et al. (1996) conducted an experiment using advertisements with strong and mild fear appeals in order to answer two questions:

1. Do consumers perceive the strong fear appeal as less ethical than the weak fear appeal?
2. How effective is a strong fear appeal compared to a weak fear appeal when it comes to positive consumer attitudes toward the ad itself, the brand of item being advertised, and the intent to purchase?

PARTICIPANTS

The participants in this study consisted of 305 women who were shopping in a large shopping mall in the southeastern United States. Their mean age was 28 years. Sixty percent of them were single, 34 percent were married, and the rest were divorced or widowed. Their median household income was between $30,000 and $40,000, and they had an average of 14 years of education. Seventy-nine percent of them were white, 17.4 percent were African American, and 3.6 percent belonged to other races or ethnicities. They were randomly chosen from shoppers in the mall by female doctoral candidates who served as researchers. The researchers stopped people and asked if they would be willing to take part in a study. Some mall traffic was allowed to pass between each attempt to recruit participants. About half of those who were selected for inclusion in the study agreed to participate. To help ensure a representative sample, the selection of participants was done in a way to eventually include people from across the hours of operation of the mall. The data collection for the entire study required 9 weeks of work in the mall.

PROCEDURE

The technique used was an example of what is called the *mall intercept technique*. This has become a popular method of testing advertisements in the past few years because it has been shown to produce quality data (Bush & Hair, 1985). In this study, a strong and a mild version of a videotaped advertisement was constructed by editing an actual television infomercial for a "stun gun" device. The stun gun was targeted for sales to women as prevention against assault and rape. A stun gun is a small handheld device that, through small prongs on one end, is able to deliver an attention-getting 200,000-volt shock to an attacker. Focus groups were conducted before the study to assist in choosing material from the infomercial that would send a strong and a mild fear message. A focus group is a group organized to discuss a particular issue. In this instance, a focus group was used to collect opinions about research procedures. In the end, the *mild* advertisement consisted of testimonies from actual police officers talking about the utility of the stun gun in preventing assaults. The *strong* fear appeal consisted of the same set of testimonies followed by a written statement on the screen saying that the material to follow was a recording from an actual 911 call to police made by a woman from a suburban neighborhood who had discovered a prowler in her house. In her case, the police arrived too late, and she was brutally attacked and raped. This notice was followed by scenes of a housing suburb at night with a voice-over of an actual emergency call. To make sure she could be understood, the victim's words appeared on the screen as subtitles. She became progressively more frantic in her pleas on the phone. Finally, as the assailant broke into her bedroom, the woman's last frantic and desperate words are heard: "Why are you here?! Why?! Why?! . . . ."

Because the advertisements involved the stun gun, any women who already owned a firearm or a stun gun, as well as any who had seen or heard about the original infomercial on TV, were screened out and did not participate in the study. The researchers used three different locations in the mall to set up a small television and videotape player that had headphones for listening to the sound. The researchers also set up movable partitions that allowed sufficient privacy so that only one participant at a time would be exposed to a stimulus videotape. People who agreed to participate were asked to sign consent forms. They were assured that their responses to the stimulus tapes would be anonymous, confidential, and used only for academic research. Next, they were taken to one of the partitioned areas to view either the strong or the mild version of the advertisement for the stun gun.

Dependent Measures

The dependent measures were questions on a questionnaire that asked about the participants' (1) perceptions of the ethical nature of the ad, (2) other attitudes toward the ad, (3) attitudes toward the particular brand of the product, and (4) intention to buy the product. Perceived ethicality of the ad was measured with a scale called the Reidenbach and Robin Multidimensional Ethics Scale. This instrument was reported to have a high level of validity when checked against other accepted measures (Reidenbach & Robin, 1990). It measured two kinds of ethical thought: a *moral* dimension and a *relativistic* dimension. Participants were asked to make ratings on a 7-point scale anchored at the ends by adjectives of opposite meanings. The moral dimension was measured using adjectives reflecting absolute moral standards, such as *fair/unfair, just/unjust, morally right/not morally right,* and *acceptable to my family/not acceptable to my family.* The relativistic dimension assessed ethical judgments made with reference to the society or the culture such as: *culturally acceptable/not culturally acceptable* and *traditionally acceptable/traditionally unacceptable.* A direct single item, which asked the participants to rate the ad as *ethical/unethical,* completed the measures of ethics.

Other attitudes toward the advertisement were measured by asking participants to rate ad characteristics on a 6-point scale running from *no, definitely not* to *yes, definitely*. The ad characteristics that were rated in this way were *good, distinctive, appropriate, easy to understand,* and *objective*. Attitudes to the particular brand of stun gun featured in the ad were collected on the same kind of 6-point scale. The brand characteristics were *high quality, interesting, appealing, desirable, good,* and *useful*.

Researchers also assessed intent to purchase the product. Participants were told that the stun gun was typically sold in the local area for between $60 and $80. Purchase intention was measured by asking participants to respond to a single 6-point item that read *I plan to purchase [brand name]*. This statement was rated with a 6-point scale anchored at the ends by *no, definitely not* and *yes, definitely*.

As a check to see that people were paying attention and that the experimental manipulation was doing what it was supposed to, two additional items were asked. On a 6-point scale from *no, definitely not* to *yes, definitely* participants were asked to rate whether the ad clearly featured an actual violent crime. As a further manipulation check, they were asked to rate how tense the ad made them feel on a 4-point scale from *definitely do not feel* to *definitely feel*. Last, participants were asked to rate, on a 6-point scale, how confident they were of their own ability to use a stun gun to stop an assailant.

Results

Participants were randomly assigned to either the strong or the weak group and, as would be expected with random participant assignment, there were no significant demographic differences between the group that saw the mild ad and the group that saw the strong version. There were also no significant differences between the groups in their reported confidence in their ability to use a stun gun to stop an attack on themselves. Preexisting attitude differences between groups on this question would have constituted an important confound. Ideally, the groups should be similar in every way except in exposure to the independent variable or variables.

Manipulation Check

The data in the manipulation checks (having noticed the violent crime or not and having experienced tension) should be different for the two groups if the advertisements were doing what they were supposed to do. These data are presented in Figure 30.1.

The differences seen in Figure 30.1 are in the predicted direction. The *strong* group had noticed the violent crime and experienced more tension. If this manipulation check had failed to produce these differences, it would have been difficult to interpret other results from the study. This would have indicated that participants had not responded to the different levels of the independent variable. As can be seen, the manipulation check was successful and differences between groups on both manipulation check questions were statistically significant ($p < .001$).

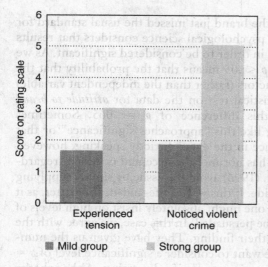

FIGURE 30.1   Manipulation Check. Participants' mean ratings on a 4-point scale of the amount of tension they experienced watching the advertisement and their recollection, on a 6-point scale, that the advertisement featured a violent crime.

Attitude about Ad and Brand

The independent variable did make some difference to attitudes toward the advertisement and to the brand of product. The data are presented in Figure 30.2.

These data are the result of adding together the scores on the six different 6-point scales that were used to assess attitudes to ad and to brand. These scales were scored in such a way that higher numbers reflect more positive attitudes on the descriptors that were words such as *good*, *appealing*, and *appropriate*. The attitudes toward the advertisement are significantly different

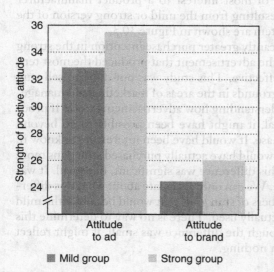

FIGURE 30.2   Attitudes to Ad and Brand by Group. Mean ratings on six different 6-point scales (summed), each reflecting the extent of positive attitudes toward the advertisement and the brand of the product.

(p = .005). The attitudes toward the brand just missed the usual standard for statistical significance. Ordinarily, psychological science considers that results have to meet a criterion of $p < .05$ in order to be considered significant. As we have described in other chapters, $p < .05$ means that the probability that the difference is the result of chance factors (rather than the independent variable) is 5 percent, or 1 in 20. The statistical test on the data for *attitude to brand* found a significance level for this difference of p = .065. Sometimes researchers will say that a finding like this "approaches significance" or that there is "a trend toward significance in the data." Strictly speaking, however, this outcome is not significant. It has not met the accepted criterion, regardless of how close it is. LaTour et al. (1996) avoid this issue by simply supplying the data and letting the reader decide. If this were a life-and-death matter, as it might be in the test of a new drug, one might absolutely insist on high levels of statistical significance in order to be persuaded. In this case, we agree with the way the researchers have handled their finding. They have given us the numbers and allowed us to decide if we want to consider a significance level of p = .065 to be adequate in a questionnaire study of advertising. Although the research question about attitudes to brands is interesting, it is not so important that calling this significant or not will have earth-shattering consequences. This is a reason why replications of studies can be useful. If this study were to be replicated a few times, we might gain a more clear picture of the significance, or lack thereof, for these data.

Purchase Intention

Probably the data that would be of most interest to a product manufacturer would be the purchase intention resulting from the mild or strong version of the advertisement. Responses to this item are shown in Figure 30.3.

The data here show a significantly greater purchase intention in the strong group ($p < .001$), suggesting that the advertisement that produced the most tension, or even fear, was the most effective. This study was not done to sell stun guns. These researchers had backgrounds in the areas of marketing and management. They were interested in understanding how advertisements work. If product sales had been part of the goal, it might have been possible to go beyond purchase intention to actual purchase. It would have been interesting to know if, given the chance, the *strong* group would have actually purchased stun guns more frequently than the *mild* group. This difference was significant, but small. It was less than 1 point on a 6-point scale. We can only speculate about what this difference would mean in terms of numbers of stun guns that would be sold if the mild and strong advertisements were actually used. There is no way to determine this from the data presented. Even though the difference was small, it might reflect millions in sales, or it might reflect nothing.

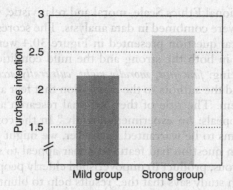

FIGURE 30.3   Purchase Intention by Group. Purchase intention ratings of the statement "I plan to purchase [brand name]" from *no, definitely not* to *yes, definitely* on a 6-point scale.

Ethics

The last major question asked by this research was if the mild or strong version of the advertisement would be rated as different from an ethical standpoint. The data are presented in Figure 30.4.

Outcomes were not significantly different for either the multidimensional ethics scale or the single item about ethics. At least in this study, it would seem that people did not perceive a frightening advertisement to pose an ethical problem. Responses to the two ethical dimensions measured by the Reidenbach and

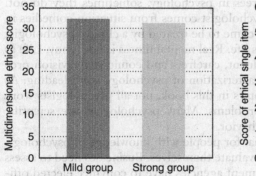
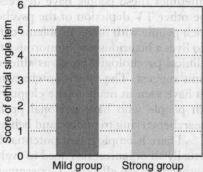

FIGURE 30.4   Dependent Measures That Were Ratings of the Ethics of the Mild and the Strong Advertisement. Differences between groups were not significant on either measure.

Robin Multidimensional Ethics Scale, moral and relativistic, were similar so the two types of scales were combined in data analysis. The scores on both this scale and the single ethical question presented in Figure 30.4 were quite high, suggesting that people in both the strong and the mild condition were rating the advertisement as being: *fair, just, morally right, culturally acceptable,* and *ethical.* These outcomes lead the authors to the conclusion that fear appeals are not seen as an ethical problem. The title of their original research article is "Don't be afraid to use fear appeals: An experimental study." In the context of this study, that conclusion seems to be warranted. However, we might see it differently if the advertisement in question had featured a fear appeal to sell some unnecessary, or even dangerous, product to impoverished elderly people. The abstract of the original research study says that the "results help to blunt 'blanket' criticism of fear appeals and provide evidence for advertising executives who wish to argue for serious consideration of fear appeal use." We might also want to consider this message carefully. The fear appeal can be useful. There are some things about which people should be afraid. People who engage in high-risk behaviors should be afraid of HIV infection and subsequent AIDS. People who drink alcohol should be afraid to drive a car or operate other machinery. Perhaps fear appeals in advertisements should be used when fear is appropriate. It is a matter of personal judgment whether fear should be considered as just one more ordinary tactic to make people buy things.

One reason why we chose to include this study is because it illustrates an area of applied psychology that offers employment opportunities for people with backgrounds in psychology. Popular culture sometimes seems to think that psychology is the same thing as counseling or that its main mission is to treat mental illness. Probably this image is formed by television portrayals of psychologists on talk shows or situation comedies. On talk shows, psychologists are seen as those people who analyze problems on stage, dealing out simple and glib solutions. Sometimes these people have degrees in psychology, sometimes they do not. The other TV depiction of the psychologist comes from situation comedies in which people with funny problems come to be treated by a clinical psychologist who lives a luxurious and humorous life. Real mental illness is not funny. Life as a clinical psychologist is not as affluent, carefree, and comic as television programs suggest. The television characterization of psychology is misleading. As you have seen in many of the chapters in this book, not all psychologists work with people who have personal problems. Many psychologists are scientific researchers trying to understand behavior.

There is employment potential for people with knowledge of psychology. Virtually all organizations need to evaluate themselves. Businesses need to assess whether they are effective. Government agencies have to convince elected officials that they should continue to receive funding. There are good jobs in these domains for people who are curious about behavior, creative in their thinking, and skilled in scientific psychology. Psychology is more than a collection of facts;

it is also a set of skills. People with good sets of skills are likely to find good careers. That is what we want to happen to you.

REFERENCES

Bush, A. J., & Hair, J. F. (1985). An assessment of the mall intercept as a data collection method. *Journal of Marketing Research, 22,* 158–167.

Garfield, B. (1990). Good taste takes deep dive in bungee ad for Reebok pump. *Advertising Age, 61,* 51–52.

Hothersall, D. (1990). *History of psychology* (2nd ed.). New York: McGraw-Hill.

LaTour, M. S., Snipes, R. L., & Bliss, S. J. (1996). Don't be afraid to use fear appeals: An experimental study. *Journal of Advertising Research, 36,* 59–67.

Reidenbach, R. E., & Robin, D. P. (1990). Toward the development of a multidimensional scale for improving evaluations of business ethics. *Journal of Business Ethics, 9,* 639–653.

Rotfeld, H. (1989). Fear appeals and persuasion: Assumptions and errors in advertising research. *Current Issues and Research in Advertising, 11,* 21–40.

CHAPTER 31

I'M WARNING YOU

The research in this chapter focuses on important variables that influence people to follow warnings. For example, every time we travel by plane the flight attendants warn us about what to do in the event the aircraft loses pressure and we need to use the emergency oxygen system. If you have flown, your experiences probably suggests that passengers largely ignore the attendant's demonstration in favor of reading their newspapers, adjusting their luggage, or taking a snooze. Sometimes the warnings are given over the television monitors. It appeared that even fewer passengers were paying attention to the monitors, but that could be checked out in a formal research program. We are constantly receiving warnings: warnings about our diet, exercise, driving, parenting, relationships, medications, and so on. We are often noncompliant, and the warning has little impact in modifying our behaviors. It is important to note that most people would agree that the warnings given are useful and beneficial. Certainly, it would be helpful to know what to do if the aircraft lost pressure and oxygen was not readily available. Health care professionals often warn their patients about weight control, exercise, and medications, and these warnings are ignored even though they are vital for a person's health. What are the variables that impact the adherence or neglect of warnings? The series of experiments in this chapter investigate how *cost* and *social influence* impact our decision regarding acceptance or rejection of warnings. *Cost*, as defined in this research program and generally in psychological investigations, refers to the effort an individual has to expend or the convenience to the individual, whereas *social influence* refers to the impact that other people have on our behavior.

Previous research in this area suggests that warnings are often ineffective (McCarthy, Finnegan, Krumm-Scott, & McCarthy, 1984). Wogalter et al. (1987) confirmed that the location or placement of a warning affected compliance. They found that if a warning was given early in the instructions, it resulted in the highest degree of compliance. In addition, the prominence of the warning was also related to compliance. Cunitz (1981) and Peters (1984) noted that warnings have

Incorporating the research of M. S. Wogalter, S. T. Allison, and N. A. McKenna, "Effects of Cost and Social Influence on Warning Compliance," 1989, *Human Factors*, *31*, pp. 133–141.

both an informational and behavioral role. The informational function informs the consumer about the correct manner of usage of the product so as to avoid danger, whereas the behavioral role attempts to persuade the consumer to focus on the warnings and modify the consumer's actions in the direction of safety.

Cialdini (1993) stated that people are exposed to thousands of social influence attempts each day, largely from advertisers. To make sense of this bombardment of influence, Cialdini argued that we resort to heuristics to help us make decisions about how to respond to the barrage of social influence. Heuristics are simple "rules of thumb" that we employ to clarify tasks in order to come up with an effective decision in a speedy manner. For example, suppose you just moved into an apartment in an unfamiliar community and you were very hungry and wanted to find a fast-food burger restaurant. How would you go about the task? Using a heuristic that fast-food restaurants are located near interstate highway exits might well be a "rule of thumb" that would be successful. This is called a "rule of thumb" because it is usually successful, but not always. Eagly and Chaiken (1984) propose the following heuristic strategies that have been successful in getting people to comply with warnings:

- Expertise of the source: Warnings from a well-known cardiologist about diet and exercise affecting blood pressure would likely have greater impact than similar opinions from your plumber.
- Positive value of the source: Warnings from an admired person will likely have greater influence. Advertisers have capitalized on this by providing endorsements by famous entertainment and sports figures.
- Warning quality: The quality is often inferred from the quantity of specific reasons cited in the message. The more specific reasons suggested, the higher the perception of message quality and therefore warning value.
- Statistical arguments: Warnings tend to be perceived as more effective if they are upheld by statistics. If a person is told that 80 percent of dentists use Blah-Blah mouthwash, and it is further supported with figures and charts, it is likely to be an impressive warning.
- Behavior of others, social influence: People imitate the behavior and experience of others, and their experience becomes a guide for how to respond.

The research described in this chapter targets this final heuristic—social influence—as a variable that was examined in reference to its potential effect on compliance to warnings. In addition, the cost to the individual, often in terms of effort and time commitment, was studied in conjunction with social influence. The procedure for the initial three studies focused on a chemistry laboratory project in which participants mixed chemicals according to specific instructions. In the first study, the important variable was cost and the outcome variable was compliance with warnings. The second and third studies showed how social influence, in both low- and high-cost situations, effected compliance with warnings. The fourth and final investigation took the lessons learned from the chemistry laboratory experiments into a real-world setting to determine how the lab findings hold up. This final study should influence your opinion about the external validity of the laboratory findings.

RESEARCH STUDY 1

The objective of this initial study was to evaluate the effect of two levels of cost (low and high) on compliance with a warning in a chemistry laboratory. The participants in this experiment were 23 introductory psychology students. The research was conducted in a traditional chemistry laboratory with the typical assortment of beakers, flasks, measuring devices, solutions, and so forth that conveyed a sense of authenticity to participants. The lab situation was designed to portray an environment in which the participants were being asked to handle chemicals that could possibly be dangerous. In performing the chemistry assignment, participants were given their directions in written form and were told to complete the task as quickly and precisely as possible. They were also told that their work would be evaluated for correctness. After the above instructions, participants were given the following printed caution:

> WARNING: Wear gloves and masks while performing the task to avoid irritating fumes and possible irritation of the skin. (Wogalter, Allison, & McKenna, 1989, p. 135)

After the warning statement, the participants were given the specific written directions necessary to measure and mix the solutions and complete the assignment. The procedure for participants consisted of signing of consent documents in a room where safety equipment—gloves and masks—were obviously placed on a table. They were then led to an adjacent room where the chemistry project was conducted. Next they were told to be precise, to produce high-quality work, and to complete the work in five minutes. The participants were randomly assigned to one of two conditions: low cost (masks and gloves in the consent signing room as well as in the chemistry room) and high cost (masks and gloves were only accessible in the consent signing room). The manipulated variable, therefore, was cost (high or low) and the outcome variable was participant compliance with the safety warning (wearing both mask and gloves). The low-cost condition required little effort for the participants to comply because the safety equipment was in the chemistry laboratory. The participants in the high-cost condition would have had to exert some effort and leave the laboratory to obtain the safety gear. The results of this research are presented in Table 31.1.

The findings provide clear evidence that low-cost conditions enhance compliance with safety directives. A statistical analysis of the results confirmed that the cost variable was indeed statistically significant at $p < .01$. As you will remember, this means that luck or other extraneous variables were not likely to

TABLE 31.1 Percentage of Compliance with Safety Warning in Three Experimental Studies

WEARING GLOVES & MASK WHILE CONDUCTING CHEMISTRY PROJECT	PERCENT OF COMPLIANCE BY PARTICIPANTS
Study 1	
Low cost ($N = 11$)	62%
High cost ($N = 12$)	17%
Study 2	
Low cost	
Compliant confederate ($N = 8$)	100%
Noncompliant confederate ($N = 9$)	33%
Study 3	
High cost	
Compliant confederate ($N = 10$)	70%
Noncompliant confederate ($N = 10$)	0%

be responsible for the effect on the outcome variable and that readers can place confidence in the findings. The finding from this study, that is, low cost facilitating warning compliance, was seen in the previous research of Wogalter et al. (1987) as well as in other studies of compliance in the field of social psychology (Piliavin, Piliavin, & Rodin, 1976).

RESEARCH STUDY 2

In this study, the participants were exposed to either a compliant or noncompliant confederate. The participants in the study were unaware of the confederate's role and were led to believe the confederate was another participant in the experiment. The general finding in the social psychology literature (Cialdini, 1993) is that people who are exposed to others who comply tend to comply in similar situations. In the same way, being exposed to noncompliant examples leads to noncompliance in participants. This second experiment sought to determine if the general findings stated previously occurred in a warning compliance situation. The 17 students in this research were introductory psychology students. The chemistry laboratory setup was similar to the first study, except that more equipment was required to accomplish the task. The necessary safety equipment was in the same room as the participant and near the chemistry laboratory setup. It was therefore low cost for all participants. Procedures were the same as the first study with one exception—a confederate, who acted like another student, worked near the participant and demonstrated compliance (i.e., wore safety mask and gloves) or did not comply (i.e., did not wear safety equipment). Table 31.1 (Experiment 2) shows that participants were highly influenced by the extent of confederate compliance in a low-cost situation. A statistical analysis of the results confirmed that the cost variable was indeed statistically significant at $p < .001$. Simply put, when a confederate complied, the participants always complied, and when a confederate did not comply, two-thirds of the participants followed the confederate's lead and did not wear safety equipment.

RESEARCH STUDY 3

This third study followed the same pattern as the second study with one change—high cost was substituted for low cost. Would participants comply with the social influence of a confederate in a high-cost context where safety equipment was located in a room adjacent to the chemistry laboratory? The participants were 20 introductory psychology students. The results can be seen in Table 31.1 (Experiment 3). The findings clearly show that warning compliance is significantly ($p < .001$) impacted by the influence of a confederate, under conditions, of high cost to the participant. Under the high-cost conditions, 70 percent of participants complied with warnings when working beside a compliant confederate. In contrast, if the confederate was noncompliant, not a single participant followed the warnings.

In summarizing the data from the three investigations, the following major conclusions can be drawn: (1) low cost is much more effective than high cost in getting individuals to comply with warnings when there is no model for the behavior, and (2) social influence is a powerful factor, and individuals tend to follow the lead of others under both low- and high-cost conditions.

FIELD STUDY

Studies in laboratories are an excellent method of obtaining useful data in understanding such issues as the variables affecting warning compliance. It is vitally important however to determine whether the results obtained in the experimental lab operate outside the lab in the real world. It is laudable that the research described in this chapter chose to provide an out-of-lab field study to investigate the generalizability of the findings discovered in the three laboratory investigations

The field study was done in a women's dorm at a university. The three-story dorm had an elevator that traveled from the basement to the third story. On the ground floor, a handwritten sign was affixed to the wall adjacent to the elevator controls. The sign stated:

CAUTION: Elevator may stick between floors. Use the stairs. (Wogalter et al., 1989, p.138)

A stairwell was located about 10 feet from the elevator. The study collected data on elevator and stair usage, with warning sign posted, under three conditions:

- No confederate (essentially a baseline condition to ascertain typical usage)
- Compliant confederate
- Noncompliant confederate

The actual procedure for conducting this study involved a confederate who either (1) chooses to use the stairs after reading the warning sign or (2) reads the sign and chooses to use the elevator. In each condition, a single participant observed the confederate's actions. The data recorded, the outcome variable, consisted of the frequency of warning sign compliance in the three conditions. Table 31.2 presents the percentage of compliance in the three conditions.

In both the baseline condition (no confederate) and the noncompliant confederate condition, the percentage of participant compliance was approximately the same, 28 to 32 percent. However, when a participant was confronted with a confederate who was compliant with warning messages, it was likely (89 percent of the time) that the participant also complied. This study confirms the findings of the laboratory research and shows the powerful impact of social influence to comply. Probably noncompliant confederates had little impact on participants largely because the baseline response was quite low and could not be further decreased even through social influence.

IMPLICATIONS

The outcomes of this series of studies can be usefully applied in many nonlab situations. For example, the research suggests that it is desirable for organizations, manufacturers, and institutions to make warnings as easy and convenient to follow as possible. Reducing the cost (i.e., effort) for an individual is an issue for designers and engineers to implement so that the product or service is used in the safest manner. If a product requires considerable effort to operate in the

TABLE 31.2 **Percentage of Compliance With Elevator Warnings in Three Conditions**

CONDITION	PERCENT OF COMPLIANCE WITH ELEVATOR WARNING SIGN
No confederate ($N = 18$)	33%
Compliant confederate ($N = 18$)	89%
Noncompliant confederate ($N = 18$)	28%

safest manner, individuals will likely have low rates of compliance. For example, if a paint and varnish remover requires plastic gloves for safety, this research would recommend that the gloves be included with the product in order to lower the effort of compliance and ultimately enhance safety. Wogalter et al. (1989) noted that hair coloring products typically include protective plastic gloves with the product to enhance consumer compliance with the safety instructions. It is also likely that organizations that use strategies requiring low effort to gain compliance will benefit by having their products used in a safe manner and therefore avoid possible legal issues. Our students have informed us that condoms are conveniently available in many dorm bathrooms. The ready availability certainly meets the test of low cost and would likely increase usage to avoid the potential dangers of unsafe sex.

The research described in this chapter certainly supports the view that observing a single person complying with a safety warning facilitates compliance in others. The converse, observing a person who fails to comply with warnings, also has a powerful influence in inhibiting compliance among observers. These findings argue that employers should not allow a single example of noncompliance in safety situations because it can serve as an effective model for increasing noncompliance in other workers.

The impact of cost and social influence can operate and can be seen in a wide range of human interactions. If you are interested in seeing how these variables and others operate, the work of Latané (1981) and Cialdini (1993) are excellent resources.

REFERENCES

Cialdini, R. B. (1993). *Influence: Science and practice* (3rd ed.). New York: HarperCollins.

Cunitz, R. J. (1981). Psychologically effective warnings. *Hazard Prevention, 17,* 5–7.

Eagly, A. H., & Chaiken, S. (1984). Cognitive theories of persuasion. In L. Berkowitz (Ed.), *Advances in experimental social psychology* (Vol. 17, pp. 268–359). New York: Academic Press.

Latané, B. (1981). The psychology of social impact. *American Psychologist, 36,* 343–356.

McCarthy, R. L., Finnegan, J. P., Krumm-Scott, S., & McCarthy, G. E. (1984). Product information presentation, user behavior, and safety. In *Proceedings of the Human Factors Society 28th annual meeting* (pp. 81–85). Santa Monica, CA: Human Factors Society.

Peters, G. A. (1984). A challenge to the safety profession. *Professional Safety, 29,* 46–50.

Piliavin, I. M., Piliavin, J. A., & Rodin, J. (1976). Costs, diffusion, and the stigmatized victim. *Journal of Personality and Social Psychology, 32,* 429–438.

Wogalter, M. S., Allison, S. T., & McKenna, N. A. (1989). Effects of cost and social influence on warning compliance. *Human Factors, 31,* 133–141.

Wogalter, M. S., Gofrey, S. S., Fontenelle, G. A., Desaulniers, D. R., Rothstein, P. R., & Laughery, K. R. (1987). Effectiveness of warnings. *Human Factors, 29,* 599–612.

CHAPTER 32

DOES TV VIOLENCE SELL?

In the United States, the television is a basic feature of the home, with more than 98 percent of households having one or more sets (American Psychological Association, 1993). It is also the dominant force for commercial advertising according to Bushman (1998). Data from Huston et al. (1992) indicated that adults spend more time in front of the television that any other single activity outside of working and sleeping. Children spend more time watching TV than they do in school. Television clearly is a dominant activity for American family life.

TELEVISION IS VIOLENT

Comprehensive research on television programming (National Television Violence Study, 1996, 1997) found that approximately 60 percent of programming on cable and network television consisted of violent content. Before children become teenagers they are likely to be exposed on television to more than 8,000 murders and more than 100,000 various incidents of violence on television (Huston, Donnerstein, Fairchild et al., 1992). Surveys indicate that the American public is consistent in its belief that violent programming should be reduced or eliminated (Fischer, 1994; Zipperer, 1994). The television industry, in response, appears to believe that television just mirrors our culture and is not exaggerating or overemphasizing violence. However, research (Oliver, 1994) suggests that television violence far overestimates the violence that can be found in the real world. It is possible that television executives believe that violence is an effective way to capture greater numbers of viewers and, therefore, will be more attractive to commercial advertisers. However, as Bushman (1998) related, increasing violence does not necessarily increase the viewership of a program (Diener & Defour, 1978; Diener & Woody, 1981; Sprafkin, Rubinstein, & Stone, 1977).

Incorporating the research of B. J. Bushman, "Effects of Television Violence on Memory for Commercial Messages," 1998, *Journal of Experimental Psychology: Applied, 4,* pp. 1–17.

The research described in this chapter explores the effectiveness of commercials during both violent and nonviolent programs. Does a viewer remember the content of a commercial better if it is placed in a program of violent content or nonviolent content? Bear in mind that the content of a commercial must be remembered in order to sell the product. Although Bushman's research does not assess whether actual purchase decisions are altered by placement during violent/nonviolent programs, memory for commercial details is certainly a very desirable characteristic.

WHY VIOLENCE MAY AFFECT MEMORY

Two suggestions have been made about why commercials might be ineffective in violent programs:

- Violent programs put viewers in a bad mood and may make them angry (Anderson, 1997; Bushman, 1995). Anger generated by watching violence may activate other anger-related concepts and inhibit the information from the commercial, therefore decreasing the value of the information contained in the commercial (Bower, 1981; Isen, Clark, Shalker, & Karp, 1978).
- Mood management theory (Isen, 1984; Parrott, 1993) suggests that violence might put viewers in a negative mood. Viewers placed in a negative mood by programming engage in an active process to improve their negative mood. In contrast, viewers in a program-initiated positive mood seek to continue their positive mood without the need for an active cognitive process to make changes. The mood change or mood repair process, demands that individuals devote more cognitive energy toward themselves rather than directing this energy outward. Therefore, in repairing a mood, individuals would be less focused outwardly on commercial messages, thereby minimizing the impact of the commercials. This is probably not something that advertisers would want to happen.

BUSHMAN'S RESEARCH

The previous theoretical explanations are interesting, but Bushman's (1998) research does not test them directly. The first two studies focus on the impact of television violence on memory for commercial information. The third study examined whether anger induced by a violent program impairs a person's memory for details of a commercial.

STUDY 1

This research was designed to examine the impact of television violence on participants' memory for brand name of the product and specifics of the commercial. The participants were 200 volunteers who were undergraduate psychology students (100 males and 100 females). They received additional course credit for being in the study. The participants were randomly assigned to watch either a 15-minute violent or nonviolent video movie segment. The movie segments were determined by previous research not to differ on participants' self-reported arousal or on objective measures of physiological arousal (e.g., blood pressure, heart rate). The videos used were determined to be equally arousing and exciting, but different in violence. The 15-minute videos used in this experiment were taken from the films *Karate Kid III* (violent) and *Gorillas in the Mist* (nonviolent). The violent video showed a karate tournament in which an arrogant opponent repeatedly broke the rules and fought in a dirty manner. The nonviolent video depicted a scientist observing and interacting with gorillas. Each 15-minute video was interrupted at the 5-minute and 10-minute point for a 30-second commercial. The commercials used were for Krazy Glue and Wisk detergent. The order of the commercials was counterbalanced and therefore half the participants watched the Wisk commercial first, and half saw the Krazy Glue commercial first. To make the 15-minute video and commercial sequence even more realistic, a network station identification logo and message were also made part of the video. After watching the video the participants:

1. Listed the brand names of the products shown in the commercials
2. Listed all the details they could recall about the commercials
3. Reported the number of television hours in various categories that they watched per week
4. Reported whether they had seen the film or commercials shown

After collecting these data, participants were debriefed.

RESULTS OF STUDY 1

The presentation order of the commercials, the sex of participant, habitual exposure to television violence, previous exposure to the film segments, and previous exposure to the commercial used were *not* related to the dependent variables. The results of this research are presented in Table 32.1. In terms of brand name recall, participants who watched the nonviolent video had significantly higher rates of recall than those who watched the violent video film segment did. When asked to recall commercial details, participants in the nonviolent situation had higher scores than the group that watched the violent film segments. The

TABLE 32.1   Study 1—Impact of Television Violence on Recall of Commercial Brand Names and Commercial Details*

OUTCOME MEASURE	VIOLENT FILM (MEAN SCORE)	NONVIOLENT FILM (MEAN SCORE)
Brand name recall**	1.22	1.50
Commercial details***	6.69	8.61

*Differences between violent and nonviolent groups for both dependent measures were significant at $p < .05$.

**Scores on brand name recall ranged from 0 (no brands recalled) to 2 (both brands recalled).

***Scores on commercial details ranged from 0 to 22.

findings indicate that watching commercials in a context of violence impairs memory for commercials

STUDY 2

Bushman (1998) conducted a second investigation to replicate the initial study and to investigate another dependent measure, visual brand recognition. The decision to purchase a product may not require a person to remember the brand name, but only to be able to recognize it on the store shelf. This acknowledges the fact that shoppers frequently make choices between brands in the store at the time of purchase (Bettman, 1979). In this situation, consumers are faced with many competing brands, and if prior advertising is effective they need only to recognize the product. This is different than having the product name stored in memory and seeking it out while shopping.

The participants and general procedure for this second experiment were similar to the first study with the addition of the visual brand recognition test. Participants were shown the videos and commercials and given the same brand name recall and commercial message recall as in Study 1. In addition, the third dependent measure, visual brand recognition, was accomplished in the following manner. Participants were informed that the video segment they watched had two commercials, one for a laundry detergent and the other for a glue product. The participants then watched slides of six different glue products (Krazy Glue and five other glue products) and six different laundry detergents (Wisk and five other detergents). The task for the participants was to write the brand name seen in the video segment. This measure did not require that they recall the brand name because it was presented along with five other competitors. They only needed to be able to recognize it.

TABLE 32.2   Study 2—Impact of Television Violence on Brand Name Recognition, Recall of Commercial Brand Names, and Commercial Details*

OUTCOME MEASURE	VIOLENT FILM (MEAN SCORE)	NONVIOLENT FILM (MEAN SCORE)
Brand name recognition**	1.66	1.85
Brand name recall**	1.21	1.56
Commercial details***	7.10	8.01

*Differences between violent and nonviolent groups for brand name recognition and recall were significant at $p < .05$.

**Scores on brand name recognition and brand name recall ranged from 0 (no brands recalled) to 2 (both brands recalled).

***Scores on commercial details ranged from 0 to 17.

RESULTS OF STUDY 2

The results of this second study are presented in Table 32.2. Participants who watched the nonviolent video segment *recognized* more brands than participants who watched violent videos ($p < .05$) and also *recalled* more brand names ($p < .05$). In this study the differences between violent and nonviolent groups on the commercial message recall outcome measure were in the predicted direction (i.e., the nonviolent group recalled more details), but were not significant ($p > .05$).

This second investigation replicated the findings of the initial study and provided some new findings. The added recognition measure in particular provided an even more realistic appraisal of how consumers make decisions, giving the research greater ecological validity.

STUDY 3

The goal of Study 3 was to see whether or not anger mediates how television violence influences memory for commercials. In other words, does anger resulting from watching violence impair memory? Bushman (1998) also explored how positive affect (the opposite of anger) served as a possible intermediary variable affecting memory. The advantage of exploring polar-opposite emotions was that information could be gathered on whether anger impairs memory and conversely on whether positive affect facilitates memory. In this experiment, the researchers used the same general procedures except that four video segments of violent and nonviolent films were used. Violent video segments included the films *Cobra, Die Hard, Single White Female,* and *The Hand That Rocks the Cradle*.

Nonviolent video segments included *Awakenings, Chariots of Fire, Field of Dreams*, and *Never Cry Wolf*. Participants were randomly assigned to watch one of the possible eight videos. After watching the video segment participants filled out a rating form to assess anger and positive affect. Anger was determined by the number of adjectives endorsed on subscale of the Multiple Affect Adjective Checklist (Zuckerman & Lubin, 1985). Some of the anger items were *angry, annoyed, furious*. Positive affect was assessed on participants' endorsement of adjectives (e.g., *alert, enthusiastic*) from the Positive and Negative Affect Schedule (Watson, Clark, & Tellegen, 1988). Based on the results of the first two experiments, the researchers expected higher brand recognition, brand recall, and commercial message memory scores for participants watching nonviolent videos than the group who observed the violent video segments. The researchers used a complex statistical analysis to determine whether television violence increases viewer anger and thus decreases a viewer's ability to retain information about commercials. This line of reasoning was based on the views discussed previously suggesting that anger interferes with the commercial information presented and that the viewer has to use his or her cognitive resources to cope and "repair" their negative mood (mood management). Arousal and positive affect were not hypothesized to have negative effects on mood and therefore would not decrease commercial recall.

RESULTS OF STUDY 3

As you can see in Table 32.3, the participants watching nonviolent video segments had significantly higher rates of brand recognition, recalled more brand names, and recalled more details of the commercials than the participants who watched violent video segments. This is consistent with the results of the previ-

TABLE 32.3 Study 3—Impact of Television Violence on Brand Name Recognition, Recall of Commercial Brand Names, and Commercial Details*

OUTCOME MEASURE	VIOLENT FILM (MEAN SCORE)	NONVIOLENT FILM (MEAN SCORE)
Brand name recognition**	1.65	1.79
Brand name recall**	1.14	1.31
Commercial details***	5.10	6.28

*Differences between violent and nonviolent groups for all three dependent measures were significant at $p < .05$.

**Scores on brand name recognition and brand name recall ranged from 0 (no brands recalled) to 2 (both brands recalled).

***Scores on commercial details ranged from 0 to 18.

ous experiments and provides a valuable replication. The complex data analysis from this third experiment discovered that anger was a very important mediator of the effect of television violence on a participant's memory for commercials. General arousal and positive affect did not have the significant impact that anger had. This finding provides insight into why television violence diminishes participants' ability to recall important details of a commercial. It looks as if television violence makes a person angry, and that anger decreases the ability of the person to remember commercial details. This research suggested that television advertisers should be aware that if they present commercials during violent programming, viewers may actually have to focus on mending and repairing their own emotional and cognitive states. They may have to calm down from the anger generated and therefore have less available time to focus on the commercials. This research should send a cautionary note to advertisers—placing commercials in a violent context might not pay off in sales. Bushman (1998) points out that this series of investigations does not directly examine whether or not television violence impacts the actual purchasing behavior of viewers. However, because the decision to purchase is often based on information from commercials, lack of memory for important commercial details added to arousal of anger is likely to have a negative effect on purchasing.

In summing up this research, Bushman (1998) states the following three reasons why advertisers might want to avoid placing commercials for their products in violent programming:

1. Most viewers voice upset toward the amount of violence presented on television (TV Guide, 1992; Zipperer, 1994).
2. Film and television violence may increase violence in viewers through observational learning and therefore contribute negatively to our society (National Institute of Mental Health, 1982; Paik & Comstock, 1994).
3. Based on the research conducted by Bushman, placing commercials in the context of violent programs may not make economic sense for advertisers. Viewers of such commercials get angry and have decreased memories for many important aspects of the commercial message.

REFERENCES

American Psychological Association. (1993). *Violence and youth: Psychology's response*. Washington, DC: Author.

Anderson, C. A. (1977). Effects of violent movies and trait hostility on hostile feelings and aggressive thoughts. *Aggressive Behavior, 23,* 161–178.

Bettman, J. R. (1979). Memory factors in consumer choices: A review. *Journal of Marketing, 43,* 37–53.

Bower, G. (1981). Mood and memory. *American Psychologist, 36,* 129–148.

Bushman, B. J. (1995). Moderating role of trait aggressiveness in the effects of violent media on aggression. *Journal of Personality and Social Psychology, 69,* 950–960.

Bushman, B. J. (1998). Effects of television violence on memory for commercial messages. *Journal of Experimental Psychology: Applied*, *4*, 1–17.

Diener, E., & DeFour, D. (1978). Does television violence enhance program popularity? *Journal of Personality and Social Psychology*, *36*, 333–341.

Diener, E., & Woody, L. W. (1981). Television violence, conflict, realism, and action: A study in viewer liking. *Communication Research*, *8*, 281–306.

Fischer, R. L. (1994, July). Is it possible to regulate television violence? *USA Today*, 72–75.

Huston, A. C., Donnerstein, E., Fairchild, H., Feshbach, N. D., Katz, P. A., Murray, J. P., Rubinstein, E. A., Wilcox, B. L., & Zuckerman, D. (1992). *Big world, small screen: The role of television in American society.* Lincoln: University of Nebraska Press.

Isen, A. M. (1984). Toward understanding the role of affect in cognition. In R. Wyer, Jr., & T. Srull (Eds.), *Handbook of social cognition* (pp. 179–236). Hillsdale, NJ: Erlbaum.

Isen, A. M., Clark, M., Shalker, T. E., & Karp, L. (1978). Affect, accessibility of material in memory and behavior: A cognitive loop? *Journal of Personality and Social Psychology*, *36*, 1–12.

National Institute of Mental Health. (1982). *Television and behavior: Ten years of scientific progress and implications for the eighties (Vol. 1), Summary report.* Washington, DC: U.S. Government Printing Office.

National Television Violence Study. (1996). *National television violence study* (Vol. 1). Thousand Oaks, CA: Sage.

National Television Violence Study. (1997). *National television violence study* (Vol. 2). Studio City, CA: Mediascope.

Oliver, M. B. (1994). Portrayals of crime, race, and aggression in "reality-based" police shows: A content analysis. *Journal of Broadcasting and Electronic Media*, *38*, 179–192.

Paik, H., & Comstock, G. (1994). The effects of television violence on antisocial behavior: A meta-analysis. *Communication Research*, *21*, 516–546.

Parrott, G. W. (1993). Beyond hedonism: Motives for inhibiting good moods and for maintaining bad moods. In D. M. Wegner & J. W. Pennebaker (Eds.), *Handbook of mental control* (pp. 278–305). Upper Saddle River, NJ: Prentice Hall.

Sprafkin, J. N., Rubinstein, E. A., & Stone, A. (1977). *The content analysis of four television diets* (Occasional Paper 77-3). Stony Brook, NY: Brookdale International Institute.

TV Guide. (1992, October 10–16). TV Guide poll: Would you give up TV for a million bucks? *TV Guide*, *40*, 10–13, 15, 17.

Watson, D., Clark, L. A., & Tellegen, A. (1988). Development and validation of brief measures of positive and negative affect: The PANAS scales. *Journal of Personality and Social Psychology*, *54*, 1063–1070.

Zipperer, J. (1994, February 7). Violence foes take aim: Advertisers and affiliates caught in the crossfire. *Christianity Today*, pp. 40–42.

Zuckerman, M., & Lubin, B. (1985). *Manual for the MAACL-R: The Multiple Adjective Checklist Revised.* San Diego, CA: Educational and Industrial Testing Service.

SUBJECT INDEX